THE

MEGHAN METHOD

THE STEP-BY-STEP GUIDE TO DECORATING YOUR HOME IN YOUR STYLE

MEGHAN CARTER

PHOTOGRAPHS BY BRENT WALTER

GEM MULTIMEDIA

{ why this book }

MANY BOOKS — and magazines and interior designers, for that matter — will try to tell you that changing your paint color and rearranging your furniture will fix all the problems in your life. But I'm going to be straight-up with you. Not so much.

Decorating your home is no more a solution to your life problems than going to the plastic surgeon. All you'll get is temporary problem amnesia. And once the newness of your fresh facade fades, you'll remember. Every one of those original problems will come flooding back.

Now that's not to say decorating isn't important. It's highly important. Just not fix-all-your-problems-and-make-you-deliriously-happy important.

You see, our happiness works like a car. To drive, a car needs fuel. Just as to be happy, we need fuel. Only, we don't need just one type. We need nine: health, safety, relationships, self-regard, food, work, enjoyment, spirituality and home. And if any of those tanks run low, so will our happiness.

Of course, we all think we can cheat the system. We figure if we keep filling one of the tanks, the overflow will fill the rest. But it doesn't work that way. I don't care how spectacular your home is, if you're in a terrible relationship or have a life-threatening illness or hate your job, you're not going to be blissfully happy. Having a gorgeous home is not enough to make up for the bad in your life. All it can do is bring you some joy. Just some.

Because decorating is only one piece of the happiness puzzle. You've got to fill all your tanks — work through all your issues and come to peace with each one — to be truly happy.

Doesn't work that way. You must fill each tank individually.

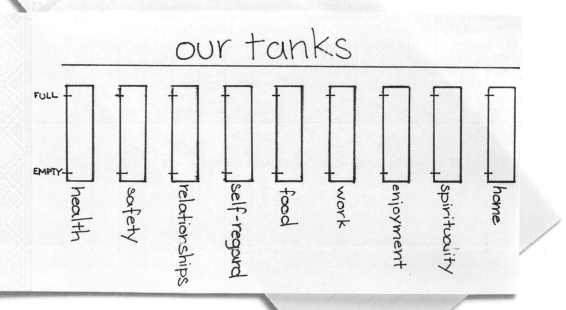

our tanks

FULL

EMPTY

health · safety · relationships · self-regard · food · work · enjoyment · spirituality · home

But rarely do you fill all tanks at once. Which means, when going for happiness, you've got to start someplace. And that's where this book comes in.

Of all the types of fuel we need, our home is the only one that affects all of our other tanks, because our home is our life headquarters. It's where we organize our life. It's where we recharge our weary bones. And most importantly, it's where we feel free to be ourselves.

That's why we fill the majority of our tanks at home. Because it gives us a safe place to do it. To rebuild our health. To protect us from danger. To gather with loved ones. To regain our confidence. To nourish our empty bellies. To prepare before a big day at work. To pray our most intimate prayers.

We do all of that at home. And if we don't, we should. Our home is the only place on earth we have to make our very own. Which means, we should take advantage of it and turn our home into a place that works for us. A place that helps us keep our life — and tanks — in order and gives us the strength, energy and sanity needed to wake up each day and fill those other tanks.

But that's all our homes can give us. So if you go into decorating expecting it to fix all your problems, you'll be sorely disappointed. Decorating can't fix the problems in our lives.

All it can do is fill one tank. But that one tank — our home — is the tank that best enables us to fill all our other tanks. Which means, once you get your home in order, it's far easier to get your life in order.

That's why I wrote this book. Because when it comes to building happiness, the best place to start is your home.

And that's the best thing I could wish for anyone. Happiness.

For all those told they weren't
talented, artistic or stylish
enough to decorate.
It's time you learned the truth.

CONTE

current reads→

sexy

peaceful

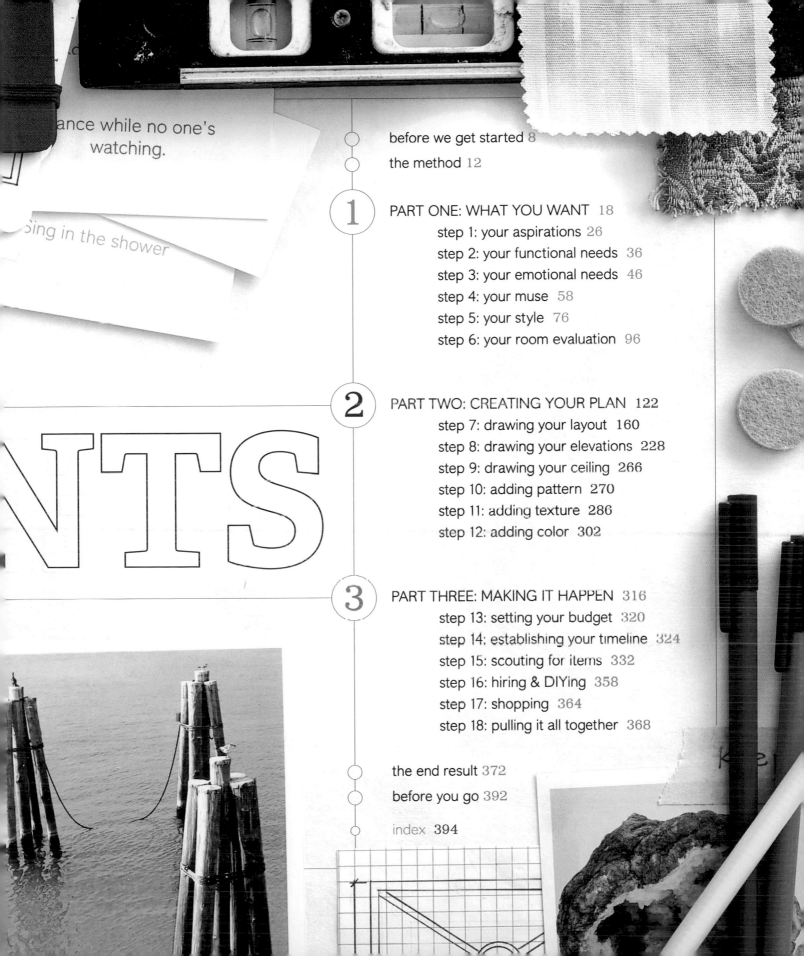

...ance while no one's watching.

...sing in the shower

NTS

ALL YOU NEED
TO DECORATE:

- confidence ← what you bring
- Know-how ← what I'll give

AND YOU'LL HAVE
PLENTY OF BOTH BY
THE TIME WE'RE DONE.

before we get started

WHEN I WAS JUST SIX, my mom decided it would be a good idea to let me pick out the wallpaper for my room. Hand in hand, we walked into a small décor shop and found seats at a long table in front of a giant wall-to-wall, floor-to-ceiling bookshelf. And I do mean giant. There were so many wallpaper books stuffed on that bookshelf you could have easily killed an entire weekend looking through all of them. But, it only took me a handful of minutes to find the wallpaper I wanted. The second I saw it I put my hand on the page, pointing to the pattern. And without missing a beat, my mom immediately scrunched up her face.

You know the look. You can probably even hear the tone of her voice when she said, "Meghan, are you sure *that's* what you want?"

"Yes," I said innocently.

And that innocent yes launched us into a 15-minute discussion about other wallpapers I could choose.

"Are you sure you wouldn't rather have the bunny one? Or what about that flower one?" my mom desperately fished.

But I wasn't having any of it. Fortunately, at six, I was still young enough not to let my mom's dislike sway my decision. And it paid off.

A few weeks later I had red, yellow and blue hot air balloons floating on my walls.

But had I been just ten years older, the story would have been very different. For one, I definitely wouldn't have been looking at hot air balloons and bunnies. I'd moved on to polka dots and butterflies by then. And more importantly, when I heard that disapproving tone in my mom's voice, I would have taken it to heart. In fact, I probably would have asked for her opinion and based a large part of my decision on what she thought.

Why? Because at some point while growing up, I stopped believing in myself. I stopped listening to my own voice and tuned into everyone else's because I thought I wasn't talented, creative or artistic enough to have a good opinion. But I was wrong.

ANYONE CAN DECORATE.

And yes, that means you. You don't have to be ridiculously artistic. You don't have to be extraordinarily stylish. You don't even have to be creative. All you have to be is you. Just you, because decorating is simply about creating a home that makes you happy. And you are the only person on earth who knows what that is.

Some editor at a home magazine can't tell you which sofa will make you happy. Just as some interior designer on TV can't tell you which color will put a smile on your face. And God love your mother, but she doesn't always know what's best for you. Although, if she's anything like my mom, she's shockingly right the majority of the time.

But not about those balloons. I liked those balloons. They made me happy — very happy, and if I had not stood up for myself, I wouldn't have had anything to count as I drifted off to sleep. And if you don't listen to yourself — if you don't tune into you, you may miss out on the home of your dreams.

Decorating is half self-confidence and half know-how. The know-how I can give you. In fact, by the end of this book you will have so much decorating know-how you will never need to ask a single person for his or her decorating opinion again.

But the self-confidence? That, unfortunately, I can't give you. It must come from within. And I know it's in you. Everyone has that six-year-old inside waiting to be heard. All you have to do is give yourself a chance.

If you can do that, I can show you the rest.

the method

WHEN IT COMES TO DECORATING, most people feel deficient. Like they were skipped over by the creative fairy and missed out on getting hit with the artistic stick. But the truth is, there's no such thing as a creative fairy. Magical artistic sticks don't exist. And, as much as you'd like to think you're deficient, you're not. You can decorate just as good as anyone else — if not better. You just don't know where to start.

In fact, most people don't even realize there's a right place to start when decorating. They just do the first thing that comes to mind — shopping.

They go to the paint store, the furniture store, the carpet store, and during the course of their shopping escapades, they buy half the things they need for their rooms and figure they'll find the other half later. But when later finally comes around, they panic, because they can't figure out what will look good with the things they've bought.

What color couch will work with the fresh coat of paint on my wall? What backsplash will look best with the countertops and cabinets I had installed? Is there a single drape in existence that goes with the bedding and rug I just bought?

Maybe. Maybe not. That's the problem with shopping first. You almost always end up working your way straight into a partially decorated corner with no way out in sight.

And it's while stuck in those corners that many — *if not most* — people give up and think they're just not talented, artistic or creative enough to decorate. But the truth is, the only reason they end up stuck is because they skipped the first two parts of the decorating process.

You see, decorating a room is like making an omelette. You have to perform certain steps in the right sequence for it to turn out perfect. And while the things you put inside may change each time, the basic method is always the same.

Of course, when you're stuck in those corners desperately looking for help, you won't find that method. All you'll get are a bunch of interior design experts handing out silly — and often contradictory — decorating rules that essentially just tell you to "do what I do." Only use three patterns in a room. Only paint your woodwork white. Only pick neutral wall colors. But if you were to open any home magazine, you'd find those so-called "rules" broken time and time again.

For one very simple reason. "Do what I do" isn't a method. It's just a bunch of politely stated— *and all too often not-so-politely stated* — suggestions. Simply someone else's opinion of what looks good and what doesn't. Which only helps if you love that person's style. If you don't, tough luck. They won't help you, because all they do is show you how to mimic one style. They don't teach you how to decorate. They don't help you find your style. And that's what we really need when we're stuck in those corners. Yet you can't find that type of advice anywhere. And to be completely honest, I don't know why.

Maybe the experts feel the rooms they decorate are so amazing that, seriously, how could you not want your room to look like that? Maybe they just don't know how to articulate their decorating processes, so they tell you what's worked for them in the past and hope it will also work for you. Maybe they don't want you to know their processes because they're afraid of losing their superiority and oh-so-important paycheck. Yeah, that one may be a bit too conspiracy theory. Maybe it's simply because they think you don't have what it takes to decorate — only those hit with the artistic stick do — so they figure they have to dumb it down for you. They figure the best you can do is just mimic them.

Well, that's bull.

If that last one's the reason — if they really think you don't have what it takes — they're wrong. Dead wrong. You're not deficient. You don't need a dumbed-down version. You have all the talent

PROFESSIONAL'S DECORATING ADVICE METHOD

Do this and your room will look fabulous.

[lw]ays [paint] [wo]odwork [w]hite.

• Never use overhead lights.

• Put something black in every room.

• Don't ever buy the matching set.

• Never paint your room white.

• Save bright colors for accents only.

• Never leave windows bare.

• Always paint your walls a neutral color.

• Always group things in threes.

• Don't use busy patterns on large furniture pieces.

• Don't display family photos.

• Only u[se] three p[ieces] in arc[h] One [sits] one m[?] & on[e]

• Don't all ex[?] leg fu[?] in a[?]

• Pu[t] th[?]

The True Decorating Method

Determine what
you want.

↓

Create a
plan.

↓

Make it
happen.

and creativity needed to decorate. They're just giving you the wrong instructions.

So forget everything they've told you. All the opinions. All the dumbed-down rules. Everything. You don't need them. All you need is to learn how to decorate.

All you need is that step-by-step method that walks you through each part of the decorating process without ever — not even once — imposing a style on you.

And that's exactly what I'm giving you.

I spent well over three years boiling decorating down to it's very basics, and here's what I found. You can't wing it. Walking into a store, picking out items and hoping your room will magically come together doesn't cut it. When you decorate, you must have a plan. A good plan. A detailed plan. One that clearly shows what furniture, lighting, accessories, patterns, textures and colors you will use.

And I'm guessing you never made one of those. Most people don't. That's why they end up stuck in those corners. But if they'd only had a plan, that wouldn't have happened. They would have known exactly what would fit and look good together before they bought a single item for their room. That's why making a plan is essential.

Of course, you can't divine one out of thin air. You need inspiration. You need direction. You need to know what you want. And when it comes to decorating, most people don't have a clue what they want. They just walk into stores hoping something will jump out at them. But impulse buys rarely lead to long lasting love. If you want a room you'll thoroughly enjoy, you've got to take the time to pinpoint exactly what you want.

And that's all there is to it. No artistic sticks involved. No creative fairies necessary. No silly rules needed.

When you strip decorating down to its core, the process is simple. Determine what you want. Create a plan based on those wants. Then, make it happen. If you do that, you'll end up with a room perfectly tailored to you and your style. So let's get to it.

EDGY

GLAMOROU

PART ONE: WHAT Y WAN

ROOM: BREAKFAST/SIT

ENT LAYO

(1)

your
pirations

RANK: YOUR ASPIRATIONS:

ecorating
is not
bout what
ou put in
your
home.

It's
about what
you
get out
of it.

YOU
T

maybe

Practice

Chillax while catchi
weekly favorites
tube.

der the c
d, snowy p

Everyone's got it wrong. They think we decorate because we want a good-looking home. But I assure you, that's not what we want.

If it were, we'd flip through room photos in magazines thinking, "I want to look at this room for hours."

But no one does that. We don't fantasize about staring at those rooms. We fantasize about having them — about what our life would be like in them. And we think, "If only I lived there. Then, I could do all those things I want to do. Then, I could have that life."

And it's that life we're after.

The sleeping in on Sunday mornings. Staying up late swapping stories. Curling up with a book by the fire. Romancing through the midnight hour. Baking cookies and fixing soups. Hosting dinner parties for big groups. The laughing. The chatting. The dancing. The singing. Sharing all those moments that give life meaning.

That's what we want. That's why we decorate. To make all those dreams come true.

Not to create a good-looking room. So ditch the idea that decorating is about looks or beauty or anything else superficial like that. Because it's not. Any room can be beautiful. But only one can make all those dreams happen. That's why decorating your room for looks doesn't work. Because it doesn't give you what you really want. It doesn't make your dream life happen. And that's what decorating is all about.

We decorate to make our aspirations possible. And if you focus on that — your aspirations — you'll get the room you really want. The one that enables the life in your dreams.

THE "YOU" IN WHAT YOU WANT

Now wait a minute. Just because we've determined the "what" — your dream life — in what you want doesn't mean we're ready to jump ahead. There's still one thing we've got to clarify. The "you." Because it doesn't mean just you. It means you and everyone else who lives in your home. Of course, if you live alone, none of this applies to you. But if you don't, listen up.

Decorators tend to be on the selfish side. And for far too long we've been allowed to run wild doing whatever the heck we wanted. Partly because the home has always been the woman's domain, which meant she was free to decorate however she pleased. Partly because the men of the household insisted they couldn't care less about decor. And partly because no one cared about what the kids had to say. After all, they don't pay the bills.

But they do live in your home. All of them. And if you decorate your home only taking your wants into consideration, the rest of your family may end up feeling uncomfortable in their own home.

Now, more than likely, they won't say anything. They probably won't even realize they feel uncomfortable. They'll just react. They won't stay as long at dinner. They'll migrate to their rooms instead of hanging out with everyone. They'll spend more time away from the home than in it. And don't even get me started on the bedroom.

How many men feel sexy surrounded by a bunch of pink flowers? Not many. And people wonder why their love life fizzles out. Sure there are probably other problems. But the decor sure as hell isn't helping.

So if all those things you dream of doing — your aspirations — involve other people, you'll want to take their wants into consideration as well. Because if they don't feel comfortable, they're not going to stick around. And your dream life will stay a dream.

CO-DECORATING

If multiple people in your home will be using your room, every single one of them old enough to talk should be involved in the decorating process. The first six steps of the method should be completed by each person individually. That way, no one gets influenced by anyone else's opinion.

But that doesn't mean each person should steam ahead and finish all six steps at once. It doesn't work that way. The wants from each step build on the next. So after everyone finishes each step, you must discuss your wants and combine them together. Then each person should take those combined wants and finish the next step. And so on.

Once you've completed steps one through six, the rest of the steps can be done together. If some people are too busy, one person can run point and complete each step from seven to 18 on his or her own. But after finishing each step, be sure to run what you've done by everyone else. That way everyone can give his or her input. And you know how important receiving their input is.

Now if someone in your home refuses to partake and insists they don't care what you do with the house, remind them that their wants won't be taken into consideration. Which means if they want to watch football on a big screen TV, tough luck. Or if they want to play video games with their friends, too bad. Or if they want to enjoy spa days with the girls, oh well. You only get a say if you participate.

Of course, be aware that some may not want to participate because they're afraid of being judged or ignored. So you need to set some ground rules. One, have an open mind. No disparaging or judgmental remarks made about anyone's wants. Two, what's shared at home stays at home. No Twittering or Facebooking or telling other people about a housemate's wants. Three, be nice. No making fun of anyone's wants. Okay. Maybe there are some exceptions to that last one if it's in a kind way.

But otherwise stick to the ground rules. If you do, everyone will feel far more safe, which is very important. Because sharing our innermost dreams is scary. No one wants to be rejected. So listen. Really listen. When you do, people will open up.

BLENDING YOUR WANTS

Now I realize most people don't get too thrilled about the idea of codecorating. In fact, the second I mention it, most people immediately throw up their arms in protest.

"We'll never agree on anything. We have completely opposite tastes."

"If I let him have a say, the whole house will be black."

"All she ever wants are flowers, flowers, flowers."

But I'm not asking you to let them bully you into getting their way. I'm asking you to work together as a team. And when you work together as a team, everyone has an equal say. Which means, no one gets his or her way every time. Instead, all of your wants are blended in a such a way that everyone likes the end result.

Of course, you probably think that's impossible. But if you do the following two things, you'll be amazed by the result.

Ask why. Before dismissing what someone else wants, ask them why. Why do you like that?

Most people have a very good reason for liking what they do. So give them a chance to explain. Because often times it's not the actual thing they're in love with, but one of its qualities. And once you know what qualities they're after, you can come to a compromise both of you thoroughly enjoy.

For example, maybe he finds the color black sexy. Instead of using black everywhere, find something you both feel is sexy and use that instead.

Or maybe she likes flowers because of their bright, cheerful colors. And while you don't like the flowers, you do love the bright colors. So use those.

So ask why. Because once you know why someone likes what they do, it's far easier to find some common ground.

Focus on what you have in common. While you may think there's absolutely nothing you can all agree on, I assure you there is. If there wasn't, you wouldn't have chosen to live together. But you did, because you have something in common.

Focus on those things, because they're what brought you together in the first place. Which means, they can bring you together again.

THE "YOU" IN BABY, KID, TEEN & GUEST ROOMS

When it comes to decorating baby, kid, teen and guest rooms, people get a little confused about who the "you" is. So let's break it down.

Baby rooms. Obviously, when you decorate a newborn's room, he or she hasn't even entered the world yet. So you can't really get his or her opinion. Which means, the "you" is you. After all, you'll be using that room a lot. Changing diapers. Reading books. Rocking your bundle of joy back to sleep at three in the morning. So your wants should the main focus. Just be sure to consider what your baby will need and want as well. Because he or she will be using the room too. And as a new parent, I'm sure you want his or her first view of the world to be enjoyable.

Kid Rooms. When it comes to kid rooms, once they can talk, let them be the "you." They'll only be young once. Let them live it up. If they want hot air balloon wallpaper, so be it. It's their room. You don't spend that much time in there. So who cares what they choose? Your job isn't to tell them what to pick, but to help them discover what they love and turn it into a reality.

Teen Rooms. Teen rooms work just like kid rooms, except you don't need to hold their hands through the process. Instead, give them some responsibility. It's the perfect chance for them to learn how much things cost in the real world and how to stay on budget. Plus, you'll be helping them to develop their own style.

Guest Rooms. Technically, in guest rooms, your guests should be the "you." But because you'll potentially have a conveyor belt of guests coming through your home, that won't work. Asking everyone what they want would drive you insane because you can't please everyone. Instead, create what you think would be the best guest room ever. And as long as you put true care and concern into it, your guests will have nothing to complain about. After all, they're lucky to have a bed to sleep on — let alone, a well-appointed room.

CHOOSING A ROOM

I completely understand the appeal of decorating your entire home at once, because when it's done, it's done. And the end result is absolutely spectacular. But getting there is far from it.

Decorating one room is hard enough. You've got to make hundreds of decisions while keeping track of hundreds of things. And let's not even bring up the chaos of ripping your room apart or how many clams you have to spend to make it happen.

So throwing another room — or God help you more — into the mix is like begging for a beating. You've got to be a true glutton for punishment to step inside that whirlwind — especially if you plan to do all the DIY work yourself on top of raising a family or working a nine to five. You may need to be committed afterwards.

Not to mention that when you're a newbie, you're bound to make a mistake or two. And it's far better to make a mistake on just one room than every single room in your home. That's why I've set up this book to only take on one room at a time. Because if you do any more, you'll be biting off more than you can chew.

Now, after you've got a few rooms under your belt, that's a completely different story. The hundreds of decisions will no longer phase you due to your increased confidence and know-how. Which means, you'll be able to breeze through rooms in no time flat.

But for now, while you're still green, stick to one room. And I'd recommend starting with the smallest, least-used room of your home. Like a hallway, guest room, home office or storage room. That way you make all your mistakes — or at least most of them — where it least matters. Then, once you have more experience, you can move on to the more expensive, highly-used rooms. Like your kitchen, bathroom and family room.

But enough logistics. Let's move on to the main event: *figuring out what you want.*

llax while catching your
weekly favorites on the
tube.

ty.

der the covers
d, snowy night.

The
entire
point of
decorating.

step:

1

your
aspirations

Luxuriate while a
rejuvenating face m
goes to work

As you already know (page 20 for those who don't), your aspirations — the things you dream of doing in your room — are the reason why you decorate. Which makes them your decorating goal. Your mission. Your ultimate purpose.

Everything you do from this point on will solely be to make your aspirations happen. Every single decision you make — every single item you choose — will be based on them. So you've got to get them right because your aspirations are the very foundation of your entire room.

THE POINT OF ASPIRATIONS

We've been trained to believe decorating is all about what we put in our rooms. The sofas. The chandeliers. The dishwashers. So when it comes to listing our aspirations, we sometimes default to listing the things we wish we had. But that's the last thing you want to do, because decorating is not about what you put in your home. It's about what you get out of it.

The tickle fights and movie nights. The afternoon naps and late-night chats. The holiday soirees and pancake Sundays. That's what decorating is about. Those moments.

Not getting stuff. The things we cram in our rooms are simply a means to an end. And if you just list those things, you won't plan for those moments. You'll just plan for enough space. And that's not what we really want. We don't want rooms full of stuff. We want rooms custom tailored to our dreams.

So if you find yourself starting to list a bunch of things like a double oven or soaker tub, stop and ask yourself why you want them. Because your answer — whatever activity it may be — is your aspiration. And that is what you should write down.

Not things, but the things you want *to do*.

Decorating is not about what you put in your home.

It's about what you get out of it.

GO BEYOND THE STANDARD

I don't know if it's because we're bashful or boring, but when listing our aspirations, we tend to only list the standards. Like I want to cook in my kitchen. Or I want to sleep in my bedroom. Or I want to shower in my bathroom.

But I know that's not all you want to do. No one is that boring. So it must be that we're all bashful. Scared stiff of listing something that might be weird or uncool or wussy. But there is no shame in having a dream. And there is definitely no shame in going for it. If you want to do something, own it. This is your one shot to make your dream life come true. So don't hold yourself back by only listing the safe things. List what you really want.

And just in case you need a little push, turn the page.

Lose track of time catching up with old friends.

Know exactly where your shoes and keys are when running late.

Soak in a warm, bubble bath.

Hole up for an all-day, movie marathon.

Watch th drifti

Narrate the nightly bedtime story.

Share heart-to-hearts over cookies and milk.

Romance over a candlelit dinner for two.

Have a girls' night full of chit-chat and guilty snacks.

Enjoy get

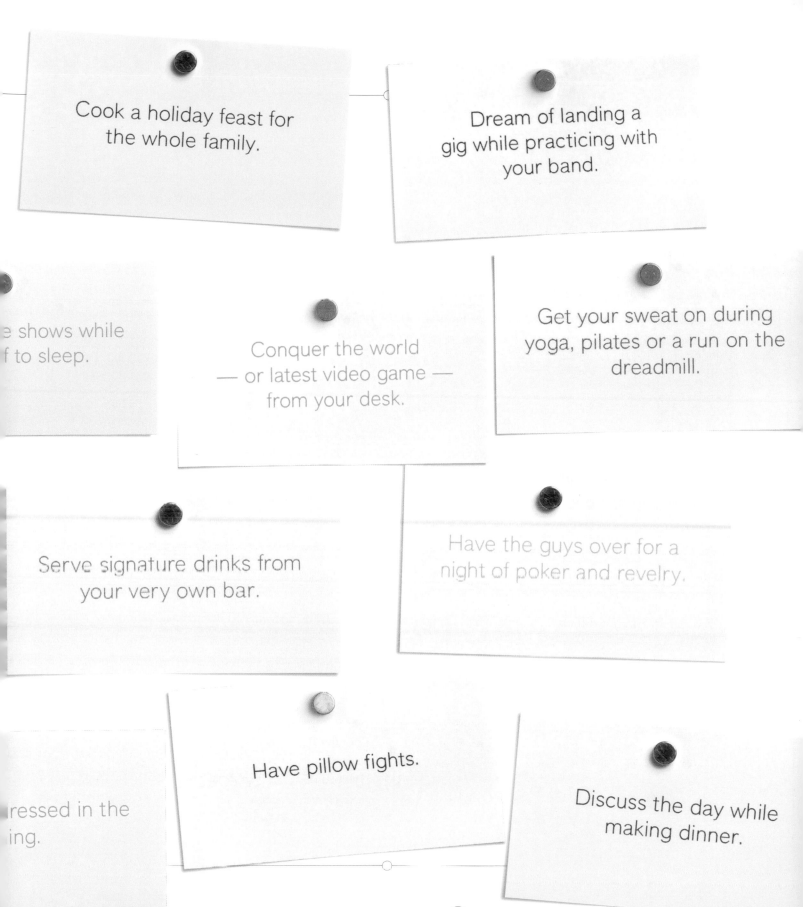

Cook a holiday feast for the whole family.

Dream of landing a gig while practicing with your band.

e shows while f to sleep.

Conquer the world — or latest video game — from your desk.

Get your sweat on during yoga, pilates or a run on the dreadmill.

Serve signature drinks from your very own bar.

Have the guys over for a night of poker and revelry.

Have pillow fights.

ressed in the ing.

Discuss the day while making dinner.

DITCH THE IDEALIZED YOU

Now, hold up. As soon as people start thinking about their dreams, the floodgates bolt wide open, and everything they ever wanted — even for only a fleeting moment — comes pouring out. But you've got to reel that back in.

Listing every single thing you ever dreamed of doing won't get you anywhere. Because most of those things we only half want. And half wanting means we'll only half do it — if that.

For example, I'd love to play the piano. But if I had a piano in my home, I wouldn't start taking piano lessons. Not even if the piano dropped down straight from Heaven. Because at the end of the day, I don't really *want* to play piano. I just like the *idea* of it.

And if you list a bunch of things like that — things your idealized self would do — you'll end up with a house filled with things that never get used. And most of us can't do that. Because we're working with limited real estate and need to use every single square inch to its maximum potential. There's no room for idealized aspirations. We've only got space for the ones we really want to do with our whole heart and soul.

So after you've opened your floodgates and poured every

Play the piano like a virtuoso.

Not going to happen. At least, not in my case.

last dream you've ever had onto your page, look over each one and ask yourself, "Do I *really* want this?"

If you answer yes, then ask yourself, "Will I really *do* this?"

If you answer yes again, then you have a bona fide aspiration. If you answer no, cross that sucker off the list. Because what's the point of planning for an aspiration you'll never do?

DON'T FORGET THE SMALL STUFF

There are a number of small activities we do that keep our days running smoothly. Like putting on shoes. Making coffee. Brushing our teeth. Folding laundry. Paying the bills. Feeding the fishes. Answering e-mail. Doing the dishes.

And while they may seem like insignificant stepping stones to the bigger things we want to do in our day, believe me, they're not. Those little activities are what make the bigger activities possible. It's not fun cooking in a kitchen full of dirty dishes. Just as, turning your clothes inside out only works for so long.

So while you may not yearn with every fiber of your being to do those activities, on some level you do want to do them. Because they're what grease the gears for your bigger aspirations. They're what give you the good breath needed for a little lovin'. And what make you chipper and alert first thing in the morning.

So don't skip adding them to your aspiration list. Because despite what you think, you do want to do them. And if you don't add them to your list, you won't plan for them. And if you don't plan for them, they won't be easy to do. Which means, there will be a lot of moaning and groaning every day when it comes time to do them.

Whereas, if you write them down and plan for them, you can make them as effortless and enjoyable to do as possible. And when you do write them down, take the time to think of how you want to do them.

Deck the halls for the holidays.

For example, wouldn't folding laundry be a lot nicer if you could stare at a gorgeous view or watch TV while doing it? Or wouldn't putting on and taking off shoes be much easier if you had a place to sit while doing it?

So be specific when listing the small things you want to do. Don't just say you want to do dishes. Say I want to listen to music and sing along while doing dishes. Or I want to exercise while catching up with my favorite shows.

A ROOM FOR ALL SEASONS

Either we have extremely short-term memories or the seasons put a trance on us, because when it comes to listing aspirations, we always forget other seasons exist. In the winter, we want to sit by the fire, curl up with a movie and bake batch-after-batch of warm gooey cookies. But if we get sucked into thinking that's all we want to do, we'll be miserable come summer. Because we'll decorate our home to be warm and cozy and fireplace-centric. Yet all we'll want is the sun pouring in and the windows wide open.

So when listing your aspirations, you must consider what you want for *all* seasons. Because what we want to do drastically changes depending on the weather.

Of course, if you own a weekend ski chalet or summer beach house, you can completely ignore this section because your home is a one-season home. But the majority of us live in the same home year-round. Which means, our rooms must be fit for every season. Spring, summer, winter, fall and the holidays.

Especially the holidays, because the holidays aren't the holidays without traditions. So if you want it to be the most magical time of year, complete with a giant Christmas tree in your hall and a table full of hungry relatives, you better write those aspirations down. If you don't, you won't plan for it. And if you don't plan for it, it won't happen. And if it doesn't happen, it won't feel like the holidays.

LISTING YOUR ASPIRATIONS

It should go without saying, but when you list your aspirations, only list what you want to do in the room you plan to decorate. So think of your room. Then think of what you want to do in it.

If you have trouble figuring out what you want, think about your daily routine. What do you do when you wake up in the morning? How do you get ready? Where do you eat breakfast? What do you do during the day when you're at home? Where do you eat lunch? Where do you work out? What about dinner? How do you relax in the evening? What do you do before bed?

Thinking about how you spend your time will jog your memory as to what you enjoy doing. It may even help you think of how you wish you spent your time. If not, ask yourself how you wish you spent your time. Are there any things you'd like to do more? Things you'd like to do less? Things you'd like to try?

If there are, list them. And don't try to rush the process. Remember, your aspirations are the foundation of your entire room. You must get them right. Don't expect to finish in five minutes. It can take hours — even days — to think of them all. Once you have a list, don't charge ahead. Let them soak in for a few days. After some time has passed, ask yourself if you still want to do those things. That way, you don't end up falling for a fling. Instead, you only end up with aspirations you truly want.

1

your aspirations

FOR ROOM:

You'll want this — and all the sheets from Step 1 through 6 — in front of you during the entire decorating process. So don't fill out the versions found in this book. Instead, print your own copies from TheMeghan Method.com.

DIRECTIONS:

(1) List all the things you want to do in your room.

(2) Double check to make sure you actually want to do each thing you listed. Cross off any you don't.

(3) Rate all aspirations left according to importance. The aspiration you want most should be rated 1. The aspiration you want second most should be 2. And so on.

GET YOUR OWN COPY AT TheMeghanMethod. com.

RANK: YOUR ASPIRATIONS:

1

your aspirations

DIRECTIONS:

1 List all the things you want to do in your room.

2 Double check to make sure you actually want to do each thing you listed. Cross off any you don't.

3 Rate all aspirations left according to importance. The aspiration you want most should be rated 1. The aspiration you want second most should be 2. And so on.

GET YOUR
OWN COPY AT
TheMeghanMethod.
com.

RANK: | **YOUR ASPIRATIONS:**

RANK	YOUR ASPIRATIONS
4	read while snuggled under the covers
1	sleep blissfully & peacefully
2	get dressed & ready to go
5	write letters, postcards or e-mails
3	wake up early to catch the sunrise -or- a flight
7	hang towels and swimsuits after a day in the lake
6	store luggage & belongings out of sight

1

your aspirations

DIRECTIONS:

1. List all the thin[...]
   want to do in y[...]

2. Double [...]
   sure y[...] [...]to
   do[...]sted.
   [...]don't.

   [...]spirations left
   [...]g to importance.
   [...]aspiration you want
   [...]ost should be rated 1.
   The aspiration you want
   second most should be 2.
   And so on.

RANK: YOUR ASPIRATIONS:

2 gather for casual
   Sunday brunches ___ or lunch

1 eat breakfast while
   reading the latest news

4 curl up with a book
   and fresh scone - or
   whatever other goodies
   can be found in the kitchen

5 enjoy the spectacular
   lake view

6 sit by the fire on
   chilly days

7 play board games
   on rainy days

3 enjoy cocktails & conversation
   while dinner is being made

8 share heart-to-hearts

9 savor a midnight snack

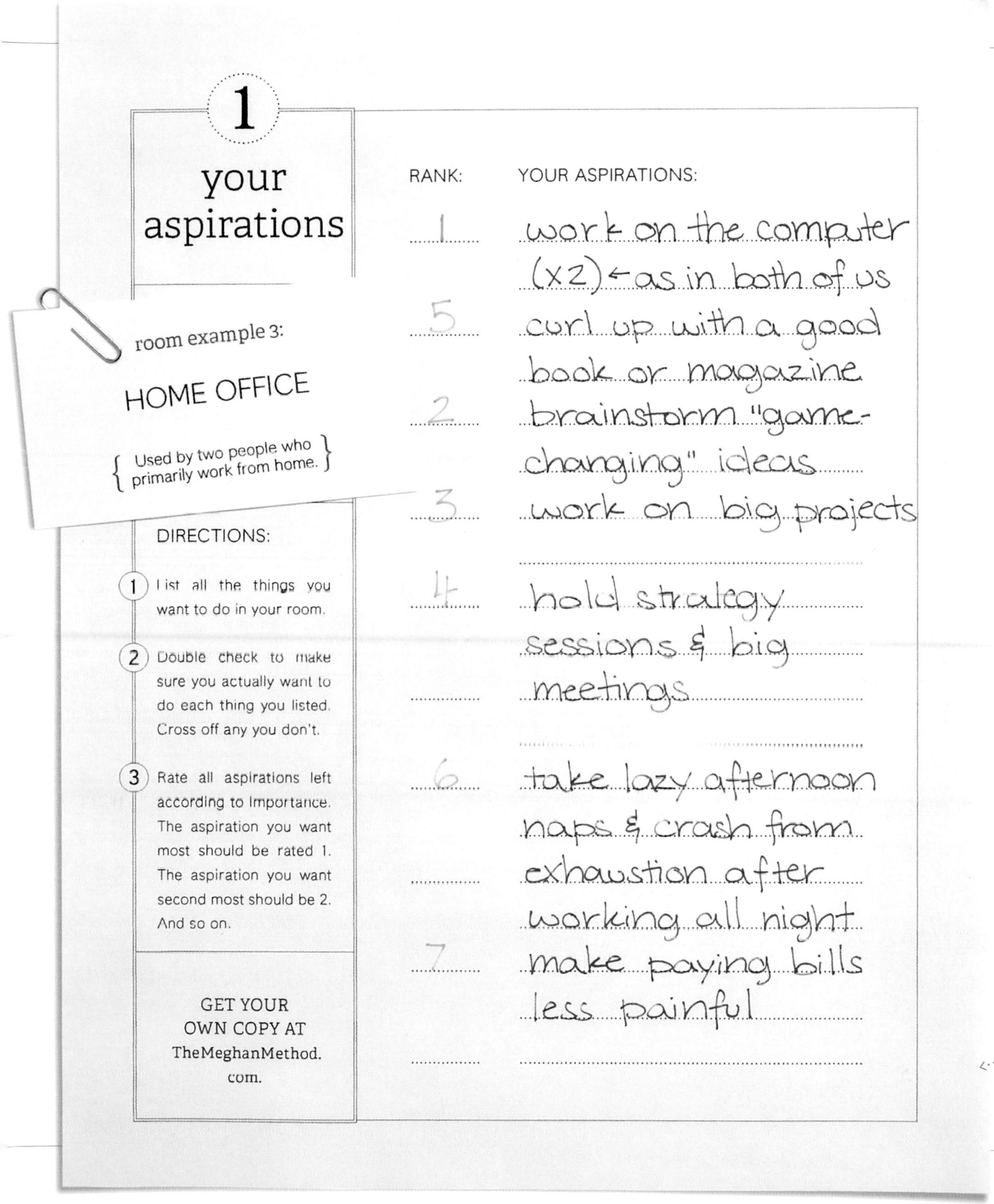

your aspirations

room example 3:

HOME OFFICE

{ Used by two people who primarily work from home. }

DIRECTIONS:

(1) List all the things you want to do in your room.

(2) Double check to make sure you actually want to do each thing you listed. Cross off any you don't.

(3) Rate all aspirations left according to Importance. The aspiration you want most should be rated 1. The aspiration you want second most should be 2. And so on.

GET YOUR
OWN COPY AT
TheMeghanMethod.
com.

RANK: | YOUR ASPIRATIONS:

1 — work on the computer (x2) ← as in both of us

5 — curl up with a good book or magazine

2 — brainstorm "game-changing" ideas

3 — work on big projects

4 — hold strategy sessions & big meetings

6 — take lazy afternoon naps & crash from exhaustion after working all night

7 — make paying bills less painful

All of the sheets — from step 1 through 6 — are the blended versions of each person's wants for each room.

What you need for your room to work.

step: **2**

your functional needs

D ecorating is no different than cooking. You can't make what you want until you know what ingredients you need. And the ingredients you need to make your aspirations happen to fall into two categories. The first is function.

WHY FUNCTION MATTERS

Function simply refers to how well an object assists you in doing what you want to do. The better it assists, the better it's said to function. And you want the things in your room to function really well. Extraordinarily well. Because if they don't, doing your aspirations will be hard. And when things are hard, we don't do them.

Take cooking for example. You can cook without a stove or oven. But it's extremely inconvenient. You've got to build a fire. Tend the fire. Bend over the fire. And after a few times of cooking like that, you're bound to give up and order takeout, because it's easier.

And we like easy. When things are hard or uncomfortable, we avoid them. That's why people camping in the wilderness don't take showers all that often. Because it's too hard to find clean, private water, and when they do, it's normally freezing.

So if you want all your aspirations to happen, you must have all the things needed to make your aspirations both easy and comfortable to do. Which boils down to having the right tools.

If you want to do laundry, you need a washing machine and dryer. If you want to host dinner parties, you need a dining table and chairs. If you want to watch the game, you need a chair and a TV.

But let's be honest. Not just any chair will do. If your chair is hard as concrete, you'll go somewhere else to watch the game. Because having the right tool isn't enough. You must have the right tool with the right characteristics. If you don't, it's like trying to carve a Thanksgiving turkey with a plastic knife. Frustrating. Terribly frustrating.

We decorate to get:

The decorating flow chart.

OUR ASPIRATIONS

We make our aspirations happen by fulfilling our:

To be revealed on page 47.

1. FUNCTIONAL NEEDS

2

RIGHT
TOOLS

+

RIGHT
CHARACTERISTICS

———————

A
FUNCTIONAL
ROOM

Having the right tool only makes your aspiration possible. It doesn't ensure that doing it will be comfortable. The characteristics of your tool do that.

So if you want your aspirations to stand a chance of happening, you must have the right tools with the right characteristics. Because then — and only then — will your aspirations be easy and comfortable enough to be enjoyable.

THE TOOLS YOU NEED

Every single aspiration on your list requires certain tools. Most — if not all of those tools — fall into one of the following categories.

Lighting. When it comes to lighting, you don't need to decide whether or not you need it. That's a given. Every room needs some type of lighting because without it, we can't see. And you need to see for most aspirations.

So you need lighting. The question is *how much*. Because not all aspirations require the same amount of lighting. Which means, you must determine the intensity of light you functionally need.

TASK LIGHTING. The brighter the light, the easier it is to see details. So if you're doing close-up work — such as sewing or reading — you'll want very bright light, known as task lighting.

GENERAL LIGHTING. For most activities — such as walking, talking or eating — we don't need bright lights. Because there are no small details we must see. So in those situations, we use medium-intensity lighting, known as general lighting.

MOOD LIGHTING. This is the type of lighting we use when seeing clearly isn't a concern. because all we're after is adding a bit of romance or drama — such as during dinner parties or bubble baths.

To determine which of those three types of lighting you need, think about how clearly you must be able to see during each of your aspirations. Sometimes, an aspiration requires a combination of lighting types. Other times, you only need one type of lighting.

Window Treatments. Window treatments serve two functional purposes. The first is to keep peeping Toms from grabbing a peek. So if your room has windows that are easy to peep in, and your aspiration is something you don't want the whole world to see, then you'll need some sort of window treatment.

As for the second reason, the sun doesn't come with an off switch. Which can be incredibly inconvenient when you want to sleep in, watch a movie or use your computer without fighting a glare. So if your room has windows facing the sun and your aspirations require darkness or no glare, then you'll need a window treatment.

If you do need a window treatment, be sure to note why you need it — whether it's for privacy or sun blockage. That way, when the time comes, it'll be easier for you to determine which type of window treatment you need.

Furniture. Very rarely does an aspiration only require one piece of furniture. Typically, aspirations require at least a few. So if you only list one piece, you're probably missing some.

For example, people tend to say they only need seating to read a book. But where do you put a drink? Or what about your feet? And where do you get your books from?

To be comfortable when reading, at bare minimum you need some sort of seating and a table or flat surface within arm's reach. That way you have a place to put a snack, a drink or your book. To make your reading spot extra comfortable, you should also have a place to rest your feet, such as an ottoman. And of course, you need a place to store your books.

So when thinking about what types of furniture you need, don't list only the main pieces. List every piece of furniture — down to the smallest detail. Because if you don't list it, you won't plan for it in your room.

Electronics. In this age of technology, it seems we can't walk five steps without running into an electronic device. We've got microwaves and toasters and blenders in our kitchens. TVs and DVD players and speakers in our family rooms. Computers and scanners and printers in our home offices.

You can find technology in practically every room of our homes. And as much as we don't want to admit it, we've become dependent on it. So to avoid a wicked bout of gadget withdrawal, think about what electronic equipment you'll need for each of your aspirations. Even if it's something as small as an alarm clock. If you need it, plan for it.

Appliances & Plumbing Fixtures. Of all the tools we put in our homes, these are the ones we should praise the high heavens for. Without them, we'd spend our whole day slaving over hot fires, plunging our hands in soapy water and peeing in a ditch. That's why I can't imagine any sane person forgetting about a single one of those all-so-important, miracle devices they need. But just in case, consider yourself reminded.

Storage. There's no way getting around it. Many of our aspirations require a lot of stuff. And if you don't want that stuff lying on your floor or cluttering up your workspace, then you'll need storage.

If your aspiration is cooking, where you need a bunch of little doodads and thingamajigs, then be sure to include storage on your list. Don't worry about being too specific about what type of storage you need. We'll get to that later. For now, a general idea is just fine.

Accessories. When it comes to tools, there are the big ones. Like sofas, sinks and refrigerators. And then, there are the small ones — the little tools that everyone forgets about. Like a pad and paper near the phone for jotting messages. Or a soap dish near the sink for washing hands. Or a bedside tray for corralling jewelry taken off before bed.

Now I realize some people may think those tiny tools aren't important to list. But if you don't list them, you won't create a place for them. Which means, you'll end up squeezing them in wherever they'll fit afterwards. And that won't necessarily be the most convenient or attractive place.

I'm sure everyone's seen a random phone cluttering up an otherwise gorgeous kitchen counter or a desk covered by chargers and gizmos. All because no one thought ahead and planned for those all-so-important, small tools.

Don't let that happen to you. Carefully think about all of the little tools you need for each of your aspirations. Like pen holders and file folders. Hair dryers and curling irons. Place mats and serving bowls. All those small accessories.

Space. Technically, this isn't a tool. But for some aspirations, it's most definitely needed. Like kickboxing. Or ballroom dancing. Or any type of activity that requires you to move around a lot or flail your arms. So for each aspiration that requires movement, be sure to ask yourself how much wide-open space you need.

THE CHARACTERISTICS YOU NEED

As you know, having the right tools is not enough to make your space function well. Those tools themselves must also be functional. So for each tool you list, you must also note which of the functional characteristics it must possess. That way, when it comes time to choose what to use in your room, you'll know exactly what you need.

Accessibility. Ideally, everything in our home would be equally easy to access. But that's not the case. There will always be top shelves and farthest corners. Which means, not all tools will be equally easy to get to.

That's not such a big deal if you don't plan to use a tool frequently. But if you do, you'll want it to be easy to access. That way you'll spend less time getting what you need and more time doing what you want.

Amount. If you don't have enough of the right tool, you might as well not have the tool at all. A single chair at a dinner party won't do you much good. That's why you must know how much of each tool you need.

In private rooms, such as bedrooms and bathrooms, answering that question is easy. The same number of people use the room day-in and day-out.

It's the public areas of our home, such as living and dining rooms, that can be difficult. If you plan to entertain often, then base your needs on the largest number of people you plan to entertain frequently. An easy way to gauge that number is to think back to the holidays. How many people do you typically have over? That's how much seating you need.

If you don't entertain often, then having extra seating beyond those who live in your home isn't as crucial. But it's always nice to have extra in case friends drop by. So plan accordingly.

Comfort. Few people enjoy sitting in uncomfortable chairs or sleeping on uncomfortable beds. In fact, I can't think of a single person. So if any of your tools require someone to stay in a stationary position for an extended period of time, comfort should be a big priority.

Now how comfortable does it have to be? Well, that depends on how often you plan to use it and how long of a time you plan to use it for. The more often and longer you use it, the more comfortable it should be.

Cleanability. If you spend all your time cleaning, you'll have no time left for your aspirations. That's why it's so important for the things in your room to be easy to clean.

And don't be fooled into thinking you only have to worry about cleanability if you have kids and dogs. Dinner guests and clumsiness have been known to stain things from time to time. Which means you can't avoid a mess.

So if you don't enjoy cleaning — which most people don't — you'll want your tools to be extremely easy to clean. Especially in places such as kitchens — where making a mess is practically a requirement — and family rooms — where your items must withstand a daily barrage of abuse.

Durability. They say wear is a sign of love. But it's also a sign of using the wrong material. So if you want your tools to last, you'll want them to be durable.

How durable they need to be depends on how often you plan to use them and what type of use they'll be getting. If they'll be used often and you don't plan to pussyfoot around, they'll need to be extremely durable. Especially if children will be launching themselves — among other things — at them on a daily basis.

Safety. For the most part, you don't really have to worry about safety. Except if you have very small children or are getting up there in age. Then safety becomes an issue.

If you have small children, sharp corners and small objects can be a hazard. So be sure to note that all tables and storage units must be childproof.

If you're up in years, you'll want to avoid storing heavy things up high. That way, you'll protect yourself from having something crush you. You'll also want to include grab bars in bathrooms. That way, you'll avoid slipping. So next to all storage or bathroom items, be sure to note they need to be safe.

Size. Despite what people claim, size matters. Especially when it comes to tools. Just ask anyone who's had to take a shower in 30" by 30" space. Or lounge on a tiny stool. Or share a twin size bed with someone else. It's no fun.

We need our tools to be a certain size for them to be comfortable to use — and in some cases to be useable. Imagine trying to fit your weekly groceries into a refrigerator the size of a shoe box. It's not going to happen.

Granted, most things we put in our homes come in a standard size. So you don't really have to worry about writing down the size for every tool. But if you want a tool to be a special size, be sure to make note of that. Like I want a giant freezer or desk or soaker tub. That way you'll know to make extra room for that super special item.

DOING A RUN THROUGH

The absolute best way to ensure you have everything you need for your aspirations is to do a run-through. Pretend — or actually do — the activity you plan to do. Because when you do it, all the things you need — and may have forgotten — start popping into your head.

Like a place to put the remote control. Or a spot to sit down while tying shoes. Or a buffet for serving holiday dinners.

Whatever it may be, you'll think of it during a run-through. So don't skip this step because you think you'll look silly. Because there is nothing worse than putting the finishing touches on your room only to realize it doesn't function as well as you hoped because you forgot to include something.

So do those run-throughs. Even if it's only for a handful of minutes. Often, that's all it takes to jog your memory and remind you of everything you need.

LISTING YOUR FUNCTIONAL NEEDS

The very first thing you should do when creating your functional needs list is write down all of your aspirations. Then, for each aspiration, write down what tools — lighting, window treatments, furniture, electronics, appliances & plumbing fixtures, storage and space — you will need to do that aspiration.

Once you've written down all the tools you need, go back over each one and write down any functional characteristics — comfort, cleanability, durability and safety — it must have.

Creating your list may take some time, and be sure to take all the time you need. Because every item you write on that list will end up in your room. So you must get it right. Forgetting something now could mess up your entire plan. So before you move on, be sure you've written down everything you could possibly need.

CHARACTERISTICS

- ☐ accessibility
- ☐ amount
- ☐ cleanability
- ☐ durability
- ☐ safety
- ☐ size

TOOLS

- ☐ lighting
- ☐ window treatments
- ☐ furniture
- ☐ electronics
- ☐ fixtures
- ☐ storage
- ☐ accessories
- ☐ space

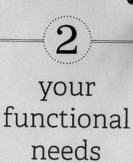

your functional needs

FOR ROOM:

DIRECTIONS:

1. List each of your aspirations.

2. Write down what tools you'll need for each aspiration.

3. Next to each tool you need, list the functional characteristics it must possess.

4. Double check you've listed everything you need.

GET YOUR OWN COPY AT TheMeghanMethod. com.

ASPIRATION:...

TOOLS: CHARACTERISTICS:

2

your functional needs

room example 1:

GUEST BEDROOM

{ Used by two kid or adult guests who may or may not be related. }

DIRECTIONS:

(1) List each of your aspirations.

(2) Write down what tools you'll need for each aspiration.

(3) Next to each tool you need, list the functional characteristics it must possess.

(4) Double check you've listed everything you need.

GET YOUR
OWN COPY AT
TheMeghanMethod.
com.

ASPIRATION: sleep blissfully

TOOLS:

CHARACTERISTICS:

bed — durable & cleanable (x 2)

pillows — comfortable & cleanable (x 4)

sheets — CLEANABLE durable & comfy (x 2)

blankets — CLEANABLE durable & comfy (x 2)

water carafe — big enough for 2 glassfuls

mattress — COMFORTABLE

2

your functional needs

room example 2:

BREAKFAST/SITTING

{ Used by a couple and any guests they may have. }

DIRECTIONS:

1. List each of your aspirations.

2. Write down what tools you'll need for each aspiration.

3. Next to each tool you need, list the functional characteristics it must possess.

4. Double check you've listed everything you need.

GET YOUR OWN COPY AT TheMeghanMethod.com.

ASPIRATION: eat breakfast / lunch

TOOLS:	CHARACTERISTICS:
table	big enough for 4
seating	enough for 4 comfortable cleanable
lighting	general
salt & pepper	
storage	for linens & small serving items (medium)

2

your functional needs

room example 3:

HOME OFFICE

{ Used by two people who primarily work from home. }

DIRECTIONS:

1. List each of your aspirations.

2. Write down what tools you'll need for each aspiration.

3. Next to each tool you need, list the functional characteristics it must possess.

4. Double check you've listed everything you need.

ASPIRATION: work on computer

TOOLS:	CHARACTERISTICS:
computer, keyboard & mouse	BIG monitor (x2)
seating	durable & comfy (x2)
desk	large w/ storage for files (x2)
lighting	task (x2)
pen & paper	
backup hard drive	small yet mighty (x2)
reference books	easy access

Where are the rest of the functional needs sheets for each example? No room! But that doesn't mean you should fill out only one. Be sure to fill out a sheet for each of your aspirations. That way you will know exactly what you need.

happy

calm

EXCITED

step:

3

your emotional needs

Savvy

If you want your aspirations to happen, you must set the right mood.

As you're well aware (or should be, page 37), you need two ingredients to make your aspirations happen. The first is your functional needs, with which you're already well acquainted. It's the second we've got to talk about.

And while everyone thinks it's form, because we've been told over and over again that when it comes to decorating, the two parts are function — *the way things work* — and form — *the way they look*. The truth is the second ingredient we need is *emotion*.

So listen up. Because the way you look at things — literally — is about to change.

WHY EMOTION MATTERS

Our emotional state dictates what we do. If we feel stressed, we skip cooking and order takeout. If we feel unsexy, we fake a headache and go to bed. If we feel tired, we sit on the couch instead of working out. Because we only do things when we're in the mood. And if we ain't in the mood, it ain't gonna happen.

That's why emotion matters when decorating. Because if our room doesn't make us feel the way we want to feel while doing our aspirations, we'll never do them. No one parties in a room that makes them feel depressed. Just as no one romances in a room that creeps them out.

So if you want your aspirations to happen, you must set the right mood in your room. And we do that through the way our rooms look.

COMMUNICATING EMOTION

We're hardwired to visually read emotion. That's what body language is all about. The different ways we contort our faces communicates certain emotions. A smile communicates happiness. A dropped jaw communicates surprise. A lifted chin communicates smugness. And we don't even have

The decorating flow chart continued.

We decorate to get:

OUR ASPIRATIONS

We make our aspirations happen by fulfilling our:

1. FUNCTIONAL NEEDS

2. EMOTIONAL NEEDS

For those who feel the Cheskin research is too old, I hear you. That's why I called up Cheskin's company, Cheskin, and spoke with the current CEO, Darrel Rhea. Unfortunately, he was unable to give me any more recent examples due to confidentiality agreements with clients. However, he assured me what Cheskin found continues to be proven today. And while he couldn't say how he knows, he did offer this anecdote: If a sofa looks uncomfortable, people will actually think it's uncomfortable — even if in a blind test they thought it was incredibly comfortable.

to think about it. We naturally read the changing shapes of other's faces and instantly understand how they feel.

And we read emotion in more than just shapes. We see emotion in colors, textures and sizes as well. A red face communicates embarrassment or anger. Smooth, supple skin communicates health and youthfulness. A large bosom communicates sexiness and fertility. And we see all those emotions for a very good reason. Survival.

If we couldn't read emotion, we wouldn't be able to decide who to trust, who to run from and who to procreate with. But because we can see sincerity and deceit, kindness and rage, sickliness and health, we know with whom to align ourselves.

Now most people would think we only need to be able to read human appearance for survival. But that's not true. If we didn't have an emotional response to our environment as well, we'd be screwed. Just imagine if we didn't feel scared when we saw dark, ominous swirling clouds. We'd stay standing in the middle of the field and get sucked up by a tornado. But because we read danger when we see that, we run. We run as fast as we can.

And it's not just fear we feel from our environment. We feel relieved when we see water. Happy when we see sun. Cautious when it's dark. Because the way our environment looks evokes an emotional reaction from us.

Of course, we only think of the sky and clouds and trees and rivers as being our environment. But we're so wrong. Everything around us is our environment. God or man-made. Which means the way everything — absolutely everything — looks evokes an emotional reaction.

But don't take my word for it. There have been plenty of scientific studies to back up that claim. Some of the earliest are due to a marketer and researcher by the name of Louis Cheskin. In the 1930s he conducted a series of experiments to determine the effect a product's packaging had on consumers. In one test, he asked housewives to use three different boxes of detergent and report which worked best. Unbe-

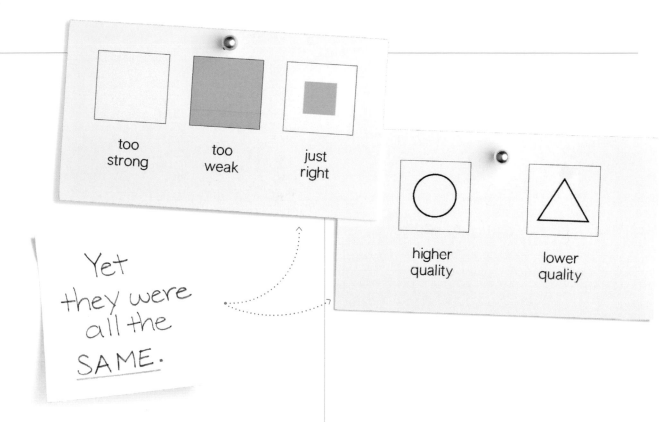

too strong   too weak   just right

higher quality   lower quality

Yet they were all the SAME.

knownst to the women, the detergent in the boxes were all the same. The only difference was their packaging. One box was yellow, one was blue and one was both yellow and blue.

Now you'd think the women came back saying all worked equally well because it was the same detergent in every box. But that was not the case. They claimed the detergent in the yellow box was far too powerful, and some even said it ruined their clothes. They reported the detergent in the blue box wasn't powerful enough, and some claimed it left their clothes dirty. All seemed to praise the detergent in the yellow and blue box. Some even described its cleaning ability as "wonderful."

Yet the only difference between the three boxes was their color. Which means, the color of the packaging alone influenced how the women felt about the product. And if the color of a small package can drastically influence how well we think a product works, what effect do you think the color of our room has on us?

The answer: a lot. Far more than we want to admit. The color of our room influences how we feel and how well we think our room works. Even what we do in it and how we use it. And it's not just color that influences that.

Cheskin also did a number of studies regarding shapes. In one, he gave consumers packages with the identical product inside. The only difference was one package displayed a circle and the other had a triangle. Over 80 percent — yes, 80 percent — favored the one with the circle and believed it was higher quality.

Not willing to trust the results, Cheskin conducted that same test over and over again, only changing the product inside the packaging, and every time, the results came back the same. Which means, like it or not, the way things look — their colors, shapes, textures, patterns, sizes — strongly influence the way we feel.

That's why the way our room looks matters. Not for some superficial reason. But because it actually elicits an emotional response from us. A deep, raw emotional response.

You know what I'm talking about. I'm sure you've been

in a room that made you feel uncomfortable or antsy like you couldn't wait to leave. Just as I'm sure you've been in a room — or at the very least, seen a room — you absolutely loved and never wanted to leave. And it wasn't because it functioned so well. It was because of how it looked.

The way every object in your room looks communicates an emotion to you. Your lamp. Your chair. Your table. Your bed. They all affect how you feel. Which means, if you want your aspirations to happen, the way all those things look must communicate the emotions you want to feel. Because if they don't, your aspirations probably won't happen.

That's why you must know how you want to feel during each one of your aspirations. And once you know how you want to feel, you'll know how your room should look. Because we communicate emotion through the shapes, colors, textures and patterns we use in our room.

HOW THINGS LOOK

The idea that emotion dictates the way things look is hard for many people to grasp, because we're stuck thinking that things either look ugly or beautiful. Not cheerful or sassy or energetic or rugged or any of the other things we can feel. But that is really how we perceive looks. Emotionally.

Just think about why you find something beautiful. Is it because it's the epitome of aesthetic perfection? No. If it were, everyone would find the identical things beautiful. But we don't. We each find different things beautiful. Because beauty is simply anything that makes us feel good. That makes us feel something we want to feel. Whatever that may be. And because we all like feeling something different, we all have a different idea of what is beautiful.

Just as we all have a different idea of what is ugly, which is simply anything that makes us feel something we don't want to feel — something bad.

When it comes down to it, we innately understand that looks simply communicate emotion. We just don't articulate

ugly
(adjective)

any object whose physical appearance makes you feel bad

it that way. Instead we use the all-too-vague and completely judgmental words "beautiful" and "ugly." And we need to stop.

For one, they don't communicate what we really feel. And two, they make people think there is a good or bad when it comes to how a room looks. But there is no good or bad looking room. Just as there is no good or bad emotion. Beauty is in the eye of the beholder. So forget about what everyone else thinks. If they dislike the way your room looks, it's simply because they don't want to feel what you want to feel. Not because your room is ugly or bad.

And if you're really worried about your room looking beautiful, stop. As long as you make your room feel the way you want it to feel, it will look beautiful to you. Because beauty is the byproduct of making a room feel the way you want it to feel.

So stop worrying about beauty and focus on emotion. Because that's all that matters.

THE RANGE OF EMOTIONS

When I say the way an object looks communicates an emotion, I'm not talking just about the typically defined emotions that philosophers and psychologists talk about. Looks can communicate far more than those standard emotions. They can communicate anything you can feel. Happy.

beautiful
(adjective)

any object whose physical appearance makes you feel good

Sad. Cozy. Airy. Warm. Cold. Sophisticated. Down-to-earth. Bright. Dark. The possibilities go on and on. Just turn the page to see what I mean.

WHAT YOU WANT TO FEEL

The emotions you want to feel completely depend on what you want to do in your room. If you want to exercise, the last thing you'll want is to feel sleepy. Just as if you want to sleep, the last thing you'll want is to feel energized.

So when it comes to determining what emotions you want, look at your aspirations. Think about the ideal emotions you want to feel while doing each one. Those emotions are the ones your room must communicate in order for your aspirations to happen.

Sometimes deciding exactly what you want to feel can be a bit difficult. That's why I always start by first listing what I don't want. Because we often feel far stronger about what we don't want to feel. So listing those emotions is easier. And once we know what we don't want to feel, figuring out what we do want becomes a breeze. After all, it's just the opposite of whatever repulsed us.

But be careful. Sometimes our brain gets in the way because we feel foolish, silly or embarrassed by the emotions we truly want to feel. But there is no shame in what you want. You deserve to feel however you want to feel. So own it. If you're worried about what other people will think, turn back to page 22 and remind them of the ground rules when decorating. No trash talking or making fun of what anyone wants. Especially how they want to feel. Because that is often what we're most sensitive about.

LISTING YOUR EMOTIONAL NEEDS

When listing emotions, we expect it to just come to us within a matter of seconds. But that's not always the case. Sometimes it takes days for the emotions we want to feel to bubble to the surface. So take your time.

Don't feel like you have to list a gazillion emotions. Sometimes we only want to feel one or two emotions in a room.

If you're having a particularly hard time, read emotional words. As you read each one, listen to your gut. Does it respond positively or negatively? The emotions your gut roots for are the ones you more than likely want to feel.

And whatever you do, don't think about it. Logic won't get you anywhere. To determine what emotions you need, you just have to feel. So let go, and use your gut.

Once you've created a list of emotions, sit on it for a day or two. It's very important you get them right. The way your room looks will be based entirely on those emotions. So be sure they're the ones you really want to feel before you move on to the next step.

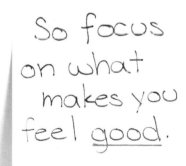

So focus on what makes you feel good.

GLAMOROUS

EDGY

dr

inspired

cheerful

mysterious

soothed

fest

CAPABALE

TOUGH

amy

POWERFUL

cool

peaceful

sensual

e

SOPHISTICATED

energized

elegant

GOOFY

your emotional needs

FOR ROOM:

DIRECTIONS:

1. List each of your aspirations.

2. Under each aspiration, list all of the emotions you do not want to feel while doing each.

3. Then, list all the emotions you do want to feel.

4. Double check you really want to feel all the emotions you listed.

GET YOUR
OWN COPY AT
TheMeghanMethod.
com.

ASPIRATION:..

I DON'T WANT TO FEEL: I WANT TO FEEL:

....

....

....

....

....

....

....

ASPIRATION:..

I DON'T WANT TO FEEL: I WANT TO FEEL:

....

....

....

....

....

....

....

3

your emotional needs

room example 1:

GUEST BEDROOM

{ Used by two kid or adult guests who may or may not be related. }

DIRECTIONS:

1. List each of your aspirations.

2. Under each aspiration, list all of the emotions you do not want to feel while doing each.

3. Then, list all the emotions you do want to feel.

4. Double check you really want to feel all the emotions you listed.

GET YOUR
OWN COPY AT
TheMeghanMethod.
com.

ASPIRATION: sleeping & reading

I DON'T WANT TO FEEL:	I WANT TO FEEL:
energized	relaxed
overwhelmed	soothed
	cocooned
	welcomed

ASPIRATION: wake up/get ready

I DON'T WANT TO FEEL:	I WANT TO FEEL:
gross	clean
sluggish	crisp
dark	refreshed
somber	glamorous

3

your emotional needs

DIRECTIONS:

1. List each of your aspirations.

2. Under each aspiration, list all of the emotions you do not want to feel while doing each.

3. Then, list all the emotions you do want to feel.

4. Double check you really want to feel all the emotions you listed.

ASPIRATION: *eat breakfast*

I DON'T WANT TO FEEL:	I WANT TO FEEL:
sluggish	energized
gloomy	optimistic
tired	cheerful
stressed	fresh
	sunny
	structured
	fun
	calm

ASPIRATION: *gather for brunch*

I DON'T WANT TO FEEL:	I WANT TO FEEL:
tense	happy
	relaxed
	playful
	energized
	soothed
	cozy
	comforted

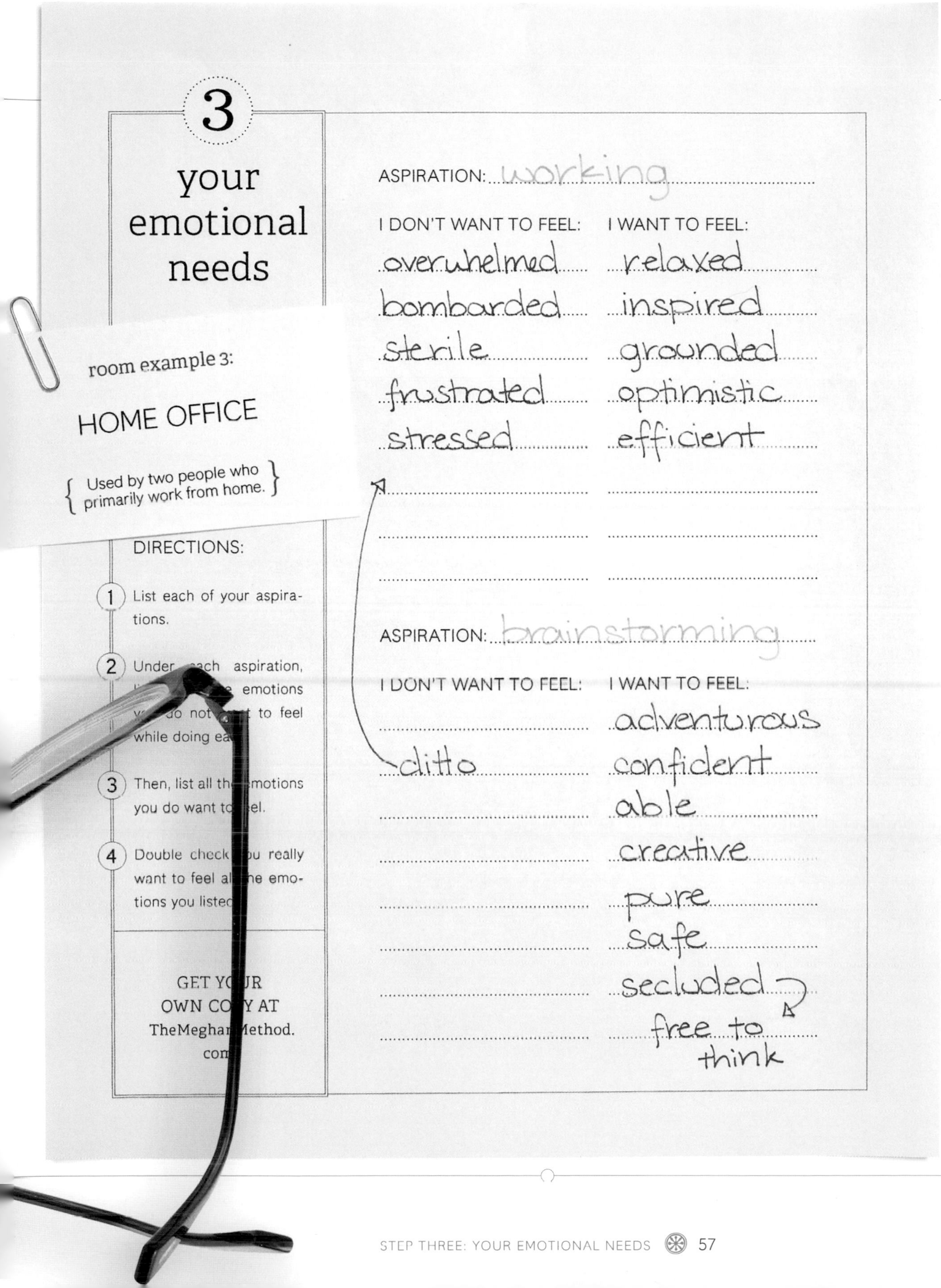

your emotional needs

room example 3:

HOME OFFICE

{ Used by two people who primarily work from home. }

DIRECTIONS:

(1) List each of your aspirations.

(2) Under each aspiration, list the emotions you do not want to feel while doing each.

(3) Then, list all the emotions you do want to feel.

(4) Double check you really want to feel all the emotions you listed.

GET YOUR OWN COPY AT TheMeghanMethod.com

ASPIRATION: working

I DON'T WANT TO FEEL:

overwhelmed
bombarded
sterile
frustrated
stressed

I WANT TO FEEL:

relaxed
inspired
grounded
optimistic
efficient

ASPIRATION: brainstorming

I DON'T WANT TO FEEL:

ditto

I WANT TO FEEL:

adventurous
confident
able
creative
pure
safe
secluded
free to think

Where are all the emotional needs sheets for each example? Again, no room!

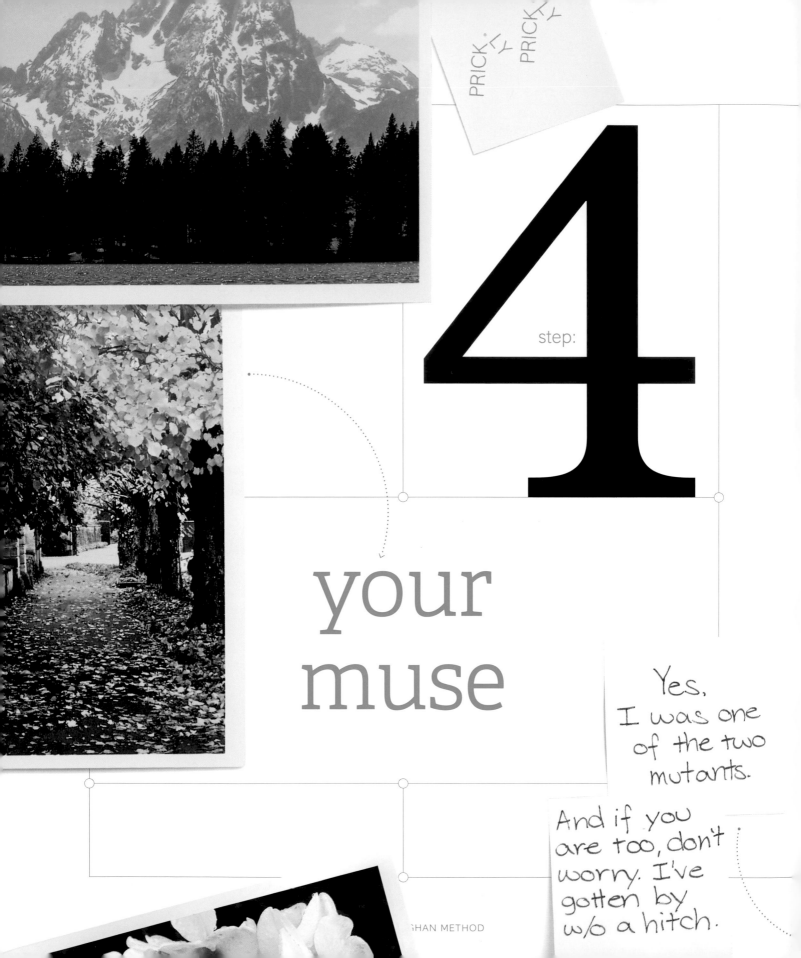

PRICK. PRICK.

step:

4

your
muse

Yes,
I was one
of the two
mutants.

And if you
are too, don't
worry. I've
gotten by
w/o a hitch.

During college I attended a guest lecture given by neurologist Vilayanur Ramachandran. Part way through, he displayed two images and asked, "Which is Kiki, and which is Bouba?"

a.

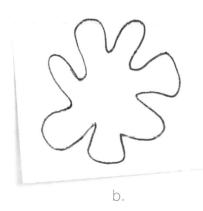

b.

The shapes above are similar to the ones he showed. So go ahead. What do you think?

After giving us a few seconds, he pointed to shape B and asked, "Who thinks this is Kiki?"

Two out of over a hundred people raised their hands.

"Well, there's one or two mutants," he joked.

Because practically everyone — 95 percent to 98 percent of the population — believes Kiki is the sharp shape and Bouba is the rounded one. Which is remarkable, because there is no dictionary or cheat sheet telling us which is which. We all — well almost all of us — just happen to assign the same make-believe name to the same make-believe object. Which means only one thing. There's nothing random or arbitrary about the way we name things.

If there was, we wouldn't all agree on the same names. But we do. And we do for a reason. Because we name things based on how they look.

Kiki sounds sharp. That's why we assign the name Kiki to the sharp shape. Whereas, Bouba sounds soft. That's why we assign the name Bouba to the rounded shape.

And we don't do it with just make-believe words. We do it with all words. "Circle" sounds rounded and continuous. "Triangle" sounds pointed and incremental. "Sleek" sounds straight and harsh. "Prickly" sounds sharp and pointed. "Joy" sounds uplifted and bright. "Gloom" sounds downtrodden and overcast.

We could do this all day because most words look like they sound. Which means, you already know what all the emotions you want to feel look like.

If you didn't, you'd never be able to understand anyone else's description of something. But we do. When someone says a hotel looks rustic, we have a general idea that it will look rough and worn. Just as when someone says a restaurant looks chic, we have a general idea that it will look streamlined and sexy.

But here's the problem. We only have a general idea. If we see a picture of something, we can tell you whether or not it looks like a certain emotion. But we can't do it in reverse. We can't hear an emotional word and tell you exactly what it looks like.

For example, draw magical.

You'll probably have a hard time. Whereas, if I show you a picture of a winter wonderland and ask you if it looks magical, you probably won't even hesitate before saying yes. It will just pop out. Because winter wonderlands look magical. Period.

Now why our brains can't do it in reverse, I don't know. There are a few rare people who can hear an emotion and picture exactly what it looks like. But the majority of us can't. That's part of the reason why so many people struggle

with decorating. Because we can't take an emotion and tell you exactly what it looks like.

But just because we can't picture emotions like those rare few doesn't mean we can't decorate. It just means we need a translator. Something that turns those emotional words into a physical form.

Fortunately, when we decorate, there are two different things that translate emotions for us. The first is a muse. The second, well, we'll get to that later. For now, let's just talk about muses.

WHAT IS A MUSE

You'll often hear interior designers talk about their inspiration for a room. The thing that was the guiding force behind their choices. Well, that thing is their muse.

Now I know, muses are traditionally women. But I'm using the term loosely.

When decorating, a muse is any object whose physical appearance makes you feel the way you want to feel in your room. Think of it as the physical embodiment of your emo-

Magical looking.

happen by fulfilling our:

The decorating flow chart continued.

1.

FUNCTIONAL NEEDS

2.

EMOTIONAL NEEDS

tional wants. Because it's the characteristics of your muse — its colors, textures, shapes and patterns — that make you feel the way you do.

And it only follows that if you use those same characteristics in your room, you will evoke all those emotions you want to feel. That's why people use muses when decorating. They act like a cheat sheet — telling you exactly what colors, textures, shapes and patterns communicate the emotions you want to feel.

POSSIBLE MUSES

Like I said, your muse can be anything. Absolutely anything. Something you've seen in person. Something you've only seen in photos. It doesn't matter. As long as the way it looks makes you feel what you want to feel, it's fit to be your muse.

Of course, given that there are thousands upon thousands of potential muses, it can be a bit hard to think of the right one. That's why I've collected a bunch of pictures of potential muses, taken by friends and family, to help get your brain juices flowing. Now, by no means do they represent all of the possible muses out there. They're just a very small tip of the iceberg.

To determine what our emotional wants look like, we use two translators:

• *To be revealed on page 77.*

1.

A MUSE

2.

FINDING YOUR MUSE

Given that we can't picture what our emotions look like, finding your muse is like playing a children's memory game. You have to keep flipping over cards until you find the picture that matches. Only instead of matching identical pictures, you have to match your emotions to the picture that evokes them.

Now that can be difficult — considering there is no standard stack of muse cards to flip through. Anything in the entire world can be your muse. A place. An object. A food. A flower. Anything. Which means you've got to weed through a lot of options to find your muse. Fortunately, I've developed a system to make narrowing down the choices a bit easier.

1. LIST ALL THE POSSIBILITIES. List everything you can possibly think of that makes you feel your emotional wants. If you struggle to think of something that makes you feel all of them, tackle each emotion individually.

Now I've said this before, and I'm going to say it again. There is no shame in what you like. So don't feel awkward or embarrassed by what you're drawn to as a muse. You feel what you feel. You can't change it. So you might as well embrace it. Better yet, celebrate it. And don't worry about what anyone else thinks. Worry about what you think. That is your No. 1 priority.

2. GATHER PHOTOS. Once you have a long list, you need to see exactly what each item looks like. If you have the items on hand, great. Go get them. If not, you need to find pictures of each one.

The easiest way to find good photos is to head to your computer and do an image search. Google (google.com), Picasa (picasa.google.com) Flickr (flickr.com) and Webshots (webshots.com) are all great places to start. Find a few pictures of each of the items on your list. That way you have a good representation of what it looks like.

3. WEED OUT THE WRONG ONES. Once you have pictures of your potential muses, ask yourself, "Does it look like I expected?"

Sometimes our memory of how something looks is affected by other associations we have with it. Like its smell, taste or sound. And when we find one of those things especially good, we project that onto how it looks and we end up thinking the item looks better than it really does. Sometimes we think it's brighter. Other times we think it's richer. Either way, when we see it, we feel disappointed because it doesn't look as good as we expected.

So if you feel that way about any of the items on your list, cross it off. Because it's not its appearance that makes you feel those emotions. It's another one of its qualities. And when you choose a muse, you must find one whose physical appearance makes you feel those emotions.

4. SELECT THE RIGHT ONE. When you find the right muse, you'll know it. You'll feel it in your gut. You'll have a sensation of, "Wow. That's it." And you'll feel all those emotions you want to feel wash over you.

But not if you think about it. Turn your brain off, and turn up your gut. That's the only way to decide whether or not you've chosen the right muse. You have to just feel it.

Now, you may feel it for more than one thing. And that's okay. You can have more than one muse. Just try to limit it to no more than three. Because if you get too many, you'll have too many characteristics to choose from. And then it becomes very difficult deciding how your room should look. So keep your muses to three or less. The fewer choices you have, the easier it is to decorate.

Once you've found the muse or muses that evokes all the emotions you want to feel, you're ready to move on. But before you do, make sure you've chosen the right one. If you have even the slightest hesitation, it's not right. You need to love your muse through and through. Because the way your room looks will be based on it. So take the time to get it right.

orange & juicy

green & leafy

DISSECTING YOUR MUSE

When we use a muse, we don't take pictures of it and put them all over our room. That would look cheesy and defeat the whole purpose. To evoke the emotions we want to feel, we must use our muse's characteristics. Which means, we need to determine what they are. So that when it comes time to create your plan, you'll know exactly what to use.

Keep in mind that the more pictures you have of your muse, the easier it will be to list all of its characteristics. Because try as it may, a picture can't show you what your muse looks like in real life. It can only show you one side of it. So the more pictures you have, the more sides you can see. And the more sides you see, the better idea you have of what your muse truly looks like.

Also, the pictures you choose to use of your muse will drastically change the characteristics you list. For example, if your muse is an orange, its colors, shapes and textures will differ depending on whether you use a picture of it cut in half or on the tree. So take your time when determining which picture — or pictures — to use when listing your muse's characteristics. Use the ones that best evoke the emotions you want to feel.

Turn the page to see the characteristics you should look for in your muse — or muses.

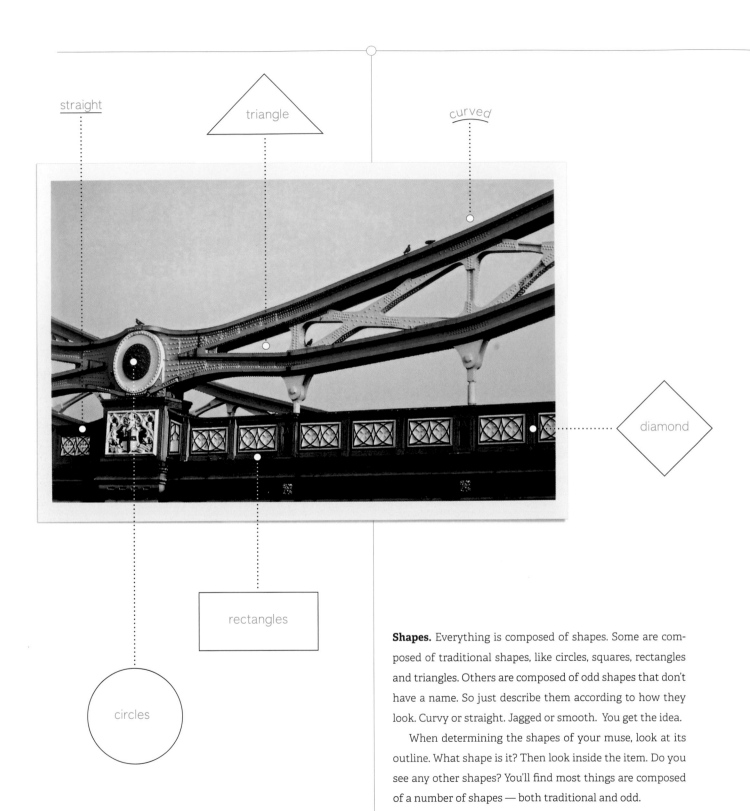

straight

triangle

curved

diamond

rectangles

circles

Shapes. Everything is composed of shapes. Some are composed of traditional shapes, like circles, squares, rectangles and triangles. Others are composed of odd shapes that don't have a name. So just describe them according to how they look. Curvy or straight. Jagged or smooth. You get the idea.

When determining the shapes of your muse, look at its outline. What shape is it? Then look inside the item. Do you see any other shapes? You'll find most things are composed of a number of shapes — both traditional and odd.

diamonds

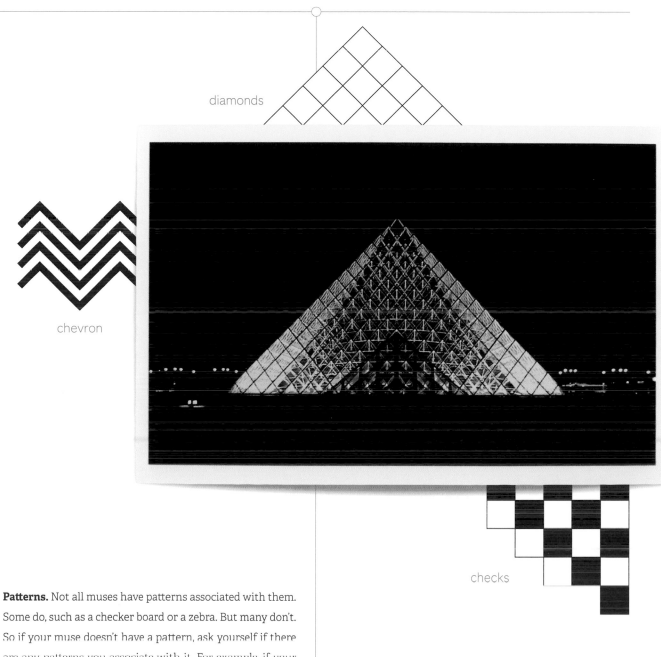

chevron

checks

Patterns. Not all muses have patterns associated with them. Some do, such as a checker board or a zebra. But many don't. So if your muse doesn't have a pattern, ask yourself if there are any patterns you associate with it. For example, if your muse is a pine cone, you may associate plaid with it. Or if your muse is a pie, you may associate picnic checks with it.

If you don't associate any patterns with your muse, don't worry. Just leave that section blank.

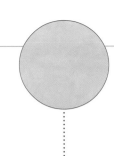

smooth & matte

bumpy & matte

rough

glassy & shiny

Textures. Texture refers to the surface quality of an object. And considering all objects have surfaces, your muse most definitely has a texture. So look at its surface. What does it look like? Rough or smooth? Wet or dry? Hard or soft? Fluffy or prickly? Silky or scratchy?

Your muse will have at least one. And often, it will have more than one. So look closely. You don't want to miss one because it's the combination of those textures that evokes the emotions you want

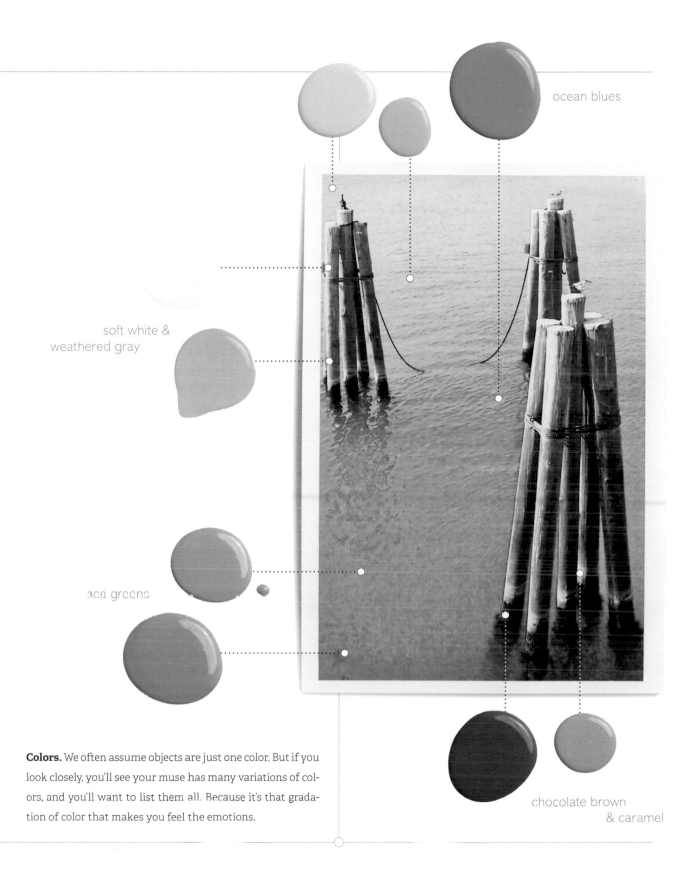

ocean blues

soft white &
weathered gray

sea greens

chocolate brown
& caramel

Colors. We often assume objects are just one color. But if you look closely, you'll see your muse has many variations of colors, and you'll want to list them all. Because it's that gradation of color that makes you feel the emotions.

not seen: wood, seagrass, seaweed, shells & glasss

rocks   sand

glass   wood   leather   metal

like wood   like leather

Materials. Some muses are easy to list materials for. Such as a sailboat. You just list all the materials that its composed of: wood, canvas, metal and rope.

Others, such as mountains, are a bit more difficult because you don't necessarily see all the materials you associate with them. But if you think about it for a bit, they'll come to you. Stone and wood.

Then there are those muses, such as a plum, that are practically impossible. Because they're not composed of things we'd use in a room, there are no materials we associate with it. So for those, you can either leave the materials section blank, or think of what materials it reminds you of. For example, maybe the skin of a plum reminds you of silk or satin.

4

your muse

FOR ROOM:

DIRECTIONS:

1. Write down your muse.

2. Get your muse, or find a few photos of your muse.

3. Use your actual muse or the photos of your muse to list all the characteristics — shapes, patterns, textures, materials and colors — you associate with it.

✱ If you have more than one muse, fill out a sheet for each one.

GET YOUR
OWN COPY AT
TheMeghanMethod.
com.

MUSE: ....

SHAPES: PATTERNS:

....

....

....

....

....

....

TEXTURES: MATERIALS:

....

....

....

....

....

....

COLORS:

....

....

....

Soothing & cocooning.
Clean & crisp.
While still being glamorous.

your muse

MUSE: seashell

SHAPES:
curved
pointed
straight

PATTERNS:
stripes

room example 1:

GUEST BEDROOM

{ Used by two kid or adult guests who may or may not be related. }

DIRECTIONS:

① Write down your muse.

② Get your muse, or find a few photos of your muse.

③ Use your actual muse or the photos of your muse to list all the characteristics — shapes, patterns, ...ures, materials and ... you associate

...ve more than ... out a sheet ...e.

TEXTURES:
smooth
rippled
jagged
coarse

MATERIALS:
glass
ceramic
silk
wool

COLORS:
dark brown   white
caramel
cream

GET YOUR
OWN COPY AT
TheMeghanMethod.
com.

4

your muse

room example 2:

BREAKFAST/SITTING

{ Used by a couple and any guests they may have. }

DIRECTIONS:

1. Write down your muse.

2. Get your muse, or find a few photos of your muse.

3. Use your actual muse or the photos of your muse to list all the characteristics — shapes, patterns, textures, materials and colors — you associate with it.

※ If you have more than one muse, fill out a sheet for each one.

GET YOUR
OWN COPY AT
TheMeghanMethod.
com.

MUSE: *spring tulips*

SHAPES:
straight
curved
circle

PATTERNS:
stripes
dots

TEXTURES:
smooth
soft

MATERIALS:
fabric
-like silk
wood
ceramic

COLORS:
yellow   green
red
pinkish red

*Fresh & cheerful,
yet elegant
& sophisticated.*

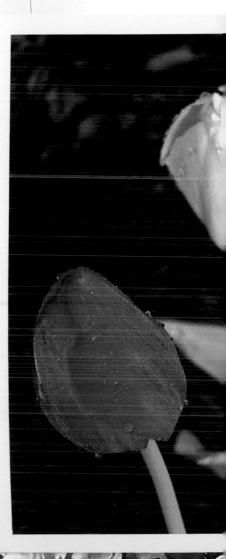

Inspiring & optimistic.

MUSE: malachite meets

SHAPES:
curvy
jagged

PATTERNS:
blotchy dots

Grounded & pure.

room example 3:

HOME OFFICE

{ Used by two people who primarily work from home. }

Efficient, confident, able & adventurous despite having shipwrecked.

1. Write down your muse.

2. Get your muse, or find a few photos of your muse.

3. Use your actual muse or the photos of your muse.

TEXTURES:
rough

MATERIALS:
stone

Takelung.

Fünfmastiges Schiff „Potosi", 6150 Tonnen Tragfähigkeit. Erbaut für F. Laeisz in Hamburg von Joh. C. Tecklenborg in Geestemünde.

Bibliographisches Institut in Leipzig.

Meyers Konv.-Lexikon, 5. Aufl.

Zum Artikel »Takelage« (Bd. 19).

COLORS:
green
white

Relaxed, secluded & safe in my dreams.

MUSE: shipwrecked

SHAPES:
straight
rectangles
curved

PATTERNS:
geometric

TEXTURES:
rough
smooth
shiny
matte

MATERIALS:
wood
metal
canvas

ORS:
llow
ack

MUSE: on a deserted island

SHAPES:
jagged
straight

PATTERNS:
lines
stripes

TEXTURES:
rough
bumpy

MATERIALS:
wood
seagrass
sand
shells/coral
rocks
glass

COLORS:
brown   white
green   blue
cream

step:

5

your style

YOU
HAVE
STYLE.

It's true.
You do.

A muse alone is not enough to translate our emotions into a complete physical form. Because muses only tell us what general characteristics to use. They don't specify the details. And the details matter.

Both you and I could have the identical muse and use the same shapes, patterns, textures, colors and materials. Yet our rooms could look completely different all because of the details. Your room may have tons of ornamentation. Mine might have none. Or vice versa. And that difference in our rooms all comes down to our individual style, which is the second emotional translator we need when decorating.

WHAT IS STYLE

People think style is something you either have or you don't. So when the topic is brought up, they get all nervous because they don't think they have it. In fact, most people spend their entire lives thinking they have to mimic those who do have style.

But guess what. You have style. You've always had style. And you always will have style. You're probably just not in tune with it.

Style is simply the visual representation of our core values. And we all have core values. They're the things we believe to be true no matter what. Like cleanliness is a virtue. Or honesty above all else. Or hard work equals reward. And so on.

Typically, we're completely unaware of our core values. But they're there. They're our internal compass guiding every one of our decisions. And to figure out what they are, all you have to do is look around. As crazy as it may

aspirations happen by fulfilling our:

The decorating flow chart completed.

1. FUNCTIONAL NEEDS

2. EMOTIONAL NEEDS

To determine what our emotional wants look like, we use two translators:

1. A MUSE

2. YOUR STYLE

sound, we surround ourselves with things that confirm what we believe.

In communication theory it's called selective exposure. So if you're a liberal, you probably read a liberal newspaper. Just as, if you're a conservative, you probably watch a conservative news channel. Because at the end of the day, we prefer hearing things that align with what we believe.

And it's not just news we do it with. We surround ourselves with objects that represent what we believe as well. That's why people who feel strongly about the green movement often use natural objects such as driftwood, plants and rocks to decorate their homes. Or why people who believe in hunting hang stags' heads on their walls. Because we like seeing things that reflect our beliefs.

That's all style is. And you can clearly see that when you look at historical styles. Each one is reflective of the ethos — collective beliefs — of the society at that particular snapshot in time.

Take the Victorian style for example. During that time period, people praised progress — particularly man's ability to create machines. That's why mass-produced, overly-ornate products became so popular. Because they represented man's progress. And the more ornate, the better. Because the more ornate an object was, the more sophisticated the machine needed to be that made it. So Victorians stuffed their rooms with as many ornate things as they could get their hands on. That's why the Victorian time period became known for its tawdry decadence.

But not everyone liked the progress. Around that time, a growing number of people became disgusted by the opulence and inauthenticity of the Victorian period. They wanted to return to a simpler time when things were hand-made out of natural materials. So they started building homes with clean lines, exquisite workmanship and local materials. And the Craftsman style was born.

When you look at each of those styles — the Victorian and Craftsman — you can clearly see what they believed to be good. It's reflected in the way they look. Just as what you believe is reflected in the way your personal style looks. Because as I said, style is simply our core beliefs communicated through the way things look.

THE IMPORTANCE OF YOUR STYLE

No matter how much we'd like to believe we're open to other opinions, when it comes down to it, we only feel comfortable when surrounded by things that reflect what we believe. That's why it's so important to determine your style and hold on to it. Because if you don't decorate your home according to your style, you'll always feel uncomfortable.

Just imagine an animal rights activist living in a home filled with taxidermy. Or an eternal optimist living in an all black home. It'd cut across the grain of their very being, irritating them day after day. And no one — at least not that I know of — wants to feel frustrated at home.

The only way you'll feel comfortable in your home is if you decorate it according to your personal style. And you need to feel comfortable in order to make your aspirations happen.

USING YOUR STYLE

Our style is like a pair of glasses. They change the way we see the world. That's why you and I could have the identical muse, yet our rooms would look completely different. Because we see the world through different glasses. And those glasses are always on. Which means, they influence the way we see everything — including our emotional wants and muse.

You see, our style glasses act like a filter. When we look at our emotional wants and muse through them, we get a sharper, more refined picture of exactly what our room should look like. How we should use the colors, textures, shapes, patterns and materials of our muse. How much ornamentation we should incorporate and layer throughout our room. What type of lighting and materials we should favor or avoid. That's what our style tells us. It clarifies the details and gives us a precise idea of the way our room should look in order to make us feel the way we want to feel.

OWNING YOUR STYLE

In order to use your style, you must accept it. Which can be exceptionally hard for some people. Because we've spent our entire lives being told some styles are better than others. With the trendy styles earning the gold star of approval.

But here's the truth. No style is better than any other style. Just as no one's beliefs are better than anyone else's. They're just different. And no matter how hard you try, you'll never get everyone to love your style. It's impossible. Because some people don't share your core values, which means they'll feel uncomfortable in your room. Just as you'd feel uncomfortable in their rooms.

So don't take it personally. Instead, learn to celebrate the different styles for what they are: an expression of a differing opinion. And most importantly, learn to celebrate your own.

Your style is uniquely you. Be proud of it. Don't let the trends make you feel like your style isn't good enough. Trends are simply a reflection of what our society currently believes. Well, more like what the media and product designers believe. And you don't have to agree with them. They're simply posing another perspective, not giving a dictum of what is stylish.

The most stylish thing for you will always be your own style. So ditch the trends, and own what you like.

STEERING CLEAR OF OTHER STYLES

Many people would say that to understand your own style you must study those that came before you. But I whole-

style
(noun)

the physical representation of your core values

heartedly disagree. Decorating according to specific styles is all about intellect, because you have to know the context in order to understand the room.

Which means the room will speak to your head, not your heart. And when decorating it's the heart — the gut emotional reaction — that matters. Not some pretentious idea. Because we only do our aspirations when we feel in the mood. And in order to be in the mood, we must feel how we want to feel. And emotion gets us in the mood far better than intellect ever will. That's why I don't believe you must be fluent in the historic styles to be able to decorate. I actually think they just get in the way.

Knowing all the styles makes it harder for you to listen to your gut emotion. Because instead of just seeing an object, you see its style and all the labels other people have placed on it. Which makes it difficult to determine whether you like that object because it feels good or because other people have said it looks good.

So forget about all the design styles. Decorating is not about copying someone else's style. It's about finding your own.

Now there are two exceptions. One, if you're doing a historic restoration, then you'll want to learn all about the style you're trying to recreate. Two, if you're fascinated by design styles and want to take that up as a hobby, then by all means research away. But other than that, steer clear of them. That way you don't risk being influenced by what other people think.

FINDING YOUR STYLE

You'd think that when it comes to finding your style, all you have to do is list your beliefs and values. But it doesn't work that way. For one, most of us don't know what our core values are. They're buried too deep in our subconscious.

And two, even if we could list them, we wouldn't be able to figure out what they looked like. Remember, our brains don't work in reverse. We can't draw what a belief looks like. But if we see an image, we can tell you if it feels right to us. (Page 60, if this isn't ringing a bell.)

That's why when it comes to finding your style, you've got to work backwards. You've got to look through tons of room images until you find ones that feel good to you. And those — the ones that feel good — are the ones that communicate your core values and represent your style.

And don't worry about not knowing whether or not a room feels good. You'll have an instant gut reaction. Just like on Christmas morning. You don't have to contemplate whether or not you like a gift. You know instantaneously. Just as you won't have to contemplate whether or not you like a room. If you do, you'll know. You'll feel an intense "Wow" for it.

So as you go through all the photos, listen to your gut. It's your style barometer. And it will never lead you wrong. So let's get to it.

1. FIND TONS OF ROOM PHOTOS. Magazines and books have spectacular room photography. But if you want to find a lot of photos fast, go online. Most magazines have large photo archives, and blogs are a treasure trove of room photography. For a list of where to start your search, turn the page.

Whatever you do, don't censor yourself and go to the places you think you'll like. No. No. No. Expose yourself to as much diversity as possible. For one, you never know what you may like. And two, the more looks you expose yourself to, the better you'll understand your style. Because you'll start to notice a pattern as to what you hate and what you love. And that's exactly what we're trying to figure out. So look at rooms of every style imaginable.

2. SORT THE PHOTOS. It's obvious that you should put all the photos you like in a pile, because they represent your style. But you should also put the ones you hate in a pile. Because they help you to gain a deeper understanding of exactly what your style is by telling you what it's not. And most importantly, what to avoid.

If you're looking through magazines, putting the photos you love and hate into piles will be easy. All you'll have to do is rip them out.

But that doesn't work if you're looking for photos online. So instead, you'll need to create two folders on your desktop. One for the photos you love and another for the photos you hate. When you find a photo you either love or hate, you'll want to place it in its corresponding folder.

If you have a hard time finding photos you want to save, don't worry. That just means you have a very unique style. But don't give up either. You need to have at least a dozen photos in each pile, if not more. The more photos you have, the easier it will be to clearly define your style. So go through hundreds.

Plus, the more photos you go through, the better you'll get at decorating. Think of it as learning through osmosis.

3. HONE YOUR STYLE. Some people have very staunch, clearly-defined core values that never change. Their style is exceptionally consistent and precise. If you're one of those people, when you look through the pile of photos you like, they'll all look extremely similar. And you won't need to hone your style because it's already clear cut and straightforward. So feel free to move on.

But everyone else, you need to stick around. Because your style needs some honing. You see, some people have a broad scope when it comes to their core values. That's why the photos you like seem to run the gamut. Because you have a very broad style spectrum. And which part of your style spectrum you choose to use depends completely on what you're doing. That's because we favor the values that align with what we're doing.

Think of it in terms of clothes. People with a very precise style have a closet filled with pretty much identical things. All black or all white or all formal. So when they go out, they always wear pretty much the same thing.

Whereas, people who have a broad scope of core values have closets with a wide variety of different kinds of clothes. They change the type of clothing they wear depending on the occasion. One day it might be brights. Another all black. One day extremely formal. The other ultra casual. You get the idea.

If you're a person like that, the same thing will go for your rooms. The part of your style spectrum that you use depends completely on what you plan to do. That's why many people who have a home in both the city and the country decorate them completely differently. Not because their style changes, but because a segment of their style spectrum shifts depending on what they're doing.

When we're in the city, we spend more time inside. So we tend to favor our core beliefs that fall on the man-made side. Whereas, when we're in the country, we spend more time outside. So we tend to favor our beliefs that fall on the natural side.

When determining which part of your style spectrum to use in your room, look at the photos and ask yourself, "Does this environment feel right for my aspirations?"

If so, set those photos in a pile labeled "current style." Those photos represent the style you'll use in your room.

If not, don't throw them away. Set them aside in a pile labeled "alternative style." Those photos represent a part of your style you may use sometime. Once you've gone through all the photos in your love pile, you're ready to move on.

DISSECTING YOUR STYLE

Having a stack of photos won't do you any good. You have to figure out what drew you to them. What you love and what you hate about them. So first look through all of the photos you hate. What do they have in common? Those things are the antithesis of your style. They're the things to avoid.

Now look through all the photos you love — or your "current style" pile, if you had to hone your style. What do they have in common? Those things are the elements of your style. They're what you'll want to use in your room.

So start spotting those similarities. These are the things you should be looking for:

Shapes. Look at the shapes of the furniture, rugs, patterns, accessories and artwork. Do you see the same types of shapes in many of the rooms? If so, what are they? Circles? Squares? Curvy? Straight? Jagged? Smooth?

Then, look at the shapes of the rooms. Are they square? Round? Oddly shaped with lots of juts?

Patterns. Look at the patterns used throughout the rooms. How many do you see? Is there a lot of pattern? A little? None?

If you see pattern repeatedly used, is there any particular type? If so, what is it? A floral? A geometric? A stripe? Something else? Don't know the name of it? Flip to page 202.

Textures. Look at all the surfaces in the rooms. What textures do you predominantly see? Rough or smooth? Shiny or matte? Fuzzy or prickly?

Colors. There are three things to look for when it comes to color. First, do you see the same colors used in many of the rooms? If so, make note.

Second, what types of colors do you see in many of the rooms? Bright, bold colors? Dull, lackluster colors? Dark, moody colors? Light, pastel colors?

blogs

6th Street Design School
6thstreetdesignschool.blogspot.com

79 Ideas
79ideas.org

A Life's Design
alifesdesign.blogspot.com

A Merry Mishap
amerrymishapblog.com

A Perfect Gray
aperfectgray.com

Absolutely Beautiful Things
absolutelybeautifulthings.blogspot.com

Aesthetic Oiseau
aestheticoiseau.com

An Indian Summer
anindiansummer-design.blogspot.com

Anh Minh
anh-minh.com

Alkemie
alkemie.blogspot.com

All the Best
allthebestblog.com

Apartment #412
apartment-412.blogspot..com

Apartment Diet
apartmentdiet.tumblr.com

Apartment Therapy
apartmenttherapy.com

Aphro Chic
aphrochic.blogspot.com

Architect Design
architectdesign.blogspot.com

Automatism
lorilangille.blogspot.com

Beach Bungalow 8
beachbungalow8.blogspot.com

Belle Maison
bellemaison23.com

Belle Vivir
bellevivir.blogspot.com

Bijou and Boheme
bijouandboheme.blogspot.com

Bijou Kaleidoscope
bijoukaleidoscope.blogspot.com

Birch + Bird
birchandbird.com

Black. White. Yellow.
blackwhiteyellow.blogspot.com

Bromeliad
bromeliadliving.blogspot.com

Brunch at Saks
brunchatsaks.blogspot.com

Carolina Eclectic
carolinaeclectic.blogspot.com

Carrie Can
carriecan.blogspot.com

Casapinka
casapinka.typepad.com

CasaSugar
casasugar.com

Chapman Interiors Blog
champmaninteriorsblog.com

Chinoiserie Chic
chinoiseriechic.blogspot.com

Chutzpah
chutzpahrummage.tumblr.com

Chic Coastal Living
chiccoastalliving.blogspot.com

Coco + Kelley
cocokelley.blogspot.com

Coco Cozy
cococozy.com

Coco Pearl
cocopearl.blogspot.com

Color Sizzle
porterhousedesigns.com/colorsizzle

Copy Cat Chic
copycatchic.com

Cote de Texas
cotedetexas.blogspot.com

Cottage and Vine
cottageandvine.blogspot.com

Creative Influences
creativeinfluences.blogspot.com

Daily Imprint
dailyimprint.blogspot.com

Daisy Pink Cupcake
daisypinkcupcake.blogspot.com

Decor 8
decor8blog.com

Decorology
decorology.blogspot.com

Design Addict Mom
designaddictmom.blogspot.com

Design Chic
mydesignchic.com

Design Dump
mydesigndump.blogspot.com

Design Milk
design-milk.com

Design Sponge
designspongeonline.com

Desire to Inspire
desiretoinspire.net

Driftwood Interiors
driftwood-interiors.blogspot.com

Dwellers Without Decorators
dwellerswithoutdecorators.blogspot. com

Effortless Style
blog.effortless-style.com

Elements of Style
elementsofstyleblog.com

Elle Oh
elleohblog.blogspot.com

European Chic
europeanchicdesign.blogspot.com

Flights of Whimsy
myflightsofwhimsy.blogspot.com

For the Love of Gold
fortheloveofgold.blogspot.com

Gramercy
shopgramercy.blogspot.com

Green Street
greenstreetblog.blogspot.com

Habitually Chic
habituallychic.blogspot.com

Happiness Is
shannoneileenblog.typepad.com

Haven and Home
havenandhome.blogspot.com

Hooked on Houses
hookedonhouses.net

House of Turquoise
houseofturquoise.com

i suwannee
isuwannee.com

In my House
inmyhousedesign.blogspot.com

Inspired Design Daily
inspired-design-daily.com

Interiors
kikette-interiors.blogspot.com

Jamaica Byles
jamaicabyles.blogspot.com

Jessia Claire's World
jessicaclairesworld.blogspot.com

Katiedid
katie-d-i-d.blogspot.com

Knight Moves
knightmovesblog.blogspot.com

La Dolce Vita
paloma81.blogspot.com

La Maison Boheme
maisonboheme.blogspot.com

Layers of Meaning
layersofmeaning.com

Little Blue Deer
littlebluedeer.com

Little Green Notebook
littlegreennotebook.blogspot.com

Live Breathe Decor
livebreathedecor.com

Living in Andyland
livinginandyland.blogspot.com

Love Nordic Design Blog
lovenordic.blogspot.com

Luphia Loves
luphia.blogspot.com

Lush Lee
lushlee.com

Made by Girl
madebygirl.blogspot.com

Material Girls
materialgirlsblog.com

Meade Design Group
meadedesigngroup.blogspot.com

Mochatini
mochatini.org

Mrs. Blandings
mrsblandings.blogspot.com

Mrs. Howard Personal Shopper
mrshowardpersonalshopper.com

Mstetson Design
mstetson.com

My Little Apartment
mylittleapartment.blogspot.com

Obsessilicious
Obsessilicious.blogspot.com

Peppermags
peppermags.blogspot.com

Just a small sampling of the many, many design blogs.

Peppermint Bliss
peppermintbliss.com

Pink Wallpaper
pinkwallpaper.blogspot.com

Plush Palate
plushpalate.blogspot.com

Porchlight Interiors
porchlightinteriors.blogspot.com

Realestalker
realestalker.blogspot.com

Remodelista
remodelista.com

Room Envy
roomenvy.wordpress.com

Rose and Hudson
roseandhudson.blogspot.com

Sacramento Street
sacramentost.blogspot.com

Savvy Home
savvyhome.blogspot.com

Sfgirlbybay
sfgirlbybay.com

Simplified Bee
simplifiedbee.blogspot.com

Simply Grove
simplygrove.com

Slipcover Your Life
slipcoveryourlife.com

Small Place Style
smallplacestyle.blogspot.com

So Haute Style
sohautestyle.com

Strange Closets
strangeclosets.com

Studio Annetta
studioannetta.blogspot.com

Stylebeat
stylebeat.blogspot.com

Style Carrot
stylecarrot.com

Style Court
stylecourt.blogspot.com

Urban Grace Interiors
blog.urbangrace.com

The Boo and the Boy
thebooandtheboy.com

The City Sage
annesage.com/blog

The Decorista
thedecorista.com

The Glam Lamb
glamlamb.com

The Goods Design
thegoodsdesign.blogspot.com

The Peak of Chic
peakofchic.com

The Selby
theselby.com

The Style Files
style-files.com

Things that Sparkle
*thingsthatsparkleblog.
blogspot.com*

So Haute Style

Things the Inspire
thingsthatinspire.net

This is Glamourous
citified.blogspot.com

Tobi Fairley
tobifairley.com/blog

Trouvais
trouvais.com

Urban Style Vibes
urbanstylevibes.com

Velvet & Linen
brookegiannetti.typepad.com

Vintage + Chic
vintageandchicblog.com

White & Wander
emmaclements.com

Wisteria,
wisterianyc.blogspot.com

Young House Love,
younghouselove.com

Adore Home
adoremagazine.com

American Bungalow
americanbungalow.com

Anthology
anthologymag.com

Architectural Digest
archdigest.com

Arts & Crafts Home
artsandcraftshomes.com

At Home
mofflymedia.com/Moffly-Publications/atHome/

Atomic Ranch
atomic-ranch.com

Better Homes & Gardens
bhg.com

Cabin Life
cabinlife.com

Canadian House & Home
houseandhome.com

Coastal Living
coastalliving.com

Country Living
countryliving.com

Country Sampler
sampler.com

Dwell
dwell.com

Elle Decor
elledecor.com

Fresh Home
freshhomemag.com

Good Housekeeping
goodhousekeeping.com

High Gloss
highglossmagazine.com

Home & Design
homeanddesign.com

House Beautiful
housebeautiful.com

Interiors
shelterinteriors.us

Living Etc.
livingetc.com

Log Home Living
loghome.com

Lonny
lonnymag.com

Luxe Magazine
luxesource.com

Martha Stewart Living
marthastewart.com

Midwest Living
midwestliving.com

Old House Interiors
oldhouseonline.com

Real Simple
realsimple.com

Romantic Homes
romantichomes.com

Rue
ruemag.com

Southern Accents
southernaccents.com

Southern Living
southernliving.com

Style at Home
styleathome.com

Sunset
sunset.com

The Nest
thenest.com

Traditional Home
traditionalhome.com

Veranda
veranda.com

Victorian Homes
victorianhomesmag.com

Curbed
curbed.com

Decor Pad
decorpad.com

HGTV
hgtv.com

Houzz,
houzz.com

Luxist
luxist.com

My Home Ideas
myhomeideas.com

iVillage
ivillage.com

Shelterpop
shelterpop.com

Third, how much of each type of color do you see? Small punches or big swathes?

Materials. Focus on the materials in the rooms. What do you see most? Fabric? Wood? Tile? Stone? Where are those materials primarily used? On furniture? The floors? The ceilings?

Sizes. There are two sizes you should look at. First, look at the size of the rooms. Are they narrow or wide? Do you they have tall ceilings or low ceilings?

Then look at the size of the furniture and objects. Are they petite, average or oversized?

Moldings. Look at the decorative molding used on the walls and ceilings. Are there any? If so, how much? What type is frequently used? Wall panels? Crown molding? Columns? Chair rail? Beams? Don't know? Turn to page 237.

Ornamentation. Ornamentation refers to the amount of decorative flourishes and details in a room. The less ornamentation in a room, the more streamlined and plain it will appear. The more ornamentation in a room, the more ornate it will appear. How much ornamentation do you see in the rooms? Are there any types you see repeated?

Furniture. Pay close attention to each piece of furniture used in the rooms. Do you see any particular types repeated? Such as chaise lounges? Sectional sofas? Ottomans? A certain type of chair? If so, be sure to describe the pieces.

Layout. Look at how the furniture is arranged. Do you tend to see the same arrangements used throughout your photos? If so, do they look symmetrical or asymmetrical? What pieces of furniture are used in them?

Accessories. The accessories in a room are all the little chachkies like boxes, bowls, specimens, statues, mirrors and artwork. Do you see any particular types of accessories used in many of the rooms you saved? If so, what are they?

Electronics. Look for all the electronics in the rooms. Do you see any, or are they hidden? If you see any, what do they look like?

Light. First, look at the types of lighting used. Do you see lots of chandeliers? Pendants? Lamps? Sconces?

Then look at how much overall light there is. Are the rooms very bright? Are they dark? Do they have lots of windows?

What you find when looking through the photos will give you a very good idea of what you should and shouldn't use in your room. So take your time when searching for similarities. It's very important for you to accurately describe what you find because you'll use your style to guide every design choice you make.

OVERALL STYLE DESCRIPTION

After spotting all of the similarities in the photos, you should have a very good idea of what your style looks like. Now, it's time to describe it.

Very rarely does someone's style fall into an actual design style, such as French country or mid-century modern. Most of us are mutts. We like a little bit of a few, and the resulting mix is a style of our own creation. Which means describing it will come down to using your own words.

So look at all the common elements you love. Are they formal? Casual? Rustic? Modern? Traditional? Grand? Down-to-earth? Romantic? Glam? Feminine? Masculine? Classic? Hip? Edgy? Refined? Fun? Sophisticated?

Knowing the overall description of your style will help you find stores and places to shop. It will also help you to better understand your style. So take your time when figuring out what words best sum up the look you love.

5

your style

FOR ROOM:

DIRECTIONS:

1. Look at the photos you love. Write down the characteristics you see repeated in many of those photos.

2. Then, look at the rooms you hate. Write down the main similarities you see under, "Things I Hate."

3. Fill out "My Style" using a few words to describe your style based on the characteristics you love and hate.

GET YOUR
OWN COPY AT
TheMeghanMethod.
com.

MY STYLE: ....

SHAPES: PATTERNS:

....

....

....

....

....

TEXTURES: MATERIALS:

....

....

....

....

....

COLORS:

....

....

....

5

your style

FOR ROOM:

SIZES:

....
....
....
....
....
....

LAYOUT:

....
....
....
....
....
....

LIGHTING:

....
....
....
....
....
....

ORNAMENTATION:

....
....
....
....
....
....

MOLDINGS:

....
....
....
....
....
....

FURNITURE:

....
....
....
....

ART:

....
....
....
....

ACCESSORIES:

....
....
....
....

5

your style

FOR ROOM:

WINDOW TREATMENTS:

....

....

....

....

....

....

ELECTRONICS:

....

....

....

....

....

....

THINGS I HATE:

....

....

....

....

....

....

....

....

....

....

....

....

5

your style

room example 1:

GUEST BEDROOM

{ Used by two kid or adult guests who may or may not be related. }

DIRECTIONS:

1. Look at the photos you love. Write down the characteristics you see repeated in many of those photos.

2. Then, look at the rooms you hate. Write down the main similarities you see under, "Things I Hate."

3. Fill out "My Style" using a few words to describe your style based on the characteristics you love and hate.

GET YOUR OWN COPY AT TheMeghanMethod. com.

MY STYLE: cottage glamour

SHAPES:
curved
straight
square
rectangle

PATTERNS:
botanical
natural
novelty
geometric
   * all very faint
      in color

TEXTURES:
silky
smooth
crisp
nubby
rough

MATERIALS:
* fabric
wood
glass
metal (brass)
ceramic

COLORS:
neutral   bold
gold
brown

5

your style

FOR ROOM:

GUEST
BEDROOM

SIZES:

standard

LAYOUT:

mostly
symmetrical

LIGHTING:

table lamps
* wall sconces
chandeliers

ORNAMENTATION:

simple
refined
classic
slightly
masculine

MOLDINGS:

baseboards
casings
chair rail

FURNITURE:

tufted
upholstered
-chairs &
headboards
wood

ART:

natural objects
simple

ACCESSORIES:

ceramics
books
shells
glass
pillows & blankets

Notice something missing?
I skipped the "What I Hate" sheets
to avoid offending anyone.
Plus, I'm sure you can figure out how
to fill it out on your own.

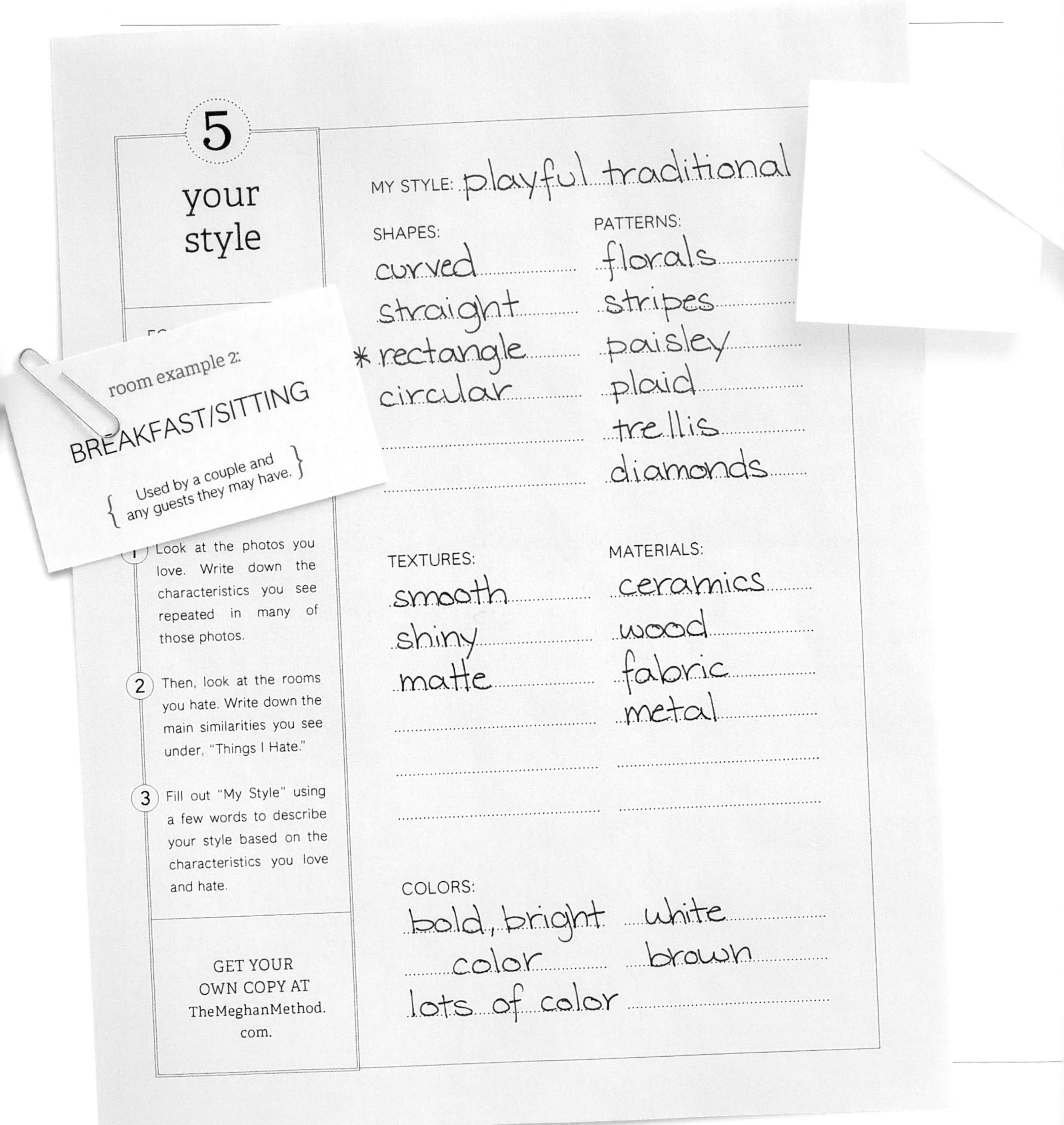

5

your style

room example 2:

BREAKFAST/SITTING

{ Used by a couple and any guests they may have. }

1) Look at the photos you love. Write down the characteristics you see repeated in many of those photos.

2) Then, look at the rooms you hate. Write down the main similarities you see under, "Things I Hate."

3) Fill out "My Style" using a few words to describe your style based on the characteristics you love and hate.

GET YOUR OWN COPY AT TheMeghanMethod. com.

MY STYLE: playful traditional

SHAPES:
curved
straight
* rectangle
circular

PATTERNS:
florals
stripes
paisley
plaid
trellis
diamonds

TEXTURES:
smooth
shiny
matte

MATERIALS:
ceramics
wood
fabric
metal

COLORS:
bold, bright color
white
brown
lots of color

5 your style

FOR ROOM:

BREAKFAST/
SITTING
ROOM

SIZES:

standard
some petite
some stuffed

LAYOUT:

symmetrical

LIGHTING:

chandeliers
pendants

ORNAMENTATION:

classic
traditional
not-over-
    the-top
a bit preppy
*roped detail

MOLDINGS:

crown
base
casings
firplace
    surrounds

FURNITURE:

painted wood
big arm chairs
ottomans

ART:

*botanicals
country sides

ACCESSORIES:

*plants
pottery
books
oriental rugs

5

your style

room example 3:

HOME OFFICE

{ Used by two people who primarily work from home. }

DIRECTIONS:

1. Look at the photos you love. Write down the characteristics you see repeated in many of those photos.

2. Then, look at the rooms you hate. Write down the main similarities you see under, "Things I Hate."

3. Fill out "My Style" using a few words to describe your style based on the characteristics you love and hate.

GET YOUR OWN COPY AT TheMeghanMethod. com.

MY STYLE: raw classic — yet fun

SHAPES:
straight
squares
rectangles
circle (some)

PATTERNS:
MINIMAL
· geometric
· exotic

TEXTURES:
* rough
smooth
bumpy
shiny

MATERIALS:
* wood
glass
metal
seagrass
* stone
plaster

COLORS:
* white
brown
green
blue
yellow
* small pops of bright color

5

your style

FOR ROOM:

HOME
OFFICE

SIZES:

grand
large

LAYOUT:

symmetrical
structural

LIGHTING:

task lamps
grand
chandeliers
pendants

ORNAMENTATION:

classical
minimal

MOLDINGS:

beams
columns
crown
base
casings

FURNITURE:

rough wood
tables
stools
daybeds
bookcases

ART:

maps
architectural
prints
animals

ACCESSORIES:

chunky hardware
specimens
glass
baskets

6

your room
evaluation

*Seeing
what
you're
working
with.*

*And taking
some
measurements.*

keeper

ROOM: BREAKFAST/SITTING

If decorating were like baking — where you start with a completely blank slate and make everything from scratch — you could move straight on to planning right now. This is because your aspirations, functional needs, emotional needs, muse and style give you all the direction you need to start creating.

But decorating is not like baking.

It's like getting dressed in the morning. You've got to work with what you've got. Sometimes, you get lucky, and love it. Other times, you loathe it. Either way, you must become well acquainted with your space before creating your plan — for three very good reasons.

One, if you don't, you won't know which parts of your room to highlight and which parts to downplay — *or in the worst-case scenario, ditch.*

Two, our rooms are already filled with a bunch of stuff. If some of it still works, there's no reason to throw it away. So you've got to go through it all and decide what you want to keep and what you want to pitch. That way, you'll know what pieces to include in your plan.

Three, try as we may, we often forget to list a few things we functionally need. But one look at our worn sofas and stained countertops reminds us that more durable fabric and impenetrable surfaces might be a better idea this time around.

And that's why it's so incredibly important to evaluate your space before making your plan. But enough chit-chat. Let's get to it.

HOW TO LOOK

When I first started wearing glasses, they drove me crazy. My nose constantly felt agitated, and I couldn't understand how people wore them all the time. But after a few days, the awkward sensation went away, and I no longer noticed them. Now, I accidentally fall asleep in them — all thanks to the way our brains work.

If our brains receive the same signal over and over again, they eventually stop responding and we no longer notice the sensation. And it doesn't just happen with things touching our skin — like glasses. Once we've seen the same thing a few times, we stop noticing the small details and only pay attention if something big changes. Think of it as our brains' safeguard against information overload. By not noticing the details, we can focus on more important matters.

Most of the time that's a good thing. But not when it comes to evaluating our rooms because we no longer see them for what they are. We don't notice the small scratches, scuffs, dings and dents our homes accumulate — just as we forget how spectacular some of our pieces truly are. All we see is a glossy overview.

And a glossy overview doesn't cut it when it comes to evaluating. You must see your space for exactly what it is — the good, the bad and the ugly — in order to know how to improve it.

So slow down. Take the time to look in every, single corner of your room. Notice all the details, and most importantly, be honest about what you see. If you do that, you'll walk away with a solid evaluation.

GETTING STARTED

The first thing most people want to do when evaluating their room is clean everything up and move furniture out of the way. But that is the absolute worst thing you can do. The best way to learn exactly what you need is to see how you really live — mess and all.

So don't move a single item. Not even an inch. No cleaning. No sweeping up. No tidying at all. While it may be hard to accept how you really live, you need to see it as is. As is on its worst day is even better, because it will be far easier for you to see what is and isn't working for you — especially when it comes to conquering clutter.

TAKE A PHOTO

Better yet, take a few. Take a shot from every angle of your room. If your room is messy or worn out, those pictures will serve as a reminder of why not to compromise on any of your functional needs. If you do, your room may end up like that again.

Plus, once you're in your brand-new room, you'll find it difficult to remember what your room used to look like. And you'll want to remember. Because the picture you take right now will prove how far you've come, and what you're capable of. So snap away. Those pictures are going in the archives.

WHAT'S NOT WORKING

I'm not talking about things that are actually broken. I'm talking about what items and parts of your current layout aren't working for the way you live.

For example, if people regularly sit on the floor during conversations, your current seating isn't working for you. You need more of it. If you feel like you're running a marathon every time you cook dinner, your kitchen layout isn't working for you. You need things to be better arranged. If you spend more time scrubbing your shower than scrubbing yourself, your tile or grout isn't working for you. You need something easier to clean.

And all those things — those terribly inconvenient things — need to be noted, because they're what to avoid when creating your room plan. Think of it like learning from your mistakes. You've got to know what's wrong in order to fix it.

So take your time looking around your room for everything that's not working, and use this handy little sheet as a guide.

Get your own copy at: TheMeghanMethod.com

6 your room evaluation

WHAT'S NOT WORK

DIRECTIONS: Check all boxes that ap

LAYOUT:
- ☐ I have too much empty space in my room. I need to fill it better.
- ☐ My room is too cramped. I need to use less stuff.
- ☐ I don't have enough space to do:
- ☐ I have to walk back and forth too much, because my stuff is too far awa
- ☐ It's too hard to have a conversation because:
- ☐ I hate the view from my:
- ☐ I need to get rid of this, because people never use it:
- ☐ People don't use this because it's inconvenient. But I wish they used th
- ☐ It's hard to walk around my room. There's bad traffic flow.

It's too hard to see the:
- ☐ TV
- ☐ View out the Window
- ☐ Computer
- ☐ Mirror
- ☐ Clock
- ☐ Fireplace
- ☐ Other:

LIGHTING:
- ☐ I don't have enough light to see what I'm doing. I need:
- ☐ I have dark corners in my room, and I don't like it.
- ☐ My lighting is too bright. I need it to be:
- ☐ I wish there was more natural sunlight in my room.
- ☐ I wish there was more candle or firelight in my room.
- ☐ I need window treatments. The sun is too bright when I'm:
  - ☐ Trying to Sleep
  - ☐ Working on my Computer
  - ☐ Watching TV
  - ☐ Other:

GET YOUR O

6

your room evaluation

WHAT'S NOT WORKING

ROOM: **BREAKFAST/ SITTING**

DIRECTIONS: Check all boxes that apply to your room, and fill in any details.

LAYOUT:

- ☐ I have too much empty space in my room. I need to fill it better.
- ☒ My room is too cramped. I need to use less stuff.
- ☐ I don't have enough space to do:
- ☐ I have to walk back and forth too much, because my stuff is too far away from where I use it.
- ☐ It's too hard to have a conversation because:
- ☒ I hate the view from my: so fa
- ☐ I need to get rid of this, because people never use it:
- ☐ People don't use this because it's inconvenient. But I wish they used this more:
- ☒ It's hard to walk around my room. There's bad traffic flow.

It's too hard to see the:

- ☐ TV
- ☒ View out the Window
- ☐ Computer
- ☐ Mirror
- ☐ Clock
- ☐ Fireplace
- ☐ Other:

LIGHTING:

- ☒ I don't have enough light to see what I'm doing. I need: more light in the center of room.
- ☐ I have dark corners in my room, and I don't like it.
- ☐ My lighting is too bright. I need it to be:
- ☐ I wish there was more natural sunlight in my room.
- ☒ I wish there was more candle or firelight in my room.
- ☐ I need window treatments. The sun is too bright when I'm:
    - ☐ Trying to Sleep
    - ☐ Working on my Computer
    - ☐ Watching TV
    - ☐ Other:

6 your room evaluation

WHAT'S NOT WORKING

ROOM:

DIRECTIONS: Check all boxes that apply to your room, and fill in any details.

SEATING:
- ☐ I don't have enough seating. I need this much more: ....
- ☐ I have too much seating. I only need this much: ....
- ☐ My seating isn't comfortable. It's too: ....
- ☐ I need more durable seating, because my current stuff is dirty and worn out.

SURFACES:
- ☐ I need more counter or work space. I need: ....
- ☐ I have too much counter or work space. I only need: ....
- ☐ I don't have enough space to eat. I need: ....
- ☐ I don't have enough places to set drinks, snacks, books and other things. I need: ....
- ☐ My surfaces are too hard to clean. They are: ....
- ☐ My countertops or work spaces are too low. They need to be: ....
- ☐ My countertops or work spaces are too high. They need to be: ....

APPLIANCES:

I don't want another appliance like: ....

    because: ....

BEDDING:
- ☐ I want a new mattress. My current one is too: ....
- ☐ I want new bedding. My current bedding is too: ....
- ☐ My bed is too high.
- ☐ My bed is too low.
- ☐ My bed is too small.
- ☐ My bed is too big.

OTHER THINGS NOT WORKING:

....

....

6

your room evaluation

WHAT'S NOT WORKING

ROOM: **BREAKFAST/ SITTING**

DIRECTIONS: Check all boxes that apply to your room, and fill in any details.

SEATING:

☐ I don't have enough seating. I need this much more: _____

☐ I have too much seating. I only need this much: _____

☒ My seating isn't comfortable. It's too: *stiff. I want big and stuffed.*

☐ I need more durable seating, because my current stuff is dirty and worn out.

SURFACES:

☐ I need more counter or work space. I need: _____

☐ I have too much counter or work space. I only need: _____

☐ I don't have enough space to eat. I need: _____

☒ I don't have enough places to set drinks, snacks, books and other things. I need: *more side tables*

☐ My surfaces are too hard to clean. They are: _____

☐ My countertops or work spaces are too low. They need to be: _____

☐ My countertops or work spaces are too high. They need to be: _____

APPLIANCES:

I don't want another appliance like: _____

because: _____

BEDDING:

☐ I want a new mattress. My current one is too: _____

☐ I want new bedding. My current bedding is too: _____

☐ My bed is too high.

☐ My bed is too low.

☐ My bed is too small.

☐ My bed is too big.

OTHER THINGS NOT WORKING:
The current wall color. Too drab.

PREFERENCES

While living in our rooms, we build up a lot of preferences, like putting our feet up when relaxing, or sitting while baking cookies. And having a list of those preferences is incredibly important because then it's super easy to customize your room according to your likes, which will make it far more enjoyable and comfortable for you. So take the time to think about what you truly prefer, and use the sheet below as a guide.

Get your own copy at: TheMeghan-Method.com

6 your room evaluation

MY PREFERENCES

ROOM:

DIRECTIONS: List all of your preferences under each category.

FURNITURE & ACCESSORIES: I prefer these types:

FURNITURE & ACCESSORIES: I hate these types:

STANDING ACTIVITIES: I prefer to stand when:

SITTING ACTIVITIES: I prefer to sit when:

LYING ACTIVITIES: I prefer to lie when:

6

your room evaluation

MY PREFERENCES	HOME OFFICE
	ROOM:

DIRECTIONS: List all of your preferences under each category.

FURNITURE & ACCESSORIES: I prefer these types:

daybeds
stools
open shelving

big, magnetic whiteboard for
writing & hanging inspirations,
ideas, projects & notes
↳ the bigger, the better

FURNITURE & ACCESSORIES: I hate these types:

short tables you have to bend over when
working standing up

STANDING ACTIVITIES: I prefer to stand when:

writing on whiteboard
creating collages & picture boards
working on projects - sometimes

SITTING ACTIVITIES: I prefer to sit when:

working on computer
discussing tactics
working on projects - sometimes

LYING ACTIVITIES: I prefer to lie when:

reading - in a half sit/lie
media scanning - half sit/lie
napping

YOUR STORAGE NEEDS

I purposefully left storage out of both the "What's Not Working" and "Your Preferences" sections, because it's such a force to be reckoned with that it must be tackled alone. And heed my warning, you do not want to skip this part. Planning for the proper amount of storage may be the most important thing you do when decorating, because if you don't, you'll end up with clutter. And clutter is the No. 1 all-time nemesis of any room, because it obscures the spectacular view you worked so hard to create and gets in the way of your activities. So you must — and I do mean must — address your storage needs.

Now I realize most people believe you must be naturally neat to have a clutter-free home. But that's not true. Not even in the least. I am the antithesis of a naturally neat person. I hate everything to do with cleaning. I don't mind living in chaos. And I refuse to spend a morning — or even an hour — tidying up each week. Yet if you were to look in my closet or drawers, you would think I was the queen of neat freaks. And it's not because I force myself to do those things I hate doing. It's because I finally discovered the secret of perfect organization.

And I promise, it has nothing to do with guilt. I know many people use it as a motivator — making you feel like a bad person who doesn't care about your family or yourself — and expect that knowledge to keep you organized.

But that doesn't work, because messy people aren't bad people. We're just economical. We realize the cost benefit isn't in our favor. Having a perfectly clean house doesn't give us as much joy as playing with our kids, chatting on the phone, reading a book or relaxing on the sofa. So after a long, hard day where we've worked our fingers to the bone, why come home and put ourselves through more terrible, mind-numbing work — especially when the world won't end if we don't do the dishes or hang up our jackets? It just doesn't make sense. Given our little time and demanding schedule, there are much more important things for us to do — even if

it's just taking a well-deserved, sanity-restoring break.

So if you want to stay organized, you must make it effortlessly easy — as easy as being messy, because that's the only way we'll do it. That's the secret. And here's how.

ONE: Only Store What You Need. Nothing else. We only have so much storage space and if you stuff it full of things you *don't* need, you won't be able to see what you *do* need.

So get rid of those unwanted gifts you hold onto compulsively. Get rid of those tennis rackets you swore you'd use someday and never did. Get rid of those old worn-out, beat-up shoes. Get rid of them all, because you either don't use them, or they're past their prime, which means you don't need them. So give them to someone who does. That's what Salvation Army, Goodwill, Craigslist (craigslist.org) and eBay (ebay.com) are for.

Once all that stuff is gone, you'll be amazed by how easy it is to find exactly what you need and how uncluttered and clean your drawers and closets look.

TWO: Everything You Need Must Have a Home. When things don't have a specific home, we don't know where to put them, so we leave them out in the open. Then, when we have to tidy up, we run around like chickens with our heads cut off, not knowing where to put things. So we stuff it all in any empty nook and cranny we can find. But that never ends well, because the next time we actually need those things, we don't know where they are.

That's why everything must have a designated home — a place where it belongs. Because then, you never have to think about where it goes. Putting it away becomes automatic. The scissors go here. The mail goes here. The keys go here. And when you need those things, you know exactly where they are: in their home, where they belong.

THREE: Those Homes Must be Easy to Access. And I do mean *easy*. If a "storage solution" is too hard to use, we won't use it. Don't listen to those experts who say you must train yourself to use those systems. We're not dogs. No one's going to give us a treat each time we put our laundry away. Which means, if a storage system isn't extremely easy to use, we're not going to use it.

And we shouldn't. There is no reason to put yourself through the pain and misery of using a storage system that wastes your time. Time that could be better spent doing something you enjoy. So stop blaming yourself. Stop thinking you're a horrible person for not being able to stay organized. Realize the truth. It's not you. It's your storage.

If you want to conquer clutter and stay effortlessly organized, you must choose storage systems that are easier to use than being messy.

For example, after a hard day at work or school, who doesn't feel like throwing his or her bag and coat on a chair? It's so much easier than hanging it up in the closet, which requires so many actions:

1st action — put your bag down

2nd action — take off your coat

3rd action — open the closet door

4th action — take a hanger off the rod

5th action — put your coat on the hanger

6th action — put the hanger and coat back in the closet

7th action — pick up your bag

8th action — put your bag where it belongs in the closet

9th action — close the closet door

That's way too hard. Only someone who's extremely disciplined would do that. Everyone else throws their coats and bags on chairs, because it's so much easier. It takes a third of the effort. Just three actions:

1st action — throw your bag on the chair

2nd action — take your coat off

3rd action — throw your coat on the chair

That's all most of us are willing to do when it comes to putting our coats and bags away. Just three actions. Anything more is too hard. So if you don't want coats and bags littering all the chairs in your home, find a storage system that only requires three actions. And don't worry, it's possible. It takes just as much effort to throw a coat and bag on a chair as it does to throw your coat on a hook or your bag in a cubby.

1st action — throw your bag into a cubby: its home

2nd action — take off your coat

3rd action — hang your coat on a hook: its home

When determining what home is best for each item, first determine how many actions it takes to be messy. Write that number down. Then brainstorm storage solutions that require the same amount of actions or less. Those are the ones that will work as a home for your items.

Now, there are some times when you can't find a satisfactory storage solution that requires as few actions as it takes to be messy. In those cases, people are typically willing to do one to two extra actions above what it takes to be messy — especially if the item is rarely used. But that action must be easy — very easy. Just remember, the less actions required, the better. So work hard to keep them to a minimum.

If you do those three things — only store what you need, have a home for each item and make that home easy to use — there will be no excuse for being messy. Being organized will be just as easy. Plus, you have the long-term benefits of:

One, being able to find your stuff whenever you need it.

Two, being able to see the gorgeous home you worked so hard to create.

Three, being able to enjoy your activities because there's no clutter in the way.

No economical person would pass up on that because it's a win-win. You put in the same amount of effort as being messy, yet you get far more from being neat. So you might as well be neat.

That's the secret to staying organized.

Of course, where do you start? Especially when your home is filled with clutter and difficult storage solutions? Right here:

1. TACKLE THE STUFF IN PLAIN SIGHT. If you did what I asked and kept your room as is on its worst day, more than likely you have clutter scattered around your room. Like mail, keys and half-eaten bags of pretzels on the counter. Soccer cleats, backpacks and toys on the floor. Papers, boxes and notebooks on the dining table. And you need to sort through it all to figure out what you really need.

First, pick up all the trash, and throw it away or recycle it.

Next, pick up everything you no longer need — all the things you've worn out or will never use. What you no longer need is a judgment call. Some people say to get rid of practically everything to free yourself from material possessions. Others will tell you to hold onto practically everything for sentimental reasons. Here's what I know: the more you hold onto, the harder it will be to fit everything into your room. So get rid of as much as you can because the more free space you have, the easier it will be to see the things you need and truly love. Once you've decided on what you no longer need, sort those items into two piles — donate and sell. Then, set them aside to deal with later.

Everything that's left is what you truly need. And don't touch a thing. There's a reason I told you to leave your room exactly how it is. The placement of your clutter tells you one of three things.

A. The item doesn't have a home and desperately needs one. Think mail. It ends up on the kitchen counter because no one knows where else to put it.

B. The item has a home, but it's too hard to use. Think back to the coat. It ends up on the chair or floor because hanging it up in the closet is too hard.

C. The item has a home but it's in the wrong room. Think of dirty clothes. We end up with a big pile on our bathroom floors because that's where we take our clothes off before showering. Yet, many people insist on keeping their hampers in their closets. But if you have a pile of dirty clothes in your bathroom, your hamper obviously shouldn't be in your closet. It should be in your bathroom, corralling that big pile of clothes on the floor.

Go around your room, and ask yourself why each item is laying out. All the items that don't belong in your room should be taken to the place where they are best stored. All the items you plan to keep in your room should be listed on the worksheet on page you'll see when you flip the page under the heading "Items to Store."

Next to each item, list how often you use the item. Daily? Weekly? Monthly? Yearly? Knowing how often you use each item will make it easier when it comes time to determine where each item should be stored. The things you use most often should be the easiest to access.

Then, for each item, list the maximum number of actions you're willing to do when putting it away. Remember, that's simply how many actions it takes to be messy. So if you throw mail on the counter — which is one action. You know, the maximum number of actions you're willing to do is one.

Finally, based on your maximum number of actions, list two or three optimal places for each item to be stored. Such as drawers, on shelves, in a basket or on a hook. That way, you'll know what type of storage you should incorporate in your room. Remember, the place you store it should require as many or less actions as it takes to leave that item laying out. Otherwise, you'll never put it away.

2. TACKLE THE STUFF HIDDEN FROM VIEW. Now it's time to tackle all of the stuff that's actually put away where it belongs — like in drawers and on shelves — or stuffed out of sight — like under the couch cushions or behind the armoire. We're going to do it the same way as we did the stuff laying out.

First, pick up all trash and throw it away or recycle it.

Then, pick up all the things you don't need. Place the things you plan to donate and sell on the piles you already have going.

Next, go through each item left, one by one, and ask yourself if it belongs in that room. Everything that doesn't belong should be taken to the room where it's best stored.

Everything that's left is what you need to store in your room. Add each item to your list. If you already have that item on your list, there's no need to write it again. Only list the new items you need to store.

3. GROUP & MEASURE. Knowing how often you plan to use an item and the best way to store it isn't enough when it comes to making your plan. You must also know how much you need to store. If you don't, you may try to cram a room full of books onto one tiny shelf. And no matter how hard you push, that ain't going to happen.

So group all like items together in a pile. Put books in one pile. Magazines in another. Writing instruments in another. You get the idea.

To make things easier, group the piles in another room. That way, you don't have to step over a bunch of piles during the rest of the evaluation.

Then arrange all the items in each pile according to how you plan to store them. If you plan to put books on a bookshelf, line them up. If you plan to put cooking tools in a drawer, arrange them in rows. If you're stacking sweaters on a shelf, fold, stack and line them up. Keep in mind that stacking more than three items on top of each other makes them difficult to use. So stack more at your own risk. For individual items — like a vacuum cleaner or a TV, you obviously don't need to do anything. Leave them as is.

Once you have all of your items arranged, measure the overall length and maximum width and height of each grouping. If you're not sure how to measure accurately, look

WHEN USING A TAPE MEASURE:

1. Always select one with an overall tape length longer than what you're measuring. And if you don't have one, don't think a ruler or yard stick can stand in. When you use a measuring device smaller than what you're measuring, you're far more likely to get the wrong measurement.

2. Be sure the beginning of the tape measure aligns perfectly with the beginning of the object. The number that lines up with where the object ends is the overall measurement.

3. Keep the tape measure as straight as possible. If it sags or bends, you'll get the wrong measurement.

4. Don't round up or down when recording your measurement. You need to know the exact number.

3.5"

5. You can write the overall measurement in either feet or inches. It's up to you.

6. If you're measuring anything wider than your arm span, ask for help. If you don't, the tape measure may slip, bend or pull away from the beginning of where you're measuring, which will cause you to get the wrong measurement.

at the card above. After measuring each grouping, write the measurements down next to each item on your list. Those numbers tell you how much linear storage you need for each type of item, and how tall and wide that storage must be.

For example, if you have 15 feet of books that are 10 inches wide and 9 inches deep, you know the depth of your bookshelves must be at least 9 inches. The space between each shelf must be at least 10 inches, because you need enough room to put your finger on top of each book. And you must have at least 15 feet of shelves, which could be three 5-foot-long shelves, five 3-foot-long shelves or any other variation that adds up to a total of 15 feet.

Once you've finished measuring the last items, breathe a deep sigh of relief. You're finished evaluating your storage needs. Hooray.

6 your room evaluation

MY STORAGE NEEDS

ROOM:

DIRECTIONS: Fill in the chart below with the details of what you plan to store.

ITEMS TO STORE	USE FREQUENCY	MAXIMUM # OF ACTIONS	OPTIMAL STORAGE SOLUTIONS	STORAGE SPACE NEEDED
	☐ daily ☐ weekly ☐ monthly ☐ yearly		1. 2. 3.	
	☐ daily ☐ weekly ☐ monthly ☐ yearly		1. 2. 3.	
	☐ daily ☐ weekly ☐ monthly ☐ yearly		1. 2. 3.	
	☐ daily ☐ weekly ☐ monthly ☐ yearly		1. 2. 3.	
	☐ daily ☐ weekly ☐ monthly ☐ yearly		1. 2. 3.	
	☐ daily		1.	

MY STORAGE NEEDS

HOME OFFICE
ROOM:

DIRECTIONS: Fill in the chart below with the details of what you plan to store.

ITEMS TO STORE	USE FREQUENCY	MAXIMUM # OF ACTIONS	OPTIMAL STORAGE SOLUTIONS	STORAGE SPACE NEEDED
books	☐ daily ☐ weekly ☒ monthly ☒ yearly	1 - 2	1. open shelf 2. out on table (display) 3. in cabinet	12" T 9½" D 38½" W
magazines	☐ daily ☒ weekly ☐ monthly ☐ yearly	1 - 2	1. open shelf 2. magazine holder 3. basket/bin	12" T 9½" D 70¾" W
files	☐ daily ☒ weekly ☐ monthly ☐ yearly	1 - 2	1. file drawer 2. file box 3.	9" T 12" D 45" W
tapes	☐ daily ☐ weekly ☐ monthly ☒ yearly	1 - 3	1. open box/bin 2. lidded box/bin 3.	4¼" T 3¼" ☒ D 84" W
mail	☒ daily ☐ weekly ☐ monthly ☐ yearly	1	1. open sorter 2. tray 3.	always changing
post-its	☒ daily ☐ weekly ☐ monthly ☐ yearly	1 - 2	1. open jar/bowl 2. hinged box 3. tray	2" T 2" D 6" W ↖ more or less

NEED TO STORE MORE ITEMS? PRINT OFF EXTRA SHEETS AT:
TheMeghanMethod.com

HOW YOUR ROOM MEASURES UP

Keep that tape measure out. That little bit of measuring you just did was only a warm up. It's now time for the real measuring to begin, and I cannot stress enough how vitally important it is to accurately measure your room.

Many people skip this part because they think it's a pain. But spending 10 minutes measuring your room is nowhere near as painful as spending a boatload of money on a sofa that won't fit in your room, or cabinetry that's an inch too small. And don't think those things work like pants or pumps. Often times, if you order the wrong size, there are no returns.

So do yourself a favor, and measure. Not just once. Not just twice. But three times. And once you've gotten the same exact number three times, write it down. That way, you know for sure that you have the accurate measurements. And those measurements are crucial to your decorating plan because every decision you make — every item you buy — will be based on those measurements. So you must get them right.

Here are all the measurements you must take:

1. The Bird's-Eye View. Knowing the overall size of the room tells you how much stuff you can put in it. Draw the shape of your room on a piece of paper. Include the location of your windows, doors, walkways and fireplaces in your drawing. And don't worry, there's absolutely no need for your drawing to be perfect. Rough is fine.

Once you've created the bird's-eye view of your room, measure the overall length of each wall, and write it down. Remember to measure three times to make sure the number is correct.

If you have a baseboard in your room, you should also measure the length of each wall from baseboard to baseboard. The length will be a little less.

Next, measure the width of each door, window, walkway opening and fireplace — including the trim around them.

Write those measurements down.

Now measure the width of each section of empty wall. Write those measurements down. When you're finished, your paper should look like this:

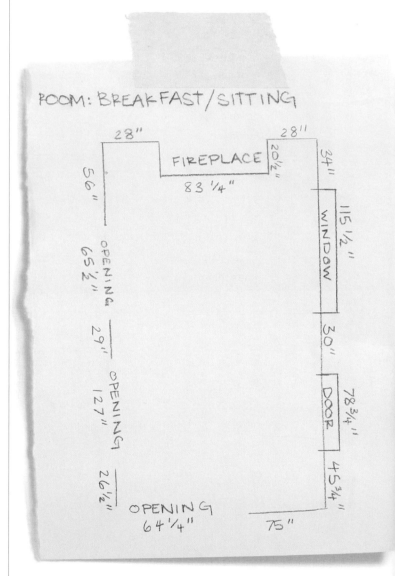

2. Your Current Layout. Having a drawing of your current layout gives you a better understanding of its flaws and strengths. This makes creating a new layout much easier because you'll know what to avoid and what to do again.

Duplicate the bird's-eye view drawing you just created. Only this time, draw where your furniture is located in the room. Again, it can be rough.

Measure the length and width of each piece of furniture. Write those numbers down. Knowing the actual sizes of your old furniture will give you a concrete baseline when deciding how big your new furniture should be.

Measure the distance between each piece of furniture and the wall. Knowing the actual distances between your current furniture arrangement will help you to determine how much space should be between the items in your new floor plan. If your current layout feels too tight, you'll need more space between your items than you currently have. If your layout feels too empty, you'll need less. If it feels just right, then duplicate the spacing.

3. The Ceiling. In order to create a decorative ceiling or good lighting scheme, you must know the location of all of your current lights and items on your ceiling. If your ceiling is completely blank, you can skip this part. Otherwise, draw the bird's-eye view of your room again. Roughly estimate where the light fixtures, skylights, architectural moldings or beams are located on the ceiling, and draw them in.

Now measure the location of each light fixture, skylight, beam or piece of molding. When you're finished, your paper should look like this:

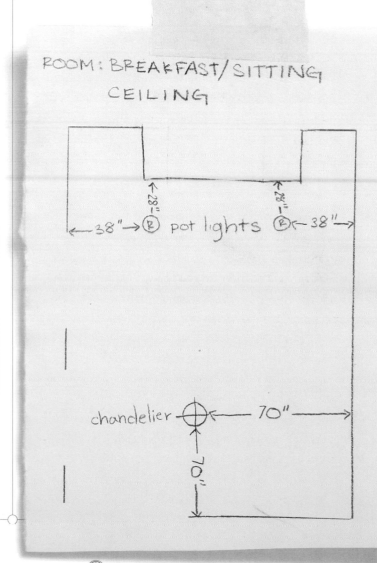

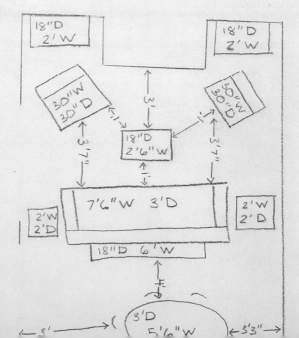

4. Your Wall Anatomy. Knowing exactly where the windows, doors and other items are located on your walls will tell you where you can place pieces of furniture and electronics.

Draw the rough shape of each wall in your room. If your room is a square or rectangle, you will have four walls to draw. If your room has weird juts, you'll have more. Label each wall either with the direction it faces or a nickname you'll remember, like "TV wall" or "window wall." Use the measurements from the bird's-eye view drawings to fill in the width of each wall.

Measure the overall height of each wall. Write that down.

On each wall, roughly draw where all the windows, doors, fireplace, heating units, air conditioning units and other permanent fixtures are located — if any. Measure the location of each of those items.

Draw in any decorative trim, and measure the width of each piece.

Draw the location of wall lights, light switches, electrical outlets, phone outlets, cable outlets and heating or AC controls. Measure the location of each of those.

Whew. You're finally finished with measuring. Hooray.

Now, put those papers in a safe place — like in a big, red folder labeled, "Don't touch."

Better yet, make a copy. Scan them. Take a photo. Do whatever you have to do to make sure you either A, don't lose those papers, or B, have a backup copy. Because I'm sure you don't want to do that all over again.

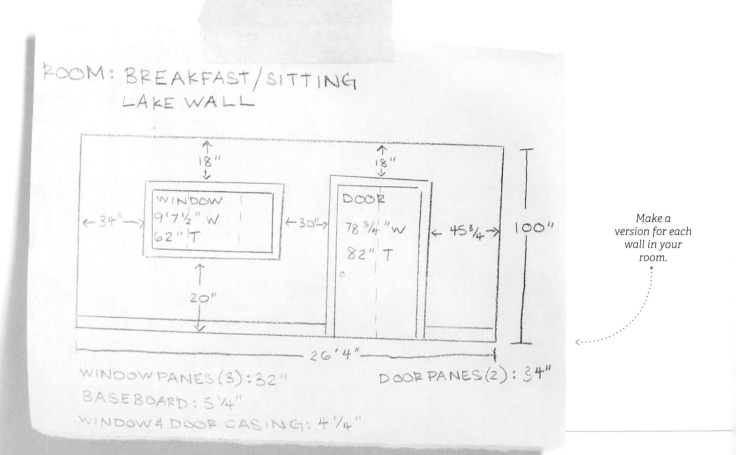

Make a version for each wall in your room.

YOUR CURRENT ITEMS

Many people assume that when you redecorate you ditch everything and buy all new stuff. But that's not even remotely true. More often than not, you'll find a gem or two among the things you own. Which means you've got to sort through your stuff to see if you have any diamonds in the rough.

Sometimes, you'll get lucky and have tons of things to reuse. Other times, you'll have none. Either way, it's a good idea to sort. For one, if you find things to reuse, it saves money that you can spend on splurge items. And two, it's convenient. You don't have to schlep around town or spend hours online searching for the perfect item, because you already have it.

But don't let those two benefits persuade you to keep things you don't truly love.

When you decorate, the only tools you have are the things you put in your room. That's it. In the end, decorating is just filling a room with objects, and the objects you choose tell the whole story. They're what dictate what you can do in your room. They make you feel good. They are everything, which means you must choose the objects wisely.

So no compromising. Don't hold onto things out of guilt or because they're convenient. Every single item you put in your room must fit the criteria to the right.

If a piece doesn't fit those criteria, it's not right for your room. Get rid of it. Give it to a friend. Donate it to charity. Sell it at a garage sale, on eBay (ebay.com) or Craigslist (craigslist. org).

Of course, saying that is easy. Actually doing it, that's another story. Especially when we're talking about getting rid of Grandma's rocker or a painting from a dear friend — even if we never liked them in the first place. But remember, it's the memories and sentiment we've attached to those things — not so much the things themselves. And while you may feel like you're losing a piece of the past, you're really trading in for the future. The "what could be."

If you're feeling guilty, take photos and videos of the item

Furniture & Other Tools
must be:

☐ COMFORTABLE and/or EASY TO USE.

(If it's a storage item, it must be the type listed on your storage needs sheet.)

Test the item. Sit on it. Open it. Use it. If it doesn't easily work or is terribly uncomfortable, get rid of it. Keep in mind if you truly love the item, it can be fixed. So don't ditch something you love simply because it wobbles or needs new padding.

☐ FUNCTIONALLY NECESSARY.

Look at your functional needs sheet. If you don't see the item on your list, ask yourself if you forgot to include it. If not, it needs to go. You don't need it.

☐ CONGRUENT WITH YOUR EMOTIONAL WANTS.

Look at each item and see if its characteristics are similar to those listed on your muse and style sheets. If not, it's not right for your room.

If they are, ask yourself if you like the item. Keep in mind, you can have things reupholstered and refinished in different colors. So focus on the shape and texture of the item — not its color or pattern.

If you're having a tough time deciding, move the item to another room. Seeing it in a new setting will help you to see it with fresh eyes. Why? The stuff around your item influences the way it looks to you. So it may be the combination of it with your current decor that you don't like — not the item itself.

Decorative Accessories
must be:

☐ CONGRUENT WITH YOUR EMOTIONAL WANTS.

See card above for instructions.

before sending it off. Or do what my Granny did — keep it in the attic, and only bring it out when that person comes to visit.

Either way, get all the things that don't fit functionally and emotionally out of your room. That way, you'll have space for all the things you want and need.

So get to it. Sort all of your items — your furniture, accessories, light fixtures and everything else — into three groups: the keepers, the maybes and the goners.

The Keepers. Without a doubt, these things perfectly fit all of the necessary criteria. They're the items you truly love.

Use the sheet below to make a list of all those keepers. Take a picture of each one. Write down each depth, width and height. Make note if any need repairs, refinishing or reupholstery.

The Maybes. These things fit all of the necessary criteria, but you're not in love with them. However, you don't hate them either. If your budget is tight or you can't find anything better, these items could work.

Use the sheet you'll see when you flip the page to make a list of all those maybes. Take a picture of each one. Write down each item's depth, width and height. Make note if any needs repairs, refinishing or reupholstery.

The Goners. These are the things that don't fit the necessary criteria and need to go. For each, decide whether it can be used elsewhere in your home, or if it should be given to a friend, donated or sold.

Print off your own copy from: TheMeghanMethod.com

6 your room evaluation

THE KEEPERS

ROOM:

DIRECTIONS: Fill in the details of what items you definitely want to keep.

THE KEEPERS	DIMENSIONS	NEEDS REPAIRS	NEEDS REFINISHING	OTHER NEEDS:
		☐ no ☐ yes, it needs:	☐ no ☐ yes, it needs:	
		☐ no ☐ yes, it needs:	☐ no ☐ yes, it needs:	
		☐ no ☐ yes, it needs:	☐ no ☐ yes, it needs:	

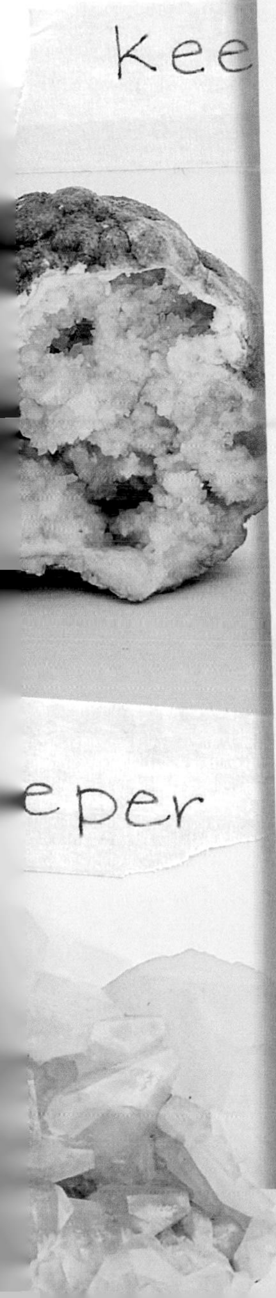

6 your room evaluation

THE KEEPERS

DIRECTIONS: Fill in the details of what items you definitely want to keep.

THE KEEPERS	DIMENSIONS	NEEDS REPAIRS	NEEDS REFINISHING	OTHER NEEDS:
architect's table	42 ½" W 30 ¾" D 32 ½" T	☐ no ☒ yes, it needs: *a new top*	☒ no ☐ yes, it needs:	
malachite specimen	8 ½" W 1 ½" D 6 ½" T	☒ no ☐ yes, it needs:	☒ no ☐ yes, it needs:	a stand
quartz specimen #1	8" W 5" D 6 ½" T	☒ no ☐ yes, it needs:	☒ no ☐ yes, it needs:	
quartz specimen #2	7" W 2" D 5 ¾" T	☒ no ☐ yes, it needs:	☒ no ☐ yes, it needs:	
mica specimen	12" W 4" D 8" T	☒ no ☐ yes, it needs:	☒ no ☐ yes, it needs:	a stand
calcite specimen	11" W 6 ½" D 6 ¼" T	☒ no ☐ yes, it needs	☒ no ☐ yes, it needs	a stand (maybe)

PLAN TO KEEP MORE ITEMS? PRINT OFF EXTRA SHEETS AT:
TheMeghanMethod.com

6 your room evaluation

THE MAYBES

ROOM:

DIRECTIONS: Fill in the details of what items you might want to keep.

THE KEEPERS	DIMENSIONS	NEEDS REPAIRS	NEEDS REFINISHING	OTH
		☐ no ☐ yes, it needs:	☐ no ☐ yes, it needs:	
		☐ no ☐ yes, it needs:	☐ no ☐ yes, it needs:	
		☐ no ☐ yes, it needs:	☐ no ☐ yes, it needs:	
		☐ no ☐ yes, it needs:	☐ no ☐ yes, it needs:	
		☐ no ☐ yes, it needs:	☐ no ☐ yes, it needs:	
		☐ no ☐ yes, it needs	☐ no ☐ yes, it needs	

PLAN TO KEEP MORE ITEMS? PRINT OFF EXTRA SHEETS AT:
TheMeghanMethod.com

6 your room evaluation

THE MAYBES

DIRECTIONS: Fill in the details of what items you might want to keep.

THE KEEPERS	DIMENSIONS	NEEDS REPAIRS	NEEDS REFINISHING	OTHER NEEDS:
Office Chairs	3' T 20½'D 22 ¼ W	☒ no ☐ yes, it needs:	☒ no ☐ yes, it needs:	
Yellow & white Pillows	18" x 18" ~~12"x12"~~	☒ no ☐ yes, it needs:	☒ no ☐ yes, it needs:	
Wood Crates (x3)	8 ¾" T 11" D 17" W	☒ no ☐ yes, it needs:	☒ no ☐ yes, it needs:	
Wood Lion Box	4 ½" T 8 ¾" D 14" W	☒ no ☐ yes, it needs:	☒ no ☐ yes, it needs:	
		☐ no ☐ yes, it needs:	☐ no ☐ yes, it needs:	
		☐ no ☐ yes, it needs	☐ no ☐ yes, it needs	

YOUR ROOM

There's a magical sense of anticipation that fills a room when everything has been removed and all that is left is space. Wide-open, empty, luxurious space that's waiting for you to transform it into something spectacular. Something amazing.

It's like when a painter sees an empty canvas, or a carver sees a chunk of untouched stone.

It's an invitation to let your imagination run wild. To visualize all of the different ways the space could be used. To see the potential of what could be.

So as much of a pain as it is, you really should move everything out of your room. Because then — and only then — will you see what you're really working with.

If you try to evaluate your space with the stuff in it, you won't get an accurate read. All those things in your room drastically influence the way you see your space. They may make it seem bigger or smaller, darker or lighter, and wider or narrower than it really is. So the only way to find out how your room really looks is to move it all out. Every single piece.

Once you've got it all out of there, magic will happen.

You'll see your room in a completely new way.

Or, you may just see an empty room. And that's okay. Once you've got a few rooms under your belt, that will change. But for now, I'll let you in on the secret of why I — and so many other people — get excited when they see an empty room.

All rooms — along with canvases and chunks of stone — have one very important thing in common: limitations. They're only so big. They're shaped in a certain way. And it's those limitations — those things we must work around — that excites people. It's a challenge.

But the challenge is not what exhilarates them. It's thinking of how they'll overcome it that makes their fingers tingle and brains buzz with excitement. Because they start visualizing all of the things they can do to turn that empty shell into a masterpiece.

Of course, I don't expect you to feel that right now. You will someday. But for now, let this sheet guide you in evaluating your space.

6
your room evaluation

MY ROOM

ROOM:

DIRECTIONS: Check all boxes that apply to your room, and fill in any details.

Print off your own copy from: TheMeghanMethod .com

MY ROOM'S SIZE:

☐ My room feels too big. I need to make it feel more intimate.

☐ My room feels too small. I need to make it feel bigger.

☐ My room feels too narrow. I need to make it feel wider.

☐ My room feels too wide. I need to make it feel narrower.

☐ My room feels too tall. I need to make the ceiling feel lower.

☐ My room feels too short. I need to make the ceiling feel taller.

☐ My room feels just right. I like the proportions exactly how they are.

☐ I want to make my room bigger by knocking down a wall and stealing space from an adjoining room.

MY ROOM

GUEST
BEDROOM
ROOM:

DIRECTIONS: Check all boxes that apply to your room, and fill in any details.

MY ROOM'S SIZE:

- ☐ My room feels too big. I need to make it feel more intimate.
- ☐ My room feels too small. I need to make it feel bigger.
- ☐ My room feels too narrow. I need to make it feel wider.
- ☐ My room feels too wide. I need to make it feel narrower.
- ☐ My room feels too tall. I need to make the ceiling feel lower.
- ☒ My room feels too short. I need to make the ceiling feel taller.
- ☐ My room feels just right. I like the proportions exactly how they
- ☐ I want to make my room bigger by knocking down a wall and st

MY ROOM'S SHAPE:

My room's shape is: _awkward_

- ☐ I want people to notice the shape of my room because I like it s
- ☒ I want to disguise the shape of my room because I find it boring
- ☒ My room has weird juts that I don't like.

MY ROOM'S FEATURES:

- ☒ My room has special architectural features, such as: _built-in dresser & bookcase_
  - ☒ I like them and want to feature them.   ☐ Hate them and want to get rid of them.
- ☐ My room doesn't have enough architectural features.
- ☐ My room has a fireplace, and I:
  - ☐ Like it and want it to be a main feature.   ☐ My room doesn't have enough windows. I want more.
  - ☐ Hate it and want to get rid of it.   ☐ My room has too many windows. I want less.
  - ☐ Hate it and want to change the way it looks.   ☒ My room has the perfect amount of windows.
- ☐ My room's fireplace is off-center in the room.   ☒ The windows in my room are off-center.
- ☐ My room's fireplace is centered on the wall.   ☐ The windows in my room are centered.
- ☒ The doors in my room are off-c   ☐ The windows in my room are off-center.
- ☐ The doors in my room are cent

6 your room evaluation

MY ROOM

DIRECTIONS: Check all boxes that

BREAKFAST/
SITTING
ROOM:

MY ROOM'S SIZE:

- ☐ My room feels too big. I need to make it feel more intimate.
- ☐ My room feels too small. I need to make it feel bigger.
- ☒ My room feels too narrow. I need to make it feel wider.
- ☐ My room feels too wide. I need to make it feel narrower.
- ☐ My room feels too tall. I need to make the ceiling feel lower.
- ☒ My room feels too short. I need to make the ceiling feel taller.
- ☐ My room feels just right. I like the proportions exactly how they are
- ☐ I want to make my room bigger by knocking down a wall and steali

MY ROOM'S SHAPE:

My room's shape is: _overall rectangular_

- ☐ I want people to notice the shape of my room because I like it so m
- ☐ I want to disguise the shape of my room because I find it boring or
- ☐ My room has weird juts that I don't like.

MY ROOM'S FEATURES:

- ☐ My room has special architectural features, such as: ⋯⋯⋯⋯⋯⋯⋯
  - ☐ I like them and want to feature them.   ☐ Hate them and want to get rid of them.
- ☒ My room doesn't have enough architectural features.
- ☒ My room has a fireplace, and I:
  - ☒ Like it and want it to be a main feature.   ☐ My room doesn't have enough windows. I want more.
  - ☐ Hate it and want to get rid of it.   ☐ My room has too many windows. I want less.
  - ☐ Hate it and want to change the way it looks.   ☒ My room has the perfect amount of windows.
- ☐ My room's fireplace is off-center in the room.   ☐ The windows in my room are off-center.
- ☒ My room's fireplace is centered on the wall.   ☒ The windows in my room are centered. _kind of_
- ☐ The doors in my room are off-center.   _both_ ☒ The openings in my room are off-center.
- ☐ The doors in my room are centered.   ☒ The openings in my room are centered.

GET YOUR OWN COPY AT: TheMeghanMethod.com

your room evaluation

MY ROOM

HOME OFFICE
ROOM:

DIRECTIONS: Check all boxes that apply to your room, and fill in any details.

MY ROOM'S SIZE:

- ☒ My room feels too big. I need to make it feel more intimate.
- ☐ My room feels too small. I need to make it feel bigger.
- ☐ My room feels too narrow. I need to make it feel wider.
- ☐ My room feels too wide. I need to make it feel narrower.
- ☒ My room feels too tall. I need to make the ceiling feel lower. ← it's <u>way</u> too tall
- ☐ My room feels too short. I need to make the ceiling feel taller.
- ☐ My room feels just right. I like the proportions exactly how they are.
- ☐ I want to make my room bigger by knocking down a wall and stealing space from an adjoining room.

MY ROOM'S SHAPE:

My room's shape is: *rectangular*

- ☐ I want people to notice the shape of my room because I like it so much.
- ☐ I want to disguise the shape of my room because I find it boring or awkward.
- ☐ My room has weird juts that I don't like.

MY ROOM'S FEATURES:

- ☐ My room has special architectural features, such as:
  - ☐ I like them and want to feature them.
  - ☐ Hate them and want to get rid of them.
- ☒ My room doesn't have enough architectural features.
- ☐ My room has a fireplace, and I:
  - ☐ Like it and want it to be a main feature.
  - ☐ Hate it and want to get rid of it.
  - ☐ Hate it and want to change the way it looks.
  - ☐ My room doesn't have enough windows. I want more.
  - ☐ My room has too many windows. I want less.
  - ☒ My room has the perfect amount of windows.
- ☐ My room's fireplace is off-center in the room.
- ☒ The windows in my room are off-center.
- ☐ My room's fireplace is centered on the wall.
- ☐ The windows in my room are centered.
- ☒ The doors in my room are off-center.
- ☒ The openings in my room are off-center.
- ☐ The doors in my room are centered.
- ☐ The openings in my room are centered.

GET YOUR OWN COPY AT: TheMeghanMethod.com

18'

16'

PART TWO: CREAT YOUR P

A s much as I've compared decorating to cooking (pages 14, 37, & 97), at the end of the day there's one major difference. When you cook, you just replicate a recipe. At least, the majority of us do. Whereas, when you decorate, you must create your own.

And it's that difference that causes people to cut-and-run when it comes to decorating. Because they don't think they have what it takes to create.

But I'm going to let you in on a little secret. Being creative doesn't take talent, skill or divine intervention. You don't even need the moons in alignment. All you need is desire and knowledge.

Think about how chefs create those recipes we follow. They don't sit around waiting for the "creative spark" to hit them. They eat something — let's say it's cake — and think, "This is pretty good, but if it had more chocolate and was a bit spongier, it'd be out of this world."

And once they have that desire, they access all the data they've stored in their brains to make it happen. And they *do* make it happen, because they fully understand the science of cooking.

Whereas, if we tried to make that same cake not knowing the difference between leveling and leavening agents, we'd end up with a soggy mound — or more likely, burnt crisp — and figure it was because we weren't creative enough.

But creativity has nothing to do with it. We just don't have the right data stored in our brains. And you *need* to have the right data in order to create. You must fully understand the ins and outs of what you're working with in order to come up with the creative solution that will make your desire a reality.

And when it comes to decorating, you don't have that knowledge. Which is why you've had so much trouble. Not because you're not creative, but because you don't have the right data. Well, that, and you didn't have a clear desire. But we've already figured that part out. That's what we just spent the last 103 pages honing.

Now, we've got to focus on the knowledge. And once you have that, you'll know how to turn your desire into the best decorating plan for you.

So let's stuff your brain full of know-how.

CREATIVITY:
understanding
set on fire
by desire

HOW DECORATING WORKS

When you decorate, there are only two things you have to worry about:

1. What items to put in your room.

And, 2. Where to place each of those items.

That's it. Just objects and placement. Because at the end of the day decorating is simply the art of arranging objects in a room.

To determine which objects to use and where to place them, we use two things as our guide:

1. Our functional needs.

And, 2. Our emotional needs.

As far as function goes, you should have no problem whatsoever. For one, you already know what items you functionally need to put in your room. That's why you made your functional needs list (page 41 for those with temporary amnesia). And two, you already know how to position things functionally. If you didn't, your sofas and armoires would be pushed backwards against the wall. But they're not, because you can't use them that way. It's common sense, and as long as you turn yours on, you won't have a problem figuring out where to place things functionally.

So the function part of decorating isn't hard at all. In fact, everyone's pretty much got that down. It's the emotional part that throws everyone into a tailspin. And for good reason. We don't know how to communicate emotions through looks.

Heck, we don't even know where to start, because no one has ever taught us how to speak the visual language. And it's about time we learned.

Our functional & emotional needs tell us what items to use & where to place them in our rooms.

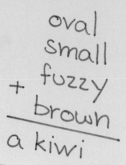

oval
small
+ fuzzy
_____
brown
a kiwi

shape + size + texture + color = an object

THE VISUAL LANGUAGE

As you already know (page 47), we communicate emotions through the way things look. Of course, most people equate emotions with being irrational. So they figure there couldn't possibly be an underlying order used when communicating them. But that couldn't be further from the truth.

We communicate emotion the exact same way we communicate ideas: through language. And there are many different languages we use to communicate emotion. One for each of our senses: touch, taste, smell, sound and sight.

But when decorating, we care primarily about the latter: the visual language. And learning it is a breeze, because it works exactly the same way as our written language. It has letters that make up words. Words that make up sentences. And sentences structured by grammar. But let's start with the letters.

Unlike in written language, the letters in the visual language aren't characters. They're characteristics: size, shape, color and texture. Now on their own, those characteristics don't have a very specific meaning. The color black could be used to communicate many things. Just like the letter S. But when you start combining those characteristics together — just as when you group letters together — you get a more precise meaning. A word. Or the equivalent of a word in the visual language, an object.

For example, black can feel dangerous, rugged, spooky or sexy. But when it's given a matte finish and put in the shape of a man's business suit, suddenly you've got an object that confidently communicates credible.

But as we all know, it's very hard to communicate a clear picture with a single word alone. That's why we string words together in sentences — to enhance the clarity of our meaning. And we do the exact same thing with objects. Only instead of creating sentences, we lump objects together in groupings. And just like with words, the meaning of each object in a grouping can drastically change depending on what you group it with.

For example, imagine you paired the black business suit with a garish purple, silky shirt, an oversized gold necklace and excessively slicked-back hair. That sense of credibility would fly right out the window.

All because of what objects were paired with the suit. Now if you'd had only one of those elements with the suit — say the bright shirt — you might not immediately discredit the person. But when you have it all together — the bright silky shirt, big necklace and greasy hair — you can't help but think shyster. Because the more objects you pair together, the clearer the emotional message becomes.

That's why the objects you choose to pair together matter so much. Because the presence of one wrong object is enough to seriously alter your message. So when you select the objects to put in your room, you must make sure they communicate the emotions you want to feel, not only on their own, but also when grouped together.

Fortunately, that should be extremely easy given that you already have a muse. You know what characteristics, when grouped together, make you feel the way you want to feel in your room. So as long as you use your muse's characteristics as a guide, you should be good to go.

But having all the right objects grouped together is not enough to perfectly communicate your emotional message. They must also be in the right place.

Just imagine if that black business suit was tied around a man's head. Forget credible or smarmy. You'd just think he was insane. Or smashed. Maybe a combination of both? Either way, the emotional message would be completely different simply because the placement has changed.

> The more objects you group together, the more specific your emotional message becomes.

WRITTEN LANGUAGE	VISUAL LANGUAGE
letters /characters	characteristics
words	objects
sentences	groupings
grammar	visual grammar (design principles)

And placement greatly matters. Think of a sentence. If the words placed were wrong all, you'd have a hard time understanding what the sentence was trying to say. Because words — and objects — must be placed in the proper order to have meaning. That's why we have grammar. It provides the structure we need to understand what everyone else is saying. And the visual language has grammar too.

Now I realize most people hate grammar. In fact, the mere mention of it often elicits moaning, groaning and the occasional hostile yell — brought on by flashbacks of terrible grade school classes spent dissecting sentences and learning the difference between present and past participles. But I assure you, learning the visual grammar is nothing like that.

For one, you don't actually need to learn it. You already innately understand the visual grammar. We just need to make you consciously aware of it.

And two, you won't have nuns slapping you across the wrist or teachers giving you dirty looks if you get it wrong. Because there is no wrong. The entire point of communication — whether it's oral, written or visual — is to have your message understood by others. And sometimes the only way to say what you want to say is to break the so-called "grammar rules."

Despite what everyone else has told us, those "rules" aren't really rules. Grammar is not a list of arbitrary dos and don'ts. It's a framework. The framework our entire communication system is based upon. And once you understand that framework, you can use it in whatever way best communicates your message. Which, like I already said, isn't necessarily what is deemed as "proper." But that doesn't matter. Your goal when communicating is to make your message as understandable as possible. Not as proper as possible.

So ditch the idea that grammar is a staunch list of absolutes, and see it for what it really is: an amazing set of guidelines that unlocks the mystery of communication. And once you understand it — the visual grammar — you will know exactly where to place all the objects in your room to communicate all those emotions you want to feel.

So let's get to it. There are only eight elements of the visual grammar — balance, proportion, proximity, repetition, contrast, movement, emphasis and white — to learn.

BALANCE

When most people talk about balance, they're typically lamenting over their struggle to bring their work and play lives into equilibrium. But there's a far more important balance to worry about. The one that keeps us standing up.

Without it, we can't work or play — let alone fret about whether we're spending enough time doing either. Just ask anyone who's had motion sickness, or even worse, vertigo. Losing your balance makes it impossible to function. And we must function to survive, which is why our bodies fight so hard to stay in balance.

The majority of that task is delegated to the hairs in our ears. But our eyes have been given a small role too: sentry duty. If they see anything that looks off, they report it to our brain. And I'm not talking about suddenly-the-horizon-is-flipped-upside-down off. Even the slightest inclination that we could be off balance — like too many pieces of furniture on one side of the room — is enough to send a warning signal to our brain. Because the disproportionate number of pieces on one side makes it look as if the floor may be sloped. And if the floor is sloped, we could fall. And if we fall, we could hurt ourselves. And that is unacceptable. So our brain responds by being on red alert, which makes us feel uneasy and uncomfortable in the room. Like we need to get out in order to be safe.

That's why it's so important to make your room balanced. If it doesn't look balanced, people will feel uncomfortable being in it. And the whole point of decorating is to create a place where people want to spend time. So if you want people to spend time in your room, it must look balanced.

The easiest way to do that is to imagine the floor of your room is sitting on a giant teeter-totter. Only instead of the teeter-totter having a giant board running down the middle

balanced

unbalanced

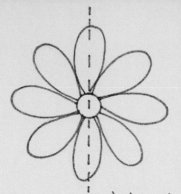

Symmetrical balance
is like a daisy.
If you split it down
the middle, the
two halves are identical.

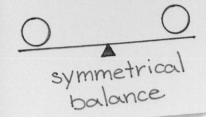

symmetrical
balance

— like most do — this teeter totter has just one tiny cone in the center supporting your entire room. Which means, if you put something in one corner of your room, you must also put something of equal weight in the opposite corner. If you don't, the whole room will look as if it's sloping down to that one object. And you don't want that. So to maintain balance, you must arrange the items in your room so that the things in opposite corners — and on opposite sides — of your room are of equal weight.

Fortunately, there are only two ways to do that. You either arrange things symmetrically or asymmetrically.

SYMMETRICAL BALANCE. The most obvious way to keep a teeter-totter in perfect balance is to put identical twins — or things — on either side. Because identical things have identical weight which means, they'll stay in perfect balance.

That type of balance is referred to as symmetrical balance, because what you put on one side is the mirror image of what you put on the other side. And achieving it in your room couldn't be any easier. You simply split your room down the middle and identically duplicate one side with the other.

But just because creating symmetrical balance is easy, doesn't mean it's the type of balance you should use in your room. First of all, not all rooms work with symmetrical balance. If your room is already asymmetrical — such as having windows, doors or weird juts in odd places, achieving symmetrical balance is extremely hard — and in some cases impossible.

But even if your room is perfectly symmetrical, you still may not want to use symmetrical bal-

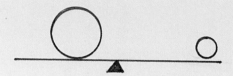

The closer an object is to the center, the heavier it must be.

ance, because it may not communicate what you want to feel. Symmetrical balance feels formal, grand and structured, and to some people, stiff or uptight. And if that's not how you want your room to feel, asymmetrical balance may be a better fit.

ASYMMETRICAL BALANCE. The other way to achieve balance on a teeter-totter is to keep piling on kids — or things — on either side until the teeter-totter becomes level. That type of balance is referred to as asymmetrical balance, because the objects on either side are not mirror images of each other.

Now, most people find asymmetrical balance far more difficult to achieve than symmetrical balance because you're not just duplicating the same things on either side of your room. Instead, you actually have to understand what balances out what. But I promise, that's not as hard as it seems. You just need to learn how a teeter-totter works.

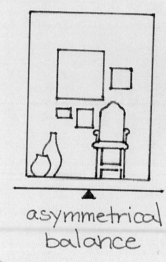

asymmetrical balance

We all understand a teeter-totter on its most basic level. For it to be in balance, both sides must be of equal weight. It doesn't matter if there are two objects on one side and five on the other — or ten objects on one side and three on the other. As long as the total weight of each side is the same, it will stay balanced.

But that's only true if the items on each side are equidistant from the center. If you were to nudge one group up a bit, suddenly the teeter-

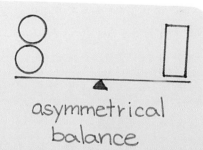

Asymmetrical balance is like a tree. Even though its two sides aren't identical, it's still in balance.

asymmetrical balance

totter would be out of balance, because the amount of weight needed to push the teeter-totter down changes the closer you get to the center.

The closer you place an object to the center, the heavier it must be. Whereas, the closer you place an object to the edge, the lighter it must be.

That's all there is to it. If the items in your room are equidistant from the center, you just have to make sure they're of equal weight. If one or more are closer to the center, just make sure they're heavier. And as long as you remember that, creating asymmetrical balance in your room will be easy. So don't let it scare you off — especially since it may communicate exactly what you want to feel in your room. Asymmetrical balance feels casual, down-to-earth and laid-back. If you want to feel those emotions, then it's the type of balance you should use.

Now what if you want to feel the emotions communicated by both symmetrical and asymmetrical balance? You use both. The amount of each depends on the degree to which you want to feel each type of emotion. The more formal, grand or structured you want your room to feel, the more symmetrical balance you'll use. The more casual, down-to-earth and laid-back you want your room to feel, the more asymmetrical balance you'll use.

Now before we stop talking about balance, there's one thing I need to clarify. When I mention weight, I'm not talking about actual weight. So don't think you need to run around your room with a scale. That'd be crazy.

When it comes to balancing the items in your room, all that matters is visual weight. How much your eyes think each item weighs. After all, when we look at a room, we don't magically know the exact weight of every object. We just estimate based on how they look. And we make those estimates based on four characteristics: size, color, pattern and texture.

Size. The bigger an item, the heavier it looks. But I probably didn't need to tell you that. We all naturally assume big things are heavy. That's why we're so shocked when we pick up a big item and realize it's light.

Color. The darker an item, the heavier it looks, because it appears more dense — like a rock or boulder. Whereas, the lighter an item, the lighter it looks, because it appears less dense — like air or water. And in our experience, rocks weigh far more than air or water. So we assume things that look dense must be heavy as well.

Texture. The more textured an item, the heavier it looks. That's because textured surfaces don't reflect as much light as a smooth surface. So they appear darker. And as we know, the darker an object, the more it looks like it weighs.

Pattern. The more patterned an item, the heavier it looks. Now this gets a bit complicated, but stick with me. We already know that objects are composed of size, shape, color and texture. Guess what? So are patterns, which means a pattern is an object. So when you have a pattern on an object, you really have an object on an object. And when you throw another object on an object, it naturally becomes heavier — which is why patterned objects appear heavier than non-patterned objects.

Now that all sounds easy enough in theory. The bigger, darker, more textured and more patterned, the heavier. But once you start comparing objects, it gets a little tricky. For example, which weighs more? A small, black and purple patterned object or a medium white one? A large black object or a large red-and-orange patterned one?

Unfortunately or fortunately — whichever way you want to look at it — there is no right answer. Determining how much objects visually weigh — and whether or not your room is balanced — is open to interpretation. And while that may drive some people crazy, I like to look at the bright side. As long as it feels good to you, you can't be wrong.

And don't worry, you'll be able to tell what does feel good. Your internal balance sensors will kick in right away, telling you what does and doesn't look balanced.

PROPORTION

For the most part, the things in our world stay the same size in relationship to one another. Mountains are always bigger than trees. Trees are always bigger than bears. Bears are always bigger than birds.

And it's not just those things that stay the same size. Their parts do as well. Trunks are always bigger than branches. Branches are always bigger than leaves. Leaves are always bigger than buds.

And because those things and their respective parts stay the same relative size, we have a sense of normal. We know how things should proportionally look. And when they're not that size, it catches our attention like fire on a mountain. Because it doesn't look right.

Now, that doesn't mean it looks bad. Quite the contrary. Being disproportional can elicit a number of good emotions: cute, whimsical, grand and quaint.

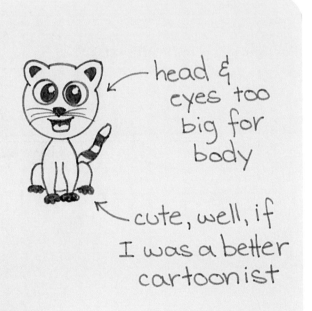

head & eyes too big for body

cute, well, if I was a better cartoonist

Cute. When part of a thing is disproportional to its whole, we often see it as cute. That's why babies and kittens and puppies look so unbearably adorable. Their heads are too big for their little bodies. And in order to survive, we've been conditioned to see that as cheek-pinching cute.

Of course, we don't always see cute when one part is disproportional to the whole. Just think of swelling or cysts. When we see that, it's just gross.

But when it comes to the items in our room, we're not worried about their health. So when we see one part disproportional to another, we normally read it as cute. Like cartoon wallpaper and silly stuffed animals.

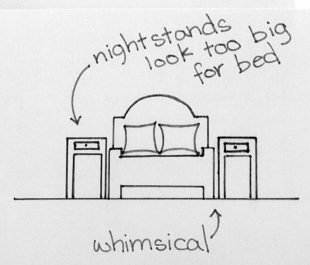

nightstands look too big for bed

whimsical

Whimsy. When one or a few items in a room is out of proportion with everything else, we see it as whimsical. Think of Alice and Wonderland. Beds too big. Doors too small. It makes us feel like we're in a fantasy world.

Just be careful. Like Alice discovered, when an item becomes too out of proportion, that whimsical feeling quickly turns to fear.

Grand. When everything in a room appears too big in relation to the human size, we see it as grand. That's why castles, cathedrals and ballrooms are built the way they are. To emphasize their importance and make us feel as though we've stepped inside something magnificent — something fit for the gods.

To create that emotion, everything in the room must be proportional to each other. Just not to a human. But be careful. If you go too big, you'll feel as if you'd climbed to the top of Jack's magic beanstalk and stumbled into a world of giants.

Quaint. When everything in a room appears too small in relation to the human size, we see it as quaint. Like the cottages in the Cotswolds of England, where you have to duck to enter, and everything looks petite.

Again, in order to evoke that emotion, everything in the room must be proportional to each other. Just not to a human. And remember, if you go too small, you'll end up with a house for ants. Not humans.

Now, if none of those emotions — cute, whimsical, grand, quaint or scary — are your cup of tea, you'll want your room to be perfectly proportional to the human size. And to do that, you must know how to tell when something is proportional. Fortunately, it's innate within all of us. Your gut will tell you. But if you don't trust your gut, you're in luck. Unlike balance — which is fairly subjective — proportion is not.

In the mid 1800s, Adolf Zeising, a German researcher, noticed the same proportion could be found repeatedly in nature. The veins of leaves. The branches on stems. Even in the human body. He called the proportion a universal law and believed it dictated whether or not we found something visually attractive.

Over a century later, Dr. Stephen R. Marquardt came to the same conclusion after developing a facial mask based on that proportion and finding that across gender and races, the faces perceived as most beautiful were those that best fit the mask.

And they're not the only ones who came to that conclusion. For centuries scholars believed that very proportion was the key to beauty. In fact, many think some of the greatest buildings of all time possess that proportion. The Parthenon, Great Pyramid of Giza, and Notre Dame Cathedral — just to name a few. Now, whether or not the builders chose that particular ratio because it's what we perceive in nature is debatable.

If you were to ask me, I would say yes. It only makes sense that we'd repeat — whether consciously or subconsciously — the proportion that's found again and again in the things we naturally feel are most beautiful. We'd be crazy not to.

So what is this magic proportion? It's aptly named the golden ratio. And it is:

1 to 1.618

Now, I realize that's not exactly an easy number to recall. Well, unless it's the digits of your birthday. But considering most of us weren't born on June 18, remembering it can be a pain. That's why most people tend to approximate it. And lucky for them, it's an easy number to estimate. If you were

golden ratio

| 1 | 0.618 |

thirds

2/3   1/3

to draw the golden ratio as a line, you'd see it's roughly 1/3 to 2/3.

So when determining the sizes of the things in your room, all you have to do is think in thirds. If you look at room photos, you'll quickly see how often that mentality is used.

Mirrors are typically two-thirds or one-third the size of whatever they're hung over — whether it's a sofa, table or mantle.

Artwork or overall artwork groupings are typically two-thirds or one-third the size of whatever they're hung over — whether it's a sofa, table or mantle.

Chandeliers are typically 2/3 the width of the table they're above.

Lamps are typically 1/3 the width of the table they're on. Their shades are typically 2/3 the width of the table they are on.

Chairs are typically 1/3 the size of sofas they're arranged next to.

Accessories grouped together are typically 1/3 or 2/3 the sizes of each other.

And so on.

Of course, sometimes using thirds as a guide isn't possible because you need something smaller. In those cases, just divide a third in half and use a sixth. Or divide the sixth in half and use a twelfth.

But above all, remember that a third is just an approximation of the actual ratio. You don't have to get it perfect. If it looks good to your eye — and most importantly to your gut — then it's right.

2/3 width of

1/3 width of

PROXIMITY

When you look at a tree-covered hill, what do you see? A green lump or each individual tree? A green lump. You only notice each individual tree after you've been gazing out at the view for quite some time — if ever. Whereas, when you gaze out at a field with one lone tree, you zero in on that tree right away. What's the difference?

Proximity. The closer like objects are together, the more likely our brain is to see them as one object. That's why we don't see 1,000 trees. We see a forest. Or why we don't see 100 waves. We see an ocean. And our brains do that for a good reason: to make processing new environments much easier.

Just imagine how hard it would be to notice every single tree, leaf and detail of a landscape the first time we saw it. Our brains would explode from information overload. Not to mention how long it would take. We'd be like sitting ducks, counting leaves while the closest bear made his move. And getting eaten by a bear isn't good for survival. That's why our brains lump together like things that are in close proximity. By eliminating the details and seeing just a swath of green, blue or brown, it makes it easier to spot the threats.

But our brains only do that if the things are close together. If you saw two trees in a field a mile

apart from each other, your brain wouldn't see a group of trees. It would see two individual trees, because there's too much space between them for our brains to see them as a swath of color. But if those two trees were just five feet apart, our brains would see them as one object. Because when things are close enough together, our brains link them together.

And not just trees and waves. Our brains link any objects within close proximity together. Chairs. Tables. Artwork. If they're close enough together, our brains will see them as a grouping rather than a bunch of random objects. And the closer they are, the more likely our brains will see them as one unit.

Now why does this matter? Because groupings soothe us — for two reasons. One, they make it easier for us to take in our environment. The more things we can group together, the less time our brains have to work at making sense of each individual item. And the less our brains have to work, the more soothed they feel. And two, they make it easier to spot danger, which makes us naturally feel safer and cozier around them.

So if you want your room to feel relaxing, calming, safe or cozy, create numerous groupings in your room by spacing items close together. If that's not what you want to feel, do the opposite. Have fewer groupings and space them further apart from each other. It'll make your room feel, energetic, lively, airy and open.

Just be warned, there's a happy medium for everything — proximity included. If you place the items in your room either too close or too far apart, it elicits bad emotions. When all of the items in a room are spaced super close together, we feel suffocated. Like we're stuck in a thicket. When we space all of the items in a room really far apart, we feel disjointed and overwhelmed. Like there are too many different things to take in and places where danger could be lurking.

How far is too far apart? It depends on the person. In general, if you space two items their width or more apart, you're getting into the territory of your brain no longer linking them together as a grouping.

So if you want your brain to link two things together, space them less than their width apart. As for how much, use proportion as your guide, and when in doubt, eyeball it. Your eyes are always your best judge. As I've already said, if it feels good to you, that's all that matters.

REPETITION

Nature loves repetition. Just look around. Leaves on branches. Petals on flowers. Sand on beaches. Trees in forests. Repetition is everywhere, and it creates two very important things for our survival: groupings and unity.

GROUPINGS. As you already know, in order for our brain to see two things as a grouping, they must be within close proximity. But that's not the only requirement. They must also look alike.

Just think back to that tree-covered hill. If each tree were a completely different color, shape and size, we'd no longer see a sea of green. We'd see a jumbled mess. Why? Because there's no repetition. And when there's no repetition, our brains can't assume all the items are alike. After all, they look different. Which means, we can't lump anything together as a grouping. Instead, our brains have to vet each item individually in case one is a threat.

And as you already know, our brains don't like doing that, because looking at each individual item takes way too long — not to mention the information overload. Which is why, whenever our brains see items repeated, they immediately group them together. That way, they only have to process each type of item once — rather than a bazillion times — which greatly cuts down on processing time.

As a result, we see like things close together as groupings. The more things look alike, the more likely our brains will group them together. Which is why we see a lawn of grass and not a million blades. Or a blanket of snow and not a trillion snowflakes. It's because all blades of grass and flakes

A ball pit. Well, a simulated ball pit. They're really just gumballs.

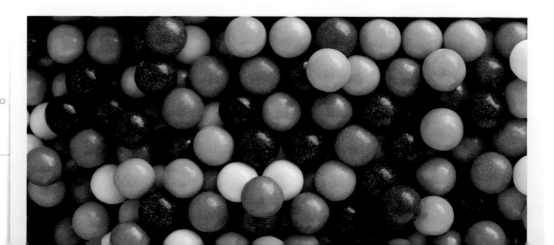

of snow look practically identical. Whereas, when we look at one of those giant children's ball pits, we have a much harder time seeing it as one — because the balls don't look identical. They're all different colors. The only thing that saves our eyes from pure chaos is the repetition of the same shape and size ball over and over again. If those balls weren't the same shape and size, our brains might explode from information overload.

So, if you want to create groupings, the more alike the things look, the easier it will be for your brain to link them together as one.

UNITY. There are tons of types of sand in the world. White. Red. Pink. Black. Tan. Brown. Yet, we never see them all on the same beach. Just as there are many different types of trees in the world. Palms. Beech. Cypress. Evergreen. Yet, you never see them all in the same forest. Nature doesn't work that way.

In each location, nature repeats itself. And not just the same items — like sand on a beach and trees in a forest. It repeats the same characteristics — shapes, colors and textures — over and over again. And it's that repetition of the same items and characteristics that gives each environment a sense of unity — the feeling that everything belongs.

The Maine coast.

Just think of the Maine coast. The rocky cliffs look as if they belong, because they're repeated over and over again. Just as the evergreens look like they belong, because they're repeated over and over again. And most importantly, they both look as though they belong together, because the

jagged, pointy, rough shapes are repeated within both.

Every place in the world works the same way. The same items and characteristics are repeated over and over. And thank goodness. If they weren't, we'd have a really hard time spotting things that didn't belong — like foreign invaders. Because our environments repeat themselves and feel so unified, spotting unusual suspects is easy.

Now, regardless of whether repetition is used to create groupings or unity, it makes us feel the same emotions: soothed and at ease. As you know, the less data we have to take in, the less work we have to do — which means we feel less on edge and far more calm. Just as, the more unified our environment looks, the easier it is to spot threats — which makes us feel like we can sit back and relax, because we don't have to be on high alert.

Whereas, when there's little repetition, there's a lot of data we have to process — which makes it harder to spot threats. So we feel on edge. Of course, being on edge isn't necessarily a bad thing. It can make a place feel more energetic and fun.

So if you want your room to feel energetic and fun, use a low amount of repetition. Whereas, if you want your room to feel soothing, calm and peaceful, use a high amount of repetition.

But be warned. If you go overboard and use too little repetition, your room will feel completely overwhelming from the sheer amount of data to take in. So to keep your brain from going into panic mode, it's a good idea to have at least some level of repetition in your room. And there are two types you can use: identical or partial.

Identical Repetition. When you repeat the same item over and over — like the steps of stairs or the tile on a backsplash — you create identical repetition, which is the most soothing type of repetition. Why? Because it's the easiest to spot. To achieve it, simply place identical items anywhere in your room.

But if you want the ultimate in soothing, you'll want to make sure those identical items are equidistant apart because it creates a visual rhythm that mimics the most soothing sound of all: the human heart beat. Thump. Thump. Thump. Thump. And when we see a place with that visual rhythm

— like a tree-lined walk or a hallway lined with pillars — we immediately feel soothed and reflective.

Now when creating identical repetition, most people assume the things must be absolutely, 100 percent identical. But that's not true. While, we as humans love that type of repetition because it's easier to create, nature? Not so much.

Rarely do you find perfectly identical repetition in the great outdoors. Every snowflake looks slightly different, as does every blade of grass. Even nature's attempt at exact replication — identical twins — doesn't come out exact. There's normally a slight discrepancy that allows us to tell the two apart.

So if you use a lot of 100-percent identical repetition in your room, it can feel a bit sterile or mechanical — because we'd never see it in nature. Whereas, when you repeat items that are just slightly off, it feels far more natural. Like repeating tiles that are ever so slightly misshaped. Or similar shades of the same color that are ever so slightly different.

Knowing that should make you feel more relaxed, because most people assume the colors in their room must match perfectly. But a subtle variation — similar to the range of color found in leaves on the same tree — will make your room feel more natural and less artificial.

Partial Repetition. When you repeat only a characteristic over and over again — a shape, color or texture — you create partial repetition. That type of repetition is used to create a sense of unity in a room, and the more characteristics you repeat, the more unified your room will feel.

But don't think you must repeat the same characteristics on the same type of object. Au contraire. When you create partial repetition, you repeat those same characteristics on any object.

You could repeat the color yellow throughout your room — on a chair, wallpaper or vase. You could use a rough texture throughout your room — on floors, a table or lamps. Where you use the characteristic doesn't matter. All that's important is that you repeat it. If you do that, your room will feel unified.

*Partial repetition.
of color
— silver —
and texture
— shiny.*

MOVEMENT

When we think of a landscape, we typically conjure up a still image. But in real life it's never still. Nature's constantly in motion. Rivers flowing. Leaves rustling. Winds blowing. Bugs bustling. Everywhere you look, there's movement, and we're used to it. So used to it, that we don't even notice it anymore — until there isn't any.

Then we notice. When things are still — too still — we feel uneasy. Because no movement is a sign something is wrong. Terribly wrong. Either a big predator is on the prowl, a tornado is on its way, or, in the very worse case, death. And if something just died, we could be next. So when things go still, we take notice. It could be a pause of activity in the forest. The calm before the storm. A ghost town. It doesn't matter. A lack of movement always means the same two things: death or imminent danger. And in both cases we feel uncomfortable — terribly, horribly uncomfortable.

That's why movement is so important. A sense of movement makes us feel comfortable and soothed. That's why we feel so relaxed at the ocean. The steady, undulating waves calm us. Just like a gentle afternoon breeze. They put our nerves at ease, and make us feel that we're safe.

But if that movement picks up speed, we immediately get unnerved because too much movement signifies danger. Terrible, horrible upheaving danger. Like tornados. Hurricanes. Stampedes. All of which could kill us in seconds, which is why we feel anxious and worried when there is too much movement.

So in order to feel safe and comfortable, there must be some movement. The less movement you have, the more calming and soothing your room will feel. Think of clouds floating by on a lazy day. Whereas, the more movement you have in your room, the more energetic, chaotic and fun it will feel. Like a carnival or soccer game — where there are tons of things to do and see.

Of course, creating any type of movement — lots or little — can be a challenge in our homes. After all, nothing moves. Not beds. Not chairs. Not rugs. Nothing. So we have to rely on the visual to create movement, and we do that by creating visual pathways through the use of lines and repetition.

Lines. When our eyes spot a line, they naturally follow it like they're on the fast lane of a highway — letting it lead them wherever it goes. And when the line comes to an end, our eyes hop onto the next closest line, and begin the journey all over again — which keeps our eyes in constant motion. And that motion of following the lines is enough to simulate the subtle motion we experience outside.

Of course, you need lines to create that motion. And in a room, our eyes read the edges of objects as lines. The mast of a model sailboat looks like two lines creating an arrow pointing up. The lines of molding in a long corridor look like straight lines pointing ahead. The curve of a rounded chair is seen as an arc pointing to the side. And those lines act as a subtle guide directing our eyes to wherever they lead.

But if you want stronger movement — the type that sucks you in and takes you for a ride — then you'll want to use actual lines in your room. Striped rugs. Zig-zag wallpaper. Anything that's bold and lined will do. And the bolder, the better. Because the easier the line is to see, the easier it is for your eyes to jump on board.

Repetition. As you already know, our brains like to link like things together. When those like items are within close proximity, it's easier for our brains because they can lump them together in a grouping. But when the items are spaced far apart, our eyes have to jump from one like object to the next, assessing each one. That action of jumping from like object to like object keeps our eyes constantly moving and simulates the subtle motion we observe outdoors.

Now you may assume that the objects have to be practically identical for it to work, but not so much. Both identical and partial repetition work. But remember, the easier it is to spot the repetition, the stronger the movement. That's why identical repetition works best at creating movement.

A close runner-up is color. Why? Move your head really fast to the side. What do you see? A blur of color? Me too. That's why it's second best at creating movement, because it's the easiest characteristic to spot in a glance.

Now whether you use lines, repetition or a combination of both depends on how you want your room to feel. Linear movement tends to be more fluid, which makes a room feel calm, serene or harmonious. Whereas, movement created through repetition tends to be a bit jerky, because your eyes bounce from object to object, which makes a room feel energetic, exciting or fun.

What happens if you want a mix of both of those emotions? Use both types of movement. Most rooms do.

But regardless of which you use, the most important thing to consider when creating movement is the shape of your path. You see, we humans have hardware restraints. Our eyes and head can't move just anywhere. They work on a swivel, which means square and rectangular pathways are awkward — and sometimes downright uncomfortable — to follow. That's why you don't see pictures hung in the four corners on a wall. It's too hard for your eyes to do that motion.

So ditch the idea of using square or rectangular pathways in your room. Instead, use straight or circular pathways, because that's how our head and eyes move best. From side to side and around and around. You can

Movement created through identical repetition.

Movement created through partial repetition.

even try using a wave-like pathway, because our eyes can easily bob up and down. Which you choose depends greatly on the shape of your room and your aspirations.

Shape. Certain pathways feel more natural in certain rooms. In a long, rectangular hallway, a straight visual path feels most natural, because it mimics the shape of the room. In a relatively square room, a circular pathway feels more natural, because it mimics the shape of the room.

Your Aspirations. If you want people to spend little time in your space and move on through, a straight visual pathway from one door to the next is your best option. It will lead them like a conveyor belt to the next room.

Whereas, if you want people to stay in the room awhile, it's better to use a circular visual pathway. With that type of pathway, your eyes are continually brought back to where they started — in the room. As a result, people feel comfortable staying in one spot, rather than bolting for the door.

To determine the shape of the room's visual pathways, follow the most prominent lines in your room — both actual and outlines. Then, draw that path. Next, connect the dots between all like objects in your room. Doing that will show you how people's eyes will most likely travel around your room.

When it comes to linear movement, everyone's eyes take a slightly different path depending on which objects his or her eyes choose to follow.

linear
movement

repetition
movement

CONTRAST

Our eyes are drawn to contrast. Think of a full moon in the night sky. Where do your eyes look? The moon? Or beyond? The moon. Because it's the point of contrast.

And we see contrast like that everywhere we look. Trees contrast with the sky. Rocks contrast with water. Flowers contrast with leaves.

There's not a place on earth where you don't see contrast. In the Sahara Desert, where all you see is sand for miles and miles, you still have contrast between that golden sand and the bright blue sky.

In the middle of the ocean, where all you see is miles and miles of blue water, you still have contrast between the blue of the water and the blue of the sky.

Even inside caves, where there is no sky and everything is rock, you still have contrast. It may be small, but the shapes of those rocks contrast with one another.

We see contrast everywhere, which is why it makes us feel safe. It's what we're used to. The only time there isn't any is during dust storms, whiteout blizzards and the dark of night. And all those things make us feel scared, because we can't see when they happen. And when we can't see, we feel unsafe because we can't spot danger. That's why we feel so uncomfortable when there's no contrast.

Just think of being stuck in an all-white room with no windows or doors. It'd make you go insane. Why? There's no contrast. It feels unnatural, which makes us feel on edge.

Of course, that doesn't mean the other end of the spectrum makes us feel any better. When there's an extreme amount of contrast, we feel just as unsafe because high contrast is usually a signal that what we're looking at is either poisonous or painful. Think of dart frogs and hornets, both of which we don't like tangling with. That's why when we see things of high contrast, we perk up to full alert.

Bear in mind, in nature things of high contrast are almost always small. And if those small doses of contrast are enough to put us on edge, just imagine an entire room of it. We'd feel jarred into outright panic.

So when it comes to contrast, you want to stay somewhere in the middle. Not too much, and not too little. Where you fall in that spectrum depends on what you want to feel.

Very low contrast — like that in a cave — is soothing and relaxing. Everything looks similar, which means most threats will be easy to spot. So our brain figures it doesn't need to be on edge and relaxes.

A high level of contrast — like that at a carnival — feels energizing and fun because there's so much to look at. So our eyes dart around trying to take it all in, which creates a sense of energy.

Now, if you move too close to the edge of too much contrast, your room will take on a sexy, dangerous feel. Think flames on a black motorcycle. Or blood red lipstick with a black dress.

Regardless of what you want, you must know how to create contrast, and it's very easy. Things contrast when one or more of their characteristics — **size, shape**, texture or color   differ. That's why a big thing contrasts with a small thing, a square thing contrasts with a round thing, a rough thing contrasts with a smooth thing and a dark thing contrasts with a light thing. Their characteristics differ. And the more a single characteristic differs, the more they'll contrast.

Contrasts less because the colors green and blue are very similar.

Contrasts more because the colors green and red are very different.

Just as the more characteristics that differ, the more two objects will contrast.

The pine cone and gumball contrast far more than either pairs of gumballs on the prior page, because they don't have any characteristics in common.

If you want a very low level of contrast, you'll want only one characteristic to differ slightly. If you want a high level of contrast, you'll want all the characteristics to differ greatly.

Most rooms mimic the contrast seen outside, which is why the ceiling, walls, furniture and floors are typically different colors. They imitate the sky, horizon, trees and ground. But you don't have to do that. Many rooms have the ceiling, furniture or floor the same color as the walls to create a feeling of less contrast.

When deciding what should contrast in your room, let your emotional wants be your guide. The more energetic, lively, sexy or dangerous you want your room to feel, the more things should contrast. The more calm, serene and peaceful you want your room to feel, the less things should contrast.

EMPHASIS

We use emphasis to communicate importance. And the more we emphasize something — the more we make it stand out — the more important it is. Just think of newspapers. How do you know which story is most important? It has the biggest headline, which tells us it's the story we should pay the most attention to.

But just imagine if newspapers didn't emphasize certain headlines. You'd have to weed through every single story in order to figure out which ones were the most important, and that takes a lot of time. Too much time. That's why emphasis is so important. It tells us — the viewer — exactly where to direct our attention so that we don't have to figure it out on our own.

But emphasis may be even more important to the communicator — which in our case is the decorator — because it allows us to draw people's attention to whatever we deem most important. The more emphasis we place on something, the more attention it will get. In a room, those things we emphasize are called focal points.

Now you don't have to have any. But most rooms do. For one, most people have something they find more important and want to place emphasize on. And two, having focal points helps to lead people's eyes through your room.

If you decide to use focal points, there are four things to consider when selecting which items to emphasize.

What should be a focal point. There are two ways to determine your focal points. The first comes from the perspective that your focal points should be the most important items in your room. After all, why else would you emphasize them?

If you decide to use that school of thought, then you'll need to determine which items in your room you deem most important. Luckily you've already figured that out. Given that the entire reason you're decorating is to make your aspirations come true, it only follows that they're the most important thing as far as your room is concerned. So your focal points should be the main things used to do your aspirations.

If you want to sleep in your room, the bed would be your focal point. If you want to cook in your room, the stove would your focal point. If you want to sit by the fire, the fireplace would be your focal point.

There's even an added bonus to using those items. Bringing attention to them encourages you to do your aspirations. After all, the more prominent they are, the more you'll be reminded to engage in those activities.

The second way to determine your focal points comes from the perspective that the things you emphasize should communicate the emotions you most want to feel in your room. After all, the only way your aspirations will happen is if you make your room feel how you want to feel. So in that vein, you'd base your focal points on your emotional needs.

If you want to feel soothed, your focal point may be a fountain. If you want to feel refreshed, your focal point may be a painting of something refreshing. If you want to feel cozy, your focal point may be a fireplace.

Which way you choose to determine your focal points is entirely up to you. Sometimes you get lucky, and your aspirational and emotional focal points overlap.

And keep in mind, an entire wall can be your focal point if you put something decorative on it — like wallpaper, fabric or tile. So don't limit yourself to furniture or accessories.

Number of focal points. For a focal point to be a focal point, it has to stand out. That means you can't have any other focal points in your immediate view — which is why rooms typically either have one large focal point in the center of the room or a focal point on each wall. Of course, if your room is very big, you can have more than one focal point on a wall. To determine if your room is big enough, stand against the opposite wall centered on your room. If you can't easily see the corners of your room in your periphery vision, there's a good chance your room could handle two focal points on one wall. After all, if you can't easily see them at the same time, they can't compete for attention.

Whether you choose to use multiple focal points or just one in the center depends on how many things you want to emphasize. Just know that the more focal points you have, the less intense each becomes.

Intensity of focal points. As you already know, for something to stand out it must contrast. So for something to be a focal point, it must contrast with its surroundings. And the more it contrasts, the more noticeable it will be.

How noticeable you want your focal points depends completely on how you want your room to feel. If you want it to feel grand, dramatic or bold, you'll want your focal point to contrast highly. Like crashing waves or majestic mountains. Whereas, if you want it to feel calm, soothing or quaint, you'll want your focal point to have less contrast. Like calm ripples or rolling hills.

Keep in mind, if you have multiple focal points in your room, they don't have to be of equal intensity. They can vary. Whether or not you want them to be equal depends on how important you feel each is. If they're equally important, you'll want them to have equal emphasis. Whereas, if one is more important than the others, you'll want it to have more emphasis to communicate its higher importance.

Adding extra emphasis. The absolute best way to highlight a focal point is to have the room's visual pathway lead directly to it. Think of a wedding. The aisle down the center directs your attention straight to the most important people in the room: the bride and groom. If the aisle wasn't there, the couple wouldn't seem nearly as important.

If you want to draw extra attention to a focal point in your room, position your furniture so that it points straight to the focal point.

WHITE SPACE

When decorating, there's a tendency to fill every single inch of wall and floor space with stuff. But doing that is like trying to listen to 30 songs at once. Completely overwhelming.

Our brains can only appreciate one thing at a time. The second we throw another item in the mix, our brains have to divide their attention. As a result, they can only take in half the details of each object.

And the more things you add, the less details your brain notices — until you get to the point where you add so many things your brain can no longer take in a single detail. Then, all you'll see is a jumbled, chaotic mess.

Think of a cramped, overstuffed store. You have to concentrate really hard on each item to tell what you're looking at. And after just a short time, your brain feels exhausted and overwhelmed from the information overload.

Whereas, when you're at a museum, you can easily see and savor each individual piece because there are so few in each room.

And the only difference between the cramped store and the museum is space. The space placed between the objects. In design, that space is referred to as white space. But don't let the name fool you. The space between objects does not need to be white. Any place free of contrast — whether it's wall space or floor space — is considered white space. Being free of contrast simply means there's no object there.

Now how much white space you use in your room depends on two things: appreciation and emotion.

Appreciation. If you want to savor every single detail of an item, you'd give it the ultimate amount of white space. An entire room alone. Like the Winged Victory of Samothrace has in the Louvre. That way, all of your attention is devoted on that object.

But if you don't care about noticing every nook and cranny of an item, go ahead and put other objects in the room with it. How many objects you add — and most importantly, the amount of space you leave between them — should be directly proportional to how much detail you want to notice in each.

The more detail you want to notice, the more white space should surround the object. The less detail you want to notice, the less white space should surround the object.

That's why decorators often cover unspectacular pieces with tons of accessories — like pillows and books and vases. They're trying to divert your attention so you don't notice the lackluster details.

Emotion. The more white space you have in your room, the more open, airy, calming and luxurious it will feel. And you get that feeling because your attention isn't being divided as much. So your brain feels as if it can relax — which is the ultimate luxury.

But be careful. If you use too much, your room will start to feel cold, austere or sterile —like you're in the middle of a barren wasteland completely exposed.

On the other end of the spectrum, when you use very little white space, your room can take on two different types of feelings. The first is cozy, cocooning and quaint. Because the less empty space there is, the more protected you feel — like you're in the middle of the forest. The second is energetic and fun, because the less empty space there is, the more things there are to look at.

But again, be careful. If you have too little white space, that energetic and cozy feeling can turn over-whelming and stifling.

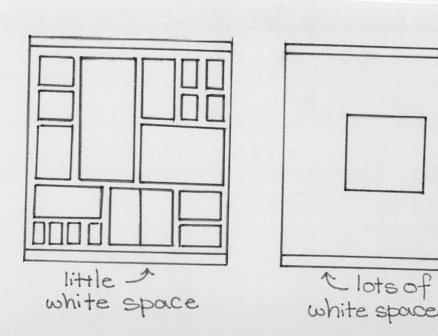

little →
white space

↖ lots of
white space

BALANCE

Symmetrical:
  formal
  grand
  structured
  stiff
  uptight

Asymmetrical:
  casual
  laid-back
  down-to-earth

PROPORTION

Proportional:
  any emotions
  other than ⟶

Out of Proportion:
  cute
  whimsical
  grand
  quaint

PROXIMITY

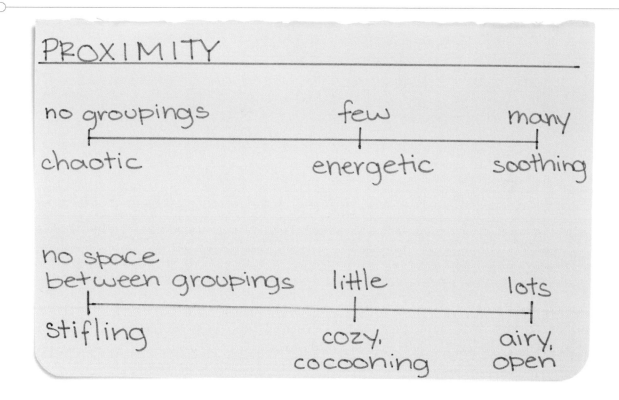

no groupings — few — many

chaotic — energetic — soothing

no space between groupings — little — lots

stifling — cozy, cocooning — airy, open

REPETITION

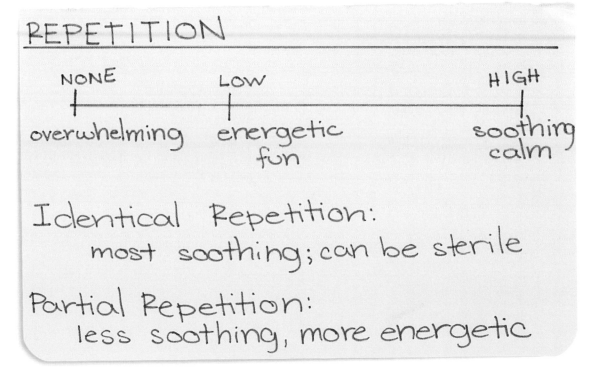

NONE — LOW — HIGH

overwhelming — energetic fun — soothing calm

Identical Repetition:
    most soothing; can be sterile

Partial Repetition:
    less soothing, more energetic

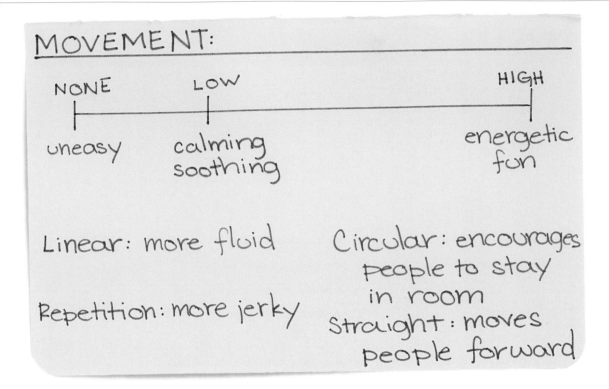

MOVEMENT:

NONE	LOW	HIGH
uneasy	calming soothing	energetic fun

Linear: more fluid

Repetition: more jerky

Circular: encourages people to stay in room

Straight: moves people forward

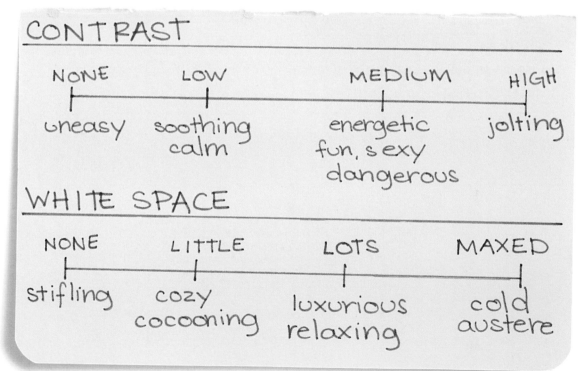

CONTRAST

NONE	LOW	MEDIUM	HIGH
uneasy	soothing calm	energetic fun, sexy dangerous	jolting

WHITE SPACE

NONE	LITTLE	LOTS	MAXED
stifling	cozy cocooning	luxurious relaxing	cold austere

GETTING THE RIGHT MIX

In order to make your room feel good to you, both the grammar and objects you choose must clearly communicate those emotions you want. So don't go playing favorites. Both parts are equally important and deserve your attention.

COMMUNICATION ERRORS

No matter how hard you try to get the right mix, some people just won't see what you see in your room. When you communicate through objects, it's open to interpretation.

After all, there is no dictionary telling you what a red sofa, blue lamp or any other object means. So we each put our own meaning on them based on our frames of reference. In most cases, our references are the same.

For instance, most people find pink girly, long drapes luscious and plaid rustic.

But even with those things, there are the exceptions. After all, plaid is also preppy. Or in my case, avoided because I had to wear it to school every day for 13 years.

So no matter what you do, people will interpret your room based on their frame of reference. Which means, you'll never satisfy everyone. So instead of worrying about what your room communicates to others, focus on what it says to you.

That is what matters most.

Everyone's emotional response to the visual grammar is slightly different. So don't be alarmed if you feel something other than what's listed on the cards. It's perfectly normal. The cards are simply generalities. Not absolutes. And as with everything, there are always exceptions. So trust your gut above all else.

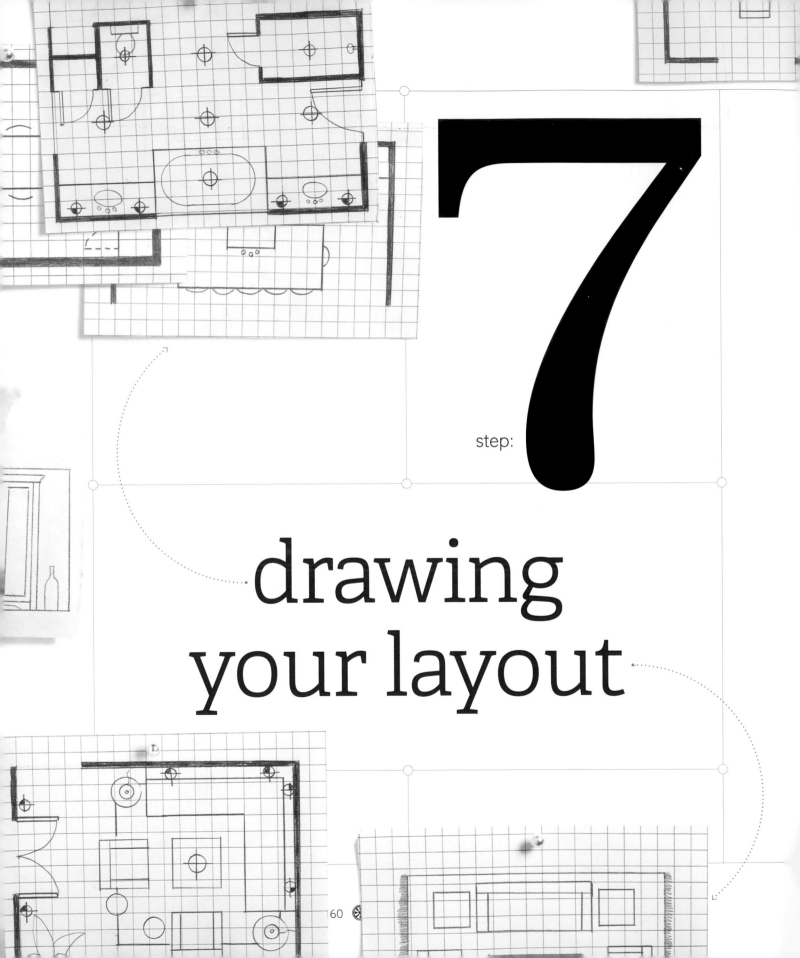

step:

7

drawing your layout

Stretch out your fingers. Roll up your sleeves. Get out a pencil. The moment we've been preparing for has finally arrived.

It's time to create.

You can do this. You know what you want. You know what you need. You know the challenges you face when it comes to your room. You even know how to wield the visual language.

You're ready. You're more than ready. You've got everything you need to create a dynamite layout. So let's do this.

THE IMPORTANCE OF A LAYOUT

Very few people take the time to create a decorating plan. And of those few, most begin the process by picking colors. But that is the absolute worst place to start. What's the point of picking colors if you don't know what you're putting in your room? That's like trying to put sprinkles on a cake you haven't baked yet. Crazy.

You can't possibly know how many and what types of colors — or patterns or textures — you need until you determine exactly what will go in your room. That's why the very first thing you should always do is draw up a layout. A layout tells you exactly what items will be in your room and exactly where they will go. Think of it like an aerial roadmap of your room.

Once you have that roadmap, you can go hog wild picking out colors. But first you've got to create it.

THE ELEMENTS OF A GREAT LAYOUT

Most people think creating a great layout is incredibly complicated. But if you've ever watched or played a team sport, you already know the secret to doing it. Put the right players in the right positions, and you'll win.

That's all there is to it. Players and positioning. And as long as you select the right players — objects — for what you

need to do, and position them where they need to be used, you'll have a great layout.

So don't stress. You've got this one in the bag — thanks to all those years of practices and watching games. And if you've never seen a team sport in your life, don't sweat it. I'm going to walk you through the entire process, and when we're finished, your players and positioning will be trophy-worthy.

WHAT YOU'LL NEED

You can use room planning software or magnetic boards with movable furniture pieces to create your layout. But I prefer to use a trusty old pencil and paper.

For one, it's cheap. Why shell out money for fancy software or special magnetic boards when you don't really need them — especially when that cash could be put towards something for your room?

Two, there's no learning curve. Everyone already knows how to use a pencil and paper, whereas all the room design software I've tested takes hours to learn. In that time, you could have drawn 10, 20, maybe even 100 layouts. So unless you plan to make a career out of interior design, what's the point of learning some software?

Three, you have a permanent record. When you hand draw your layout, you keep a copy of every draft you make, which means you can look back and see what you've already tried. But with a magnetic board, you don't get any copies. To make a new layout, you have to move your old one. So there's no way to know what you've already tested and which version is best.

That's why I kick it old-school. Now, if some snazzy software came out that was so intuitive you could learn how to use it in 3 minutes, then I may be swayed. But for now, I'm sticking with the pencil and paper. If you plan to do the same — which I highly recommend — here's what you'll need:

Graph paper: You can either buy a pad or print out free pages online. Search for "free graph paper," and a number of sites will come up that offer free printable templates.

Pencils: Preferably those with a nice sharp tip. I use mechanical pencils because the tip stays consistently sharp. But any type of pencil will do. Just don't even think about using a pen or marker. Unless you experience divine intervention while drawing up your layout, you're bound to make a mistake. More like many mistakes — which brings us to our next item.

Erasers: Lots and lots of erasers. They'll become your new best friend, especially if you choose a soft eraser — such as an art gum — that doesn't shred your paper or leave ugly marks.

Ruler: You could draw all your lines freehand, but layouts look much nicer — and are easier to read — when drawn with sharp, crisp, ruler lines. That's why I recommend using a ruler. When choosing a ruler, there are two things to look for. Length, the longer the ruler, the longer the lines you can draw, and the less time you waste moving your ruler around the page. Choose one that's at least 12 inches long. Clarity, being able to see through your ruler allows you to see exactly where the line you're drawing is in relation to everything else on the page — which makes drawing your layout much easier. So choose one that's see-thru.

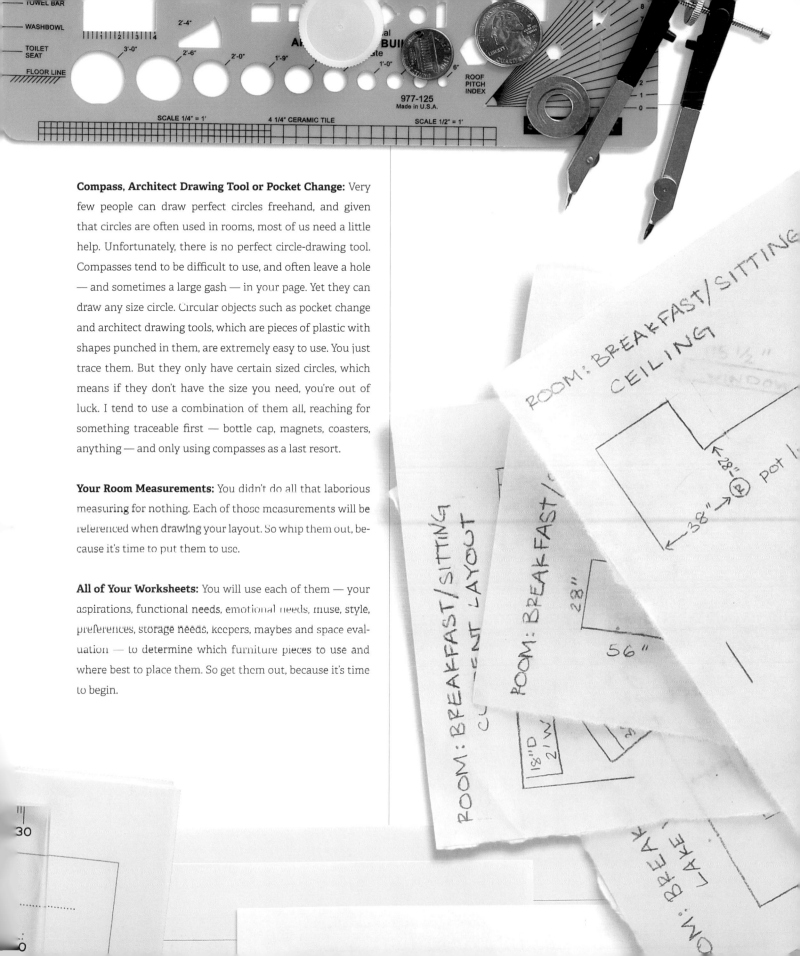

Compass, Architect Drawing Tool or Pocket Change: Very few people can draw perfect circles freehand, and given that circles are often used in rooms, most of us need a little help. Unfortunately, there is no perfect circle-drawing tool. Compasses tend to be difficult to use, and often leave a hole — and sometimes a large gash — in your page. Yet they can draw any size circle. Circular objects such as pocket change and architect drawing tools, which are pieces of plastic with shapes punched in them, are extremely easy to use. You just trace them. But they only have certain sized circles, which means if they don't have the size you need, you're out of luck. I tend to use a combination of them all, reaching for something traceable first — bottle cap, magnets, coasters, anything — and only using compasses as a last resort.

Your Room Measurements: You didn't do all that laborious measuring for nothing. Each of those measurements will be referenced when drawing your layout. So whip them out, because it's time to put them to use.

All of Your Worksheets: You will use each of them — your aspirations, functional needs, emotional needs, muse, style, preferences, storage needs, keepers, maybes and space evaluation — to determine which furniture pieces to use and where best to place them. So get them out, because it's time to begin.

SETTING UP YOUR PAPER

The entire point of creating a layout is to know with 100 percent certainty what will fit inside your room and where it will go. So guesstimating the size of your room when drawing it doesn't cut it. Your drawing must be to scale, meaning the little sketch you make of your room must be perfectly proportional to the real deal. To do that, you must properly set up your paper.

1. Label Your Paper

On the top of your page, write down the room you're working on. That way, when it inevitably gets lost in a pile of papers, you can quickly identify it. If you don't name the papers as you work through your rooms, it'll be harder to keep them straight.

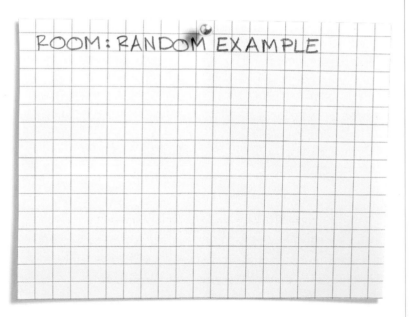

2. Choose Your Scale

Thanks to graph paper, drawing your room to scale is super easy. Each little block represents a unit of length, so all you have to do is add up however many blocks equals the overall length of whatever you're drawing.

But you can't do that until you decide how much you want each block to represent. Three feet? Two feet? One foot? Six inches.

I personally prefer using a scale of 6 or 3 inches because many furniture pieces are typically feet and some change. Which means, if you use a 1-, 2- or 3-foot scale, you'll end up having to divide your blocks — and that gets messy. If you use a 6- or 3-inch scale, you'll rarely need to divide any blocks — which makes it much easier to see the exact dimensions of each item you put in your room.

But there is one hang-up of using such a small scale. If you have a very big room, your room may not be able to fit on your page using a 6- or 3-inch scale. So before you decide on a scale, first make sure it will fit on your page — or tape a few sheets together.

To determine if your room will fit on your page, simply divide the length of your room by the scale you've chosen. If the number you get is smaller than the number of blocks running along the length of your paper, you might have a winner. To be sure, do the exact same thing for the width of your room and width of your paper. If the number comes out smaller again, you're set.

Remember, if your scale is in inches, be sure to convert your wall measurements to inches before dividing. If you don't, your number will come out wrong.

Keep in mind that it's nice to have at least three extra blocks on each side of your page for writing in dimensions and notes. So if your room will perfectly fit on your page, you may want to make your scale a bit larger.

Once you've found a scale that works, write it down.

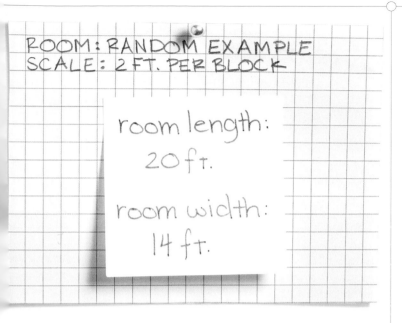

ROOM: RANDOM EXAMPLE
SCALE: 2 FT. PER BLOCK

room length:
20 ft.

room width:
14 ft.

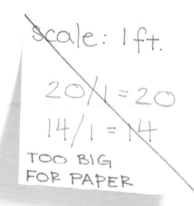

scale: 1 ft.

20/1 = 20
14/1 = 14

TOO BIG
FOR PAPER

scale: 2 ft.

20/2 = 10
14/2 = 7

PERFECT FIT!

3. Draw Your Walls.

Take the overall length of the longest wall in your room and divide it by the scale of each block. Three inches. Six inches. A foot. Two feet. Whatever you choose, the resulting number is how many blocks represent the length of your wall. To draw your wall, put a dot on the page where your wall should start. Then count the blocks until you reach the number you came up with and put a dot there, where your wall should end.

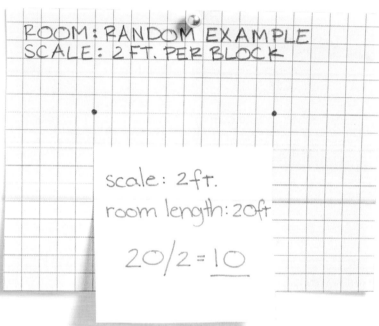

ROOM: RANDOM EXAMPLE
SCALE: 2 FT. PER BLOCK

scale: 2ft.
room length: 20ft

20/2 = 10

If your wall doesn't have any windows, doors or openings in it, draw a line with a ruler connecting the two dots. Wall sections are drawn as an extra-thick line. Be sure to draw the extra thick part on the outside of where your room will be. That way you don't take up any room space with your wall.

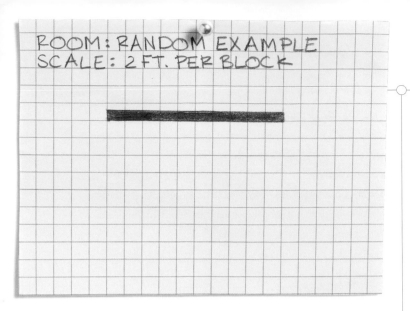

If your wall does have windows, doors or openings, hold up. You need to find the location of each before you draw any lines.

Divide the length of the wall section starting at the beginning of the wall and ending with the nearest window, door or opening by the scale of each block. The number you get is the number of blocks that make up that wall section. Count from the dot you marked to denote the beginning of your wall, over the number you just got, and make another dot there. Use a ruler to connect those two dots. That is your first wall section.

Repeat this process until you have all windows, doors, openings and wall sections marked out. Windows are drawn as a single straight line. If the window has many panes, you can mark those with small dashes.

Doors are drawn just like windows: a single straight line. A perpendicular line is used to show which way the door swings. If the door swings into your room, determine which side it opens on, the right or the left. Then draw a line the length of your door into the room. Draw an arc from the end of the line you just drew to the other side of the door.

If the door doesn't swing into your room, there's no need to draw it. The only reason to draw where the door swings is to remind you not to put any furniture in the way.

To draw an opening, do absolutely nothing. Openings are left open.

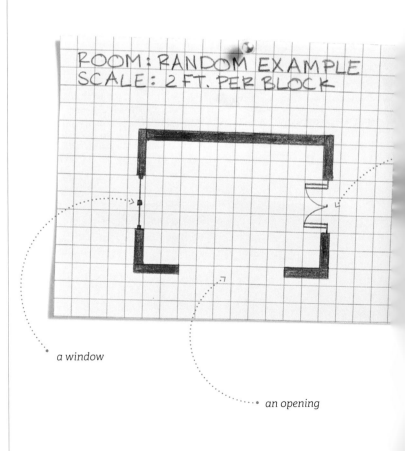

a window

an opening

Continue drawing until all walls have been drawn. If you need to draw a diagonal wall, first draw all walls that run along the lines of your paper. Then connect the dots between the two walls on either side of the diagonal. The resulting line should be the length of your diagonal walls.

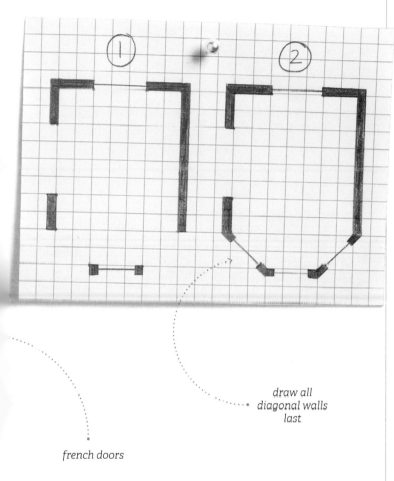

french doors

draw all diagonal walls last

When you're finished drawing all of your walls, your paper should look just like the rough drawing you did of the room when taking the measurements — only much nicer.

3. Write in Dimensions.

Once all of your walls, windows, doors and openings have been drawn, write in the overall dimensions of each wall and the individual dimensions of each wall segment, window, door and opening. That way you don't have to count each block — which can be a pain —to remember the dimension of each.

Typically, dimensions are written like this:

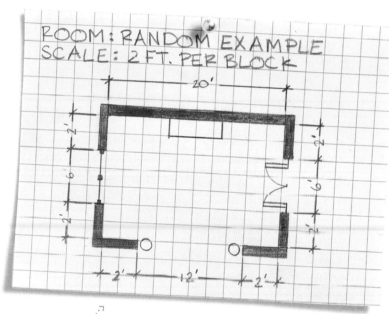

You can write your dimensions in either feet or inches. Use whichever is easiest for you.

4. Draw in Current Architectural Features.

If you have any columns, fireplace hearths or built-in cabinetry in your room that you plan to keep, you must draw them in. Otherwise, you may accidentally place something where they're located, which wouldn't work out when you put your room together.

So draw them in. And don't worry about them looking perfect. Just draw their rough shape.

5. Note Utility Locations.

The location of many things in your room — televisions, phones, sinks, toilets, etc. — depends solely on where their respective utility lines are located. You need to know where each one is in order to make your plan — even if it's just so you know how far they must be moved.

Utilities are drawn using the following symbols. If using them seems like too much work, simply jot them in with an arrow. There's no need to be formal.

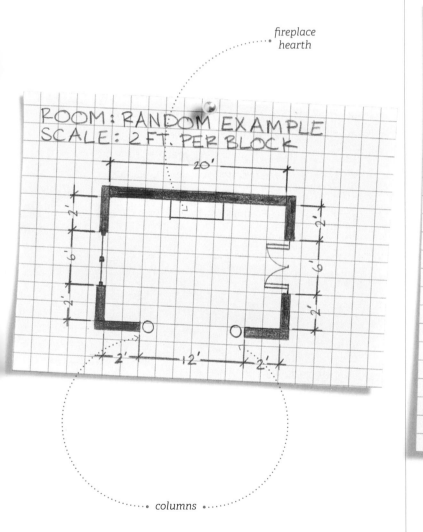

fireplace hearth

columns

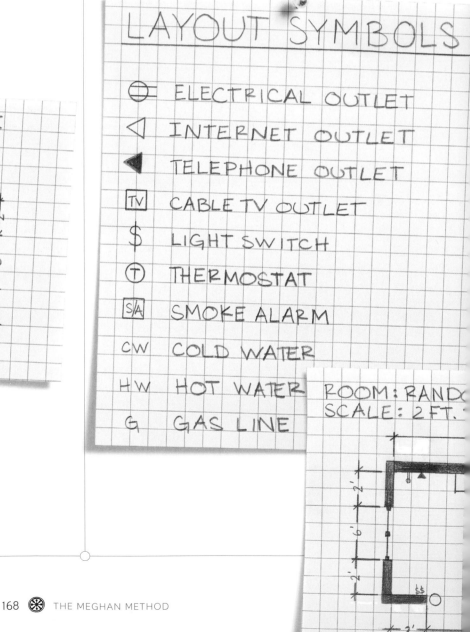

6. Copy or Scan.

Drawing a layout is like piecing together a jigsaw puzzle. It often takes a few — *or more* — tries before you get it right. And no one wants to redraw the outline of their room twice — let alone 5 or 10 times. Which is why before you draw in a single piece of furniture, you should get your paper copied. Better yet, scan it. That way you can draw layout after layout without having to redraw the outline of your room.

Of course, given that you drew your room outline in pencil, your copies and scans may not come out crisp. I know your first instinct will be to reach for a pen and trace the lines. But resist the urge. If by chance you realize during the layout process that a wall needs to be knocked down, or a door moved, the last thing you'll want to do is redraw the whole thing. Especially when you can simply erase and redraw that little bit.

If your pencil lines aren't dark enough, retrace them in pencil until they can be read by the copier or scanner. That way, you can still erase them.

As for how many copies to make? Well, that's a loaded question. You may only need five. You may need 20. I always tend to be in the double digits, because I don't stop drawing until the ideas stop flowing. And you should do the same. The only way to be sure you have the best layout possible is to flush out all the possibilities. Err on the side of caution and print more than you think you'll need. If you're lucky enough to have a scanner or copier at home, then print as needed.

DETERMINE YOUR POSITIONING

I realize you're probably itching to start drawing — especially now that you have your paper set up. But you need to hold your horses, because there's still a bit of prep work to do. You need to settle on your players and positioning. And guess what? You have to choose your positioning first.

Now I realize how crazy that sounds. After all, shouldn't you choose your players first? No. Not all players work in all positions, which is why you must first determine how to position the items in your room.

There are two things that influence positioning, and by now, you should know what they are: function and emotion.

FUNCTIONAL POSITIONING: Your Zones

If you look at your functional needs sheet, you'll quickly see that most activities require quite a few things. When it comes to positioning those things, it doesn't make much sense to scatter them all around your room. You end up bouncing around like a pinball from one thing to another.

Instead, you want to group the things you need for each activity in zones. That way, you have devoted areas in your room for each activity, which makes doing those activities much easier. Because everything you need is close at hand, while being out of the way of other activities.

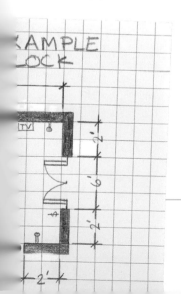

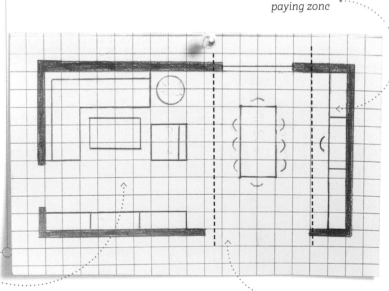

computer & bill paying zone

conversation & tv watching zone

eating zone

Now you'd think each of your aspirations would need its own zone. But that's crazy talk. More often than not, the functional needs of certain aspirations overlap. And there is no need for duplicates in your room. No one needs two beds — one for sleeping and one for watching TV. Or two tables — one for eating and one for projects. That's a waste of space and money. And considering most people don't have enough of either to throw around, you'll want to group all overlapping aspirations together in one zone.

So go through your functional needs worksheet and see if any of your aspirations require similar things. If they do, group them together in one zone. When you're finished, list each of your zones and all of the items functionally needed in that zone. Having that list will make placing the objects in your room super easy, because you'll already know what items need to be placed next to each other. Instead of placing each individual item in your room, you'll be placing each zone. The fewer zones you have, the easier it will be when it comes time to draw your layout.

But that doesn't mean you should go overboard and consolidate aspirations that shouldn't be consolidated. Only consolidate aspirations that make sense being lumped together. If that means you end up with tons of zones, that's okay. Some rooms are bound to have tons, such as kitchens with their prep, cook, clean, bake, drink, re-heat, eat and conversation zones.

So don't worry about how many zones you have. Instead, focus on making sure you group the right aspirations together. And keep in mind, some zones may partially overlap. For example, in a kitchen, the sink may be shared by both the prep and clean zone.

ZONES:

ITEMS NEEDE

HAVE MORE ZONES? PRINT OFF EXTRA SHEETS A

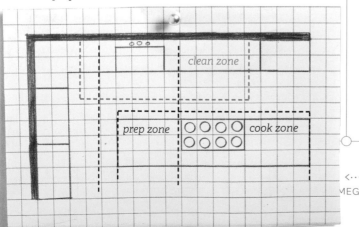

overlapping zones

ROOM:

along with the items required

thod.com

7

drawing your layout

YOUR ZONES

ROOM: BREAKFAST/ SITTING

DIRECTIONS: List the zones you need along with the items required in each.

ZONES:	ITEMS NEEDED:
eat & play games	table (for 4) seating storage (for linens, serveware, cards & other games) lighting: general salt & pepper shakers
read, talk & relax by the fire	seating ottoman side tables blanket fireplace tools storage (for books) lighting: task & general
enjoy the lake view	seating facing windows ↓ ideal view isn't straight on, but on a diagonal either left or right.

HAVE MORE ZONES? PRINT OFF EXTRA SHEETS AT: TheMeghanMethod.com

EMOTIONAL POSITIONING: Visual Grammar Cocktail

The functional part of positioning — your zones — only tells you what items need to be next to each other. What it doesn't tell you is how to position those items in your zone. And let me tell you, there are a number of ways to arrange the objects in each of your zones so that they're close together and functionally work.

So how do you decide how to arrange them? Emotion.

As you already know, your room doesn't just have to function. It must also make you feel what you want to feel, which is why the other half of positioning is all about emotion.

Fortunately, you already know how to communicate emotion through positioning. That's what those 33 pages of visual grammar were all about. Now all you have to do is figure out how you want to use each element of the visual grammar.

To do that, you'd think you'd simply look at your emotional wants and match them up with the emotions communicated by each element — as seen on pages 156-158. But not so much. You may not want to communicate all of your desired emotions through the visual grammar. Some you may want to save to communicate through objects — the words in your room.

For example, let's say you want to feel two contradictory emotions — energized yet relaxed. There's no reason why you have to communicate to both through the visual grammar. You may want to bring the energized feeling in through the objects you use, and add the relaxed feeling through the grammar. Or vice versa.

So before you can decide how to use the visual grammar, you must first figure out which emotions you want to communicate through it. Fortunately, doing that isn't all too hard. Our personal style often determines which emotions we like to communicate through visual grammar and which we prefer communicating through objects — which means, deciding how to use the visual grammar is as easy as looking at how it's used in our favorite rooms.

But don't let what you find in those photos be the only thing that guides you. Use that as your starting point, and let your muse and emotional needs be a tie-breaker of sorts, helping you determine exactly how far to go with each element. For example, maybe your muse has a high level of repetition or is symmetrically balanced, which may influence your decision of how to use those elements. Or maybe your emotional wants are all skewed toward one end of the spectrum, which causes you to sway that way.

When determining how to use the visual grammar, it's best to take all three — your style, muse and emotional wants — into consideration. And most importantly, use your gut. It will never lead you wrong. If you feel a strong inclination one way, trust it.

What you end up with — your personal visual grammar

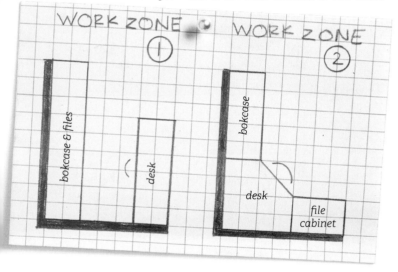

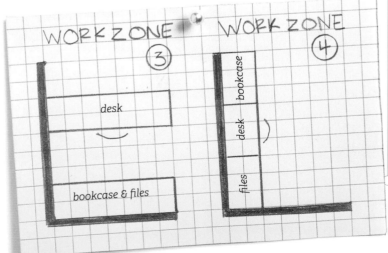

7

drawing your layout

YOUR VISUAL GRAMMAR COCKTAIL

ROOM: BREAKFAST SITTING

DIRECTIONS: Check the boxes to denote how you want to use each element.

BALANCE: ☐ symmetrical ☐ asymmetrical ☒ combination: ☐ none
70% symmetrical
30% asymmetrical

PROPORTION: ☒ proportional ☐ out of proportion
☐ cute: one part of an item out of proportion
☐ whimsy: one or more items out of proportion with room
☐ grand: room and things in it slightly too big for humans
☐ quaint: room and things in it slightly too small for humans

PROXIMITY: ☒ lots of groupings ☐ some ☐ few ☐ none
☐ lots of space between groupings ☐ some | ☐ little ☐ none
X somewhere between

REPETITION: ☒ high ☐ medium ☐ low ☐ none
☐ identical ☐ partial ☒ combination:
70 % identical
30 % partial

MOVEMENT: ☐ high ☒ medium ☐ low ☐ none
☐ line ☐ repetition ☒ combination
☒ circular ☐ straight

CONTRAST: ☐ high ☒ medium ☐ low ☐ none

WHITE SPACE: ☐ tons ☒ some ☐ a little ☐ none

cocktail — will be your guide when determining where to place each of your items in your zones. It'll even influence what items you use. So take your time when creating it. If you find yourself struggling, flip back to the visual grammar section, page 129, and review each element. The better you understand them, the easier it will be for you to create your cocktail.

When it comes to focal points, you don't need to decide how to use them. You need to decide how many you want and what they will be. To do that, flip back to page 151 to refresh yourself on how to choose focal points.

Make two lists: one of focal points based on your aspirations and one of focal points based on your emotions. If any items are listed on both, they should definitely be one of your focal points. As for the rest, it's up to you. Remember, you can always combine two different focal points, such as hanging a painting over a fireplace. And don't forget that a window, bold wallpaper, grand door, fountain or other room feature can be a focal point as well as objects. So don't limit yourself to only the items listed under your functional needs.

Once you have a list of focal points, rank them in order of importance to determine one, which you should use and two, which should be emphasized most.

Take out your aspiration sheet, and list the main item needed for each aspiration. For example, if your aspiration is to cook, you'd list a stove — or oven.

7
drawing your layout

YOUR VISUAL
GRAMMAR C〇

DIRECTIONS: List potential

RANK: POTENTIAL FOCAL POINTS BASED ON ASPIRATIC

*To rank your potential focal points, use 1 for your favorite

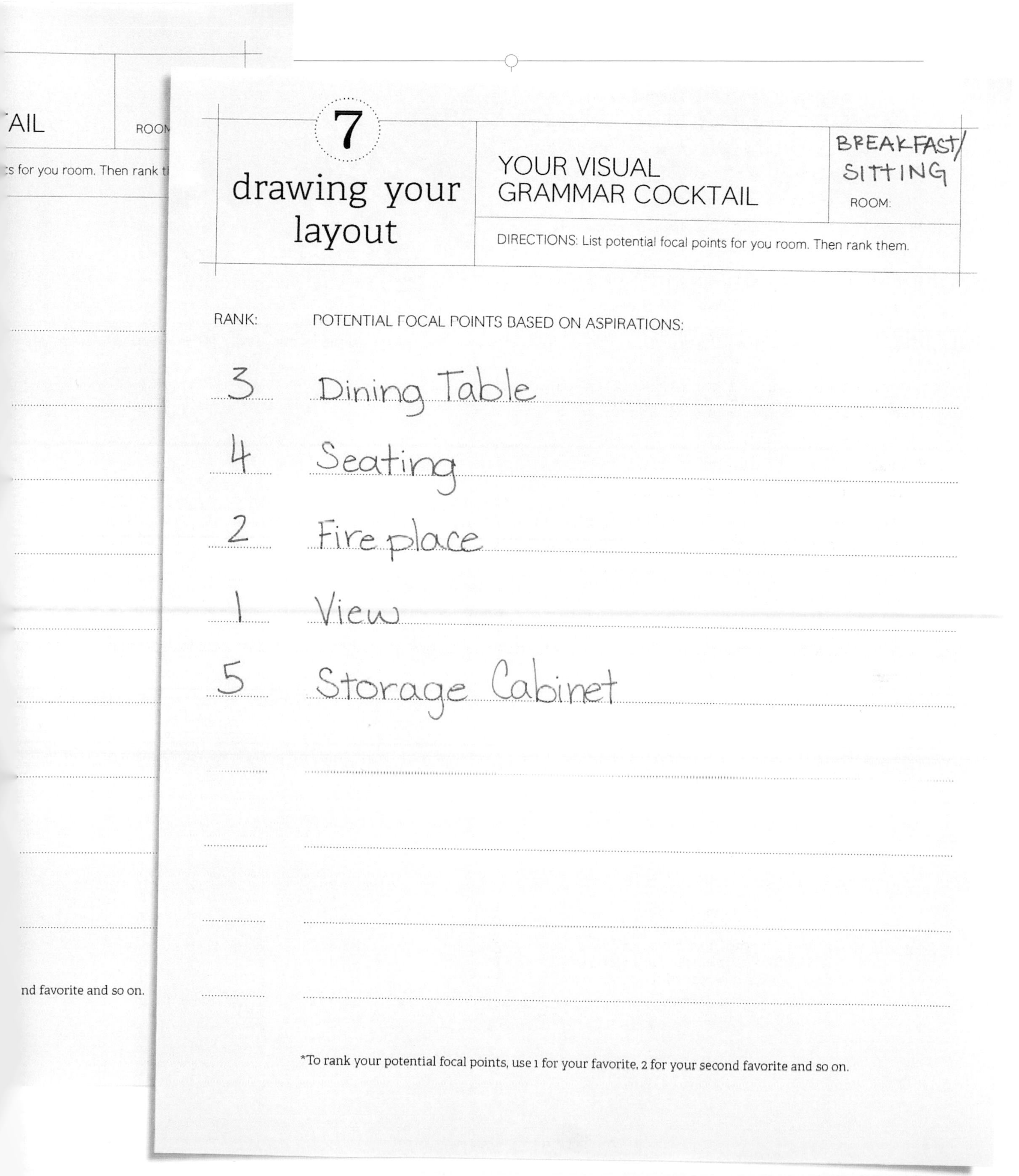

7

drawing your layout

YOUR VISUAL GRAMMAR COCKTAIL

ROOM: BREAKFAST/SITTING

DIRECTIONS: List potential focal points for you room. Then rank them.

RANK:	POTENTIAL FOCAL POINTS BASED ON ASPIRATIONS:
3	Dining Table
4	Seating
2	Fire place
1	View
5	Storage Cabinet

*To rank your potential focal points, use 1 for your favorite, 2 for your second favorite and so on.

7

drawing your layout

YOUR VISUAL GRAMMAR COCKTAIL

ROOM:

DIRECTIONS: List potential focal points for you room. Then rank them.

RANK: POTENTIAL FOCAL POINTS BASED ON EMOTIONAL NEEDS:

....

....

....

....

....

....

....

....

*To rank your potential focal points, use 1 for your favorite, 2 for your second favorite and so on.

7

drawing your layout

YOUR VISUAL GRAMMAR COCKTAIL	BREAKFAST/ SITTING ROOM:
DIRECTIONS: List potential focal points for you room. Then rank them.	

RANK: POTENTIAL FOCAL POINTS BASED ON EMOTIONAL NEEDS:

1   View

3   Artwork

2   Fireplace

If you can't think of many things you want as focal points, don't worry. You don't have to have many.

*To rank your potential focal points, use 1 for your favorite, 2 for your second favorite and so on.

PICKING YOUR PLAYERS

When picking players, your problem is never a lack of selection. In fact, it's just the opposite. For each player you need, there are almost too many options.

For example, let's say you need a bedside table. It could be round, oval, rectangular or square. It could have no drawers, one drawer or many drawers. It could have no shelves, one shelf or many shelves. It could be a nightstand, dresser, etagere or even a floating shelf. The options go on and on.

That's what drives people crazy: all the options. How in the world do you decide what to choose?

Well, lucky for you, we spent 95 pages developing a solid list of criteria each one of your players must fit — your preferences, storage needs, visual grammar, muse and style. And if each of your players don't fit all those criteria, you won't be happy with them because they won't functionally or emotionally fit what you need.

So when it comes to picking your players, all you have to do is run them through your criteria and see what fits. More often than not, you're left with just a handful of options — or even just one — which makes drawing your layout much easier. Because you'll already know exactly what will work best, instead of wasting a bunch of time haphazardly drawing in all your options not knowing which one to choose.

So let the player selection begin.

1. List Your Options

Get out your zones sheet. For each functional need, you'll need to create a list of your options. Some of your functional needs will have far more options than others. For example, if you need an oven, your options are: a single-wall oven, double-wall oven or an oven-range combo. Whereas, if you need a seating, the list goes on and on. Just look to the right.

If you need help brainstorming all of your options, think of all the different shapes your item comes in. Still need help? Flip through your style photos. Better yet, flip through tons of room photos or visit stores that sell your item. The more options you discover, the better off you'll be. After all, the best option for your situation may be one you're unaware of. So be sure to do a little research when listing all your options.

IAL PLAYERS

BREAKFAST/
SITTING
ROOM:

st the potential players for each item you need in your room.

ITEM NEEDED: seating for at least 4

RANK: POTENTIAL PLAYERS:

4 identical chairs
2 pairs of identical chairs
4 different chairs
2 identical loveseats
2 different loveseats
loveseat & 2 identical chairs
loveseat & 2 different chairs
loveseat, chaise & chair
loveseat & chaise
2 identical sofas
2 different sofas
sofa & 2 identical chairs
sofa & 2 different chairs
sofa, chaise & chair
sofa & chaise
2 identical chaise

7

drawing your layout

POTENTIAL PLAYERS

ROOM:

DIRECTIONS: List the potential players for each item you need in your room.

ITEM NEEDED:..

RANK: POTENTIAL PLAYERS:

....

....

....

....

....

....

....

....

....

....

....

....

....

ITEM NEEDED:..

RANK: POTENTIAL PLAYERS:

....

....

....

....

....

....

....

....

....

....

....

....

....

HAVE MORE ITEMS? PRINT OFF EXTRA SHEETS AT:
TheMeghanMethod.com

2. Your Preferences

It's time to start running all your options through your criteria, starting with your preferences. Take out your preferences sheet. If you spot anything you disliked as one of your current possibilities, cross it off using a blue marker or pen.

If you spot anything you liked as one of your possibilities, star it. You'll want to remember you favor that item.

If you don't spot anything in common between the two lists, no need to worry. Not every criteria will present you with the chance to cross something off your list.

3. Your Storage Needs

If the item you need doesn't offer storage — such as a sink or light — you can skip this part. But if your item could possibly be used to store something — anything — then take out your storage preferences sheet.

Look through the items you plan to store, and see if any could be stored in the object you're considering. If you find items that could be stored in your object — such as books on a bookcase — look at the ideal storage solutions you've listed underneath it. Using a green marker or pen, cross off any of your options that don't fit your top three criteria. Those options will be too hard to use, and if you put them in your room, it would probably end up messy.

Star the items that match your top storage solution criteria. Those items are the ones that will be easiest for you to use.

If you forgot to list your top three storage solutions, list them. They obviously are a good fit for you and deserve to be on your list.

Doesn't require storage.
So there's nothing to eliminate.

BREAKFAST/
SITTING
ROOM:

IAL PLAYERS

st the potential players for each item you need in your room.

ITEM NEEDED: seating for at
least 4

RANK: POTENTIAL PLAYERS:

4 identical chairs

2 pairs of identical chairs

4 different chairs

2 identical loveseats

2 different loveseats

loveseat & 2 identical chairs

loveseat & 2 different chairs

loveseat, chaise & chair

~~loveseat & chaise~~

2 identical sofas

2 different sofas

sofa & 2 identical chairs

sofa & 2 different chairs

sofa, chaise & chair

~~sofa & chaise~~

~~2 identical chaise~~

~~2 different chaise~~

U or L shaped sectional

OFF EXTRA SHEETS AT:
ethod.com

*Visual grammar cocktail specifies high
repetition and mostly symmetrical balance.
So random groupings have got to go.*

4. Your Visual Grammar Cocktail

You'd think the visual grammar only affects the placement of objects. But you can't place things in symmetrical balance unless you have two identical things. Just as you can't create repetition unless you have objects to repeat or an object with repetition. So your visual grammar greatly affects the objects you choose.

Take out your visual grammar cocktail sheet. Using an orange marker or pen, cross off any options that won't work with how you plan to place items in your room.

5. Your Muse & Emotional Needs

If we all consciously understood what items communicated what emotions, we'd be able to look at our emotional needs list and cross off options that didn't fit with what we want to feel. But most of us can't do that (page 60), which is why we have a muse. Now, you can try to use your emotional compass and cross off items that don't feel right, but it's far easier to use your muse as your guide.

So get out your Muse sheet and look specifically at the shapes you've listed. Using a red marker or pen, cross off any items that don't match the shapes you want, because those items don't communicate the emotions you want to feel.

If none of the options are listed with the shapes of your muse, double check to be sure they're not available in the shape you'd prefer. For example, if you need a storage cabinet and want curvy shapes, you could always use an armoire with a curved top.

*All the options left fit with the
shapes wanted: straight, rounded
or circular.*

BREAKFAST/ SITTING

IAL PLAYERS ROOM:

st the potential players for each item you need in your room.

ITEM NEEDED: seating for at least 4

RANK: POTENTIAL PLAYERS:

4 identical chairs

~~2 pairs of identical chairs~~

~~4 different chairs~~

2 identical loveseats

~~2 different loveseats~~

loveseat & 2 identical chairs

~~loveseat & 2 different chairs~~

~~loveseat, chaise & chair~~

~~loveseat & chaise~~

2 identical sofas

~~2 different sofas~~

sofa & 2 identical chairs

~~sofa & 2 different chairs~~

~~sofa, chaise & chair~~

~~sofa & chaise~~

~~2 identical chaise~~

~~2 different chaise~~

U or L shaped sectional

OFF EXTRA SHEETS AT:
ethod.com

Your Preferences

Your Storage
Needs

Your Visual
Grammar Cocktail

Your Muse &
Emotional Needs

Your Style

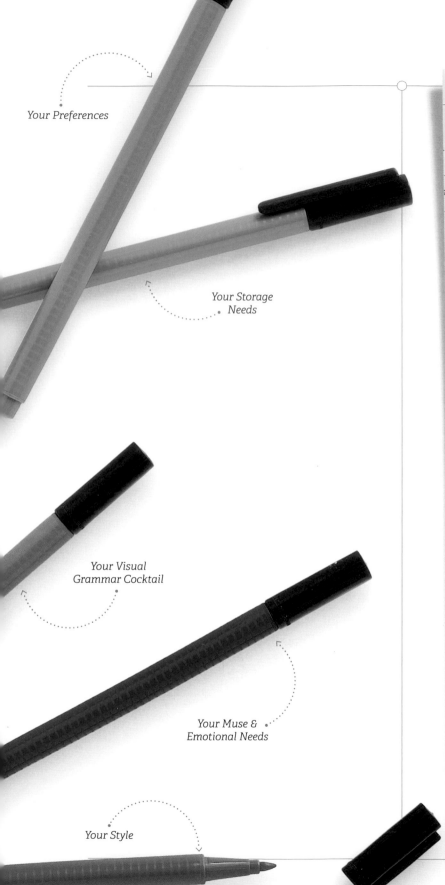

IAL PLAYERS

BREAKFAST/
SITTING

ROOM:

st the potential players for each item you need in your room.

ITEM NEEDED: seating for at
least 4

RANK: POTENTIAL PLAYERS:

4 identical chairs

2 pairs of identical chairs

4 different chairs

2 identical loveseats

2 different loveseats

loveseat & 2 identical chairs

loveseat & 2 different chairs

loveseat, chaise & chair

loveseat & chaise

2 identical sofas

2 different sofas

sofa & 2 identical chairs

sofa & 2 different chairs

sofa, chaise & chair

sofa & chaise

2 identical chaise

2 different chaise

U or L shaped sectional

OFF EXTRA SHEETS AT:
ethod.com

Sectional sofas don't fit with style preferences. So they're cut.

6. Your Style

It's finally time for your last criteria. So get out your style sheet and photos. Using a pink marker or pen, cross off any options that don't mesh with the style characteristics you have listed or fit with any of the style photos you loved.

7. Rank the Options You have Left

To create your layout as easily as possible, rank the options you have left according to which ones you like best. Put a 1 next to your favorite, 2 next to your second favorite and so on. That way you'll know which items to try first, and work hard to make fit, when creating your layout.

If you don't have any strong preferences, you can skip this part. There's no need to place importance on something you don't favor.

The options left on your sheet are your ideal players — the ones you'd prefer to have in your room. But life doesn't always fit the ideal — especially when decorating — because you have to work within the constraints of your room. That's why I had you cross off each criteria using a different color. That way, if you need to use a non-ideal item, you can go back through your list and easily find which items you don't mind compromising on.

Maybe they'll be the ones in red, because you figure you can make your room emotionally feel what you want to feel in another way. Maybe it'll be the ones in blue because your preferences weren't all that strong anyway.

Regardless, it'll be easy for you to spot, because the colors tell you why each item was eliminated. Hopefully you won't have to worry about that.

BREAKFAST/ SITTING ROOM:

IAL PLAYERS

st the potential players for each item you need in your room.

ITEM NEEDED: seating for at least 4

RANK: POTENTIAL PLAYERS:

1   4 identical chairs

~~2 pairs of identical chairs~~

~~4 different chairs~~

3   2 identical loveseats

~~2 different loveseats~~

5   loveseat & 2 identical chairs

~~loveseat & 2 different chairs~~

~~loveseat, chaise & chair~~

~~loveseat & chaise~~

2   2 identical sofas

~~2 different sofas~~

4   sofa & 2 identical chairs

~~sofa & 2 different chairs~~

~~sofa, chaise & chair~~

~~sofa & chaise~~

~~2 identical chaise~~

~~2 different chaise~~

~~U or L shaped sectional~~

OFF EXTRA SHEETS AT:
ethod.com

SIZING YOUR PLAYERS

Choosing your players isn't enough. You must also know each of their sizes. If you don't know their size, you won't know what to draw in. And when you start drawing your layout, you'll quickly find that size is everything. It affects where each item can be placed and how many you can fit in. As you try to make all the players fit in the places you want, you end up doing a little dance where you add a little here, and take a little there, until it all works.

To be able to do that dance, you need some information. You must know the minimum, maximum and optimum size each one of your players can be. Those numbers tell you how much you can give and take from each piece when trying to make it all fit. To make recording those numbers easy, I've created two worksheets for you. Turn the page to see them.

Minimum Size. In order to be functional, every piece of furniture, appliance or fixture has a minimum size. Lucky for you, I've created a list (on page 210) that makes it incredibly easy to determine what that minimum size is. All you have to to do is find the item you want and list the smallest size you see for both the width and depth on the Sizes Worksheet, which you'll see when you flip the page.

When it comes to determining the minimum size of your storage items, life gets a bit harder because it completely depends on how much you plan to store. That's why I had you measure the overall size of each item you need stored. You must have those numbers to calculate the minimum size of your storage unit. So let's get calculating.

First, decide how tall you want the storage item to be. To see standard storage unit heights, look at the chart on page 234. Remember to subtract roughly 5 inches from the height you find to account for toe room or furniture legs.

Once you know the height of the storage unit, divide it by the overall height of the item you plan to store. It's a good idea to add a couple inches onto the overall height of the items to account for the access space needed to grab it.

That number gives you the total amount of shelves you can have in your storage unit.

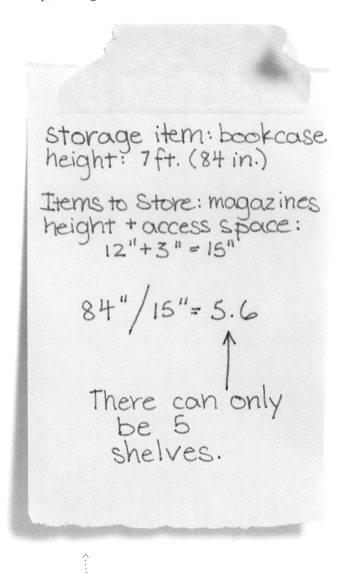

Remember, to convert all your measurements to either feet or inches. If you don't, you'll end with a bizarre number. Typically, using inches is easier. That way you don't have to deal with fractions.

Next take the linear amount of the item you need to store and divide it by the number of shelves your storage unit can have. The resulting number gives you the dimension for the minimum width your storage unit must be.

Just remember, your storage unit will need to be a bit wider than the number you get to account for the width of side panels. Also, you may want to tack on a little bit more width if you plan to expand your collection of items in the near — and even not so near — future.

If you plan to store multiple things in that storage unit, repeat the process above. Then add the minimum width of the unit needed to store each item together. The resulting number is the bare minimum width the storage unit needs to be.

If you plan to store many different sized items, keep in mind shelves are typically spaced standard widths apart. Meaning you may have some dead space in your unit, which isn't accounted for in the calculations above. So you may need a storage unit a bit bigger to actually fit all the items you want to store.

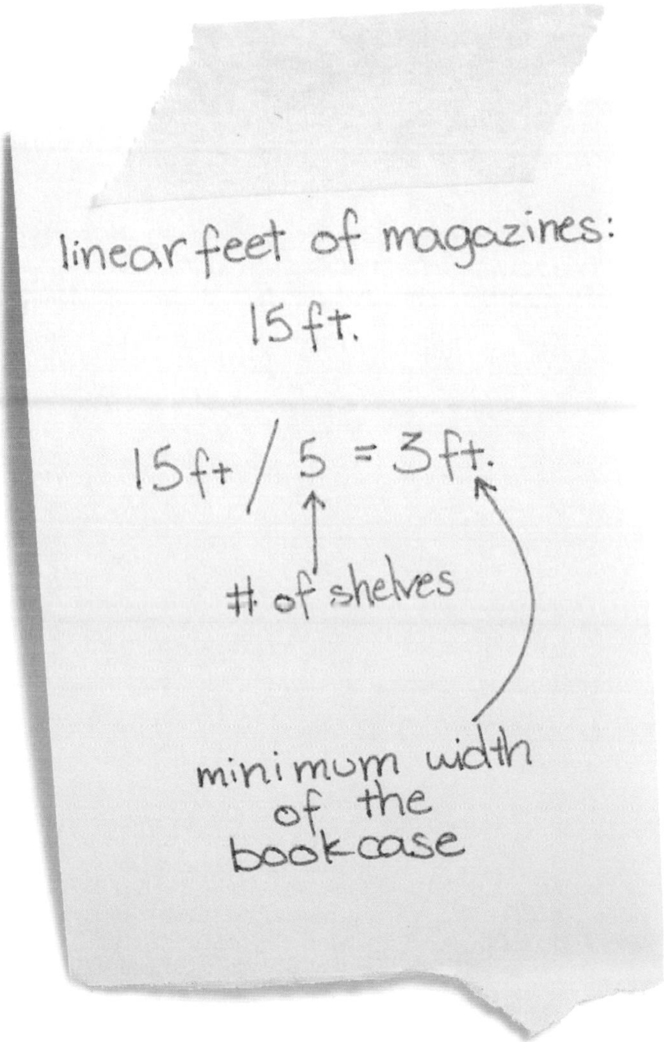

linear feet of magazines:
15 ft.

15 ft / 5 = 3 ft.

↑ # of shelves

minimum width of the bookcase

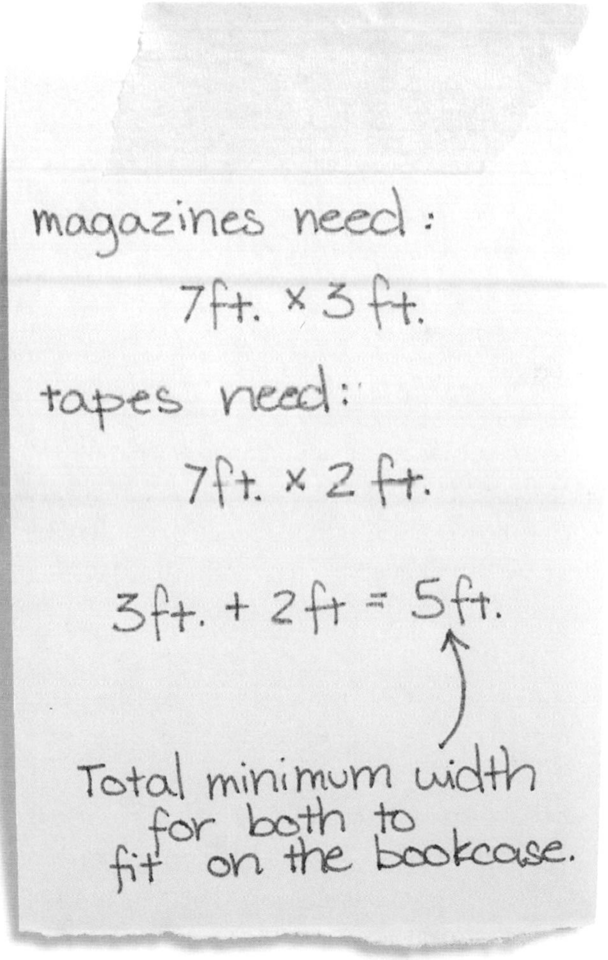

magazines need:
7 ft. × 3 ft.

tapes need:
7 ft. × 2 ft.

3 ft. + 2 ft = 5 ft.

Total minimum width for both to fit on the bookcase.

Optimal Size. There are two things to consider when it comes to optimal size: function and emotion.

Functionally, the size of your items greatly affects how much you enjoy using them. The bigger the bed, the more space you have to spread out. The larger the TV, the more immersive the experience. The longer the counter, the more space you have to work. You get the idea.

When deciding the optimal size for each item, think of what size would function best for how you want to use it. If you know the actual size you want, list it. If not, write something vague. Like the bigger the better. Having some idea of what you want is better than none. For a head start in determining the optimal size, look at your Preferences sheet from Step 6. You may have already written down what you want.

As far as emotion goes, the size of an object greatly affects how we feel about it. So when determining the optimum size of each item in your room, you should also consider what you want to feel. The smaller the item, the cuter or more refined it appears. The larger the item, the grander or more casual — if the item looks overstuffed — it appears.

Once you've chosen the optimum size for each item in your room, write under the "Optimal Size" column.

*Flip to page 210
to fill in the minimum sizes
for each of your items.*

7

drawing your layout

PREFERRED F

DIRECTIONS: List your to

ITEM	TOP PLAYER PICKS	M

HAVE MORE ITEMS? PRINT OFF EX
TheMeghanMethod.c

drawing your layout

PREFERRED PLAYERS

DIRECTIONS: List your top picks along with sizing details for each.

ITEM	TOP PLAYER PICKS	MINIMUM SIZE	OPTIMUM SIZE
desk (x2)	desk w/ drawers	28"W 24"D	at least 4'W
	desk w/o drawers	"	
	built-in desk	"	
desk chair (x2)	dining chair	17"W 16"D	on the petite
	stool	14'W 14"D	side - easy
	slipper chair	22"W 22"D	to move
storage unit	bookcase	40"W 18"D	the bigger,
	armoire	"	the better
	built-in cabinets	"	
file cabinet	built-in cabinet	18"W 24"D	the bigger,
	freestanding	"	the better
	in desk	"	
work surface	dining table	36"W 36"D	at least 4'W
	architect table	30"W 16"D	
	cabinet & counter	30"W 24"D	

HAVE MORE ITEMS? PRINT OFF EXTRA SHEETS AT:
TheMeghanMethod.com

Maximum Size. Most people forget that your furniture doesn't have to just fit in your room. It must also fit through your door, staircase, hallway, elevator — or any other place it must travel to get to your room. And if it can't, tough luck. You won't be able to use it in your room. That's why your maximum furniture size is based on what can fit through all those places in your home — not what can fit in your room.

To determine that magic number, use the worksheet to the left.

If you must use an elevator to get your items to your room, keep in mind that some buildings have a large service elevator, and if you ask nicely, they might let you use it. You may have to schedule a time, but it's worth it if it means getting the piece you want into your room.

If your maximum size ends up being smaller than you'd like, don't panic. There are ways around it. For example, you can have upholstered headboards made in two or three pieces. You can purchase a sectional sofa, which comes in individual sections rather than one giant piece. You can select a table whose legs screw off. You can even find wardrobes that collapse into multiple pieces, which are then reassembled in your room. So you still have options. You just need to be more creative about what you choose. Keep in mind the hardest items to fit through tight spaces are typically pianos, headboards, sofas, bathtubs and large armoires.

7

drawing your layout

MAXIMUM SIZ

DIRECTIONS: Fill in the dir

DOORWAYS:
Measure all the doorways your item must travel through. Write down the smallest dimension you get of each of the following.

1. Doorway Height:.................................
2. Doorway Width:.................................
3. Clearance Depth (see drawing 3):.................................

HALLWAYS:
If your items must travel through a hallway with a turn, take the following measurements.

4. Hallway Ceiling Height:.................................
5. Hallway Width:.................................
6. Hallway Sideway Depth (see drawing 6):.................................

STAIRWAYS:
If your items must travel up stairs, get the following measurement.

7. Top Stair to Ceiling Height:.................................
8. Stairway Width:.................................
9. Sideway Depth (see drawing 6):.................................

ELE
If yo
men

To be on the safe side, the maximum width or diagonal depth of the items in your room should not exceed measurements 2, 5, 8, 10 and 11.

M/
DI

To be on the safe side, the maximum height or length of the items in your room should not exceed measurements 1, 3, 4, 6, 7, 9 and 12.

M,
LE

*You may be able to get slightly larger items through,

GET YOUR OWN COPY AT: TheM

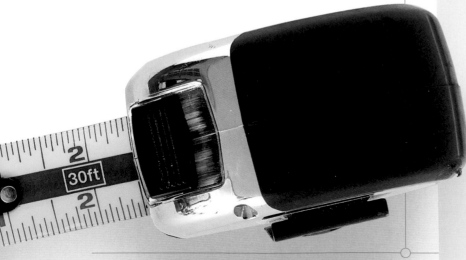

7

drawing your layout

MAXIMUM SIZE OF ITEMS

DIRECTIONS: Fill in the dimension of each place your items must go through.

DOORWAYS:

Measure all the doorways your item must travel through. Write down the smallest dimension you get of each of the following.

1. Doorway Height: 80 1/4 "
2. Doorway Width: 29 "
3. Clearance Depth (see drawing 3): 100 "

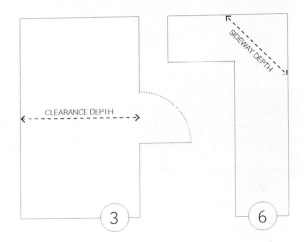

CLEARANCE DEPTH

SIDEWAY DEPTH

3   6

HALLWAYS:

If your items must travel through a hallway with a turn, take the following measurements.

4. Hallway Ceiling Height: 105 "
5. Hallway Width: 42 "
6. Hallway Sideway Depth (see drawing 6):

STAIRWAYS:

If your items must travel up stairs, get the following measurement.

7. Top Stair to Ceiling Height: 105 "
8. Stairway Width: 46.5 "
9. Sideway Depth (see drawing 6):

ELEVATORS:

If your items must travel in an elevator, get the following measurements.

10. Elevator Width:
11. Elevator Depth:
12. Elevator Height:

To be on the safe side, the maximum width or diagonal depth of the items in your room should not exceed measurements 2, 5, 8, 10 and 11

MAXIMUM WIDTH -or-
DIAGONAL DEPTH: 29 "

To be on the safe side, the maximum height or length of the items in your room should not exceed measurements 1, 3, 4, 6, 7, 9 and 12.

MAXIMUM HEIGHT -or-
LENGTH: 80 1/4 "

You may be able to get slightly larger items through, but you'll have to finagle their way in.

GET YOUR OWN COPY AT: TheMeghanMethod.com

LAYOUT FUNDAMENTALS

Now that you've got your positioning and players picked out, you're very close to being ready to draw things in. All that's left is to learn the layout fundamentals, which are the things you must consider when placing the item in your room. Fortunately, there are only ten of them: walking space, traffic flow, access space, work flow, conversation flow, utility locations, lighting, furniture size, space size, space shape and lines of sight.

WALKING SPACE.

Hands down, the most important thing a layout must have is walking space. Without it, you can't use your room because you can't even get into it. Well, unless you decide to practice your hurdling.

Fortunately, I don't need to tell you how to create walking space. You already do it naturally. Without thinking, you space your stuff far enough apart to be able to walk right up to things. You're even savvy enough to know what items don't need walking space between them — like beds and bedside tables. Just think of how inconvenient it would be to walk from your bed to your bedside table each night just to turn out the light.

You don't have to do that, because you get how to create walking space. It's the amount of walking space necessary that trips everyone up. Some leave too little. Some leave too much. So what's the sweet spot?

It depends on where you're walking. There are three types of walking space we use in a room: task, conversation and general.

TASK WALKING SPACE. Task walking space refers to the walking space between rows of cabinetry or places where you walk back and forth a lot. Typically, it's found in kitchens, bathrooms, laundry rooms and offices. Basically, anywhere you do tasks.

The sweet spot for task walking space is 3 to 6 feet, and it's not flexible. You should never make task walking space any narrower than 3 feet. Multiple people won't be able to walk by each other if you do. The space will be too narrow, and you'll really have too many cooks in the kitchen. Not to mention, if the walking space is any less than 3 feet, you won't have enough room to open any doors and drawers. So never go under 3 feet.

Likewise, you shouldn't go above 6 feet. If you have to walk three steps from counter to counter, after awhile it'll start to drive you crazy.

Ideally, the walking space between two task areas is close enough to reach within one step, but far enough apart so that two people can stand comfortably back to back. For most people, that space is about 4 feet. For some it's 3 feet. Others say it's 5 feet. I tend to side on the 3.5 to 4.5 feet range. Do what's right for you. To determine your ideal task walking space, measure the current distance between your cabinetry and use it as your baseline. If it feels too far, you know you need a bit less. If it feels too close, you know you need a bit more. Just right, well, you're set.

CONVERSATION WALKING SPACE. Conversation walking space refers to the distance between chairs, sofas and coffee tables in seating arrangements. You'd think that you would need the same amount of walking space between chairs and tables as you would between cabinetry. But you'd be wrong. Not because we don't need at least 3 feet of space to walk. We do. But we don't walk through conversation areas. We shimmy. And we shimmy for three very good reasons.

One, if we were to space our conversation areas with adequate walking space, we might have to raise our voice — or even yell — to talk to one another. And that's no way to have a conversation. Two, a coffee table does no good if you have to walk to reach it. And three, if you give people enough space to easily walk through your conversation areas, they'll use it like a hallway and your conversations will be

TASK WALKING SPACE:	3 - 6 feet
CONVERSATION WALKING SPACE	1 - 2 feet
GENERAL WALKING SPACE:	3 - 6 feet

Remember, general walking space can be less than 3 feet if needed.

constantly interrupted.

For those three reasons, we limit the amount of walking space in conversation areas to a shimmy. And to be able to shimmy, you need only 1 to 2 feet. Can you go smaller? No. One foot is definitely the lower limit. Any less and you'll be bumpin' your knees. Can you go bigger? Yes. But you start to get into the raising-voice-and-having-to-lean-really-far-to-set-your-drink-down range. Most people say 18 inches is the ideal. But again, you should always do what you prefer.

So look at the drawing you made of your current layout from Step 6: Your Evaluation. The distance between your current chairs, sofas and coffee table should be written in. Use that as your baseline. If your furniture feels too far, you know you need a bit less. If it feels too close, you know you need a bit more. Just right, and you're set.

GENERAL WALKING SPACE. General walking space refers to any walking space that's not considered task or conversation. Typically, it's the space in our rooms we use as hallways to get from one place to another.

The sweet spot for general walking space is the same as task walking space: 3 - 6 feet. But there's one difference, it's flexible.

If need be, you can have less than 3 feet. After all, some doorways are only 29" — just shy of 2 1/2 feet. But bear in mind, the reason we feel comfortable walking through that small space is because it only lasts a brief second. If we had to walk between two tall pieces for a far stretch, we'd feel a bit claustrophobic. Only use less than 3 feet of walking space for short distances, and preferably ones where the items you're walking between are no taller than waist high.

As for going bigger than 6 feet? You can do it. There's no functional reason holding you back. But emotionally, it may not communicate the right message. When you start going over 6 feet of walking space, your room begins to look a bit barren and empty. Of course, that's in standard sized rooms. If your room is gigantic, 6 feet of walking space would appear to scale and completely normal. So when deciding how much general walking space to use, be sure to consider the size of your room as well as what emotions you want to communicate.

The cozier you want your space, the smaller your general walking space should be. The more open and airy you want your space, the bigger your general walking space should be.

TRAFFIC FLOW

Designing a layout is like designing a parking lot. You have to think about the flow of traffic. How easy it is to walk around your room greatly affects how much you enjoy using it and how easy it is to do your aspirations. And since you want to do your aspirations, you need a good traffic flow.

The absolute ideal is one that gets you from point A to point B as easily as possible. That means:

No zig-zag walkways. They take too long, and endlessly frustrate people.

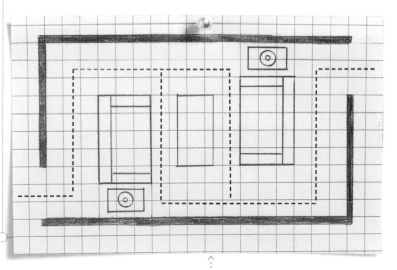

zig-zag walkway

No sharp turns. They're difficult to maneuver and often end in bruised knees.

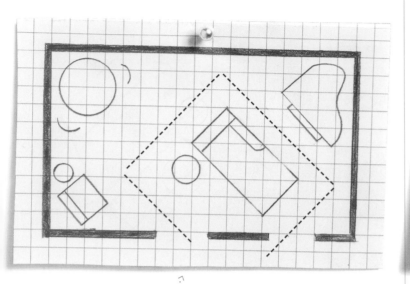

*too many
sharp turns*

No jumbled intersections. When too many paths cross, you're bound to end up with a traffic jam.

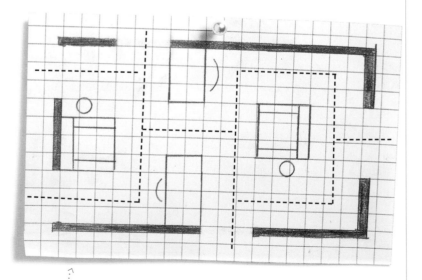

*too many
jumbled
intersections*

And no unnecessary dead ends. No one likes turning around and retracing their steps if they don't have to.

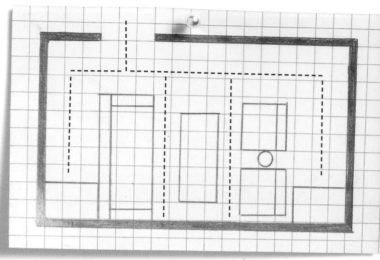

*unnecessary
dead ends*

But just because you want to avoid all those things, doesn't mean your walkways should be like Roman roads — straight and direct. The best traffic flow is one that is circular, because it offers great circulation and allows for alternative paths.

CIRCULATION. Having good circulation in your room is incredibly important because it allows you to easily move around and access all points of interest. When it comes to the best circulation, it looks like it sounds: circular. A circular flow allows you to get to all points in a room as quickly as possible without ever entering a dead end. Plus, it keeps you from getting stuck in a traffic jam, because if you encounter one, you can simply turn around and get to your destination the opposite way.

If your walkway is simply a straight line, when you hit

a traffic jam, you're stuck and have to wait until the person moves to get where you're going. Of course, in small, narrow rooms, sometimes all you can have is one straight walkway. And that's okay. Small rooms have few points of interest, which means traffic jams are less likely.

straight traffic flow •······

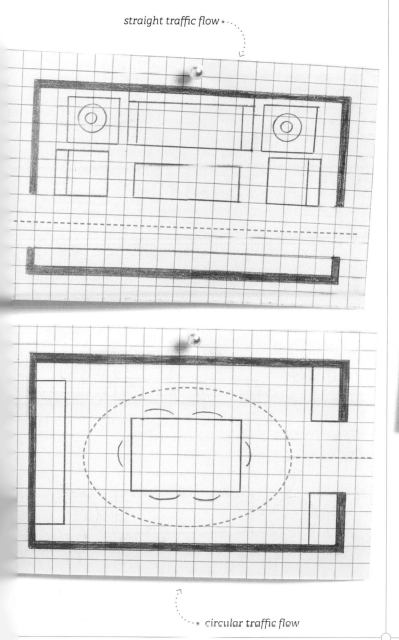

•····· *circular traffic flow*

ALTERNATIVE ROUTES. Alternative routes prevent traffic jams and keep people from getting in your way, which is especially important in task and conversation areas. You don't want people treating those places like walkways, constantly getting in the way and interrupting what you're doing. Like cooking dinner. Or folding clothes. Or watching TV. That's why it's important to incorporate alternative routes into rooms like those — if possible.

With no alternative route, the only place to •····· *walk is straight through your conversation.*

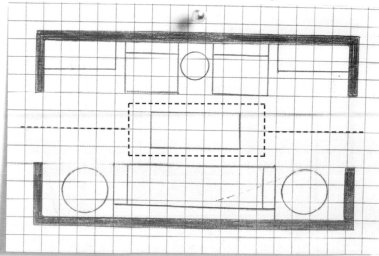

Of course, having an alternative route isn't enough to keep people from walking in your way. Your alternative route must offer a quicker route from point A to point B than the one cutting through your workspace. If it doesn't, people won't use it. We're economical creatures who always take the shortest, easiest route. Which means if the path through your workspace is easier, we'll take it.

To keep people out of your workspace, make sure the alternative path offers the easiest and shortest distance to the destination.

Bad alternative route. The main flow of traffic cuts straight through work area.

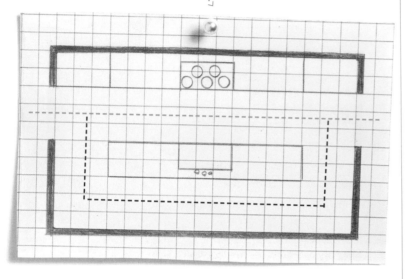

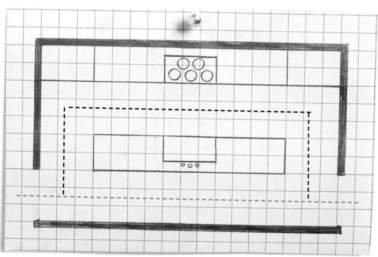

Good alternative route. The main flow of traffic keeps people out of the work area.

To determine if your room has good traffic flow, trace the pathways between all the points of interest in your room. Trace from your doorway to a chair. Or from a doorway to another doorway. Or from a doorway to a closet. You get the idea.

If your room has good flow, getting between all those points should be quick and easy. If it has bad flow, the path between points will be long, awkward and full of potential traffic jams. If that's what you've got, go back and rework your layout until you get a better flow.

Aside from function, there is one other thing to consider when it comes to traffic flow, and I'm sure you know what it is: emotion. The more streamlined and straightforward you want your room to feel, the straighter your traffic flow should be. The more rambling and cozy you want your room to feel, the more twists and turns you should have. Just remember, if you go overboard in the twisty category, your room may not function as well.

ACCESS SPACE

We all take access space for granted, but without it, you can't open anything. No doors. No drawers. You can't even take things off shelves. You need space, in order to get to things.

We already figure for that all-too-essential access space when it comes to doors leading in and out of rooms. That's why we draw the swing of the door on floor plans. It tells us don't put anything — like a dishwasher or a chair— here because it will block the door's ability to open.

But doors aren't the only things that need access space. Any item that has a door, drawer or shelf requires access space.

Fortunately, figuring out how much access space you need is fairly simple.

For drawers, it's the depth of the drawer when it's pulled out.

For doors, it's the width of the door when fully open, plus

the arc it follows to get there.

For items stored on open shelves, it's the depth of the shelf.

Now, keep in mind, it's nice to have an extra foot or so in front of doors and drawers in addition to the necessary access space. That way, you can stand in front of them — rather than on the side — when accessing what you need.

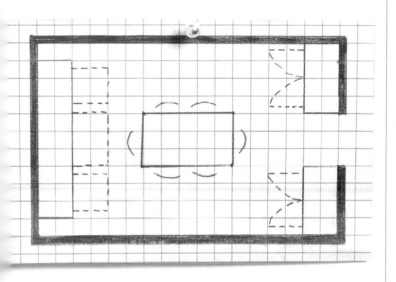

Each time you draw in a storage piece of furniture with drawers, doors or open shelves, you should also draw how much access space it needs. That way, you don't accidentally put anything in its way. And trust me, it's easy to do — especially in kitchens where you have two rows of doors and drawers facing each other.

In fact, access space in kitchens can be so tricky that professionals even mess it up from time to time. Case in point, the designer of my parent's last kitchen. Said designer arranged the dishwasher, garbage can and dish cabinet in such

a way that none could be opened at the same time. Loading and unloading the dishwasher was a hassle. A huge hassle. And it could have so easily been avoided.

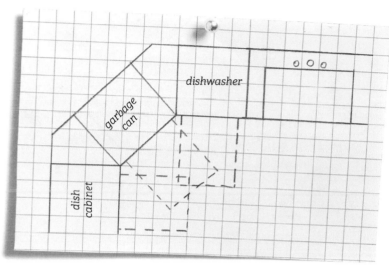

So when you have cabinetry that faces each other at a 90- or 45-degree angle, check to make sure the cabinets or appliances with overlapping access space don't ever need to be opened at the same time. If they aren't used simultaneously, you'll never have a time when one door or drawer blocks your ability to open the other.

The same goes for cabinets facing each other. Often, kitchen walkways are too narrow — typically anything less than 5 feet — to easily open the cabinets opposite each other at the same time. But as long as the two things facing each other don't need to be accessed simultaneously, it's not a problem.

So when planning for access space, don't just draw in the necessary space needed to get to your stuff. Also, check that any items across or perpendicular don't need to be accessed at the same time. If they do, come up with a different layout. Trust me. It's no fun stacking plates and bowls each time you need to load them in the dishwasher or put them away.

WORK FLOW

We like easy. The easier something is, the more likely we are to do it. Which is why it's so important to carefully plan the places where we work in our home — such as kitchens, bathrooms, laundry rooms and offices. If the layout of those rooms makes it difficult to do our daily tasks, we'll get frustrated and start to avoid — or even curse — them.

But there's no point in cursing, especially when planning a good work flow is so ridiculously easy.

1. LIST THE ORDER OF YOUR TASKS. The most ideal work flow is the assembly line, because you don't have to make any unnecessary back-and-forth trips. You just move down the line to finish each task. There's no wasted movement. There's no wasted time. The entire process is completely efficient — and most importantly, it's easy. And as I said, we like easy.

Given that we're creatures of habit, we can actually plan ahead and create assembly lines in our homes. Because we always do the same tasks in the same order, we know what items should go next to each other to create our assembly line.

So to create the perfect work flow for your room, first list the order in which you do the tasks for each job you must complete in your room.

2. DETERMINE THE ORDER OF YOUR ITEMS. Once you know the order of your tasks, you can determine which items should be placed next to each other and in what order. To do that, next to each task, list what item or items are needed. Then create a flow chart based on that list.

3. ARRANGE YOUR ITEMS. When we think of the traditional assembly line, we think of one long conveyor belt. But most of the time, our rooms aren't shaped like one long hallway that goes on forever, which means we have to get creative and stagger each step or have the assembly line turn. Nor-

mally, that's actually beneficial, because it makes it easier to incorporate multiple work flows into one space — like in a kitchen where we cook, clean, get drinks and reheat food.

Just make sure you never jumble the steps in your work flow, because then you have to double back. And when you double back, you waste time.

After creating your layout, draw your path. The line of your path should never cross over itself. If it does, your work flow is out of order. That means you need to go back and restructure things until the line of your path never doubles back.

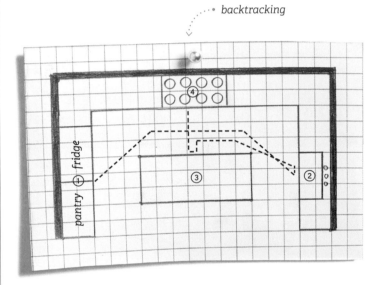

backtracking

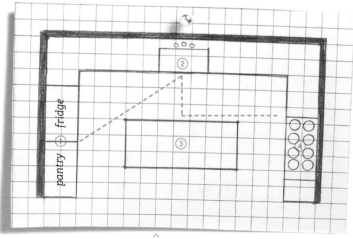

no backtracking

7

drawing your layout

YOUR WORK FLOW

DIRECTIONS: List the steps & items needed for each task in order of completion.

TASK: Cook Food

STEPS:

1. Get food.
2. Rinse food.
3. Prep food.
4. Cook food.

ITEMS NEEDED:

refrigerator & pantry

sink

empty counterspace

stove & oven

WORK FLOW DIAGRAM:

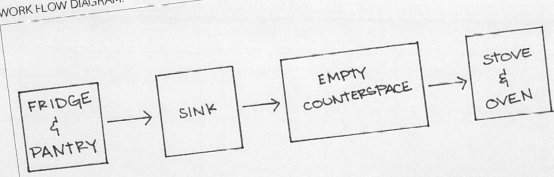

CONVERSATION FLOW

We're social creatures. We like to talk. While cooking. While cleaning. While eating. While sitting. We talk practically every chance we get, because it's what connects us to other people. And if you want to talk with others while doing any of your aspirations, you have to plan for it because not all rooms promote conversation.

A good conversation flow requires two things:

1. WE MUST BE ABLE TO HEAR EACH OTHER. There's a reason we don't hold conversations with people standing behind us or a football field away. We can't hear them. We need to hear to have a conversation. So when creating conversation areas in our homes, we must plan for people to face each other and be close enough to hear what everyone is saying.

As far as the facing each other goes, that's easy. Just make sure people mouths are located somewhere in front of everyone else's ears.

It's the "close enough" part that trips people up. Fortunately, back in 1966, a scientist by the name of Edward T. Hall determined the magic distances for conversations. And it all depends on how close of a relationship we have with the people we're speaking with.

If we have a very close relationship, we feel comfortable being 1.5 to 4 feet away. If we're just acquaintances, we prefer being 4 to 12 feet away. Bear in mind, any further than 12 feet and conversation becomes difficult, because it's hard to hear.

As long as you keep the conversation zones in your home within 12 feet, you'll be good to go. Just remember, the distance of your conversation zone is measured from person to person. Not the back of one piece of furniture to another.

2. WE MUST BE ABLE TO SEE EACH OTHER. We don't just talk with our voice. We talk with every part of our body. Our hands. Our feet. Our arms. Our face. So when we have a conversation, we need to see each other. It's the only way to get the full message — facial expression and all.

Of course, when it comes to seeing each other, we're a bit limited because we don't have eyes in the back of our heads. We can only easily see things roughly within a 120-degree range in front of us, which means to easily have a conversation with other people, they need to be somewhere within that 120 degree range.

That's why conversation areas are typically circular. It's the only arrangement where we can easily see everyone without having to drastically turn our heads. When we sit in a row — like at a long dining table — we have to constantly turn our heads from side to side to talk with the people beside us. So we end up talking more to the people across from us because they're easier to see.

····• *backs to each other*

facing each other •····

Of course, not being able to see everyone isn't always a horrible thing. In fact, some people like it better because they prefer having numerous small conversations simultaneously happening in a room, rather than one huge one. When deciding how to arrange your furniture for conversation, it's important to consider what type of conversations you want.

Numerous, Small Conversations. Any furniture arrangement that limits people to only easily seeing and hearing a few people in the room forces everyone into small conversation groups. After all, it's only easy to speak with those you can immediately see and hear. Of course, if people want to hold a conversation with everyone in the room, they can always turn their bodies or raise their voice. But it's not as easy.

One, Large Conversation. To enable a large conversation that includes everyone in the room, make sure everyone in the room can see and hear everyone else. Round tables and circular seating arrangements are best at enabling large conversations.

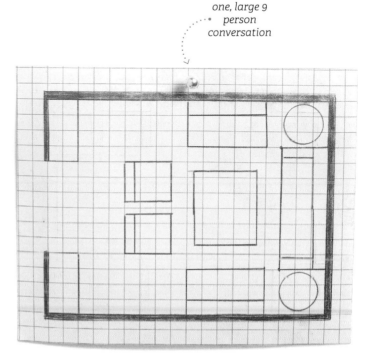

one, large 9 person conversation

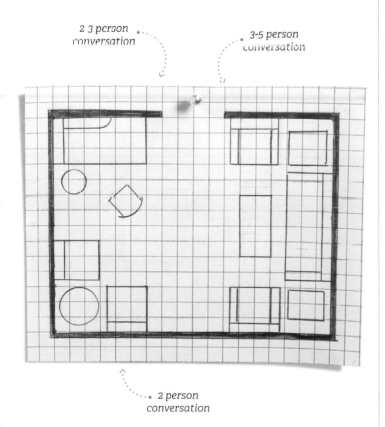

2 3 person conversation

3-5 person conversation

2 person conversation

UTILITY LOCATIONS

It should go without saying. Put your appliances and fixtures — TVs, toasters, coffee makers, lamps, chandeliers, phones, refrigerators and even toilets — directly in front of whatever it is they need to work. But you'd be surprised how often people ignore this all-too-logical axiom.

I've seen phone cords stapled up walls and across ceilings, wires exploding from the backs of entertainment centers and extensions cords stretched across rooms like booby traps. While those elaborate, bush league set-ups may make it possible for the items to turn on, they're not scoring any safety or style points.

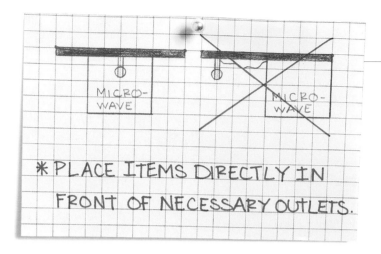

* PLACE ITEMS DIRECTLY IN FRONT OF NECESSARY OUTLETS.

It's always — always — a bad idea for cords to stretch across walkways, because they're easy to trip on. So keep cords clear of walkways.

And as far as looks go, no one — at least no one I know — likes seeing cords. That's why most shelter magazines Photoshop them out. Heck, they even Photoshop out electrical outlets and light switches because they ruin the magic. They remind us of how things work, and most people don't want to be reminded. They want lights to magically turn on, toilets to magically flush and pictures to magically appear on their television screen. How those things happen doesn't matter. That's why we don't need or want to see the cords or pipes that enable them.

Now I realize some people may want a very industrial, geeky or mechanical look. Those people may appreciate seeing cords and pipes. But everyone else, maintain the magic. Keep your cords out of sight by placing all of your fixtures and appliances directly in front of their sources of power.

If you don't have a power source where you'd like to place your item:

A. Have a new outlet installed exactly where you want it, which is always your best option.

B. Place the item on the wall where the outlet currently is, even though it's not exactly where you want it.

or C. Devise a safe, creative solution that will obscure the cord or wires from sight. For example, run them behind sofas, under rugs or behind crown moulding. Just keep in mind

that this is still a bit bootleg. But at least no one will trip over it or see it.

As for which of those three options to choose, it typically comes down to cost. It's always cheaper to leave utility lines exactly where they are — especially in bathrooms and kitchens. But if you'd like to have some of your utility lines moved, it never hurts to get a quote. Sometimes you luck out, and the way the joists run in your home makes it easy to have your utilities moved — which also makes it far less expensive. And even if it's not easy, it may still be worth it.

SPACE SIZE

For some reason, people think if they have a small room they must make it look bigger, or if they have a big room, they must make it look smaller. But truth is, you only need to make your room appear bigger or smaller if its current size doesn't communicate what you want to feel.

You see, on its own, the size of your room communicates an emotion. Small rooms feel cozy, quaint, intimate and safe — like a cave, womb or a small clearing in the woods. Whereas big rooms feel luxurious, grand, open and airy — like fields, beaches and ballrooms.

If the size of your room communicates exactly what you want to feel, there's no reason to change how its size appears. It already communicates what you want.

It's only when your room doesn't communicate what you want to feel — whether it's the complete opposite emotion or just not enough of the right one — that you need to trick the eye into thinking there's more or less space than there really is.

To do that, you must first diagnose what characteristics of your room are making it feel too big or too small. Is it too narrow? Too wide? Too short? Too tall? The answer will tell you which tricks will fix your woes.

Now as far as those tricks go, many of them come down

to the way you arrange the furniture. A few tricks have to do with what patterns, textures and colors you use, and I'll show them to you now as well. That way, you know what tricks you plan to use — which you need to know when creating your layout.

Room too Narrow -or- Want a More Spacious Feel:
tricks 1, 2, 3, 4 & 5

Room too Wide -or- Want a Cozier Feel:
tricks 6, 7, 8, 9 & 10

Ceiling too Short -or- Want More Spacious Feel:
tricks 6, 7, 8, 9, 10, 11, 12 & 13

Ceiling too High -or- Want a Cozier Feel:
tricks 1, 2, 3, 4, 6, 14, 15, 16, 17, 18 & 19

Room Overall too Small:
tricks 20, 22, 23, 27, 28, 30 & 31

Room Overall too Big:
tricks 21, 22, 24, 25, 26 & 29

This card tells you at a glance which tricks do what. That way you can focus only on the ones you need.

TRICK 1: Wide Furniture. The lower and longer your furniture is, the wider your room will appear. For the maximum effect, put your long, low furniture on your narrowest wall.

If you put it on your widest wall, your room may take on a bowling alley look.

TRICK 2: Horizontal Patterns. Horizontal patterns, like stripes, make your room appear wider by highlighting the distance between your walls. Keep in mind, the more obvious the horizontal nature of the pattern, the more powerful the effect.

TRICK 3: Horizontal Paneling or Molding. Horizontal paneling and molding works just like horizontal patterns. Although, it tends to be a bit more subtle, because you're relying on shadow lines to create the effect.

TRICK 4: Horizontal Artwork and Accessories. The more horizontal items you put in your room, the wider your room will appear. Layer on as many horizontal items as you can find. And remember, the more rectangular they are, the greater the effect.

TRICK 5: Horizontal Flooring. Horizontal flooring — such as hardwood planks or painted stripes — will make your room appear wider, just like horizontal paneling and patterns.

TRICK 6: Tall Furniture. It may seem counterintuitive, but using tall furniture can make a room feel both bigger and cozier. It all depends on the size of the room. In rooms with low ceilings, tall furniture — such as canopy beds, tall armoires and floor-to-ceiling cabinetry — extends the eye up, and fools it into thinking the space is bigger than it truly is. If those huge pieces can fit in the room, the room must be big.

In rooms with tall ceilings, tall furniture doesn't look big. It looks to scale, so putting tall furniture in your room doesn't draw attention to the room's height. It actually keeps you from noticing it — like if you were to use short furniture. Because you'd have all kinds of extra space above short pieces, which only makes the ceilings look higher.

*Which one looks taller?
Wider? Guess what?
They're the same, exact size*

TRICK 7: Vertical Patterns. Anything that looks like a stripe will make your room appear taller, because it highlights the distance between your ceiling and floor. Keep in mind, the more obvious the vertical nature of the pattern, the stronger the effect.

TRICK 8: Vertical Paneling. Vertical paneling works just like vertical stripes — only it's often a bit more subtle, because you're counting on shadow lines the create the effect.

TRICK 9: Vertical Artwork & Accessories. The more vertical items you have in your room, the taller it will appear. Remember, the taller and thinner your artwork and accessories are, the greater the impact will be.

TRICK 10: Floor-to-Ceiling Drapes. There's a reason designers love drapes. They make a space feel more grand by making a room look taller and thinner. For the maximum effect, have your drapes hung from floor to ceiling, because the taller your drapes appear, the taller your room will look.

TRICK 11: Skylights. If drawing your eye up isn't enough, create the illusion of having no ceiling at all by adding skylights. The glass not only fools your eye into thinking there's more space above than there truly is, but also allows extra natural light to pour in, which makes your space look bigger.

TRICK 12: Paint Your Ceiling a Light Color. Can't install skylights and drawing your eye up isn't enough? Avoid dark, warm colors on your ceiling. Dark colors appear visually heavy, which will make your ceiling feel lower — as if it's sagging. Light colors will make your ceiling look a bit higher than it truly is.

TRICK 13: Paint Your Ceiling a Cool Color. For the ultimate ceiling lift, make sure you paint it a cool color. Those colors appear as if they're receding away, which will make your ceiling appear higher than it is.

TRICK 14: Picture Rail. Installing a picture rail — a decorative piece of molding — around the top of your room makes your walls appear shorter, because it visually divides them. Want your room to look even shorter and feel even cozier? Paint or wallpaper everything above the picture rail — including the ceiling — the same color. It fools the eye into thinking the ceiling extends down onto the wall, which makes the ceiling look lower.

TRICK 15: Beams and Ceiling Molding. Adding beams and molding to your ceiling makes it look visually heavier. And the heavier your ceiling looks, the lower it appears. If you want to make your ceiling look even lower, place the beams as far away from your ceiling as possible. The beams will fill all that empty ceiling space, making your ceiling feel much, much lower.

TRICK 16: Pattern on Your Ceiling. The busyness of patterns makes them appear visually heavy. So if you put pattern on your ceiling, your ceiling will look lower due to the visual weight.

TRICK 17: Texture on Your Ceiling. Texture is just like pattern. The business of it makes it appear visually heavy. Sure, it doesn't look as heavy as pattern, but it's heavy enough to make your ceiling look a bit lower.

TRICK 18: Paint Your Ceiling a Dark Color. The darker the color, the heavier it looks. So if you paint your ceiling a dark color, it will look lower than it truly is.

TRICK 19: Paint Your Ceiling a Warm Color. Warm colors look as if they advance to the eye. So if you want to make your ceiling look lower, paint it a warm color. It'll visually lower your ceiling.

TRICK 20: Paint Your Walls a Light Color. Using a light color on your walls will make your room appear bigger because it reflects more light. And the lighter the color — meaning the closer it is to white — the more light it reflects and the bigger your room will appear. You'll want to stay in that very light range. The closer you get to a medium-range color, the smaller your room will look. In fact, medium intensity colors actually make your room look the smallest.

TRICK 21: Paint Your Walls a Medium Color. Medium colors are the most fattening of the bunch. They don't reflect enough light to make a room look bigger, and they don't absorb enough light to hide the edges of walls. They show your room for what it really is.

TRICK 22: Paint Your Walls a Dark Color. Dark colors work magic in a room, because they blur the lines of where one wall ends and another begins, making it extremely hard for your eye to tell how big the room actually is. That uncertainty can work to your advantage in both big and small rooms. In big rooms, if you use a dark color in conjunction with a few visually shrinking tricks, you'll fool the eye into thinking the room is smaller. Especially if you paint the ceiling dark as well. Just as in a small room, if you use a few other space-expanding tricks, you can fool the eye into thinking your room goes on much further than you can see.

TRICK 23: Paint Your Walls a Cool Color. Cool colors appear to recede, which makes them a great choice for rooms that feel too small. They make the walls appear as if they're a bit further away than they really are. And that little bit is enough to make your room appear bigger.

Which looks closer?

TRICK 24: Paint Your Walls a Warm Color. Warm colors appear to advance towards you, which makes walls painted with them appear much closer than they really are. That effect visually shrinks the room, and if you choose a warm color in a medium tone, even better.

TRICK 25: Use Pattern on Your Walls. Patterns appear visually heavy, which tricks your eye into thinking they take up more space. And the bigger and bolder the pattern, the more space it appears to take. If you want to make your room look smaller, a big and bold pattern will do the trick.

TRICK 26: Use Texture on Your Walls. Texture, like pattern, appears to take up more visual space. Just not quite as much, because texture's weight comes from shadow lines — which are typically much less noticeable than the actual lines in patterns. If you want to subtly make your room feel a bit smaller or cozier, using texture on your walls is a safe bet.

TRICK 27: Use Big Furniture. Like tall pieces of furniture, large pieces can make a room look both bigger and cozier. It all depends on the size of the room.

Most people think that using small pieces of furniture in a small room will make it look bigger. But that's not always true. Many petite pieces can make the room look cluttered, which can make the room feel smaller. Whereas, using one large piece tricks the eye into thinking the room must be bigger. How else could it fit such a large piece? Plus, the large scale piece will give your room a sense of grandeur. Keep in mind, your room will only look bigger and grander if the piece actually looks as if it fits in the space. If it looks like you had to cram it in, the effect is lost.

If you want to make a large room feel smaller, use large scale furniture pieces. They take up more space, and the more space you take up, the smaller your room will look. The key is to use several large pieces. The more stuffed your room looks, the smaller it will feel.

TRICK 28: Use Few Pieces of Furniture & Knickknacks. The fewer items you put in a room, the more spacious it feels because you have less items taking up space. If you want a small room to feel more spacious, limit the number of items you put in your room.

TRICK 29: Use Lots of Furniture & Knickknacks. The more things you stuff in your room, the smaller it will look. Think of libraries. They always appear far smaller than they really are, because there's so many things in them. If you want your space to feel smaller, stuff it.

TRICK 30: Diagonal Flooring. To visually expand your room, put flooring — such as tile — on a diagonal. The diagonal lines that fit in your room are longer than the horizontal or vertical, which fools your eyes into thinking the room is actually bigger.

TRICK 31: Use Big Mirrors. Mirrors reflective quality fools the eye into thinking there's more space beyond. So if you cover your walls in mirrors, your room will appear much, much bigger.

SPACE SHAPE

The shape of your room — just like the shape of your furniture — communicates an emotion. Round rooms feel soothing. Square and rectangular rooms feel streamlined. Rooms with juts feel jarring. Whether or not you feel your room's inherent emotion depends completely on how you arrange the furniture in your room.

If you want to enhance your room's emotion, you'll want to mimic its shape. The repetition of the shape repeats the emotion — which ultimately intensifies it.

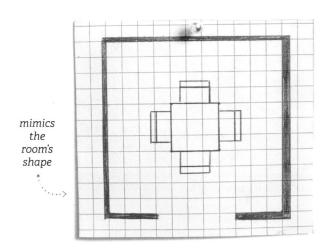

*mimics
the
room's
shape*

To soften your room's emotion, arrange your layout so that it's slightly different than your room's shape. It should still be proportional, just not exactly the same, because the contrast dilutes the room's inherent emotion by injecting another emotion to the mix.

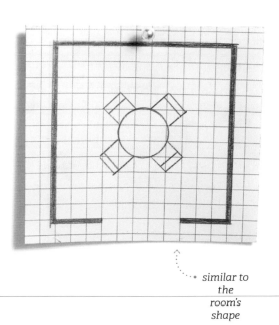

*similar to
the
room's
shape*

To override your room's emotion, your layout should strongly contrast with your room's shape. Doing that will subtly change the way your room's shape appears, which will change the overall emotion of your room. But be warned, if your layout contrasts so much that it no longer looks proportional in your room, it'll seem jarring.

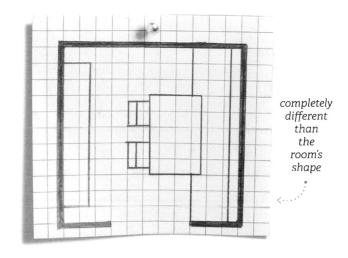

*completely
different
than
the
room's
shape*

If you have awkward juts in your room or want to completely change the inherent emotion of your room, your best course of action is to trick the eye into thinking your room is a completely different shape. There are three ways to do that.

One, hide it. Use screens, large plants or anything else big you can find to change the perceived shape of your walls.

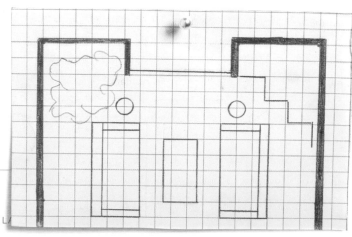

Two, fill it. Use cabinets, bookcases, shelves or anything else to fill awkward juts or entire sides of rooms. This works especially well when the cabinets, bookcases or shelves fit perfectly wall-to-wall.

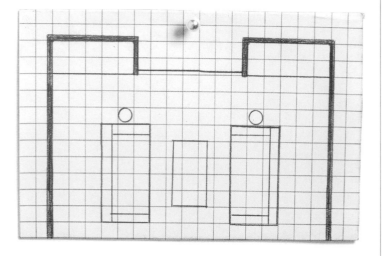

Three, accent it. This only works in rooms with juts. Place an item — such as a chair, table, lamp or piece of art — in the divot of your room. It'll fill the space, making the divot look purposeful — rather than awkward — as if it were made to show off that item. The shape of the item you choose to place in the jut depends on what emotions you want to feel. For a clean, soothing feel, choose an item that mimics the shape of the jut. For a fun, energetic feel, choose an item that slightly contrasts with the shape of the jut. For a jarring feel, choose an item that completely contrasts.

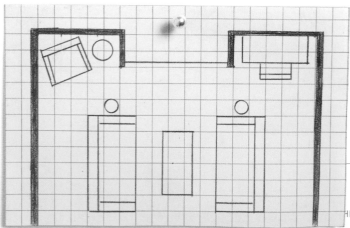

Once you've altered the shape of your room to your desire, use the shape of your room — minus the parts you've hidden — as a guide when creating the rest of your layout.

LINES OF SIGHT

When we experience a room, we don't see it all at once. That's impossible. We only see what's in our line of sight, and it's those vignettes that set the entire emotional mood for our room — not the overall look — because they're what we see.

So while most people worry about how the overall room looks when creating their layout, all you really have to focus on are your lines of sight. If you get those right, your room will not only feel the way you want to feel, but also offer you the best views from every vantage point.

To pick the right lines of sight, first determine the main vantage points. There are two types:

FIRST IMPRESSION VANTAGE POINTS. Those are the places from where you first see your room. And considering we don't walk through windows, they're always either a doorway or opening.

Now, many people believe these are the most important vantage points in your room — especially the main point of entrance — because they're where you form your first impression. In those first few seconds, you create your entire emotional opinion of the room. That's why people often put the most important feature of a room — such as a fireplace in a living room, a range in a kitchen or a bed in a bedroom — directly opposite the door.

Do you have to do that? No. For one thing, it's not always possible. But do make sure that whatever is opposite your doorway clearly communicates the main emotions you want to feel in your room. You need to hit people — including you — with that emotion when they first walk in.

To determine what to place directly in the line of sight from your doorways, look at your list of potential focal points. Those are the items you think best communicate the emotions you want to feel in your room. Go through that list and rank them in order of what would make the best first impression. That way, you know what items to try first when creating your layout.

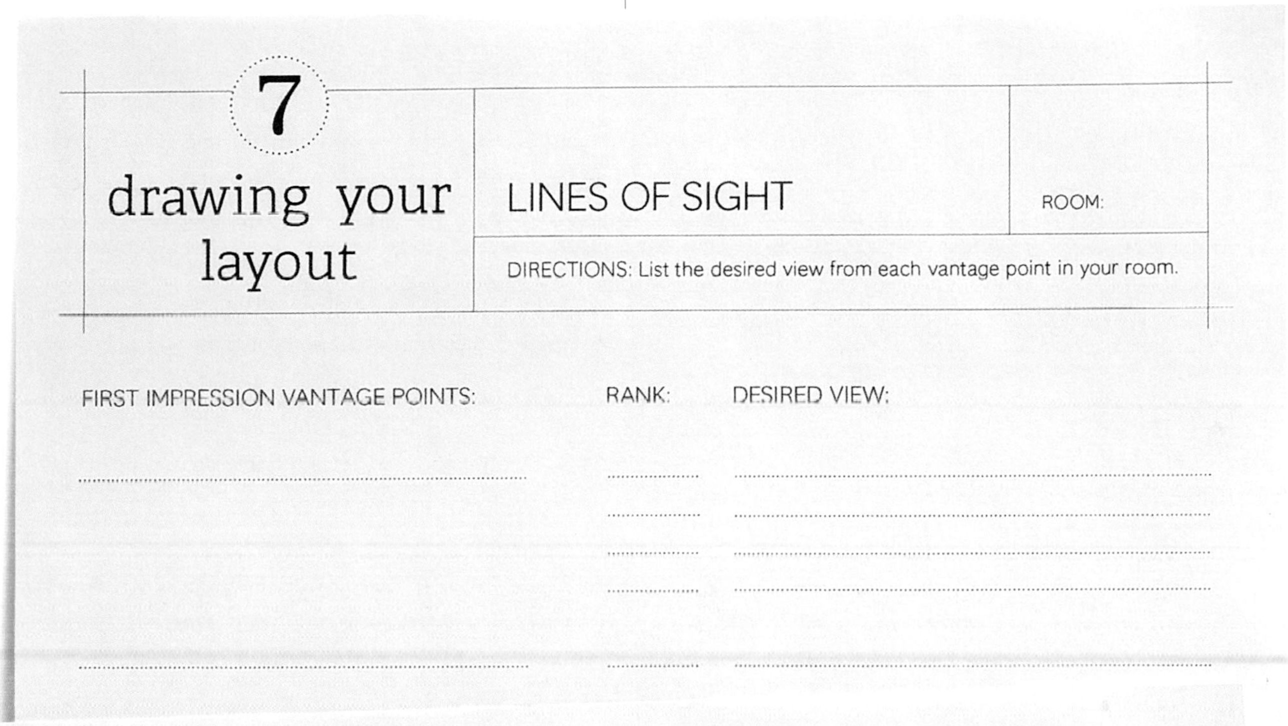

7

drawing your layout

LINES OF SIGHT

ROOM:

DIRECTIONS: List the desired view from each vantage point in your room.

FIRST IMPRESSION VANTAGE POINTS:

RANK:

DESIRED VIEW:

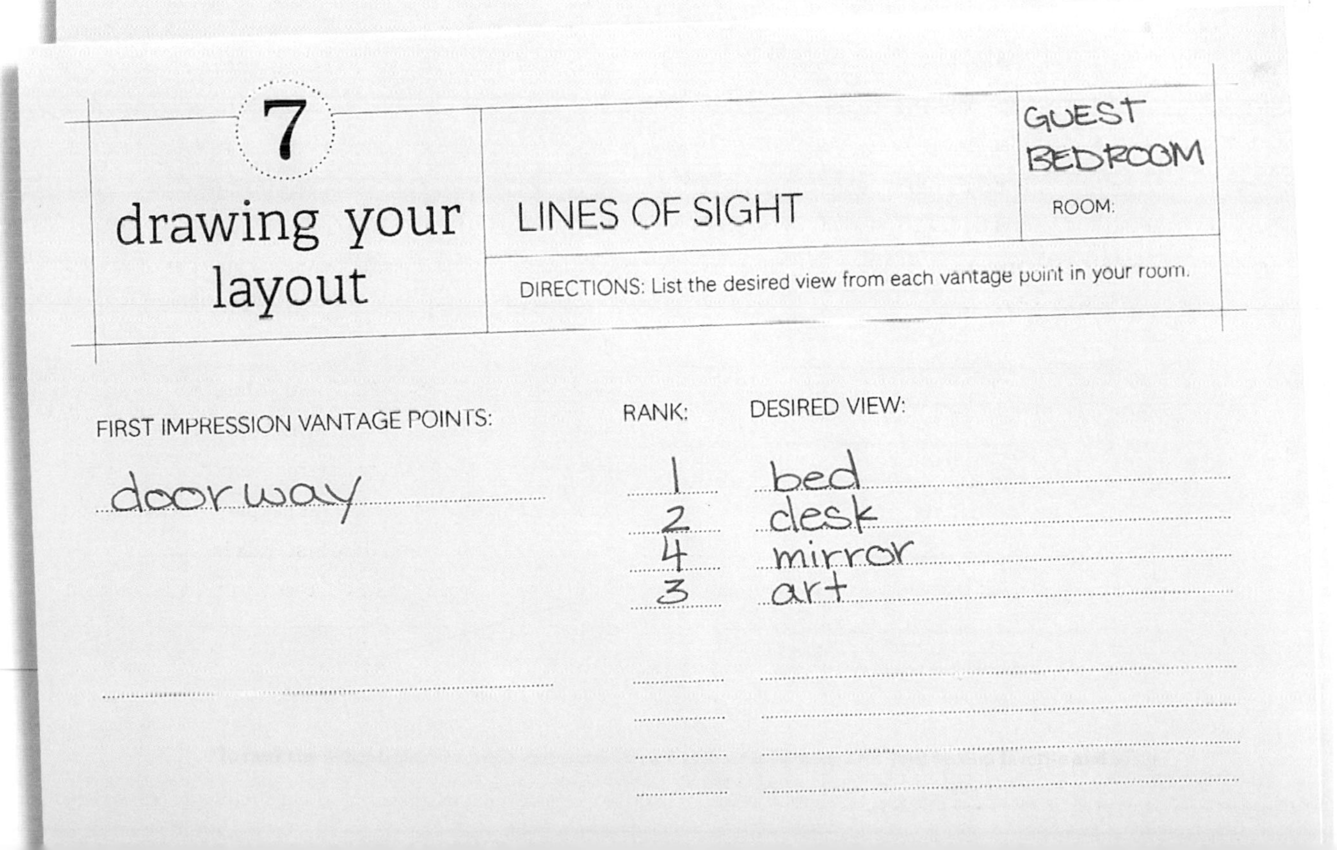

7

drawing your layout

LINES OF SIGHT

ROOM: GUEST BEDROOM

DIRECTIONS: List the desired view from each vantage point in your room.

FIRST IMPRESSION VANTAGE POINTS:

doorway

RANK: DESIRED VIEW:

RANK	DESIRED VIEW
1	bed
2	desk
4	mirror
3	art

EXTENDED STAY VANTAGE POINTS. The second vantage points are the places where we spend extended periods of time. Like standing at the bathroom sink, sitting on the sofa, eating at the dinner table and cooking at the stove. You want the views from those places to be especially good, because if they're not, you won't enjoy spending time there.

For example, who wants to sit in a chair facing a blank wall? No one. You want to see something spectacular — something that communicates emotions.

To determine what items to put in your line of sight, list all of the extended stay vantage points in your room. Use your zones list to help.

Once you've created your list, think of what you'd ideally want to see from each spot. More than likely, the items you list will be your focal points — but not always. For example, if you have a large opening that looks into your kitchen, maybe that's what you want to see from your sofa.

List and rank the top three things you'd like to see from each spot — if you can. Some spots may only have one. Having a list of your ideal lines of sight will make drawing your layout much easier, because you'll know what to try where — and that's the hardest part.

Just remember, when placing the items in your line of sight, they should be at eye level. And eye level changes depending on what you're doing. If you're standing, eye level should be at standing height. If you're sitting, eye level should be at sitting height. And you'd be surprised how many times people get that wrong. You'll see rooms where TVs are placed at standing height, which makes all the people sitting down in the room have to crane their head up like they're in the front row of a movie theatre.

So to avoid getting a stiff neck, be sure to place the items in your lines of sight at the correct eye level.

Get your own copy at: TheMeghanMethod.com.

7

drawing your layout

LINES OF SIGH[T]

DIRECTIONS: List the desi[red]

EXTENDED STAY VANTAGE POINTS: RANK:

*To rank the desired views for each vantage point, use 1 for your f[irst]

HAVE MORE EXTENDED STAY VANTAGE POINTS? PRINT OFF EXTRA SH[EETS] om each van

EW:

7 drawing your layout

LINES OF SIGHT

ROOM: GUEST BEDROOM

DIRECTIONS: List the desired view from each vantage point in your room.

EXTENDED STAY VANTAGE POINTS:	RANK:	DESIRED VIEW:
beds	1	view out windows
	2	doorway
	4	art
	3	desk
desk	1	view out windows
	3	art
	2	mirror

7 drawing your layout

LINES OF SIGHT

ROOM: BREAKFAST SITTING

DIRECTIONS: List the desired view from each vantage point in your room.

EXTENDED STAY VANTAGE POINTS:	RANK:	DESIRED VIEW:
Easy Chairs	1	Lake view
	3	art
	2	fireplace
Dining Table	1	Lake view
	3	art
	2	fireplace

*To ranl

ır second fa

HAVI

CABINETS	width	depth
Kitchen, base	9"-36"	12" or 24"
Vanity, base	9"-36"	18" or 21"
Kitchen, wall	9"-36"	12", 15" or 18"

*the width of kitchen cabinets increases in 3" increments

MATTRESSES	width	length
California King	72"	82"-84"
King	76"-80"	80"
Queen	60"	78"-80"
Double/Full	53"-54"	75"-80"
Twin	37"-39"	75"-80"

TABLES	width	depth
Dining, Rectangle	67"-108"	28"-48"
Dining Square	36"-60"	
Dining, Round	36"-96"	
Game, Poker	36"-59"	
Drop Leaf	36"-72"	21"-63"
Console, Sofa, Hall	48"-80"	14"-24"
Desk	28"-72"	24"-30"
End	14"-30"	14"-30"
Nightstand	14"-36"	14"-24"
Coffee, Rectangle	24"-53"	18"-40"
Coffee, Square/Round	24"-48"	

The dimensions listed below are averages. If you look, you'll find options both bigger and smaller than what's listed. So use these numbers as a guide. Not an absolute.

SEATING	width	depth
Sofa	80"-95"	33"-40"
Chaise Lounge	62"-90"	28"-36"
Love Seat	60"-72"	33"-40"
Settees	41"-72"	19"-40"
Chair-and-a-Half	43"-54"	33"-40"
Easy Chair	28"-36"	33"-40"
Club Chair	28"-36"	28"-40"
Slipper Chair	22"-29"	22"-35"
Dining Chair, Arm	20"-28"	16"-27"
Dining Chair, Side	17"-25"	16"-27"
Barstool	14"-25"	14"-24"
Counter Stool	14"-25"	14"-24"
Ottoman, Rectangle	24"-53"	18"-40"
Ottoman, Square/Round	24"-48"	

CHESTS	width	depth
Bookcase	36"-80"	7"-24"
Dresser	30"-74"	15"-24"
Sideboard, Buffet	48"-72"	16"-26"
Armoire	28"-60"	20"-30"
Tallboy	36"-60"	11"-24"
Lowboy	27"-40"	11"-24"

DRAWING YOUR LAYOUT

The time has finally come, and I can't even begin to tell you how excited I am. This is the part of creating a layout — of decorating — that I live for. It's the moment when you finally get to solve the puzzle. When you take all your pieces — your zones, your visual grammar cocktail and your players — and figure out how to fit them together to create the best room layout.

Ideally, all your pieces will fit together in such a way that you achieve exactly what you want as far as walking space, traffic flow, access space, work flow, conversation flow, utility locations, lighting, furniture size, space size, space shape and lines of sight.

But rarely does that ever happen. In most situations, it's just not possible. And that's life. While we may strive for the ideal, in reality it's all about making the best compromises in order to get as close as we can.

Choosing a bit smaller furniture to have an adequate amount of walking space. Sacrificing your line of sight to get a better work flow. Skipping your top furniture pick to create better conversation flow.

It's what you have to do to make it work. And in the end, as long as you make good compromises, your room will turn out great. So take your time. Monkey around with it. Rotate your items until you find the compromise that leads you to a layout you love.

Along the way, you may find yourself grow as addicted to the challenge of creating layouts as I am.

You'll need to know these when creating your layout. Without them, it's practically impossible.

1. Draw in Guides.

Being able to easily spot the center of each wall — and the room — makes it much easier to keep tabs on whether or not your room is balanced. Draw a line at the center of each wall. Then, draw a dot in the center of the room.

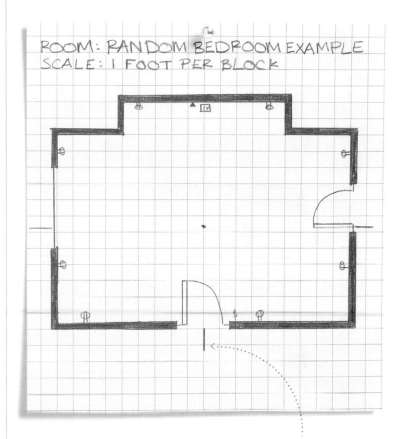

ROOM: RANDOM BEDROOM EXAMPLE
SCALE: 1 FOOT PER BLOCK

The guides are small, yet so helpful.

2. Place Your Focal Points

Since focal points are the main features in your room, they're best to place first because they should be given the optimum positions. To start, you'll need your focal points, lines of sight and visual grammar cocktail sheets.

First, draw in the focal point you want in your line of sight from the main entrance. Whether or not you place it directly centered on your door will depend on both the configuration of your room — whether there are any windows and doors in the way — and how you plan to balance your room — symmetrically or asymmetrically.

Remember to consult your utility locations before placing anything — unless you don't mind having them moved.

Then, place the rest of your focal points according to what you want in your line of sight from each location in your room. Remember, in small rooms there is at most typically only one focal point per wall, and potentially one in the center of the room. In large rooms you can get away with more. If you're decorating an open concept room with few walls, you may not have very many focal points — if any — to place. Windows or a fireplace may be the only focal point in your room.

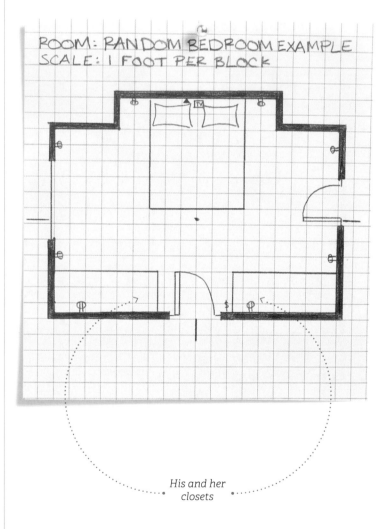

His and her closets

3. Fill in by Adding Each Zone.

Use the focal point locations to determine where to add items from each of your zones. Remember, the items from each zone should be located as close to each other as possible.

When deciding where to place each item, remember to consult what you want in its line of sight. Any that have specific things such as windows, doorways, fireplaces or TVs should be placed first. Use your visual grammar cocktail as a guide when placing each item. Don't be afraid to float items in the center of the room — especially if your room is big.

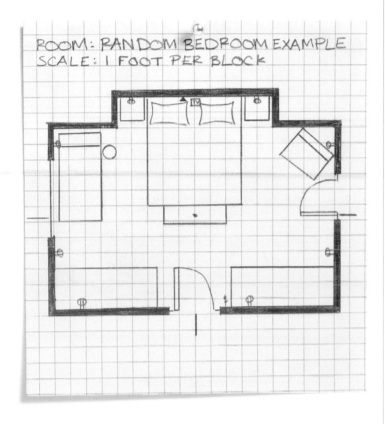

1. Switched out the swinging door leading to the bathroom for a pocket door to allow for more room.
2. Added two walls to enclose the closets.
3. Moved the light switch for easy access from the door.

4. Relocate Walls, Windows & Doors — if Needed.

If things won't fit the way you need them to fit, don't worry. It's probably not you. It's your room. Sometimes the room just doesn't work for what you want — even with compromises. When that happens, you need more than just decorating. You need a bit of renovating, and there are tons of things you can do.

Add a wall to divide a big room. Knock down a wall, and steal space from an adjoining room. Push out your wall to increase space. Put in windows. Cut in skylights. Take out a door. Install a fireplace.

Of course, many people avoid this due to the cost and hassle. But if you plan to live in your home for quite some time, it may be worth it. Small renovations can be extremely wallet friendly — especially those done inside to a non-load bearing wall. So before crossing the possibility off the list, get a few quotes. You may be surprised by how little it dents your budget — compared to the huge improvement you'll see in your room.

For now, I'd recommend not worrying about the budget. Instead, draw up a few layouts with your room exactly as it is now. Then draw a few layouts with the improvements. Choose the best of each layout, and complete both with steps 8 - 12. That way, when it comes time to get quotes and worry about the budget, you can easily decide whether or not it's worth it to make those improvements.

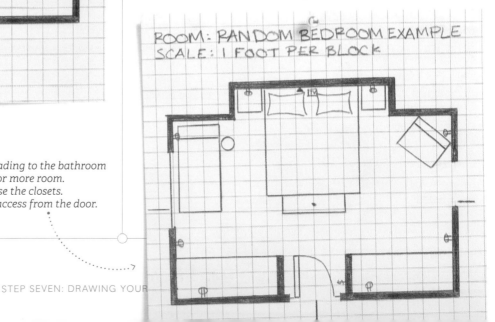

5. Add Lighting

The very first thing God said after creating Earth was, "Let there be light." Because He knew without light, no one could enjoy His creation. Just as without light, no one can enjoy your creation. So now that you have your layout created, it's time to "Let there be light."

When creating your lighting scheme, plan for the darkest time you'll be using your room — typically at night. That way, you will always have enough light. Then, when the sun is pouring through your windows, you can simply turn less lights on.

DRAW IN YOUR CURRENT LIGHTING. Before you can create your lighting scheme, see how your current lighting aligns with your layout. If you don't have any current lighting, skip ahead. But if you do, use the measurements you took of your ceiling to draw in chandeliers, pendants, flush or recessed lighting currently in your room. Then use the measurements of your walls to draw in sconces.

As far as wall sconces go, make sure nothing is blocking them — unless you no longer want them.

When it comes to chandeliers, pendants and recessed lighting, make sure you like their alignment. Typically, chandeliers and pendants are centered above tables, islands, furniture arrangements or empty walking spaces. In bedrooms, they're typically centered over beds, benches at the end of beds, or walking space. But you don't have to do it that way. Use your visual grammar as a guide when deciding how to align your lighting with your furniture.

If your current lighting aligns with the furniture in your layout, you can skip ahead to task lighting. If your current lighting doesn't align, you must decide whether you want to change the location of your lighting or your furniture.

In most cases, it's better to change the location of your lighting, because it's silly to downgrade your layout when the cost of moving lighting is almost always relatively small. If you're worried moving your lighting will break the bank, create a version with the lighting moved — and without the lighting moved — and complete both with steps 8 - 12. That way, when it comes time to get quotes and worry about the budget, you can easily decide whether or not it's worth it to move your lighting.

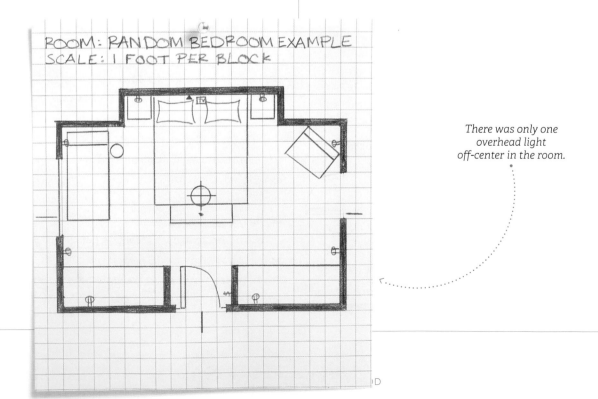

ROOM: RANDOM BEDROOM EXAMPLE
SCALE: 1 FOOT PER BLOCK

There was only one overhead light off-center in the room.

LIGHTING SYMBOLS

⊕ CEILING MOUNTED FIXTURE
(chandelier, pendant, etc.)

⊕ WALL MOUNTED FIXTURE
(sconce, picture light, etc.)

Ⓡ RECESSED CEILING FIXTURE
(pot lights, etc.)

⊢O⊣ TRACK LIGHTING

⊙ CEILING FAN with LIGHT

◯ CEILING FAN without LIGHT

⊙ LAMP (table or floor)

PLACE YOUR TASK LIGHTING. Not every room needs task lighting. You only need it if you plan to do a task that requires bright light — such as reading, cooking, sewing or applying makeup. Whether or not you need any should be listed on your Functional Needs sheet, so pull it out and see if any of your aspirations require task lighting. If they don't, skip ahead to general lighting. If they do, stick around.

When creating a lighting scheme, task lighting — if needed — is the first type of lighting you should always add, because it's the most particular in terms of where it must be located. In order to function correctly, task lighting must be placed where it can directly illuminate the surface used for doing the task. So if you're cooking, your task lighting should be placed so that it illuminates your countertops. If you're applying makeup, your task lighting must be placed

so that it illuminates you and your mirror. If you're reading, your task lighting must be placed to illuminate your book. You get the idea.

If you need to illuminate only a small space, you'll probably only need one task light.

But if your task area is large — like a kitchen countertop — multiple lights will probably be required. How many you'll need depends on the type of task lighting you plan to use.

Fortunately, any light can be a task light. A chandelier. A pendant. A sconce. A lamp. A recessed fixture. It doesn't matter. Just remember table lamps take up surface space. So if your task requires as much space as possible, a floor lamp, wall light or ceiling fixture may be a better option. Also, lamps — both floor and table — are tall, which means they'll block the view of your room if placed in the center. If you want a cozier feel in your room, that may be a good idea. But if you want your room to feel spacious and open, a different type of fixture may be a better option.

Once you've decided upon the type of fixture you want to use, you can determine how many you need. Now there is a very complicated formula you can use to determine how many lights you need in your room. But to do it, you must know the exact fixture and light bulbs you plan to use. And even then, it's hard to determine.

So to make things easy, take out your room evaluation and look at what you wrote down regarding lighting. If you felt you had enough, duplicate what you had. If you felt you need more, add more.

When placing ceiling task lights, it's best to center them on the surface they must illuminate. That way, you get even lighting coverage. Plus, if you place them too close to a wall or tall piece of furniture, the light will get cut off and appear far dimmer than it truly is.

When placing lamps, where you put them depends on how much surface area you need. If you don't need any, they can be placed anywhere on your table. If you need surface area, they're best placed to the side or back corner.

Once you've decided on how many task lights you need and where they should be placed, draw them in. If your current lighting covers all your task lighting needs, lucky you. You can skip ahead to general lighting. And remember, if you plan to use lamps as part of your lighting scheme, they must have an outlet where they can be plugged in.

Task reading lamps placed on either side of the bed and next to the chair and chaise.

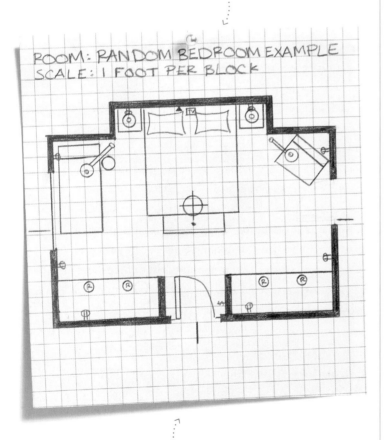

Recessed lights added in each closet to make finding items easy.

PLACE YOUR GENERAL LIGHTING. Every room requires general lighting, because it's what enables you to see everything in your room. Of course, there are many configurations that allow you to see everything in your room. You can have one center light. Numerous lights around the perimeter. Or a combination of both. Which you choose depends partly on what you functionally need and partly on what you emotionally want to feel.

As far as function goes, general lighting can either be your main light source or filler light source. In rooms with no task lighting, it is the main light source, which means it must be powerful enough to light all areas of the room that must be seen. Remember, if you have any type of storage in your room — such as dressers, armoires or cabinets — you must have enough light to see inside it.

In rooms with task lighting, general lighting is the filler light. It illuminates the dark spots in your room that task light fails to reach. For example, in a kitchen, general lighting typically is placed centered on all walkways, because without it only the countertops would be illuminated. And you need to see more than just countertops when cooking. You need to see where you're walking and into cabinets, which is why adding general lighting is so important.

As far as emotion goes, general lighting can be bright or dim. Which you choose depends on what you want to feel. If you want your room to feel bright and cheerful, have enough general lighting to clearly illuminate the entire room without having any shadows whatsoever. Doing that often takes more than one light. Typically, you need a center light in your room and a few on the outskirts — whether they're lamps, sconces or overheads.

If you want your room to feel moody or sultry, you'll want it to have low lighting with a few shadows here and there. Typically, you achieve that type of lighting the same exact way as you would for bright, cheerful lighting — with a center light and a few scattered around the room. Only instead of having them all on at full blast, you either selectively turn on a few lights or install a dimmer. Of course, you can always just have fewer lights instead. But having more lighting options is always better, because you can always turn a light off. But you can't turn on a light that's not there.

Once you've decided upon how much general lighting you need functionally and how you want your general lighting to feel emotionally, draw it in. Keep in mind, task lighting can double as general lighting in some rooms. So if you feel as if you already have enough light from your task sources, don't draw more in. If your current lighting covers all your general lighting needs, you can skip ahead to mood lighting. And remember, if you plan to use lamps as part of your lighting scheme, they must have an outlet where they can be plugged in.

PLACE YOUR MOOD LIGHTING. All rooms do not need mood lighting. You only need it if one of your aspirations requires setting "the mood," and if any of yours do, it should be listed on your functional needs sheet. If you don't need any mood lighting, you're finished with your lighting scheme and can skip ahead. But if you do, stick around.

Most mood lighting is achieved by simply turning down the dimmer on general or task lighting — but not always. There are three types of additional mood lighting you can add to your room.

The first is low lighting. These are soft, dim lights that cast a sexy glow. Typically, they're installed around ceilings or floors.

The second is accent lighting, which is lighting used to highlight special pieces in the room such as painting, objects in glass cabinetry or on shelves and fireplaces. To maximize the effect of accent lighting, use it to highlight the elements of your room that you feel best evoke the emotions you want to elicit.

The third is colored lighting. This type of lighting gives off a very cool, swanky vibe perfect for parties.

To determine which types of mood lighting you want in your room, think back to your aspirations and emotional wants. Would any of that lighting enhance the emotion while doing those activities or would dimmer switches suffice? If you decide to add special mood lighting, draw it in.

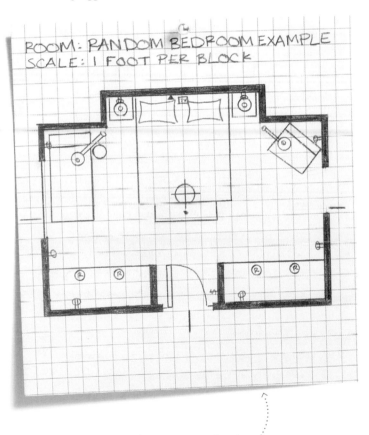

The existing overhead light works as general lighting.

Added wall sconces to set the mood.

6. Add Area Rugs

Not every room needs an area rug. But if you want one, now is the time to add it.

Typically, area rugs are used for four reasons: slip-control, comfort, anchoring and highlighting.

SLIP-CONTROL. Wood, stone and tile floors can get pretty slippery if water gets on them, which is why area rugs can be so handy. They sop up the water, while providing traction to prevent you from slipping. If you're decorating a room where water can be an issue — like kitchens, bathrooms, entries, laundry and mud rooms — having an area rug may be a good idea.

COMFORT. Area rugs offer two types of comfort. One, they keep toes from catching cold from chilly wood, stone or tile floors. And two, they offer padding which makes standing in place while doing chores — such as cooking or folding laundry — far more comfortable. If you live in a cold climate or plan to stand for long periods of time, you may want to consider an area rug.

ANCHORING. Using an area rug under furniture is the visual equivalent of drawing a circle around words. It tells you, "These things belong together."

If you have numerous different furniture pieces in your room, using that trick will unify them. Because instead of seeing a bunch of random objects standing on their own, the rug fools your eyes into seeing them a unified grouping — like flowers in a vase.

Whether or not you want your furniture to look unified depends on how you want your room to feel. If you want a soothing, relaxing, luxurious or cozy look, an area rug may be right for you. Whereas, if you want an energetic, bare, simple or airy look, an area rug may be wrong for you.

Now if you don't want an area rug because you don't want extra fabric in your room — look at the textures and materials of your muse to find out — you can always anchor your objects by having a decorative floor installed or painting your floor with a border or change of color.

AREA RUGS	
2' x 3'	9' x 12'
4' x 6'	10' x 13'
5' x 8'	10' x 14'
6' x 9'	12' x 15'
7' x 10'	12' x 18'
8' x 10'	13' x 2'

HIGHLIGHTING. Area rugs act like highlighters. They draw attention to whatever you put on them. If you have a piece of furniture in the middle of your room you want to appear more prominent, throw a rug under it.

And again, if you want to draw the attention without the use of material, you can mimic the affect of an area rug by having a decorative floor installed or painted.

If you decide to add an area rug, keep in mind you're fairly limited when it comes to which size you can use. Look above to see standard area rug sizes. If none of the standard sizes work for your situation, don't worry. You can always have an area rug made out of carpet, natural fibers — such as jute — or a custom one made. Just know, the latter gets pricey.

What size area rug you need depends completely on where you plan to put it. If it's to go under a dining table, most people recommend making the rug 2 feet larger on all sides than the table. Can it be a bit less? Yeah, you can fudge a bit. But if you go too small, the back of people's chairs will hang off the carpet causing them to feel off balance while eating. So do your best to make the rug about 2 feet bigger on all sides than your table.

If your rug is to go under a seating arrangement, you have many options. Some people only put the front legs of their furniture on the rug. Others make it so the rug is the exact size as the furniture arrangement. Some make it a foot or two bigger than the arrangement. Which you choose depends on what you want to feel in your room and how the standard sizes fit with the size of your arrangement.

If your rug is to go in a bathroom or kitchen, you can make it any size you want. Typically, people don't like having a wall-to-wall area rug. They prefer leaving a border of flooring around it.

If you want to use an area rug in your room, go ahead and draw it in. If you're not sure you want a rug, but know you want to anchor or highlight your furniture pieces, draw the border of the frame in as well.

If you're unsure you want an area rug because you don't know if you're going to use carpeting — after all, we haven't chosen flooring yet   you can hold off until we get to Step 11: Textures. But make a note that you must still decide so that you don't forget. And by the way, yes, you can put an area rug on top of carpet. Some people love the decadent, luxurious, somewhat over-the-top feeling it provides.

7. Check Your Storage

Now I realize not everyone does this. In fact, I've never heard of anyone doing this. But the only way to know 100 percent that every item you need to store has a home is to label where each item will go and double check there's enough room for it.

So pull out your Storage Needs Sheet, and make sure there's a place — with enough space — for every item listed. If there's not, you need to rework your layout until there is. Remember, the only way to conquer clutter — the No. 1 nemesis of any decorated room — is for every item in your room to have an easy-to-access home (page 104).

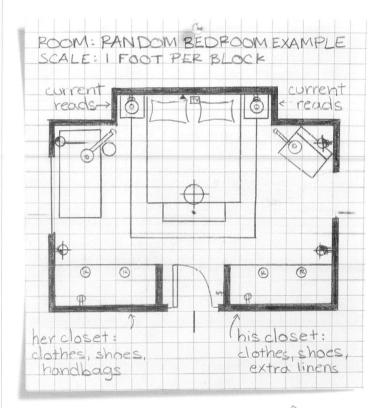

This may be the most important part. Be sure you have a place for everything that must be stored.

7

drawing your layout

LAYOUT SCORECARD

ROOM:

DIRECTIONS: Rank how well your layout fulfills each criterion.

NUMBER OF ASPIRATIONS UNABLE TO DO: ☐ 0 ☐ 1 ☐ 2 ☐ 3 ☐ 4 ☐ 5

PLAYERS:	☐ ideal	☐ less than ideal	☐ not ideal
ZONES:	☐ ideal	☐ less than ideal	☐ not ideal
VISUAL GRAMMAR:	☐ ideal	☐ less than ideal	☐ not ideal
WALKING SPACE:	☐ ideal	☐ less than ideal	☐ not ideal
TRAFFIC FLOW:	☐ ideal	☐ less than ideal	☐ not ideal
ACCESS SPACE:	☐ ideal	☐ less than ideal	☐ not ideal
WORK FLOW:	☐ ideal	☐ less than ideal	☐ not ideal
CONVERSATION FLOW:	☐ ideal	☐ less than ideal	☐ not ideal
UTILITY LOCATIONS:	☐ ideal	☐ less than ideal	☐ not ideal
LINES OF SIGHT:	☐ ideal	☐ less than ideal	☐ not ideal
SUBTOTALS: Add up the total checks in each column.			

LAYOUT #....................
OVERALL SCORE:

To determine your overall score, multiply the number in the ideal column by 3, the less than ideal column by 2 and the not ideal column by 1. Add the three resulting numbers together. Then subtract from that total the number of aspirations you're unable to do in your room. The resulting number is your layout's score.

8. Score Your Layout

The only way to know how close your layout comes to your ideal, is to score it. And I've made up an easy scorecard for you to use. Look to your left.

Keep in mind, what you rank each category is completely subjective and should be based solely on what you want. So take out your sheets for each category to use as a guide when deciding how close your layout comes to what you really wanted.

9. Go Back and Create at Least 3 More

As you already know (page 169), you don't create just one layout. You create as many as it takes until you get one you truly love. Now I realize that if you have a very tiny room, you may have only one place to put things. But if you have more than one option, you better get drawing.

SELECTING THE BEST LAYOUT

Now you'd think I'd tell you to choose the layout with the highest score. But you'd be wrong. The one with the highest score is not necessarily the one you'll like best.

You see, we favor certain elements of a layout, which means we weigh them more. And our scorecards don't account for that favoritism. They weigh everything evenly. But we don't. We irrationally hold some things to be more important. For me, it's lines of sight and work flow. For you, it may be conversation flow and visual grammar. Whatever it is, you'll weigh it more.

As a result, your scorecards may say one layout is better, but you won't agree. That's because the one thing it lacks is the one thing you want most of all — even if it means you have to sacrifice more. And that's okay. We're human. We're supposed to play favorites. I only had you score your layouts so that you could make a conscious decision about whether or not it is worth the sacrifice if the one you love isn't the most logical decision.

So look through all your layouts, and use your gut to tell you which one you like best. Don't think about it. Just feel.

If you have a hard time deciding, walk away. Give your emotions time to settle.

If you still can't decide, don't be afraid to ask for a second opinion. But don't do it for the person's response. Do it for that moment when they say what they think and you feel a pang of either disappointment or relief. In that moment you'll get your answer. You'll know what you like best.

If the score for the one you like best is highest, you're set. You have a layout. Woo hoo!

If the score isn't the highest, take some time to mull over whether the sacrifice is worth it. If it is, you've got yourself a layout. Congratulations.

If it's not worth the sacrifice, see if you can create a new layout that fits your criteria better. Sometimes if you walk away from it for a day or two, the best solution will pop into your head when you're not even thinking about it. So step away to give your brain the time it needs to mull it over, and then try to create a better version.

Every bad layout you draw gets you one step closer to "the one." So don't give up.

7

drawing your layout

LAYOUT SCORECARD

ROOM: GUEST BEDROOM

DIRECTIONS: Rank how well your layout fulfills each criterion.

NUMBER OF ASPIRATIONS UNABLE TO DO: ☒ 0 ☐ 1 ☐ 2 ☐ 3 ☐ 4 ☐ 5

PLAYERS:	☒ ideal	☐ less than ideal	☐ not ideal
ZONES:	☒ ideal	☐ less than ideal	☐ not ideal
VISUAL GRAMMAR:	☒ ideal	☐ less than ideal	☐ not ideal
WALKING SPACE:	☒ ideal	☐ less than ideal	☐ not ideal
TRAFFIC FLOW:	☒ ideal	☐ less than ideal	☐ not ideal
ACCESS SPACE:	☐ ideal ✕	☐ less than ideal	☐ not ideal
WORK FLOW:	☒ ideal	☐ less than ideal	☐ not ideal
CONVERSATION FLOW:	☐ ideal ✕	☐ less than ideal	☐ not ideal
UTILITY LOCATIONS:	☒ ideal	☐ less than ideal	☐ not ideal
LINES OF SIGHT:	☒ ideal	☐ less than ideal	☐ not ideal
SUBTOTALS: Add up the total checks in each column.	8	2	

LAYOUT # 3
OVERALL SCORE:

29

To determine your overall score, multiply the number in the ideal column by 3, the less than ideal column by 2 and the not ideal column by 1. Add the three resulting numbers together. Then subtract from that total the number of aspirations you're unable to do in your room. The resulting number is your layout's score.

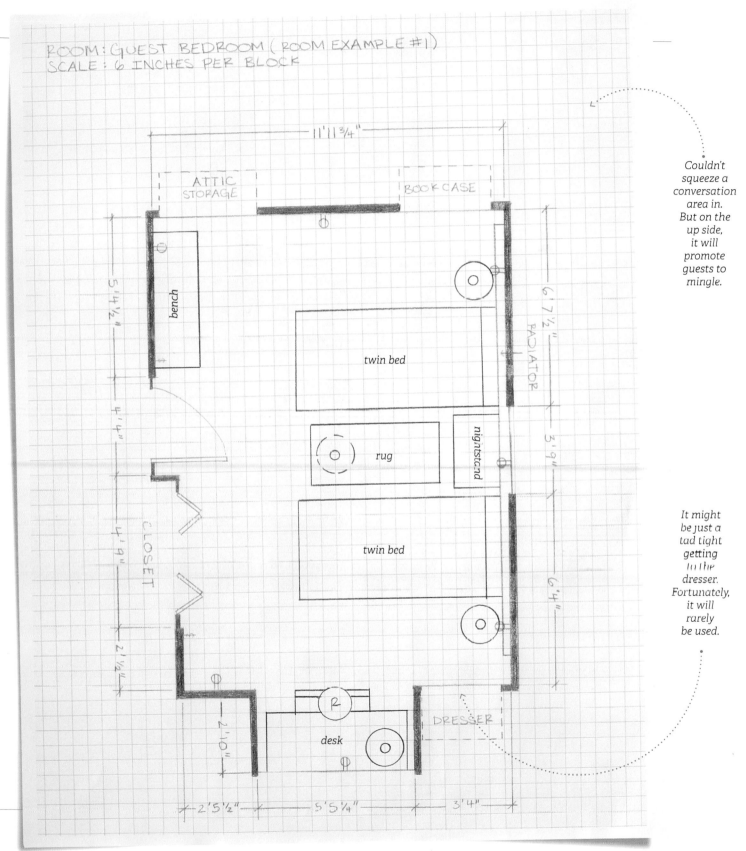

ROOM: GUEST BEDROOM (ROOM EXAMPLE #1)
SCALE: 6 INCHES PER BLOCK

ATTIC STORAGE

BOOK CASE

11'11 3/4"

bench

5'4½"

4'4"

CLOSET

4'9"

2'5½"

2'0"

twin bed

rug

nightstand

RADIATOR

6'7½"

3'9"

6'4"

twin bed

DRESSER

desk

2'5½"   5'5¼"   3'4"

Couldn't squeeze a conversation area in. But on the up side, it will promote guests to mingle.

It might be just a tad tight getting to the dresser. Fortunately, it will rarely be used.

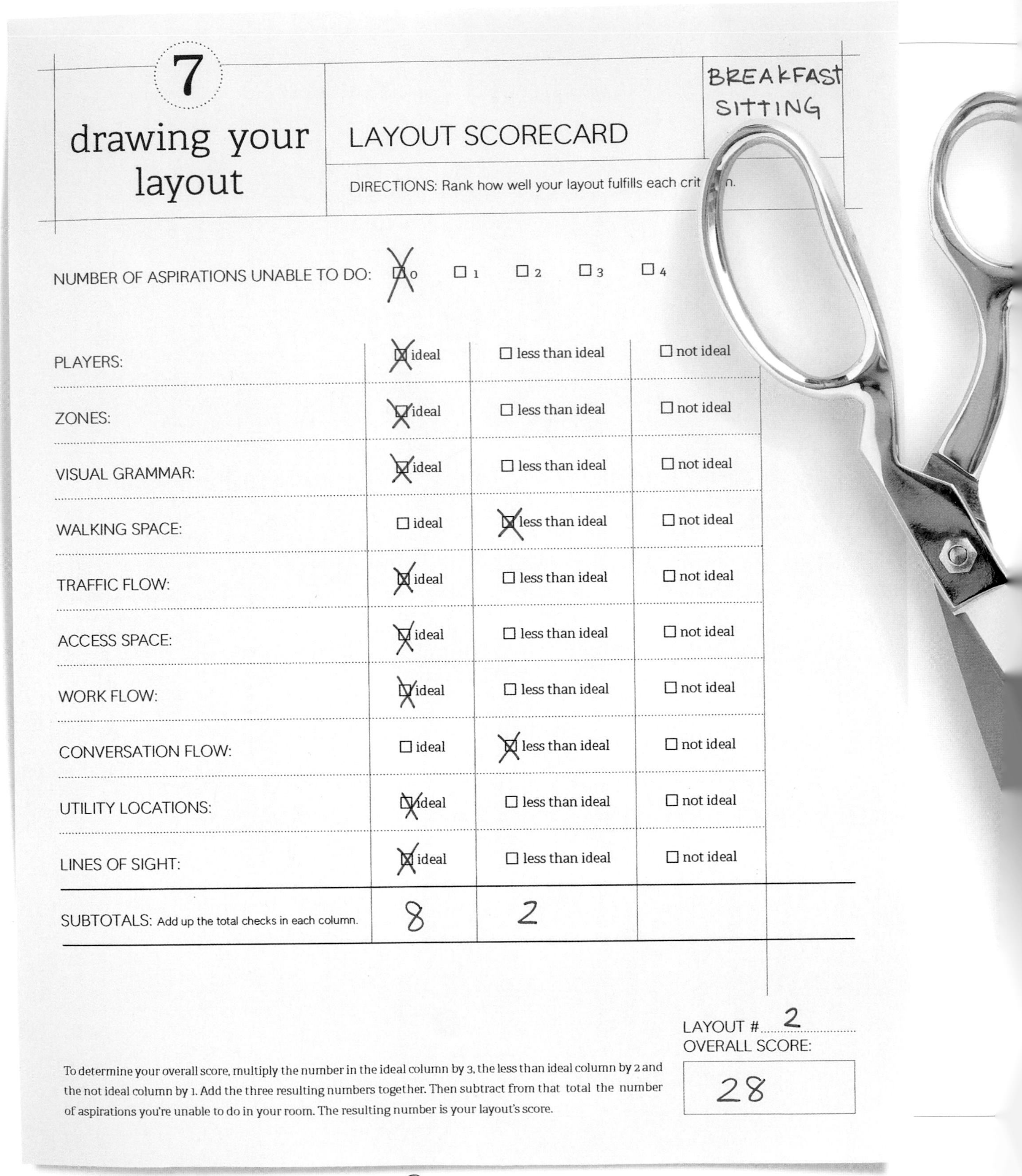

LAYOUT SCORECARD

BREAKFAST SITTING

DIRECTIONS: Rank how well your layout fulfills each crit___n.

NUMBER OF ASPIRATIONS UNABLE TO DO: ☒ 0 ☐ 1 ☐ 2 ☐ 3 ☐ 4

PLAYERS:	☒ ideal	☐ less than ideal	☐ not ideal
ZONES:	☒ ideal	☐ less than ideal	☐ not ideal
VISUAL GRAMMAR:	☒ ideal	☐ less than ideal	☐ not ideal
WALKING SPACE:	☐ ideal	☒ less than ideal	☐ not ideal
TRAFFIC FLOW:	☒ ideal	☐ less than ideal	☐ not ideal
ACCESS SPACE:	☒ ideal	☐ less than ideal	☐ not ideal
WORK FLOW:	☒ ideal	☐ less than ideal	☐ not ideal
CONVERSATION FLOW:	☐ ideal	☒ less than ideal	☐ not ideal
UTILITY LOCATIONS:	☒ ideal	☐ less than ideal	☐ not ideal
LINES OF SIGHT:	☒ ideal	☐ less than ideal	☐ not ideal
SUBTOTALS: Add up the total checks in each column.	8	2	

LAYOUT # 2
OVERALL SCORE:

28

To determine your overall score, multiply the number in the ideal column by 3, the less than ideal column by 2 and the not ideal column by 1. Add the three resulting numbers together. Then subtract from that total the number of aspirations you're unable to do in your room. The resulting number is your layout's score.

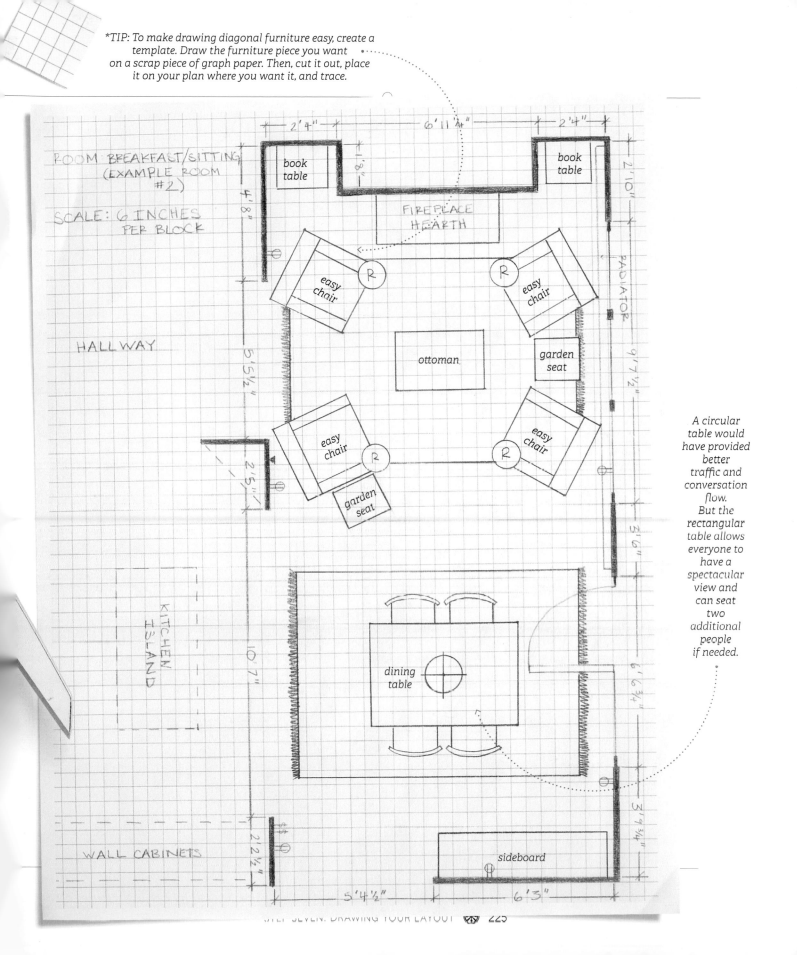

*TIP: To make drawing diagonal furniture easy, create a template. Draw the furniture piece you want on a scrap piece of graph paper. Then, cut it out, place it on your plan where you want it, and trace.

ROOM: BREAKFAST/SITTING (EXAMPLE ROOM #2)

SCALE: 6 INCHES PER BLOCK

HALLWAY

2'4"   6'11'4"   2'4"

4'8"

5'5½"

2'5"

10'7"

2'2½"

KITCHEN ISLAND

WALL CABINETS

5'4½"   6'3"

book table

book table

FIREPLACE HEARTH

easy chair

R

R

easy chair

ottoman

garden seat

easy chair

R

R

easy chair

garden seat

dining table

sideboard

2'10"

9'7½"

3'6"

6'6¾"

3'9¾"

RADIATOR

A circular table would have provided better traffic and conversation flow. But the rectangular table allows everyone to have a spectacular view and can seat two additional people if needed.

LAYOUT SCORECARD	HOME OFFICE ROOM:
DIRECTIONS: Rank how well your layout fulfills each criterion.	

NUMBER OF ASPIRATIONS UNABLE TO DO: ☒ 0 ☐ 1 ☐ 2 ☐ 3 ☐ 4 ☐ 5

	ideal	less than ideal	not ideal
PLAYERS:	☒ ideal	☐ less than ideal	☐ not ideal
ZONES:	☒ ideal	☐ less than ideal	☐ not ideal
VISUAL GRAMMAR:	☒ ideal	☐ less than ideal	☐ not ideal
WALKING SPACE:	☒ ideal	☐ less than ideal	☐ not ideal
TRAFFIC FLOW:	☒ ideal	☐ less than ideal	☐ not ideal
ACCESS SPACE:	☒ ideal	☐ less than ideal	☐ not ideal
WORK FLOW:	☒ ideal	☐ less than ideal	☐ not ideal
CONVERSATION FLOW:	☒ ideal	☐ less than ideal	☐ not ideal
UTILITY LOCATIONS:	☒ ideal	☐ less than ideal	☐ not ideal
LINES OF SIGHT:	☐ ideal	☒ less than ideal	☐ not ideal
SUBTOTALS: Add up the total checks in each column.	9	1	

LAYOUT # 4
OVERALL SCORE:

29

To determine your overall score, multiply the number in the ideal column by 3, the less than ideal column by 2 and the not ideal column by 1. Add the three resulting numbers together. Then subtract from that total the number of aspirations you're unable to do in your room. The resulting number is your layout's score.

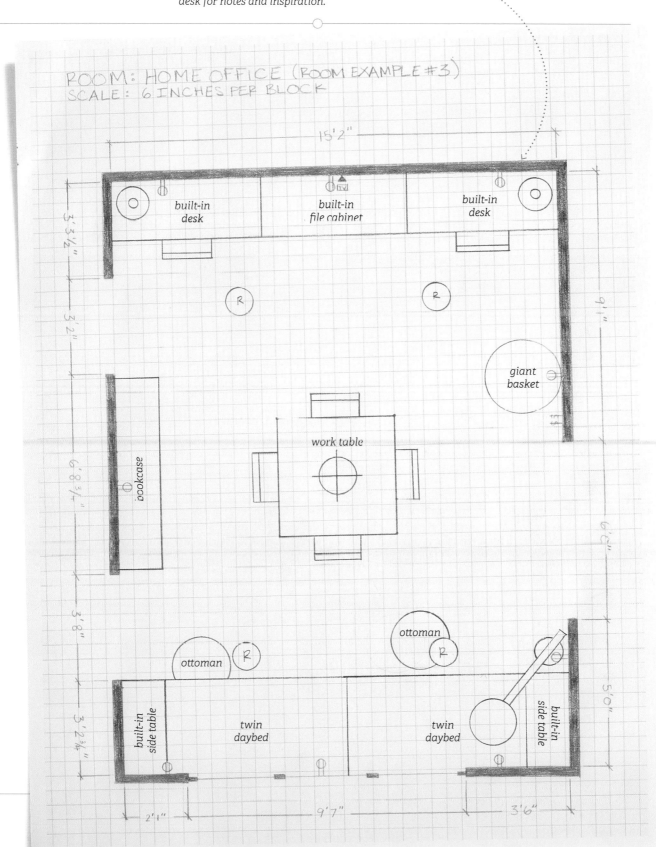

Would have prefered having the desks and daybeds facing the view, but the windows were too low. Fotunately, it's probably for the better. That way, a giant, magnetic whiteboard can be placed above the desk for notes and inspiration.

ROOM: HOME OFFICE (ROOM EXAMPLE #3)
SCALE: 6 INCHES PER BLOCK

15'2"

built-in
desk

built-in
file cabinet

built-in
desk

3'3½"

3'2"

R

R

giant
basket

9'1"

6'8¾"

bookcase

work table

6'0"

3'8"

ottoman

R

ottoman

R

built-in
side table

twin
daybed

twin
daybed

built-in
side table

5'0"

3'2¾"

2'1"

9'7"

3'6"

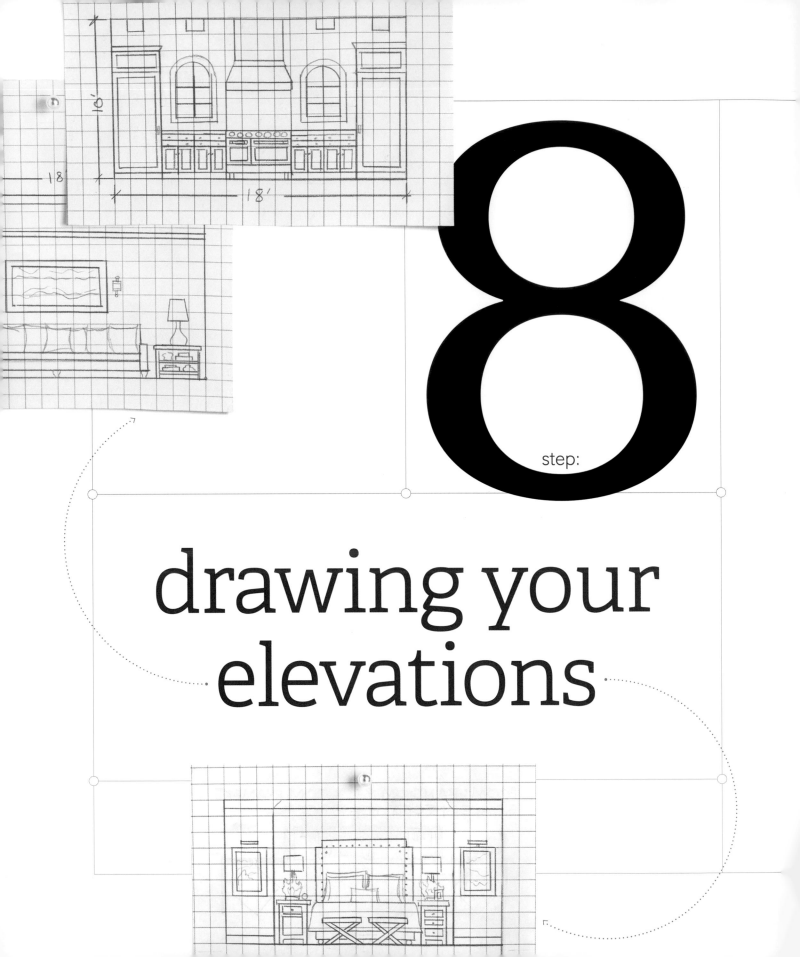

step:

8

drawing your elevations

Most people figure a room layout is all you need when decorating. But not so. A layout is like a road map. It only gives you an aerial view of your room. And that aerial view does not tell you what will be on your walls, how high your furniture will be, how low your lighting will go and what decorative accessories will adorn your tables and shelves. For that, you must draw an elevation, which is a snapshot of each location on your layout.

Now, the number of elevations you draw for your room completely depends on your artistic skill. If you're a master of perspective drawing and can whip out 3-D sketches in no time flat, then you may only need to create a couple of elevations.

But most of us aren't quite so adept with a pencil and find our artistic talent leveling off in the stick-figure range, which is why I suggest creating six 2-D stick-figure elevations of your room. One for each wall, and two additional ones for the center of your room — if you have something in the center of your room.

WHAT YOU'LL NEED

You need the same things to draw your elevations as you did to draw your layout. If you skipped ahead — naughty, naughty — flip back to page 161 to see what you need.

STEP 1. SET UP YOUR PAPER

When creating elevations, you simply need to draw each wall in your room. Fortunately, doing that will be easy considering you already know how to work with graph paper, page 164, and you already have all the measurements for your room, page 110. So let's get to it.

1. Label Your Paper

On the top of your page, write down the room you're working on.

2. Choose Your Scale.

Remember the smaller your scale, the easier it is to draw your room. Of course, you must make sure that the scale you choose fits on your page. For a refresher on how to choose the right scale, flip to page 164. Otherwise, write down your scale, and move on.

3. Name Your Wall

To remember which wall is which, name your wall. Typically, people use either the wall's directional orientation — north, south, east or west — or its main architectural feature — fireplace, door, window or closet — as its name. But you can use whatever you want. Just make sure you'll remember which wall belongs to which name.

4. Draw the Edges of Your Walls.

First, determine how many blocks you need to represent the height of your room. To do that, take the overall height of your room and divide it by the scale of each block. The resulting number is the amount of blocks that represent the height of your wall. Once you've determined how many blocks high your wall should be, draw it in.

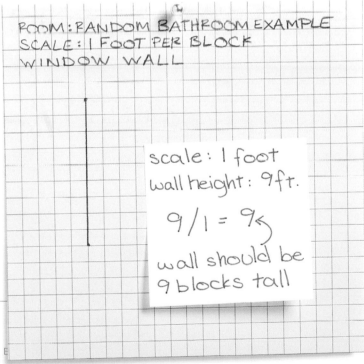

ROOM: RANDOM BATHROOM EXAMPLE
SCALE: 1 FOOT PER BLOCK
WINDOW WALL

scale: 1 foot
wall height: 9ft.
9/1 = 9
wall should be
9 blocks tall

Next, determine how many blocks you need to represent the width of your room. Do it the same way, only use the overall width of your room instead of the height. Once you've determined how many blocks wide your wall should be, draw it in.

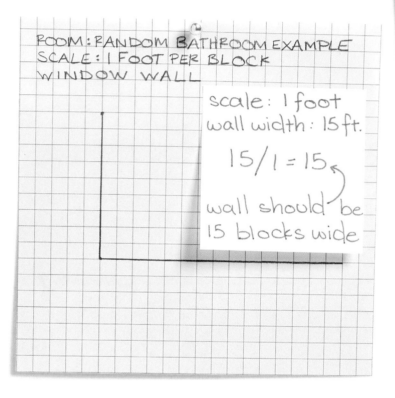

ROOM: RANDOM BATHROOM EXAMPLE
SCALE: 1 FOOT PER BLOCK
WINDOW WALL

scale: 1 foot
wall width: 15 ft.

15/1 = 15

wall should be
15 blocks wide

If your wall is a rectangle, connect the lines to create the outline of your wall.

If your wall is an odd shape, continue determining the length and location of all straight parts of your wall. Once you've filled those in, use them to connect any diagonal or rounded parts of your wall.

Then go back and do that same thing for each wall in your room. If you drew any furniture floating in the center of your room, go back and draw two extra elevations for the middle of your room. For the first, draw a single line across the bottom the length of the width of your room. Label it Room Center Widthwise.

The second should look identical, only this time it should show the length of the room. Label it Room Center Lengthwise.

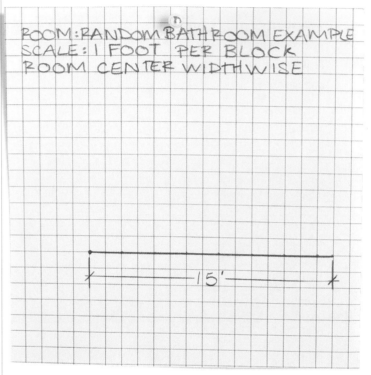

ROOM: RANDOM BATHROOM EXAMPLE
SCALE: 1 FOOT PER BLOCK
ROOM CENTER WIDTHWISE

15'

Remember, if you changed the location of any walls when making your layout, your elevations should reflect that. Once you've created all the outlines for your room elevations, you're ready to move on.

5. Write in Dimensions.

To avoid counting each block every time you want to know a dimension, write them in now. Fill in the dimensions for both the height and the width of each wall. If the wall is oddly shaped, be sure to fill in any extra dimensions.

Then, off to the side, create a line representing the height of whoever will use the room most. Having that provides a visual reminder of who you're decorating for: humans. Not giants or dwarves. Plus, it makes it easy for you to determine at what height things should be.

If you're decorating a child's room, use their height instead of yours. That way, they can actually see and enjoy what you put in their room.

If you're decorating a guest room, you can either use your height as a guide, your most frequent guest's height, or the average American height — 5'4 for women and 5'9 for men.

fireplaces — and the items you plan to keep — *if there are any*. New moldings, cabinetry and paneling will be added later.

Remember if you changed the location of any doors, windows or fireplaces when making your layout, your elevations should reflect that.

architectural details added •····

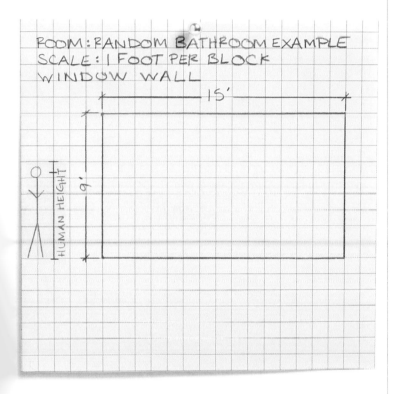

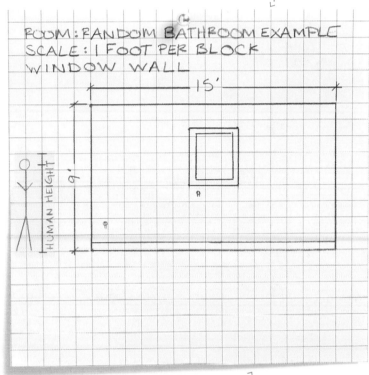

····• *utilities added*

6. Draw in Architectural Details.

If you plan to keep all the architectural details in your room — doors, openings, windows, fireplaces, cabinetry, paneling and moldings — the way they are, draw them in.

But if your current architectural details don't mesh with your style — as you figured out on page 86 — don't draw any of them in. Instead, only draw the outlines of the items you must have in your room — such as doors, windows and

7. Note Electrical, Cable and Heating Locations.

Draw in where all light switches, electrical outlets, cable outlets, phone outlets and heating or cooling controls are located. To do that, you can either use the standard labels or simply write them in with an arrow.

If you needed to change the location of any utilities to make your layout work, your elevations should reflect that.

8. Copy or Scan.

You should know the drill. You don't just create one version of each of your elevations. You create many. And to make doing that easy, either scan and print, or make copies of each of your elevations. That way you never have to redraw them.

Avoid the temptation to trace over lines with marker or pen. If the lines of your scanned or copied versions appear too faint, trace over your original versions in pencil. That way, if you need to make changes to your template in the future, you can simply erase rather than redrawing the whole thing.

STEP 2: DRAW IN FURNITURE

Thanks to your layout, you already know what furniture will be in your room and where it will go. But unfortunately, that's not enough information to draw those pieces in your elevation. For that, you must know the height of each piece and its shape from the front.

Furniture Height.

Each type of furniture comes in a range of heights. You can get a high-back, medium-back or low-back chair. A tall dresser, medium-high dresser or short dresser. The one you choose depends on five things: the size of your room, the size of nearby furniture, your lines of sight, your functional preferences and your emotional wants.

ROOM SIZE. Typically, people select furniture with a height proportional to their room. However, if you want your ceiling to appear taller, use either very tall pieces or very short pieces of furniture. The tall pieces of furniture draw your eye up, bringing attention to the height of your room. Whereas, short pieces have tons of extra space above them, which fools the eye into thinking the ceiling is taller than it is.

For the ultimate ceiling heightener, use a combination of both. The contrast between very tall and very low furniture

makes a ceiling look even taller.

NEARBY FURNITURE SIZE. We see things in terms of what they're next to, which is why an apple looks huge next to ant, yet miniscule next to an elephant.

The same thing goes for furniture. If you put a waist-high table in front of a sofa, it'll look monstrously tall. Whereas, if you put it in front of an armoire, it'll look just right. When deciding how tall each piece of furniture should be, it's important to consider what the furniture will be next to.

Fortunately, there aren't too many situations in a room where you have to worry about that. And when you do, here's the norm:

Night stands are typically a little lower, the same or a little higher than the top mattress on the bed.

End tables are typically a little lower, the same or a little higher than the arm of the neighboring sofa or chair.

Coffee tables are typically a little lower, the same or a little higher than the seat cushion of the neighboring sofa or chair.

Console tables behind sofas are typically slightly lower in height than the back of the sofa. Rarely — if ever — do you see them higher than the sofa.

Ottomans placed in front of chairs are typically the same height or a little lower than the seat cushion of the chair.

Ottomans, benches and tables placed at the end of beds are typically the same height or lower than the top mattress. Every once in awhile you'll see them a bit higher.

Which item you choose to make taller in each scenario depends on three things: emphasis, movement and emotion.

Emphasis. The taller item in a grouping appears more important, so the item you want to emphasize most should be the taller item in the grouping. That doesn't mean your end table must be taller than your sofa. That's silly. It just needs to be taller than the arm of your sofa to have more emphasis.

Movement. When the two outside items — such as night

stands on either side of a bed — are taller than the item they're next to, the movement in the room is directed up. When they're shorter, the movement in the room is directed down.

Emotion. When the two outside items in a grouping are taller than the inside item, it makes the arrangement look cozier. When they're shorter, the arrangement looks airier. The same thing goes for items placed in front of other items — such as a coffee table in front of a sofa.

LINES OF SIGHT. It doesn't take a rocket scientist to figure out that the taller an item, the more it blocks the view. So if you have items floating in the middle of your room, be careful not to make them so tall that they block your view — especially if they're directly in front of one of your focal points or main lines of sight.

FUNCTIONAL PREFERENCES. The height of your furniture greatly affects how well it functions. For example, the higher the back on the chair, the more comfortable it is to sit in, because it supports more of your back, and if you're lucky, your head as well.

Think of bathroom counters. Stock bathroom cabinets are typically about 3 inches shorter than stock kitchen cabinets. That means you've got to bend over an additional 3 inches every time you wash your face. Most people don't like doing that, which is why a number of people prefer using kitchen height cabinetry in their bathrooms.

Before deciding on the height of your furniture, ask yourself one thing: what height will be most comfortable? Also, check your Preferences sheet from Step 6: Your Evaluation (page 102). You may have listed certain heights you prefer.

EMOTION. The height of your furniture will affect how your room feels. Tall furniture makes a room feel either cozy or grand. The coziness is evoked when the taller furniture is used to create a cocoon sensation. Think of wing-back chairs and canopy beds. Grandeur is evoked when the tall furniture is used to bring attention to the height of a room. After all, the taller the room, the grander it feels.

Short furniture makes a room feel airy or down-to-earth. The airy feeling comes from a lack of furniture blocking the view, which makes a room feel more spacious. The down-to-earth feeling comes from the lack of adornment high up, which keeps the eyes lower. And when the eyes are pulled down rather than up, we get a sense of bowing our heads, which is associated with being humble and down-to-earth.

When deciding what height to make each of your furniture pieces, remember two things. One, you can mix and match. Not all of your furniture needs to be high or low. You can vary it to fit your needs.

For example, if you want your room to feel both airy and grand, you could use short pieces in the middle to keep the center of the room feeling airy and save the tall pieces for the outskirts of the room to add a sense of grandeur.

Two, emotions — such as cozy and grand — can be brought into your room in a number of other ways: pattern, texture and color. So if your functional needs conflict with your emotional wants, it's often better to go with what you functionally need. You can always add the emotion later.

Furniture Shape.

After creating your layout, you already know the shape of your furniture from above. What you don't know is the shape from straight on, and determining it is super easy thanks to your muse.

If you pull out your muse sheet, you'll remember there's a section devoted to shapes associated with your muse. Those are the shapes you should use in your room — particularly, your furniture — because they are what will evoke the emotions you want to feel.

Now, when deciding how to use your shapes, keep in mind:

Curvy is often seen as romantic, sexy and sensual. Think of an hourglass figure.

CABINETS	height
Kitchen, base	34 1/2"
Vanity, base	31 1/8"
Kitchen, wall	12-36"

*the height of kitchen wall cabinets increases in 3" increments.

CHESTS	height
Bookcase	30"-89"
Dresser	27"-62"
Sideboard, Buffet	34"-38"
Armoire	58"-80"
Tallboy	54"-80"
Lowboy	29"-39"

TABLES	height
Dining, Rectangle	29"-30"
Dining Square	29"-30"
Dining, Round	29"-30"
Game, Poker	29"-33"
Drop Leaf	29"-30"
Console, Sofa, Hall	26"-32"
Desk	26"-30"
End	20"-30"
Nightstand	26"-30"
Coffee, Rectangle	13"-21"
Coffee, Square/Round	13"-21"

SEATING	back height	seat height
Sofa	24"-40"	18"-21"
Chaise Lounge	22"-40"	18"-21"
Love Seat	24"-40"	18"-21"
Settees	24"-40"	16"-21"
Chair-and-a-Half	24"-40"	18"-21"
Easy Chair	27"-40"	18"-21"
Club Chair	27"-40"	18"-21"
Slipper Chair	24"-40"	16"-20"
Dining Chair, Arm	30"-44"	18"-20"
Dining Chair, Side	30"-44"	18"-20"
Barstool	40"-47"	29"-31"
Counter Stool	35"-43	24"-27"
Ottoman, Rectangle		13"-21"
Ottoman, Square/Round		13"-21"

MATTRESSES	height alone	height with boxspring
California King	8"-14"	16"-23"
King	8"-14"	16"-23"
Queen	8"-14"	16"-23"
Double/Full	6"-14"	14"-23"
Twin	6"-14"	14"-23"

Use these measurements as a guide when creating your elevations. They're the dimensions typically found.

Rounded is often seen as playful, jovial and fun. Think of Santa Claus.

Straight is often seen as clean, simple, direct and straightforward. Think of the horizon or spreadsheets.

You can add those shapes to furniture in a number of ways. The shapes of furniture legs, headboards, drawers, chair backs, sofa backs, dresser bodies, armoire tops — the list goes on and on. The main thing you should focus on is the amount of each type of shape you use. The more of one emotion you want to feel, the more of that shape you should incorporate.

Of course, if you find it difficult to use the shapes you want in your room — such as curvy — don't stress. Like I've already said, there are a number of other ways — pattern, texture and color — to communicate emotions. Shape is just one. So if you can't communicate exactly what you want shape-wise, you can always make up for it in another way.

Once you've decided on the height and shape of each furniture piece, draw it in. Don't worry about making them look perfect. Your elevations are just supposed to give you a general idea. A rough, stick-figure, general idea.

it in, you must first determine its height and shape from the front.

Lighting Height

There are five things to consider when determining the height of your lighting: your room size, lines of sight, vanity, functional needs and emotional needs.

ROOM SIZE. Most of the time, the height of the lighting is proportional to the height of the room. However, extra tall chandeliers and pendants can be used in rooms with super high ceilings to fill the dead space. Abnormally tall table lamps can be used to fill extra space or draw the eye up.

LINES OF SIGHT. Lighting can block your view just as much as furniture. If you have any chandeliers, pendants or table lamps in the center of your room, don't place them so that they block your lines of sight.

VANITY. You've probably heard interior designers say "never use overhead lights," and it's all for vanity reasons. Overhead lights cast ugly shadows on our faces.

To look your best, your lighting should be between face level and 45 degrees above, and off to the side. If your lighting is directly overhead, you'll get terrible raccoon eyes.

Of course, having perfectly flattering light isn't always possible. Recessed lights are necessary in some rooms. But chandeliers, pendants, table lamps and sconces can all be positioned at a flattering height.

To determine that height, figure out whether you'll be standing or sitting near that light. Then, based on where your head will be, determine the sweet spot from straight across to 45 degrees up. Your light should be positioned in that range to look your best.

FUNCTIONAL NEEDS. There are four things to consider when it comes to function and lighting.

The first is brightness. The further a light is away, the less bright it appears.

The second thing to functionally consider is blockage. If you hang your lighting too low, you won't be able to see. And

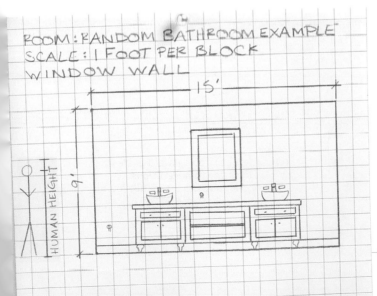

a chandelier isn't exactly what you want to see when you're sitting across the table from someone. Now, while no one hangs their chandelier that low, there are some people who don't mind having a dining room chandelier block people's view across the table while standing up. That's because it instigates people to sit down and makes the room feel cozier. So carefully consider what views you do and don't mind having blocked by lighting.

The third thing to functionally consider is walking room. If you have a hanging light over a walkway, you — and any very tall people who come to visit — must be able to walk under it. Preferably, without ducking.

The last thing to functionally consider is glare. If you place fixtures that point up — like sconces — below eye height, you'll get blasted by the exposed bulb.

EMOTION. How much your lighting blocks your view greatly affects how your room feels. If you have a chandelier, pendants, table or floor lamps partially obscuring the view, your room will feel cozy, intimate and maybe even a bit mysterious. If your lighting doesn't block your view at all, your room will feel open and airy.

When determining the height of your lighting, remember, you can always add emotion later through pattern, texture and color. So if your functional needs conflict with your emotional wants, it's better to go with what you need functionally.

To see the standard heights ceiling fixtures are typically hung above things, look below.

STANDARD LIGHTING HEIGHTS

In an Entrance	78"-84" high
Above a Table	30" or higher
Above a Countertop	30" or higher
Sconces	60" high, at least

Lighting Shape

Deciding the shape of your lighting from the front works exactly like deciding the frontal shape of your furniture. If you need a refresher, flip to page 233. Otherwise, let your muse be your guide.

Remember, chandeliers, pendants, lamps, sconces and lampshades come in a variety of shapes. Cones. Cylinders. Squares. Rectangles. Flared. So don't think you're limited to the standard circle.

Once you've determined the height and shape of each light, draw them in. And again, don't worry about making your drawings look perfect. A rough idea is all you need.

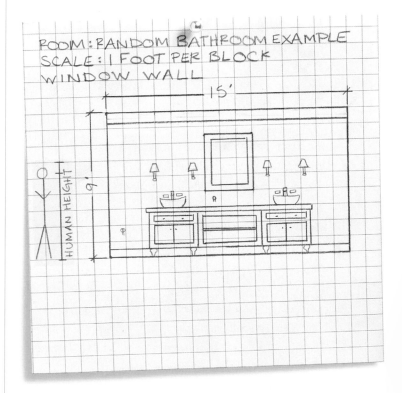

ROOM: RANDOM BATHROOM EXAMPLE
SCALE: 1 FOOT PER BLOCK
WINDOW WALL
15'
HUMAN HEIGHT

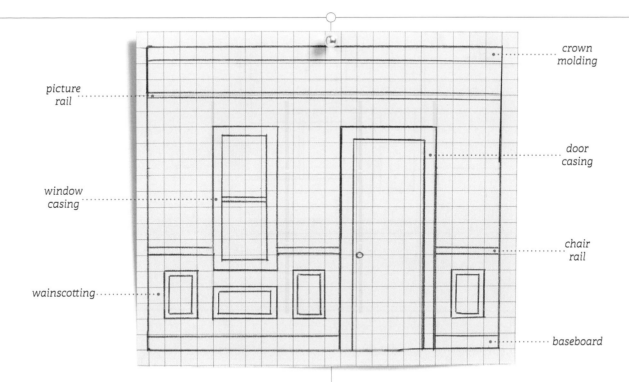

picture
rail

window
casing

wainscotting

crown
molding

door
casing

chair
rail

baseboard

STEP 4: DRAW IN ARCHITECTURAL DETAILS

Before you can draw in the architectural details, you must determine four things. First, which architectural features to use. Second, what they'll look like. Third, their size. And finally, the type used throughout your home.

Which Architectural Features to Use

The architectural features in a room can be broken down into two categories. The ones necessary for your room to *function* — doors, windows, fireplaces and structural beams and columns. And the purely *decorative* — moldings and faux beams and columns.

The number of necessary architectural features you need is easy to figure — just look at your layout.

It's the purely decorative features that you get to pick and choose. When determining which to use, there are three things to consider: your space shape, style and emotional needs.

SPACE SHAPE. If you remember when we discussed those tricks to make your space appear taller, shorter, thinner and wider, a handful of them had to do with the type of decorative molding you use — specifically tricks 5, 9, 15 and 16. If you were planning to employ any space-changing trickery, flip to page 200 to see what type of molding will suit your room best. And remember, there are many ways to fool the eye into thinking a space is a different size. The way you use molding is just one. So don't feel as though you must use it to make your space appear the size you want it to appear.

YOUR STYLE. If you look at your style sheet, there's a special section devoted to moldings. You should have listed the types commonly used in the rooms you liked. Use that as your guide to help you decide which type of decorative moldings to use. If you need help remembering which are which, take a peek at the diagram above.

YOUR EMOTIONAL NEEDS. The amount of moldings you use depends on how you want your room to feel. Typically, the more decorative molding you use, the more formal, ornate, interesting or tailored your room will look. Whereas, the less you use, the more casual, simple and clean your room will look.

Keep in mind, the emotions communicated depend greatly on the ornateness of the individual moldings. The more ornate the moldings, the less you need for your room to feel formal. The simpler the moldings, the more you can use and still have your room feel casual.

How Your Architectural Features Should Look

There are two things to consider when it comes to how your architectural features — both necessary and purely decorative — should look: ornateness and pattern.

ORNATENESS. The more ornate your architectural features, the more grand, formal and tailored your space will feel. Think of mansions and palaces. Their intricately-carved moldings make them feel opulent.

Now, the more minimal and plain your moldings, the more clean, simple, pure, raw and casual your room will feel. Think of farmhouses. They have very few moldings, which gives them a humble, simple feel.

To determine how ornate your molding should be, look at your style sheet. There's a special section labeled ornamentation. Underneath it, you should have listed the amount you want. Use what you wrote, coupled with your emotional needs, to choose the amount of ornateness in your room.

PATTERN. We're accustomed to seeing the standard molding, which is linear in style with a a bunch of graduated ripples. However, that is not the only type of molding available. You can choose molding that is:

Flat with no pattern at all.
Beaded with tiny dots running along it.
Fluted with linear grooves cut into it.
Geometric with linear designs like a Greek key.
Botanical with leaves, grapes or flowers carved into it.

Roped with an interlacing pattern.

Those are a few of the more common types. The ones you choose will depend on both your muse and style. Look at the pattern and shape sections on both your muse and style sheet. Use what you've written underneath each of those sections as your guide when deciding which type of pattern to use on your molding.

The Size of Your Architectural Features

There are two things to consider when determining the size of your architectural features: proportion and emphasis.

PROPORTION. Typically, architectural features are sized to be proportional to the room. So the taller the room, the taller the crown molding, base molding, windows and doors. The shorter the ceiling, the shorter the crown molding, base molding, windows and doors.

However, if under your visual grammar you plan to have things out of proportion to evoke either a cute, whimsical, grand or quaint feeling, you may want your architectural features to follow suit.

EMPHASIS. The larger your architectural features, the more prominent they will appear. So if you want them to be a focal point — such as a fireplace — you'll want the architectural features to be big enough to catch the eye.

The Architectural Features Used in Your Home

Typically, the same exact architectural features are duplicated throughout an entire home to create a sense of unity between the rooms. Now there are some exceptions. Architectural features such as fireplace mantles, columns and beams may only be seen in one room because they're only needed there. But when it comes to architectural features needed in every room — like doors, windows, base molding, case molding and crown molding — typically the same exact type is used throughout the home.

Of course, you don't have to do that. If you don't care

about your home looking like a unified package, then do whatever you want. But if you do, then you must decide whether to use the optimum molding for your room — which you just pinpointed — or use what you already have.

Keep in mind, you can always change the molding throughout your home to whatever you prefer. Or you can use special doors or windows in just one room to set it apart and make it a bit more special than everywhere else.

If the ideal architectural features are what you already have, consider yourself lucky. But if they're not, and you decide to skip using the ideal features, you must inject the emotions it would have communicated through something else in your room — pattern, texture, color or furniture.

Once you've decided upon what type and how many architectural features to use, draw them in.

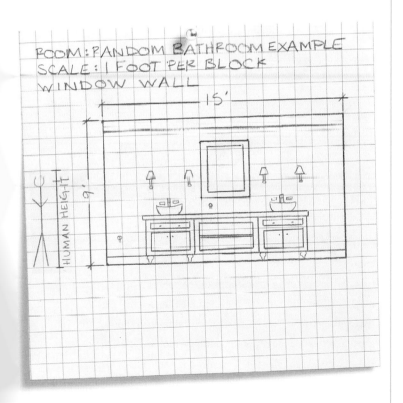

STEP 5: DRAW IN WINDOW TREATMENTS

Before you can start drawing in window treatments, you must first establish two things. One, whether or not you actually need them. And two, which type you'll use.

Whether You Need Window Treatments

Contrary to popular opinion, window treatments aren't mandatory. I grew up in a home with practically none, and if you flip through the pages of shelter magazines, you'll find bare windows from time to time. But you only get away with that if you don't need them. And I'm talking about both functionally and emotionally.

FUNCTIONAL NEEDS. If you remember, we discussed in the functional needs step (page 38 for those who don't) that window treatments are used for two reasons: light blockage and privacy. If you need window treatments for either of those reasons, it should be listed on your functional needs sheet.

EMOTIONAL NEEDS. If you don't functionally need window treatments, you may still emotionally need them. Windows with window treatments make a room feel cozier, warmer and more formal. Windows sans window treatments make a room feel open, airy and casual. Just keep in mind, some people find the look to be a bit cold — especially if they live in cold climates, because there's nothing encasing the winter landscape making it appear bundled up and warm.

Which Type of Window Treatment to Use

If you need window treatments, the type you use depends on five things: your space size, functional needs, emotional needs, style and window location.

SPACE SIZE. The type of window treatment you use can change how the size of your room is perceived. If you want your room to look wider, horizontal blinds — or any other type of window treatment that emphasizes the horizontal — is your best bet. Whereas, if you want to make your room look taller, drapes or vertical blinds should be your treatment of choice. Just remember, the longer the drapes or blinds, the taller your room will look. For optimum height, floor-to-ceiling is the ideal choice.

FUNCTIONAL NEEDS. If you need window treatments for privacy reasons, choose ones that fully block the view. Sheer drapes or curtains won't cut it. As for everything else? As long as it's opaque, it'll work great.

If you need window treatments for light blockage, the type of treatment you choose depends completely on how much control you want over the light. Blinds and shutters offer the maximum amount of control. You can completely block all light. Let in just a little by opening the slats. Let in a bit more by raising some of the slats up while leaving the others open. Or let the sun come blasting in by opening them all the way.

A combination of opaque drapes — which completely block the light — and a sheer drape or shade — which is transparent and allows light through — is your next best option when it comes to control. You can completely block the light by pulling the blackouts closed, let a little light in by closing the sheers or let the sun come blasting through by leaving both sets open. Keep in mind, using just the sheers gives you soft, diffused light — which many people enjoy.

Falling in a close third are opaque shades, which allow the same amount of control as a combination of drapes. You can completely block the light by pulling the shades down, let some light in by pulling the shade partially up, or allow the sun to come blasting in by letting it all the way up. But you won't get the soft, diffused light.

EMOTIONAL NEEDS. All window treatments — regardless of type — will feel more or less formal and cozy depending on the type of material you use. But in general, these are the emotions each one evokes. Just keep in mind, there are always exceptions.

Drapes tend to be seen as the most formal, luxurious and cozy of all window treatments due to the large amount of fabric needed. They're also seen as the most sensual and romantic of the window treatments, and the longer they are, the more sensual and romantic they appear — especially if they pool on the floor.

But that doesn't mean drapes can't look streamlined or sophisticated. Drapes hung perfectly straight that stop right above the floor are seen as both tailored and crisp.

Curtains tend to be seen as casual and cute, because they lack the drama of drapes yet still have their supple nature — which makes them short and sweet.

Blinds tend to be seen as sleek and straightforward because they're composed of numerous straight lines. Some people find that look a bit busy, which is why they prefer shades.

Shades tend to be seen as clean, casual and simple because they're typically plain when pulled down and practically invisible when let up.

Shutters tend to be seen as streamlined, yet romantic. The streamlined nature comes from the numerous straight lines. The romantic part stems from being able to throw them open like French doors.

If you want a combination of emotions, you can always layer different types of window treatments together. Drapes with blinds. Shades with drapes. Curtains with shades. Blinds with curtains. The more window treatments you layer, the more cozy your room will feel.

STYLE. If you look at your style sheet, there's a special section devoted to window treatments and under it you should have listed the types of window treatments commonly used in the rooms you loved. More than likely, those are the types you'll like best in your room. So use what you wrote on your style sheet as a guide.

SHAPE. On both your style and muse sheet there is a section devoted to shape. If under those sections you have "curved" or "rounded" listed, then drapes and curtains with a tieback — or ballooned shades, may be your best bet. If you want straight, all types of window treatments will work.

Just choose the versions of each that are straight.

WINDOW LOCATION. While it should go without saying, drapes should not be used on windows above sinks or bathtubs. Water and fabrics don't mix, plus there's a countertop in the way of the floor.

They also shouldn't be used above a radiator, because they're a fire hazard. Now, if you have to have them, you can install slightly shorter drapes that hang above the radiator — or space them from the wall a good distance away from the radiator.

Also, if your window is out of arm's reach, choose a window treatment that either has an accessible cord or a remote control that allows you to move it with the press of a button.

Once you've decided whether to use window treatments and what type you plan to use, draw them in. Keep in mind, you don't have to use the same type of window treatment on every window. For one, you can't always use the same type on every window. Not to mention, if you don't want a high amount of repetition in your room, mixing it up is a good thing

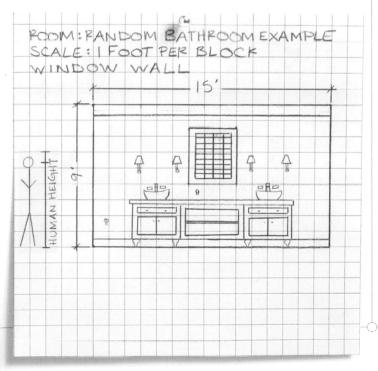

STEP 6: DRAW IN MIRRORS

There's a reason designers love mirrors. They're magical. Truly magical. They allow you to see yourself, make a room appear bigger, make your room appear brighter and add a dose of glitz and glamour.

ALLOW YOU TO SEE YOURSELF. You'd have to be living under a rock not to know that if we stand in front of a mirror our image will be reflected. But what's not so widely known is where we need to see our image.

The obvious places are bathrooms, bedrooms and closets — where we make sure we look okay and that nothing embarrassing is stuck to us. But mirrors are also nice to have in entrance halls so that you can check yourself — again for embarrassing situations — before answering the door, and so that guests can check themselves before leaving. Some people also like having a mirror by the back door for the same reasons.

If you need a mirror in order to see yourself, make sure you select one that is big enough to see everything you want to see — full body, waist high or shoulder high — and position it so that you can actually see all those things. A mirror does absolutely no good if you have to bend down or stand on your tippy toes just to be seen.

Also, be sure to consider where people may not want a mirror. For example, a full length mirror opposite a toilet can be a little disconcerting. And if you suffer from nightmares — or freak out easily — you may want to avoid placing a mirror directly opposite your bed.

MAKE YOUR ROOM APPEAR BIGGER. The ultimate way to make your room appear bigger is to cover a large part or entire wall in mirror. It fools your eye into thinking the room continues beyond, which creates the illusion of far more space.

Just remember, whatever you put up against the mirror will be reflected. So if you truly want to trick the eye, select items that appear to be cut in half. Like half moon tables and lamp shades. The reflection will fill in the other half, making them look circular.

MAKE YOUR ROOM APPEAR BRIGHTER. Mirrors magnify the amount of light in a room. Of course, that only happens if the mirror is opposite the light. When it is, your room appears brighter, because the mirror reflects the light making it appear as if there is more in the room.

And that doesn't work with just flip-the-switch lights. If you put a mirror opposite a window, it will reflect the sunlight, making your room appear brighter during the day.

Now keep in mind, the bigger your mirror, the more light it will reflect. And the more light it reflects, the brighter your room will appear.

ADD A DOSE OF GLITZ AND GLAMOUR. Mirrors are like diamonds. When they reflect light, they sparkle. And sparkly things make us feel glamourous. That's why mirrored furniture was so popular in Hollywood. It brings glitz and glamour to a room.

Of course, many things can achieve that effect — such as polished metal or shell. Mirrors are just one of them.

If you decide to use a mirror, there are three things you must determine before drawing it in. Its shape, size and whether or not you'll use a frame.

SHAPE. Mirrors come in all different shapes. The most common are square, rectangular, oval and circle. You can find curvy ones as well, just as you can find some cut in the shape of stars, hearts, flower and butterflies. Basically, whatever shape you want, you can get.

To determine what that is, use the shape sections of your muse and style sheets as your guide. Whatever you wrote down will be a good option. Keep in mind that if you have two different types of shapes written down, and have already used a lot of one, it might be a good time to inject a bit

of the other.

SIZE. The size of mirror you use will depend on both why you're using it and where you're hanging it. As far as use goes, refer above to see how big it needs to be to create the effect you want.

When it comes to where it's hung, remember if you want it to appear proportional, it should be roughly 2/3 or 1/3 the size of the available space of the item it's above.

FRAME. You don't have to use a frame. Going frameless provides an extremely minimal, clean look. But if that's not what you're going for, then using a frame will be your best bet. And when it comes to frames, they work just like moldings. The more ornate, the more formal, grand and luxurious your room will feel. The less ornate, the more casual, simple and pure your room will feel.

Don't worry now about drawing exactly how your frames should look. All you need is a rough idea of its thickness. The thicker the frame, the more prominent it will be. So if you want the design of the frame to really stand out — whether ornate or not — then you'll want a thicker frame.

Once you've decided on the shape, size and frame of your mirror or mirrors, draw them in. When placing your mirrors, keep in mind they don't need to be centered. Granted, that's what most people do. But if you chose asymmetrical balance and want your room to feel more flowing and less precise, feel free to put it off to the side or have multiple small mirrors staggered. Just remember, if you do that, balance it with something else to the side.

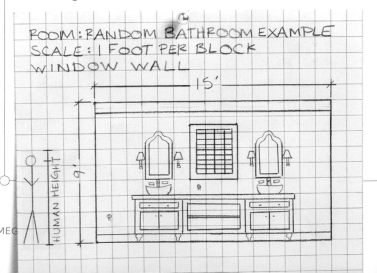

STEP 7: DRAW IN HOOKS, BARS & SHELVES

If your functional or storage needs sheet had hooks, bars or shelves listed for storing items — such as towels, coats, hats or keys — now is the time to draw them in. Remember, they must be high enough so your items don't drag on the floor. Also, keep in mind hooks and bars between hip and head high are easiest to use. Any higher and lower and we need to bend over or reach too far.

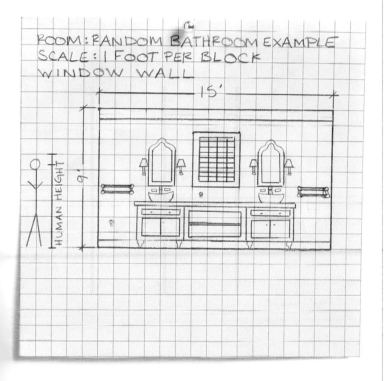

STEP 8: DRAW IN WALL ART

If you have any empty wall space that you don't want saved as white space, now is the time to fill it with art. Wonderful, evocative art.

1. Select Your Art

When most people think of art, they immediately conjure up an image of a painting or photograph. But that's just the tip of the iceberg. Tapestries, fabric, sculptures, hats, scarves, medallions, specimens — anything that can be hung can be used as wall art. So don't limit yourself to only flat things on paper or canvas. Wall art comes in many forms. When choosing which form to use, there are two things to consider: size and emotion.

SIZE. The size of your art does two things. One, it influences how much attention people will give it. The bigger it is, the more attention it will get.

Two, it communicates emotion. The bigger your art, the more grand and important it will feel.

EMOTION. Of all the things we put in our rooms, nothing has the ability to evoke as powerful of an emotion as art. Because art is solely emotional. There's nothing functional about it. So artists don't even have to think about function. Instead, they can focus solely on emotion — which means they don't have to make any compromises when creating. As a result, you end up with pure, raw, perfectly communicated emotion. Emotion far more intense than any functional object could communicate.

That's why people have such strong reactions to art, and why you must be extremely careful to choose a piece that perfectly communicates what you want to feel. Being off even slightly is enough to completely change the mood of the room. That's how strong of a communicator art is.

Now, I'm not saying this to make you afraid of choosing art. I simply want to stress the importance of being selective and listening closely to your gut. It will tell you which pieces are right. They'll be the ones you instantly fall in love with. And if there's no love, it's not the right piece.

But for now, you don't have to worry about picking the perfect piece. You just have to narrow it down to a category.

Will it be a thing? If so, what? Keys? Vintage snowshoes? Horns? Quilts? Pottery?

Will it be a painting, drawing or photograph? If so, what? A landscape? A person? An item?

For some guidance, look at the accessories and art section of your style sheet. Chances are what you have written are the types of art you'll enjoy most.

2. Choose Where to Place Each Piece

When placing art, there are four things to consider. The amount of space in front of the piece, how high you hang it, the amount of light nearby and your visual grammar cocktail.

SPACE. The bigger the piece, the further away you have to stand to be able to see the entire thing. That's why hanging huge pieces of art in tiny spaces isn't a good idea. Just think of a 17-foot-long painting hung on the side of a three-foot wide hallway. You'd never see the whole thing at once — even if you plastered yourself against the opposite wall.

HEIGHT. For art to be easily enjoyed and appreciated, it should be hung at eye level. That way, it's the first thing you see. If you hang art higher or lower, you must tilt your head to see it. The more you have to tilt your head, the harder it is to appreciate, because you're seeing it at an angle.

That's not necessarily a bad thing. If you want the art to just set a tone — not be appreciated — you can hang it at any level you please. Just remember, the further away it is from eye height, the harder it is for people to see it clearly.

As for where eye level is, it changes from person to person. So hang it at your eye level — or an average of the heights of those who most often use the room.

LIGHT. Art is a bit contradictory when it comes to light. You must have enough of it in order to appreciate your art. That means all art should be placed in a well lit area. But if it's the wrong type of light — *ahem*, the UV rays of the sun — it will damage it.

If you don't own expensive art, having it fade over time may not be the end of the world. So feel free to put it next to a window. But if your art is priceless, you have two options. One, keep it far away from any natural light. Or two, have it framed behind special glass that protects it from UV rays. That way, you can place it wherever you want.

VISUAL GRAMMAR COCKTAIL. Your visual grammar tells you three important things when it comes to placing your art. Your balance preference tells you whether you should hang it centered or off-centered. Your proportion preference tells you whether or not it should be proportional to the space where it's placed. And finally, your white space preference tells you how close it should be placed to other objects in your room.

3. Arrange It

If you decide to hang multiple pieces of art in a grouping, you need to know how to arrange it. Lucky for you, you already know how to do it. Each element of your visual grammar cocktail tells you one part of how your arrangement should be spaced and created.

Balance tells you whether your arrangement should be symmetrical or asymmetrical.

Proportion tells you how each piece should be sized compared to the others, if you plan to mix different sizes.

Proximity tells you how far apart each piece should be spaced. Remember, the closer they are together, the more they'll be seen as one object. The further away they are, the more they will be viewed individually.

Repetition tells you whether or not each piece should be the identical size and shape.

Contrast tells you how different the shape, frame — if there is any — and content of each piece should be. The more contrast, the more different. The less contrast, the more alike.

Movement tells you in what shape the pieces should be arranged. One that furthers the visual movement, like a straight line of photos down a hallway. Or one that hinders it, like a circular arrangement of photos in a hallway.

White Space tells you how much free space to leave around the arrangement so that it can be appreciated.

Finally, emphasis tells you whether you should have one piece more prominent than the others, or if they should all appear of equal importance.

So pull out your visual grammar cocktail to see what arrangement your concoction creates.

Once you've determined what art to use, where to place it and how to arrange it, you're ready to draw it in.

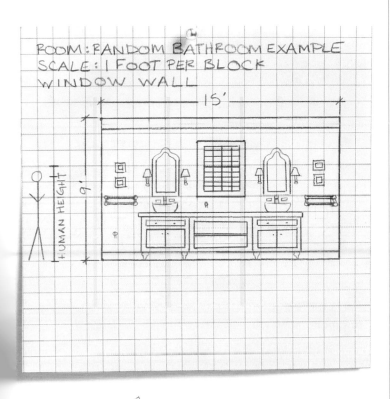

ROOM: RANDOM BATHROOM EXAMPLE
SCALE: 1 FOOT PER BLOCK
WINDOW WALL

Art doesn't have to be big.
Even small pieces
add interest,
and sometimes they're
exactly what
you need.

STEP 9: DRAW IN ACCESSORIES

We've finally reached the very last thing to add to your room — decorative accessories. Once you draw them in, you'll have a good idea as to how your room will look. So let's get to it.

Determine How Many Accessories You Want

The amount of accessories used in rooms varies widely. Some use practically none. Others use so many they're all you can see. Where you fall on the accessories spectrum depends on two things: how much emphasis you want, and which emotions you want to feel.

EMPHASIS. As you already know (or should from page 151, when you load your room full of stuff, it makes it hard to appreciate each individual item. So if you want to be able to see and appreciate each item in your room, use less accessories. There will be less things competing for your attention.

EMOTION. The more accessories you use, the more cluttered your room will look. And to most people, clutter feels cozy. Of course, everyone has their limit where too much stuff feels suffocating. But in general, the more accessories you use, the more cozy your room will feel. The less accessories you use, the more airy and open your room will feel.

Pick Which Accessories to Use

The accessories we use in our rooms can be broken down into four categories — functional, meaningful, emotional and perishable. In most rooms, you'll find a mix of them all.

FUNCTIONAL ACCESSORIES. Those are the accessories you need to complete your daily tasks. Like pen holders and letter sorters. Soap dishes and dish towels. Alarm clocks and telephones. Storage boxes and laundry baskets. And if you need any items like that, they should be listed either on your storage or functional needs lists.

Of course, all too often we forget about all those little things we need. So before moving on, brainstorm to see if there are other little things you need.

Use this sheet to list all of the functional accessories you need. Be sure to include the ones listed on your functional needs sheet as well.

When creating your list don't forget to include a wastepaper basket or cellphone charging station — if needed. They're the things people often forget to include.

8

drawing your elevations

FUNCTIONAL ACCESSORIES

ROOM:

DIRECTIONS: List the functional accessories you need in your room.

FUNCTIONAL ACCESSORIES :

8 drawing your elevations

FUNCTIONAL ACCESSORIES

DIRECTIONS: List the functional accessories you need in your room.

FUNCTIONAL ACCESSORIES :

(x2) desktop pen holder & pen

(x2) desktop notepad

(x2) keyboard & mouse

(x2) computer

(x2) mail sorter

(x2) phone

box/bowl/jar for post-its

box/bowl/jar for dry erase markers & eraser

box/bowl/jar for media scanning stickies

pen holder & pen for media scanning

baskets/magazine files for magazines

baskets/boxes for tapes

(x2) drinking mugs & coasters
⌐with lids

NEED MORE FUNCTIONAL ACCESSORIES? PRINT OFF EXTRA SHEETS AT:
TheMeghanMethod.com

MEANINGFUL ACCESSORIES. If you've lived long enough, chances are you've accumulated a number of deeply meaningful items. Photographs. Scrapbooks. Vacation mementos. Cherished gifts. Rather than hide those things away, many people like to keep them out as a reminder of happiness, hope and love. If you want a reminder of those things in your room, take some time to rummage through your stuff. Make a list of all the meaningful items you'd like to display. Then rank them according to which are most important to you. That way you know which to display most prominently. Plus, if not all can fit, you'll know which to cut and which to keep.

Now, I must mention that some people are against displaying more than a couple meaningful items in a room — especially family photographs. They say it makes guests feel like an outsider who is not part of the "cool" clique. And it may. But it's your home. You're the one who spends the most time there. So do what makes you feel happy. And if you're unhappy when guests are unhappy, then dial back on the personal photos and mementos. If you don't care if guests squirm a bit, then layer on as much as you want.

Gifts — even small ones like pen holders — and personal mascots — like octopuses — qualify as meaningful accessories.

8

drawing your elevations

MEANINGFUL

DIRECTIONS: List and ran

RANK: MEANINGFUL ACCESSORIES :

*To rank your meaningful accessories, use 1 for your favo

HAVE MORE MEANINGFUL ACCESSORIES? PR
TheMeghanMethod.co

MEANINGFUL ACCESSORIES

DIRECTIONS: List and rank the meaningful accessories you want in your room.

RANK:	MEANINGFUL ACCESSORIES :
2	Photo albums
3	Uncle J's painting
6	Inlay boxes from vacation
5	Shells found on the beach
4	Family photo
1	Granny's tureen

*To rank your meaningful accessories, use 1 for your favorite, 2 for your second favorite and so on.

EMOTIONAL ACCESSORIES. Those are the things you put in your room simply because they make you feel what you want to feel. They could be anything. A model ship. A candle. A sculpture. A specimen. A vase. A bowl. Absolutely anything you can dream up.

There are two ways to determine which accessories to use. The first is to think back to your muse. Brainstorm every item associated with your muse.

If your muse is a garden, you might say ceramic pots, baskets, fountains and wire. If your muse is the beach, you may say glass floats, seashells, coral, rope, glass bottles and model ships. Make a long list of items you associate with your muse. If you need a little brain push, look at what you wrote for the material section of your muse sheet.

You won't necessarily use all of the items, and you might not want to use them in their typical form. For example, let's go back to the garden. Instead of using the standard terra cotta ceramic pots, you may decide to use Chinese porcelain vases and urns.

You see, the idea isn't to perfectly replicate your muse. It's to use it as a guide as to what types of things and materials will evoke the emotions you want. Once you have your list created, go back through each item and see which ones you'd like to use, which you'd like to ditch and which you'd like to use as inspiration for something similar — like the pots.

The second way to determine which emotional accessories are right for your room is to look at your style sheet under the accessories section. The things you listed are the things you like, which means you'd probably enjoy having them in your room. To be sure each of those items communicate the emotions you want to feel, select a version in the materials you associate with your muse.

Get your own copy at: TheMeghanMethod.com

8

drawing your elevations

EMOTIONAL A

DIRECTIONS: List and ran

RANK: ITEMS ASSOCIATED WITH MUSE:

*To rank your emotional accessories, use 1 for your favori

If you listed items you don't want to u

HAVE MORE EMOTIONAL ACCESSORIES? PRIN
TheMeghanMethod.co

EMOTIONAL ACCESSORIES

HOME OFFICE
ROOM:

DIRECTIONS: List and rank the emotional accessories you want in your room.

RANK:	ITEMS ASSOCIATED WITH MUSE.	TRANSLATION FOR ROOM (if needed):
2	sea charts	antique maps
5	rope	woven baskets
10	sails	sailcloth/canvas pillows
4	ship pieces washed ashore	rough, wood boxes chunky, metal hardware
3	glass bottles	giant, glass jugs
9	glass floats	
1	sea creatures	antique specimen prints
11	shells	
6	coral	
8	sea fans	
5	seagrass	baskets
7	drift wood	

*To rank your emotional accessories, use 1 for your favorite, 2 for your second favorite and so on.

If you listed items you don't want to use, don't rank them.

PERISHABLE ACCESSORIES. Magazines depict an idealized version of life. One where there's fresh cut flowers in every room, colorful vegetables sitting in the sink, delicious scones and muffins and cupcakes always displayed under glass, and bowls of vibrant fruits scattered throughout the kitchen.

But that's not how it works in real life. For most, keeping that look is practically impossible. For one, it's expensive. Fresh-cut flowers and fruit don't come cheap. And two, it's a time drain. Baking fresh pastries every week — let alone every day — is enough to wear anyone out. And refilling and washing all those vases every week? Are you serious?

That's why it's very important to think long and hard before including any perishable items in your design, because they require upkeep. And if you don't want to deal with upkeep, they're not right for you.

Of course, if you're dead set on incorporating perishable items into your design because they perfectly communicate the emotions you want to feel, there are a few options that require minimal maintenance.

Fakes. There's massive controversy over whether it's okay to use fake flowers, plants and fruit in a room. Some think it's appalling because its inauthentic. Others find it wonderful because they're maintenance free. But like everything else with decorating, who cares what other people think? If you like fakes — if they make you happy — use them. If you hate fakes, don't.

A bowl of fruit or two — if you're a fruit lover. After all, many fruits need to sit out on the counter to ripen. And if you enjoy those fruits, you might as well display them in a pretty way. Just avoid making them the pivotal element that pulls your entire color scheme together. That is, unless you love that particular fruit and know it is always available. Also, avoid having too many bowls of fruit, or bowls that are too big. Most people don't eat that much fruit, and you'll end up with a bunch of rotten pieces you need to pitch.

Fresh pastries under glass. If you're an avid baker, then by all means bake away. But most of us aren't, so if you want your room to look like a pastry shop, you must be willing to buy fresh goodies each week — better yet, every couple of days — to keep your room looking stocked and inviting.

Houseplants. They're like fresh flowers, only they're often much cheaper and last far longer. Out of all houseplants, orchids tend to be the fan favorite because they require practically no maintenance, have fabulously beautiful blooms that can last as long as three months and cost very little compared to the equivalent you'd spend in three months worth of fresh bouquets.

Of course, there are many other spectacular blooming houseplants as well. Christmas cactus. Geraniums. Gloxinia. Hibiscus. Paperwhites. Narcissus. Just as there are many gorgeous green houseplants. Ferns. Palms. Citrus trees. Bonsai trees. Pothos. The list goes on and on. You've got tons of options when it comes to houseplants.

Just remember, when considering using houseplants, you must be willing to water them. They must have sunlight. They can't be too close to a heater. And they must be set in a pot or tray to keep them from leaking and damaging your furniture. If you can handle that, you can handle a houseplant.

Fresh flowers in a guest room. Let's be honest. A houseplant in a guest room is a recipe for disaster. Most people barely ever go in their guest rooms, which means the poor plant is bound to be forgotten and turn to a crisp. If you want a bit of greenery in your guest room, fresh flowers are your best bet. And considering most people don't have guests all that often, it won't dent the pocketbook much — especially if you keep the vase small or have a cutting garden.

Candy. Given that most candy has a fairly long shelf life, it's a great choice for those who want low maintenance.

Decanters. Like candy, alcohol has a fairly long shelf life, which makes it a great choice if you want low-maintenance.

Once you've decided what perishable accessories — if any — you'd like to have in your room, make a list.

8

drawing your elevations

PERISHABLE ACCESSORIES

ROOM: BREAKFAST SITTING

DIRECTIONS: List the perishable accessories you want in your room.

PERISHABLE ACCESSORIES I CAN MAINTAIN:

Plants → orchids

Fresh fruit → lemons, bananas

NEED MORE PERISHABLE ACCESSORIES? PRINT OFF EXTRA SHEETS AT:
TheMeghanMethod.com

Choose Where to Place Your Accessories

Functional accessories are extremely easy to place. They should be as close as possible to where you need to use them. A soap dish should be right next to the sink. If it's a doorstop, it should be right by the door. You get the idea.

It's the meaningful, emotional and perishable accessories that require extra consideration. When placing them, there are four things to consider: interference, visibility, concentration and your visual grammar cocktail.

INTERFERENCE. The last thing you want is for your accessory to get in the way. Whether that means hogging too much counter workspace, taking up all the foot space on an ottoman or blocking the view across the dining room table, it doesn't matter. If it gets in the way, people will be frustrated. I doubt that's what you want to feel in your room, so be sure to check that your accessories don't interfere with any of your room's activities.

VISIBILITY. The more important the accessory, the more prominent spot it should receive. That way, it will be easily visible, rather than hidden behind something else. As you plan where each accessory should go, place the most important ones first. Doing that ensures it will get one of the most visible spots in the room.

CONCENTRATION. If you plan on displaying a collection of like items such as coral, masks or vases — there are three ways to display them.

The first is to dilute their potency by evenly distributing them around the room. Doing that makes their emotional message more subtle and allows them to be enjoyed from more places in the room.

The second is to concentrate their potency by grouping them all together in one spot. Doing that creates a striking visual impact and intensifies the emotion evoked by each item.

The third option is to do a mix of both. Have one area devoted to the more — or less — spectacular of the items, and then dot the extras around the room.

VISUAL GRAMMAR COCKTAIL. Your visual grammar cocktail tells you three important things when it comes to placing your accessories.

Balance tells you whether your accessories should placed centered or off-centered.

White space tells you how close they should be placed to other objects in your room. Proportion tells you whether or not they should be proportional to the space where they're placed.

Now, if you want your accessories to be proportional, here's the main thing to remember. If they're on a table, they should be about 2/3 to 1/3 the size of their spot. If they're on a bookcase, they should be roughly 2/3 or 1/3 the size of their available spot. Just keep in mind that if all the items on your bookcase are only 1/3 the size of their space, the bookcase may appear a bit empty. But if that's what you want, go for it.

Arrange Your Accessories in Groupings

Just as with art, your visual grammar cocktail tells you exactly how to arrange your accessories in groupings. If you need a little refresher, flip back to page 244.

The only thing that is a bit different from art is movement. There are two main types of movement created with accessories. The first is a line, and the shape of the line depends on the height of the objects. If they're all the identical height, the line will point straight across. If they descend or ascend in height, the line will point either up or down. If the center item is tallest and the other items descend in height from the center, the line will point up like an arrow. If the items vary in height, the line will be curvy. Which line you choose depends on where you want to point people's attention. Up? Down? Right? Left? To the side?

The second type of movement is circular. It's created by having items of staggering heights grouped together so that the heights descend in a circular shape.

Now with both types of groupings — straight or circular

— people typically use an odd number of items. Three. Five. Seven. Because odd numbers look uneven, which causes our eyes to continue moving. Whereas, when things look even, our eyes feel as if they've completed their path and the movement tends to stop.

But honestly, you don't have to use odd numbers in your groupings. You can group as many items as you want together. As long as it looks good to you, that's all that matters.

Once you know how many accessories you want, which ones you plan to use and how you want to place them, you're ready to draw them in. If you're not 100 percent sure on what accessories, don't worry. You'll find something that wows you when you go shopping. For now, just wing it. Draw the rough shape you want the accessory to be — round, square, curvy, jagged — and make sure you draw it the correct size. That way, you'll have a rough idea of what you need when you start looking.

When drawing your accessories, don't be afraid to stack things. Books and boxes make great stands for short accessories you want to give a lift. Plus, when you stack things it makes your room look a bit more lived in. So if that's what you're going for, stack it up.

Oh, and don't worry about making your accessories look perfect. Your drawing just needs to give you a rough idea.

STEP 10: NOTE WHERE YOU'LL STORE ITEMS

Just like with your floor plan, you need to label where each item will be stored. Only this time, you need to be more specific. You need to know exactly what will be stored inside each drawer, behind each door, on each shelf, in each box, on each tray and in each bowl. That way, you know 100 percent that there's a place for everything in your room. Remember, that place should be easy to access.

Pull out your floor plan and use it to see what you planned to store where. Label on your elevations exactly where in those places each item will go. Take your time doing this. Remember to place each item as close as possible to where it will be used. Refer back to your storage preferences as far as where each item should be stored — a drawer, a box, on a peg, etc — and how much space it needs.

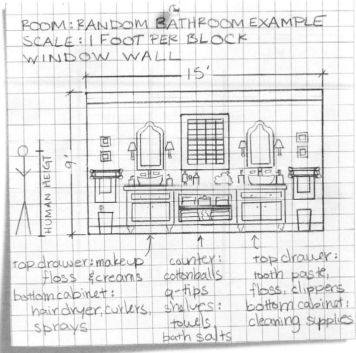

Be very specific about where each item will go.

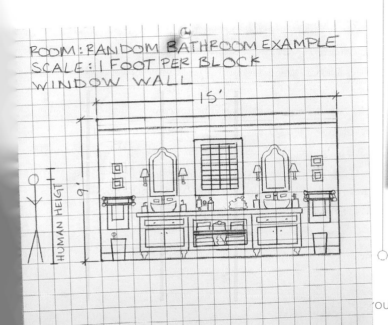

8

drawing your elevation

ELEVATION SCORECARD	ROOM:
DIRECTIONS: Rank how well your elevation fulfills each criterion.	

FURNITURE SHAPE:	☐ ideal	☐ less than ideal	☐ not ideal
FURNITURE HEIGHT:	☐ ideal	☐ less than ideal	☐ not ideal
LIGHTING HEIGHT:	☐ ideal	☐ less than ideal	☐ not ideal
LIGHTING SHAPE:	☐ ideal	☐ less than ideal	☐ not ideal
WINDOW TREATMENTS:	☐ ideal	☐ less than ideal	☐ not ideal
WALL ART:	☐ ideal	☐ less than ideal	☐ not ideal
ACCESSORIES:	☐ ideal	☐ less than ideal	☐ not ideal
LINES OF SIGHT:	☐ ideal	☐ less than ideal	☐ not ideal
VISUAL GRAMMAR:	☐ ideal	☐ less than ideal	☐ not ideal
OVERALL FUNCTIONALITY:	☐ ideal	☐ less than ideal	☐ not ideal
SUBTOTALS: Add up the total checks in each column.			

ELEVATION # ....
OVERALL SCORE:

To determine your overall score, multiply the number in the ideal column by 3, the less than ideal column by 2 and the not ideal column by 1. Then add the three resulting numbers together to get your elevation's score.

STEP 11: SCORE YOUR ELEVATION

It's time to score your elevation, and you do it the same way as you did with your layout. Only you have a different set of judging criteria.

STEP 12: DRAW AT LEAST 3 MORE

We've already been through this — page 169 — so it should need no explaining. Go back and create at least three more versions of each of your elevations. Remember, the more you create, the better.

STEP 13: PICK THE BEST ONE

As you know, the elevations with the highest score are not necessarily the best choice. So let your gut decide which one feels best. And remember, if you're not sure, walk away. If you're still not sure, ask for a second opinion — but only to help you determine how you really feel.

Then, if the one you like best isn't the one with the highest score, ask yourself if you're willing to sacrifice whatever it is the version you like is lacking.

If you are, you've got yourself a set of elevations. Hooray.

If not, then you should go back to the drawing board and see if you can create another version that satisfies what you want.

STEP 14: REDRAW YOUR ELEVATIONS

When you draw your elevations, it's important to know where all the things on your walls — light switchs, electrical outlets, baseboards, etc. — are located. That way you know what can go where. Only problem is we often block many of those things with furniture. So our elevations end up looking a bit messy. And messy is not good as we move on through the rest of the process. You need to be able to visual-

ize how your room will look. And having electrical symbols in the middle of your sofa and baseboards running through your cabinetry doesn't make that easy.

If your elevations look like that, redraw them the way you would see your room. If an electrical outlet would be covered, don't draw it. If the baseboards would be blocked, don't draw them. Only draw what you would see.

When you're finished, you should have a set of clean, crisp, beautiful elevations.

STEP 15: ADD TO YOUR LAYOUT

Now that you know what accessories will be in your room, you can add them to your layout. And don't think you can skip this part. Seeing where everything — both furniture and accessories — is in your room from a bird's eye view makes placing and balancing patterns, textures and colors around your room far easier.

So look at all the surfaces — tables, countertops, mantles — in your elevations. If there are items on them that you'd see from above, draw them into your layout. And don't worry about making it look perfect. A rough idea is good enough.

Then, look at all beds and upholstered furniture pieces. If you've put pillows, blankets, throws or anything else on them, draw it in on your layout.

Finally, look at the floor of your elevations. If you've added anything like floor vases or baskets, draw them on your layout.

To be sure you've added everything, give all your elevations one more look through.

When you're finished drawing everything in, you'll have a detailed overview of exactly how your room will look from above.

And you're finally ready to move on. At last.

ELEVATION SCORECARD

ROOM: GUEST BEDROOM

DIRECTIONS: Rank how well your elevation fulfills each criterion.

FURNITURE SHAPE:	☒ ideal	☐ less than ideal	☐ not ideal
FURNITURE HEIGHT:	☒ ideal	☐ less than ideal	☐ not ideal
LIGHTING HEIGHT:	☒ ideal	☐ less than ideal	☐ not ideal
LIGHTING SHAPE:	☒ ideal	☐ less than ideal	☐ not ideal
WINDOW TREATMENTS:	☒ ideal	☐ less than ideal	☐ not ideal
WALL ART:	☒ ideal	☐ less than ideal	☐ not ideal
ACCESSORIES:	☒ ideal	☐ less than ideal	☐ not ideal
LINES OF SIGHT:	☒ ideal	☐ less than ideal	☐ not ideal
VISUAL GRAMMAR:	☒ ideal	☐ less than ideal	☐ not ideal
OVERALL FUNCTIONALITY:	☒ ideal	☐ less than ideal	☐ not ideal
SUBTOTALS: Add up the total checks in each column.	10		

ELEVATION # 2

OVERALL SCORE:

30

To determine your overall score, multiply the number in the ideal column by 3, the less than ideal column by 2 and the not ideal column by 1. Then add the three resulting numbers together to get your elevation's score.

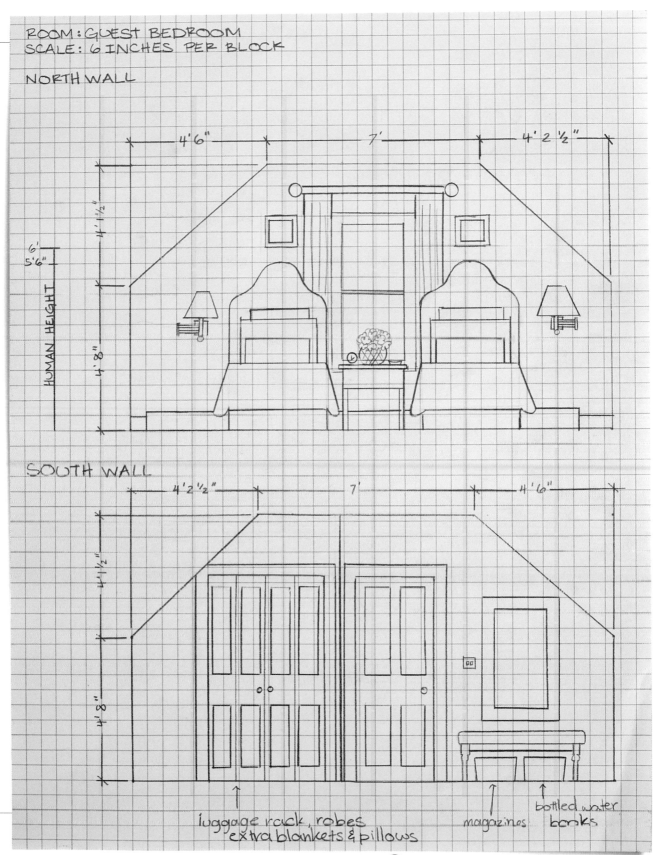

ROOM: GUEST BEDROOM
SCALE: 6 INCHES PER BLOCK

NORTH WALL

4'6"   7'   4' 2 ½"

4' 1 ½"

6'
5'6"

HUMAN HEIGHT

4' 8"

SOUTH WALL

4' 2 ½"   7'   4' 6"

4' 1 ½"

4' 8"

luggage rack, robes
extra blankets & pillows

magazines

bottled water
books

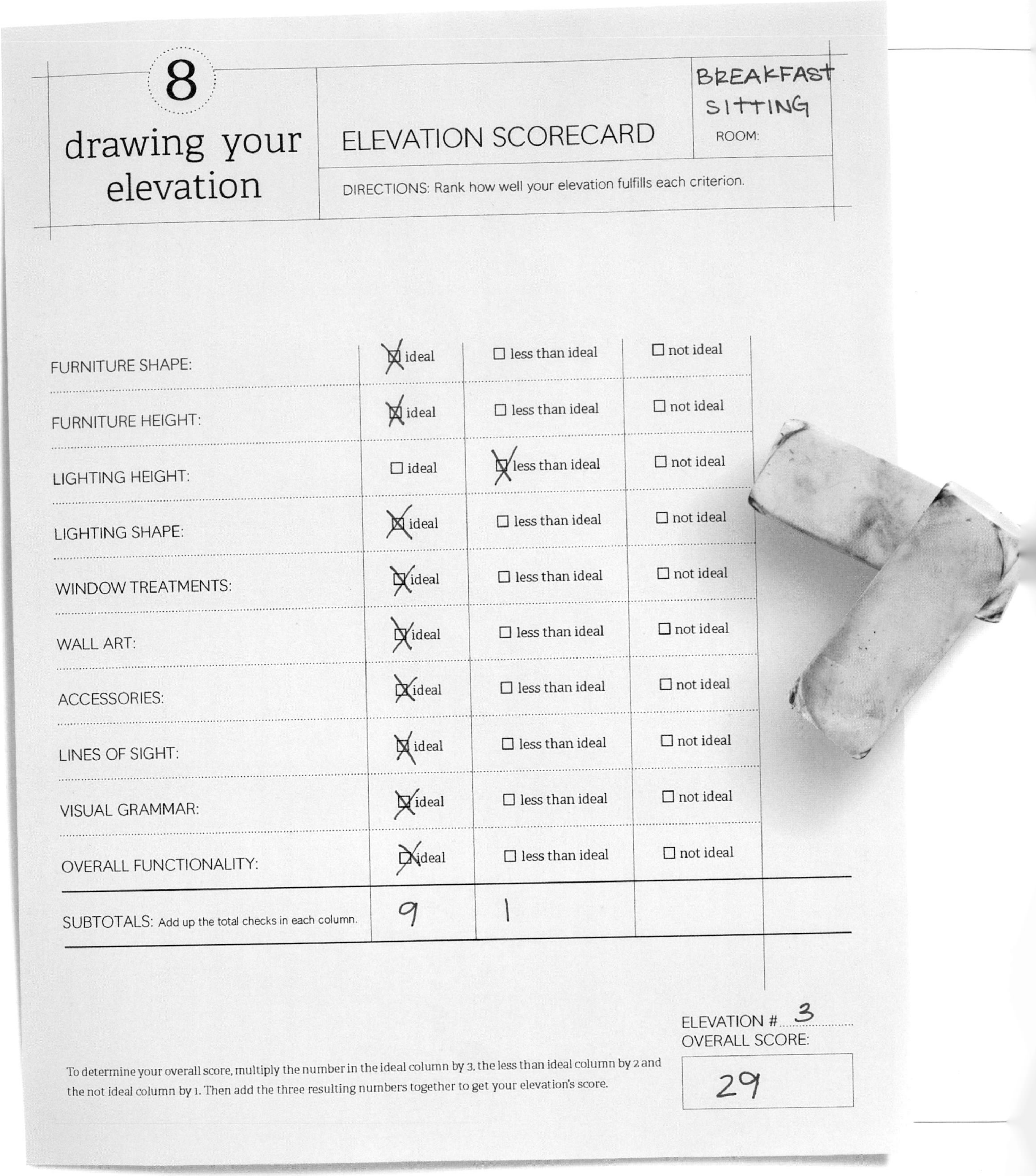

ELEVATION SCORECARD

ROOM: **BREAKFAST SITTING**

DIRECTIONS: Rank how well your elevation fulfills each criterion.

	ideal	less than ideal	not ideal
FURNITURE SHAPE:	☒ ideal	☐ less than ideal	☐ not ideal
FURNITURE HEIGHT:	☒ ideal	☐ less than ideal	☐ not ideal
LIGHTING HEIGHT:	☐ ideal	☒ less than ideal	☐ not ideal
LIGHTING SHAPE:	☒ ideal	☐ less than ideal	☐ not ideal
WINDOW TREATMENTS:	☒ ideal	☐ less than ideal	☐ not ideal
WALL ART:	☒ ideal	☐ less than ideal	☐ not ideal
ACCESSORIES:	☒ ideal	☐ less than ideal	☐ not ideal
LINES OF SIGHT:	☒ ideal	☐ less than ideal	☐ not ideal
VISUAL GRAMMAR:	☒ ideal	☐ less than ideal	☐ not ideal
OVERALL FUNCTIONALITY:	☒ ideal	☐ less than ideal	☐ not ideal
SUBTOTALS: Add up the total checks in each column.	9	1	

ELEVATION # **3**

OVERALL SCORE:

29

To determine your overall score, multiply the number in the ideal column by 3, the less than ideal column by 2 and the not ideal column by 1. Then add the three resulting numbers together to get your elevation's score.

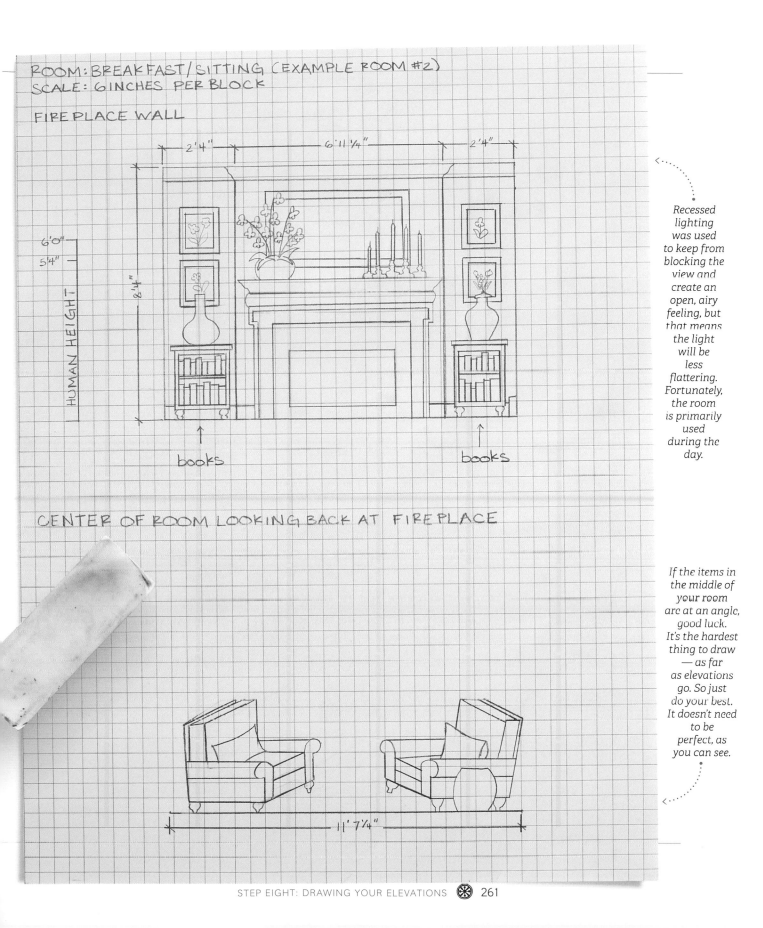

ROOM: BREAKFAST/SITTING (EXAMPLE ROOM #2)
SCALE: 6 INCHES PER BLOCK

FIRE PLACE WALL

2'4"   6'11¼"   2'4"

6'0"
5'4"
8'4"

HUMAN HEIGHT

↑ books   ↑ books

CENTER OF ROOM LOOKING BACK AT FIREPLACE

11'7¼"

Recessed lighting was used to keep from blocking the view and create an open, airy feeling, but that means the light will be less flattering. Fortunately, the room is primarily used during the day.

If the items in the middle of your room are at an angle, good luck. It's the hardest thing to draw — as far as elevations go. So just do your best. It doesn't need to be perfect, as you can see.

ELEVATION SCORECARD

HOME OFFICE
ROOM:

DIRECTIONS: Rank how well your elevation fulfills each criterion.

FURNITURE SHAPE:	☒ ideal	☐ less than ideal	☐ not ideal
FURNITURE HEIGHT:	☒ ideal	☐ less than ideal	☐ not ideal
LIGHTING HEIGHT:	☒ ideal	☐ less than ideal	☐ not ideal
LIGHTING SHAPE:	☒ ideal	☐ less than ideal	☐ not ideal
WINDOW TREATMENTS:	☒ ideal	☐ less than ideal	☐ not ideal
WALL ART:	☒ ideal	☐ less than ideal	☐ not ideal
ACCESSORIES:	☒ ideal	☐ less than ideal	☐ not ideal
LINES OF SIGHT:	☐ ideal	☒ less than ideal	☐ not ideal
VISUAL GRAMMAR:	☒ ideal	☐ less than ideal	☐ not ideal
OVERALL FUNCTIONALITY:	☒ ideal	☐ less than ideal	☐ not ideal
SUBTOTALS: Add up the total checks in each column.	9	1	

ELEVATION #: 1
OVERALL SCORE:

29

To determine your overall score, multiply the number in the ideal column by 3, the less than ideal column by 2 and the not ideal column by 1. Then add the three resulting numbers together to get your elevation's score.

To make the tall ceilings appear proportional to the room, decorative molding was added.

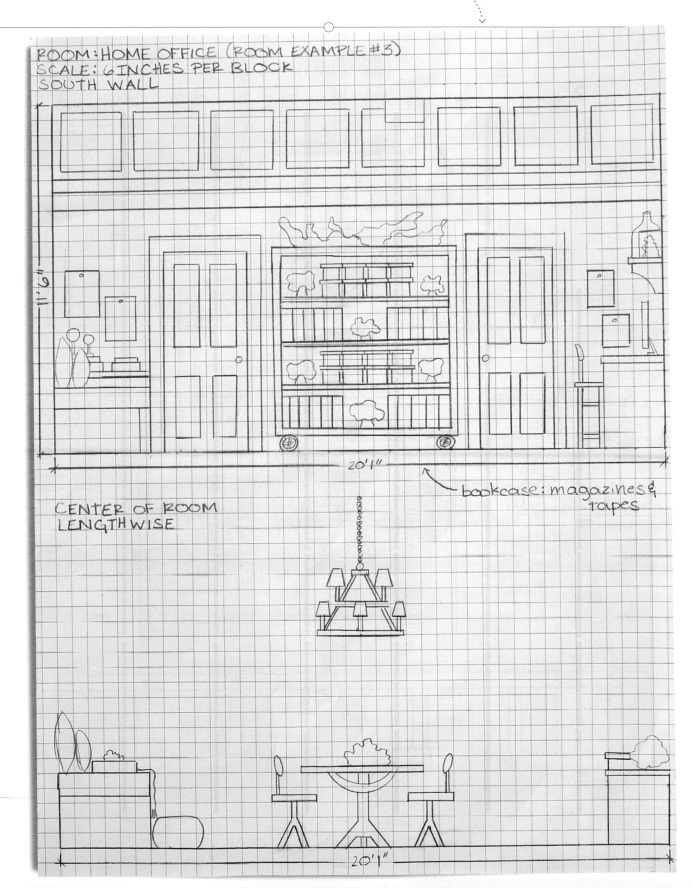

ROOM: HOME OFFICE (ROOM EXAMPLE #3)
SCALE: 6 INCHES PER BLOCK
SOUTH WALL

11'6"

20'1"

CENTER OF ROOM
LENGTHWISE

bookcase: magazines & tapes

20'1"

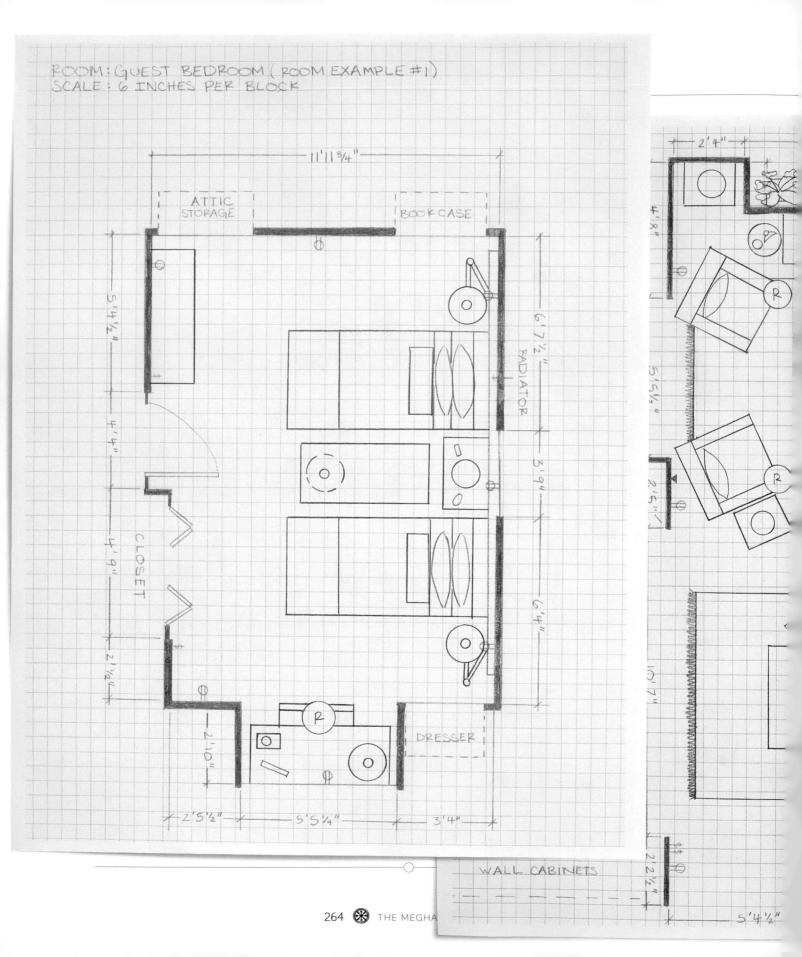

ROOM: GUEST BEDROOM (ROOM EXAMPLE #1)
SCALE: 6 INCHES PER BLOCK

ATTIC STORAGE

BOOK CASE

11' 11 ¾"

5' 4 ½"

4' 4"

CLOSET

4' 9"

2' 1 ½"

2' 0"

6' 7 ½"
RADIATOR

3' 9"

6' 4"

DRESSER

2' 5 ½"   5' 5 ¼"   3' 4"

2' 4"

4' 8"

5' 5 ½"

2' 5 ½"

10' 7"

WALL CABINETS

2' 2 ½"

5' 4 ½"

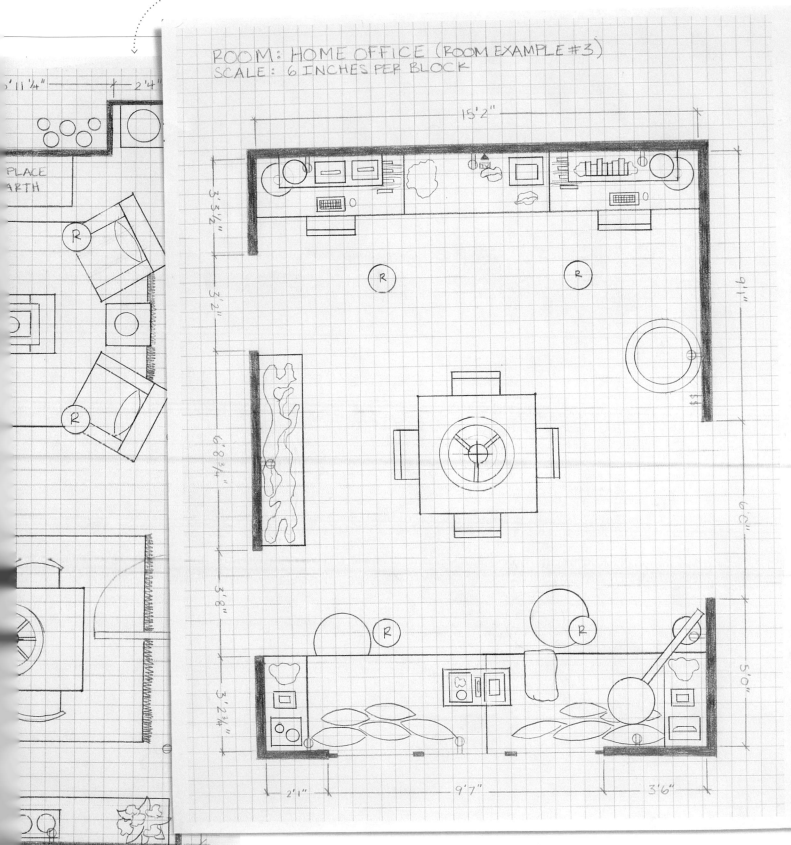

The layouts with accessories drawn in.

ROOM: HOME OFFICE (ROOM EXAMPLE #3)
SCALE: 6 INCHES PER BLOCK

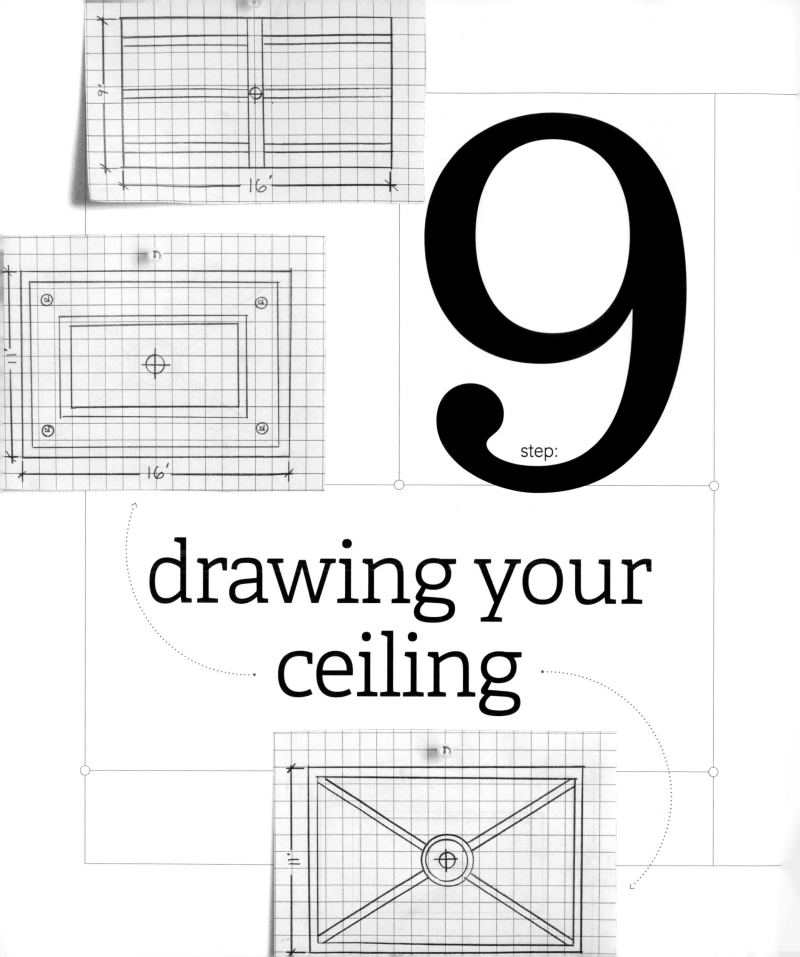

step:

9

drawing your ceiling

Most people figure it's a waste to decorate their ceiling because no one sees it. But that's not true.

When we first walk into a room, we see the ceiling in our peripheral vision. And regardless of what we see — something spectacular or blah — we carry that feeling with us when we're in the room. Think back to Cheskin and sensation transference. Page 48 for those who don't know what the heck I'm talking about.

That's why ceilings matter, because they affect how we feel in a room. And let me tell you, if a ceiling looks spectacular, people will notice. They'll look up and the positive emotions will linger on.

Very small spaces like bathroom ceilings don't matter as much, because it's harder to catch a glimpse of the ceiling in our peripheral vision. In those places, it may not be worth it. But in larger rooms and hallways, pay attention to your ceiling. You'll see it — especially in rooms like bedrooms where you lie down.

That's why it's important to create a ceiling layout. So let's get to it.

STEP 1: SET UP YOUR PAPER

You're not going to believe how easy this is. Simply redraw the shell you used for your layout. Better yet, if you have any leftover copies, use those.

If your ceiling is vaulted or sloped, draw lines to show the shape of the slope.

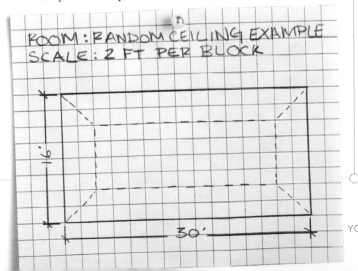

STEP 2: DRAW IN LIGHTING

Again, it couldn't be simpler. Just copy the lighting configuration you have on your layout.

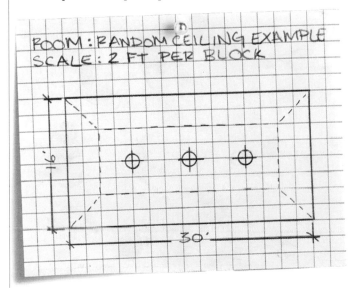

STEP 3: DRAW IN ARCHITECTURAL DETAILS

There are many ways you can decorate your ceiling. Cover it in patterned wallpaper. Paint it a solid color. Tile it. Stencil it. Put a mural on it. Add some architectural interest.

Of course, you don't have to do any of that. A plain, white ceiling may communicate exactly what you want in your room. Clean and simple. Plus, it doesn't detract attention away from everything else in your room.

If you do want your ceiling to have a bit of interest, or need to make your ceiling feel lower, then adding architectural details is a good choice. There are six main types you can add: medallions, molding, beams, tiles, planks or fabric.

Medallions. Ceiling medallions are typically round, decorative moldings used to frame a light fixture. The more ornate the medallion, the more formal and grand your room will feel. The less ornate, the more casual your room will feel.

Moldings. Typically, when people use moldings on their

ceiling, they use them to create a pattern. The most popular pattern is a grid pattern, which is referred to as a coffered ceiling. You can create any pattern you like. Diamonds. Rectangles. Circles. Stripes. A complex geometric. You name it, it can be done.

Beams. Ceiling beams can either run along the ceiling or be placed a foot or more away from the ceiling. Typically, people will use many beams running in the same direction. But you can do any configuration — like having a center beam run down the middle of your room with beams running perpendicular against it.

Ceiling Tiles. Ceiling tiles are often used in rooms such as basements where you need to access the electric and piping above. But you can use them anywhere. And don't think they all look ugly, either. You can find a wide variety of ceiling tile styles — including tin.

Planks. To give a ceiling texture, people will sometimes install beadboard planks, bamboo or old barn wood on their ceiling. Typically, when that's done, the entire ceiling will be covered like a floor.

Fabric. To give your ceiling a tent-like feel, you can have fabric hung on your ceiling. If the ceiling is super high, the fabric is sometimes hung so that it comes to a point in the center of the room, draping down just like a tent. If the ceiling is low, the fabric is typically scrunched together in pleats to give the ceiling texture since the fabric can't drape down.

Those aren't the only type of decorative ceilings you can have. You can have recessed ceilings and cathedral ceilings as well. But for those, if you don't have them, you must remodel. Whereas, the six choices above can be added to what you already have.

Keep in mind that if you choose one of those options, it must work with your lighting. You can't have a beam run halfway through a fixture. You need the light on the beam or in the white space of the ceiling.

If you need some inspiration before deciding on architectural details for your ceiling, do an image search for "decorative ceilings."

If you decide to go for it, along with some decorative detailing, draw it in.

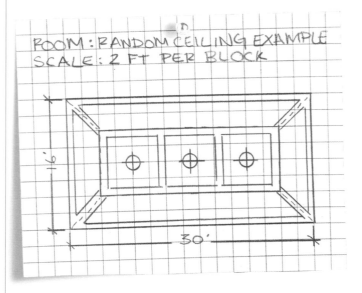

STEP 4: DRAW AT LEAST 3 MORE

You know the drill. If you decided to add architectural details to your ceiling, go back and create at least three more versions.

STEP 5: SELECT THE BEST ONE

When it comes to deciding which ceiling is best, it all comes down to gut. After all, a decorative ceiling fulfills no function. It's all about emotion. So look at your emotional wants. Which design feels the most like those emotions? If you're having a hard time deciding, walk away for a bit. Give your emotions time to bubble to the surface. If you still can't decide, ask for a second opinion. But remember, only to help you find your true feelings. Then, once you've made your decision, you're ready to move on.

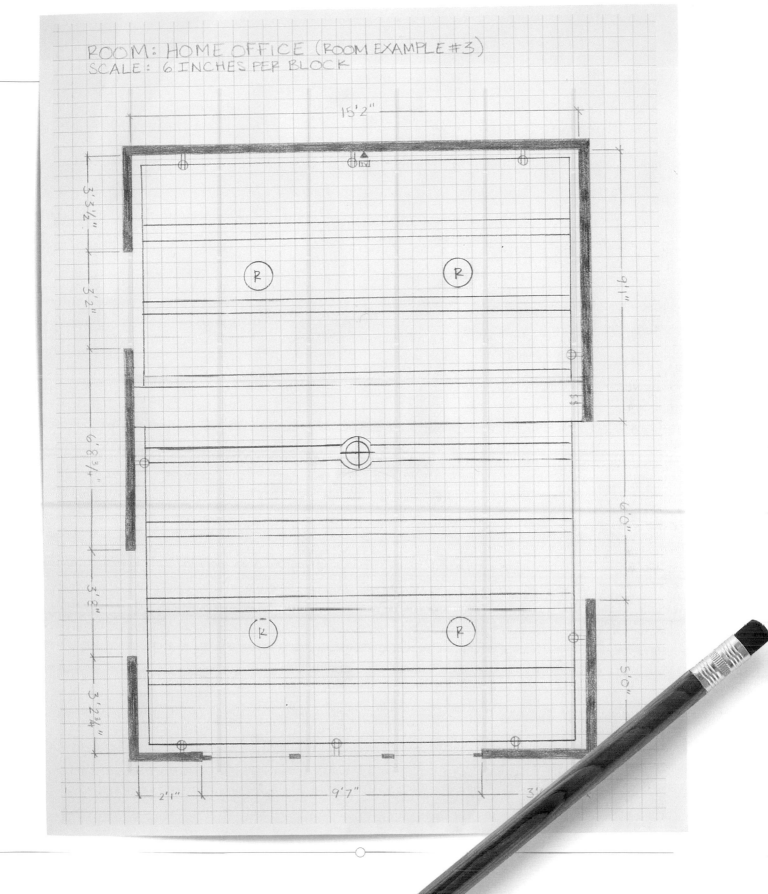

ROOM: HOME OFFICE (ROOM EXAMPLE #3)
SCALE: 6 INCHES PER BLOCK

step: **10**

adding
pattern

We're finally to the part of creating a plan that everyone loves. The icing stage, where we layer on pattern, texture and color. And first up is pattern.

Why? Because if you remember from page 133, pattern is an object in and of itself. It possesses all of the characteristics that make up an object: shape, color and texture. And you have to put all your objects into your layout before you can start picking their colors and textures. That's why pattern must be layered on first.

WHY USE PATTERN

Pattern — like texture and color — is used simply to communicate emotion. And of the three, it communicates emotion the most precisely.

Just think of the difference between orange and plaid. Orange can be seen as festive, fun, healthy, robust, energetic and a myriad of other emotions. Whereas, pattern is seen as either rustic or preppy, depending on the person.

Pattern's precision in communicating emotion stems from it being an object. It has three different characteristics to communicate emotion — shape, texture and color. Whereas, color and texture are only one characteristic. They only have themselves to communicate. That's why pattern has the upper hand in the precise department, because as you know — or should from page 120, the more characteristics you use, the more specific your message becomes.

So if you want the emotion in your room to be extremely obvious, clear and distinct, use pattern. Of course, not everyone wants that. Some people prefer having the emotion more vague and subtle, allowing how they perceive the emotion of the room to subtly change with their mood. That's why so many rooms are pattern-free.

TYPES OF PATTERNS

There are hundreds of different patterns, and when trying to select one, people often get overwhelmed by the sheer magnitude of options. But that's simply because they're looking at each pattern individually.

If you think of patterns in terms of categories, and first choose which type of pattern you want, you'll weed out tons of options — which makes selecting a pattern far easier.

Fortunately, if you were to take all the patterns in the world and classify them, you'd only have about 20 categories.

Now, I'll admit not every pattern in the world is represented by the categories on the next two pages. But practically all are. So the categories will give you a very good idea of what is available for your room.

As you look through them, keep in mind that some of the categories overlap. For example, Southwestern and Ikat could be considered ethnic. Jacobean could be considered a floral. Toile and Chinoserie could be consider pastoral.

Pattern categories are open to interpretation., and everyone has a different idea of what they are.

CHOOSING THE RIGHT PATTERNS

Which pattern — or patterns — you choose completely depends on three things: your emotional needs, stain concealment needs and room size.

Emotional Needs. Given that patterns communicate emotion, it only makes sense to choose your patterns based on what you want to feel. And lucky for you, you've already figured that out. That's why you dissected your muse and style — to determine which patterns communicate what you want to feel.

So look at the patterns and shape sections on both your muse and style sheets. What you've written under each of those categories should give you a head start when determining which patterns to use in your room.

toile

chinoiserie

damask

jacobean

botanical

floral

plaid

checks

paisley

chevron

animal print

ikat

ethnic

southwestern

novelty

abstract

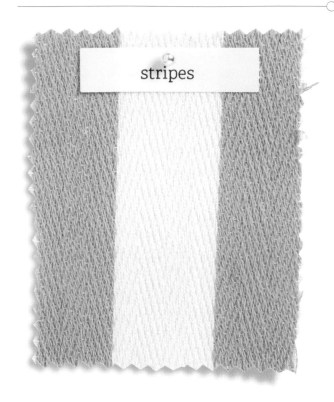

stripes

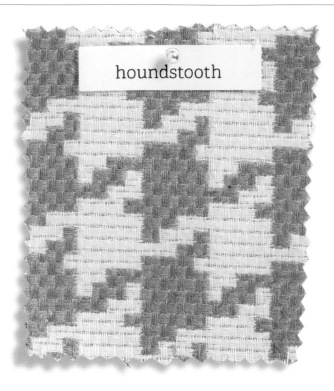

houndstooth

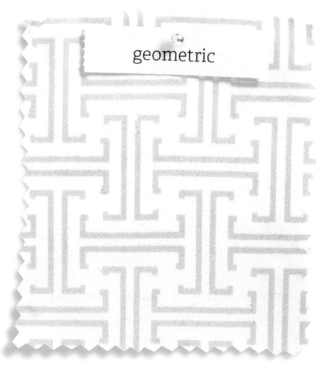

geometric

polka dot

Of course, don't feel like you must limit yourself to just those you listed. You may have forgotten a few. So if you find yourself drawn to another type of pattern and feel it communicates the emotions you want to feel, go for it. When picking patterns, always trust your gut.

Stain Concealment. There's an extra perk to using patterns in your room. They hide stains and wear. And the busier the pattern, the more it hides. That's because the more lines and colors there are, the harder it is to spot inconsistencies.

Think of "Where's Waldo." It's hard to spot him because there's so much other stuff on the page — just as it's hard to spot a stain on a complex pattern.

So if you don't want to worry about keeping the things in your room — like rugs, sofas and duvets — looking pristine, you may want to consider a busy pattern or two. Just keep in mind that pattern is not the only way to conceal dirt and wear. Texture and color can do that as well.

Room Size. If you want your room to appear a different size than it is, patterns are one way to do it.

Vertical patterns make a room appear taller (Trick 7, page 202). Horizontal patterns make a room appear wider (Trick 2, page 201). Pattern on your ceiling makes your ceiling feel lower (Trick 16, page 203). Pattern on your walls makes your entire room look smaller (Trick 25, page 204).

HOW TO MIX PATTERNS

Communicating through patterns is just like communicating through words. Sometimes you only need one to get across what you want to say. "Sweet." Other times you need a few, because what you want to say can't be communicated through just one word — or pattern — alone. "Sweet and handsome."

Of course, most people think pairing words is far easier than pairing patterns. But I assure you mixing patterns is very simple. All you need to think about is contrast.

As long as the patterns contrast enough for your eyes to easily tell them apart — but not so much that they have absolutely nothing in common — you're good to go. It's when patterns contrast too much or too little that they look bad together.

When there's too little contrast, our eyes have a hard time telling the patterns apart, which confuses our eyes. As a result, the patterns almost appear as if they're fighting with one another.

When there's too much contrast, the patterns have nothing in common. — not a shape, color or texture. So our eyes figure they don't belong together. As a result, we perceive them as out of place and visually jarring.

In both instances — too little and too much contrast — we describe the patterns as clashing because that's what they visually appear to be doing.

If you don't want your patterns to clash, all you have to do is make sure they have at least one characteristic in common — but not too many.

Typically, people do that by limiting themselves to only three patterns: one large scale, one medium scale and one small scale. But you don't have to do it that way. You can mix and match as many patterns as you want. You can even have multiple large, medium and small scale patterns if you want. As long as you stay somewhere in the middle of the contrast continuum, your patterns will look great.

CREATING YOUR PATTERN MIX

Where you fall on the pattern contrast continuum depends on what you want to feel. The closer you get to your patterns looking alike, the more artsy, eclectic and bohemian your room will feel. Because that almost-clashing-oh-so-similar look gives off the feeling that the patterns and pieces are part of a collection that has been cultivated over time. Not perfectly matched.

The closer you get to the middle of the continuum, the more clean, ordered and relaxed your room will feel, because in the middle the patterns go together perfectly, as if they were meant for each other.

The closer you get to your patterns contrasting completely, the more energetic, excited, fun and chaotic your room will feel. The high contrast causes your eyes to bounce around the room trying to figure out what's going on, which gives the room energy.

PLACING PATTERNS

When determining where to place each pattern in your room, there are five things to consider: desired emotional intensity, your room size, furniture size, stain concealment needs, and visual grammar cocktail.

Emotional Intensity. There are two things that affect the intensity of a pattern's emotional affect. The first has to do with amount. The more of a pattern you use, the louder it will scream its emotional message. Just think of the difference between a pillow covered in animal print and every single wall in your room. The pillow whispers exotic. Whereas, the room howls it. So the more you want of a particular emotion communicated by a pattern, the more of that pattern you should use.

If you find yourself wanting a large dose of a particular pattern, don't shy away. Trust your gut. People only tell you to paint walls and order upholstery in neutral because they assume you don't know what you want and will change your mind in the next few months.

But playing it safe like that doesn't communicate all emotions. Sometimes you need a bold sofa or wall, and since you've taken the time to figure out exactly what you want, you should feel secure going for it. Like I said, trust your gut. It won't lead you wrong.

The second thing that affects a pattern's emotional in-tensity is prominence. The more front-and-center a pattern is in your room, the stronger its emotional message will be, because you're placing emphasis on it.

Room Size. If you decided to use pattern to change the size of your room's appearance, make sure you put the right pattern in the right place according to the optical illusion you're trying to create. If your brain needs a boost to remember what that is, flip to page 200 and look for tricks 2, 7, 16 and 25.

Furniture Size. When you put a medium or large-scale pattern on fully upholstered pieces of furniture, it tends to disguise some of the 3-D aspects of the piece. The lines of the pattern make it hard for your eye to tell which lines are pattern lines and which are part of the furniture. As a result, the details of your piece can get a bit lost. So if you don't want to obscure the shape of your furniture's arms and cushions, you may want to save the larger, busier patterns for other items.

Cleaning Needs. As we just discussed, pattern has the wonderful ability to hide stains and wear. But that only works if you put pattern on the things that get stained and worn out — like seating, sofas, linens and floors. Remember, the busier the pattern, the more it hides.

Visual Grammar Cocktail. The elements of your visual grammar cocktail tell you four important things when it comes to placing patterns.

Balance tells you whether you should scatter your patterns symmetrically or asymmetrically around your room.

Repetition tells you how often you should repeat the same pattern in your room.

Contrast tells you how much your patterns should contrast with one another.

And movement tells you how you should place the same

patterns around your room in order to lead your eye from one place to another.

DRAWING IN YOUR PATTERNS

Now that you know how to select, pair and place patterns, it's time to draw them in. But before you do, make copies of your final layout with accessories drawn in, elevations and ceiling layout. That way you can create multiple drafts. Once you've got your copies, it's time to draw.

1. DRAW PATTERNS ON YOUR ELEVATION

Draw in the patterns you want in your room. Don't worry about making them look perfect. You just need the general idea. If you want a complex pattern like paisley or damask, just draw squiggly lines in a rough outline of the pattern.

If you don't want any patterns in your room, skip this part.

To see examples of patterns drawn on an elevation, turn the page.

2. DRAW PATTERNS ON YOUR FLOOR PLAN

Take out your layout. If you put any patterns on your furniture, draw those in. Then draw any patterns you want on your floor or rugs. Remember, the orientation of the pattern on your floor will affect how you see the room.

If you decide to use stripes, chevrons or any other directional pattern, the way you orient them will depend on three things. If you want your room to appear wider, position the pattern so that the horizontal lines run across your shortest wall. If you want to move the traffic forward, position the lines so that they point towards where you want people to go. If you want to add extra emphasis to an item, position the lines so they point your eyes straight to it.

If your pattern isn't directional in nature, you have nothing to worry about. Place it however you want.

And remember, pattern isn't used just on rugs. You can have a pattern painted or inlayed in your floor as well.

To see examples of pattern drawn on floor plans, turn the page.

3. DRAW PATTERNS ON YOUR CEILING LAYOUT

If you want pattern on your ceiling, draw it on your ceiling layout. Keep in mind that having pattern on a ceiling will make the ceiling look lower because pattern is so visually heavy. And the busier the pattern, the lower your ceiling will look.

Now if you want a pattern on your ceiling but don't want your ceiling to feel lower, you can counteract the heavy effect by making the pattern very light in color.

4. CREATE AT LEAST 3 MORE DRAFTS

You should know how this works by now. Don't settle on your first draft. Go back and make at least 3 more drafts. Test out different patterns and pattern arrangements.

5. CHOOSE THE BEST ONE

Put all the options you created in front of you, and ask yourself which one feels best. We're talking about gut instinct. And whichever one you gravitate to first is the one you should choose.

Now, if you have a hard time deciding, walk away for a bit. Give your emotions time to bubble to the surface. If you still can't decide, you know the drill, ask for a second opinion. But not to know what they think. To help you realize what you really feel.

If one still doesn't jump out at you, go back to the drawing board. More than likely, you haven't created the right combination yet.

Once you've created a plan you love, you're ready to move on to the next step: texture.

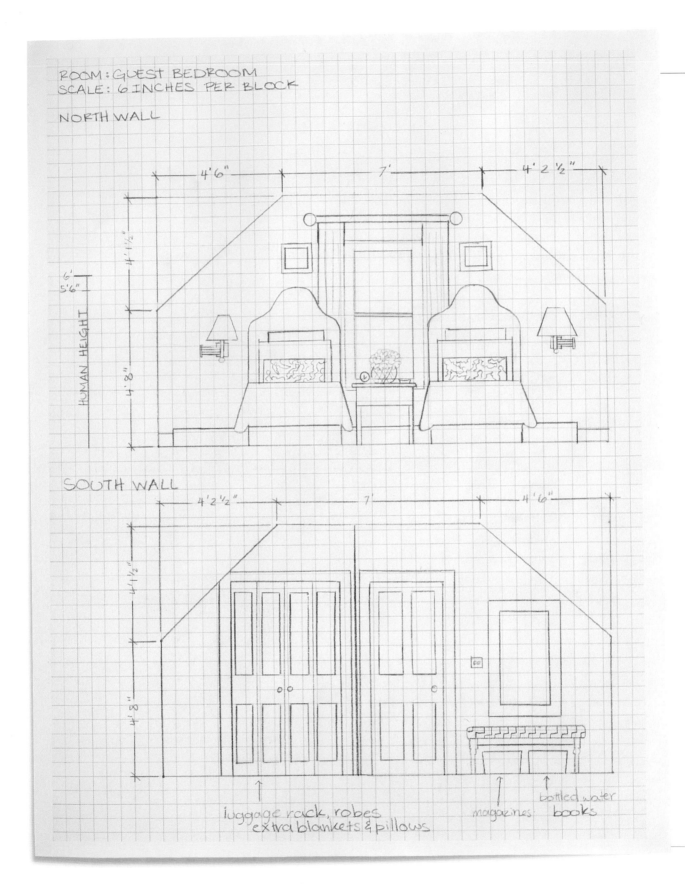

ROOM: GUEST BEDROOM
SCALE: 6 INCHES PER BLOCK

NORTH WALL

4'6"   7'   4'2½"

4'1½"

6'
5'6"

HUMAN HEIGHT

4'8"

SOUTH WALL

4'2½"   7'   4'6"

4'1½"

4'8"

↑
luggage rack, robes
extra blankets & pillows

↑
magazines

↑
bottled water
books

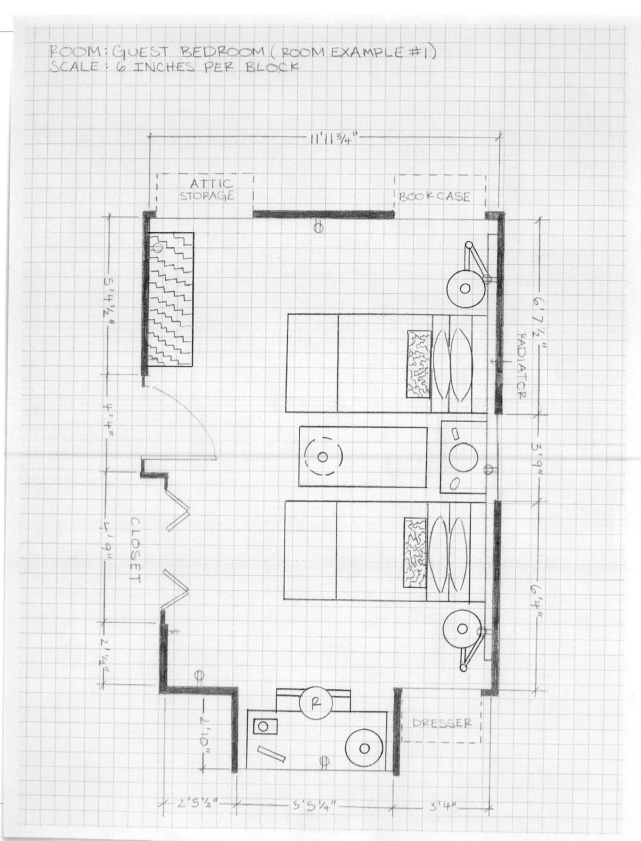

ROOM: GUEST BEDROOM (ROOM EXAMPLE #1)
SCALE: 6 INCHES PER BLOCK

11'11¾"

ATTIC
STORAGE

BOOK CASE

5'4½"

4'4"

CLOSET

4'9"

2'5½"

2'0"

6'7½"
RADIATOR

3'9"

6'4"

DRESSER

2'5½"

5'5¼"

3'4"

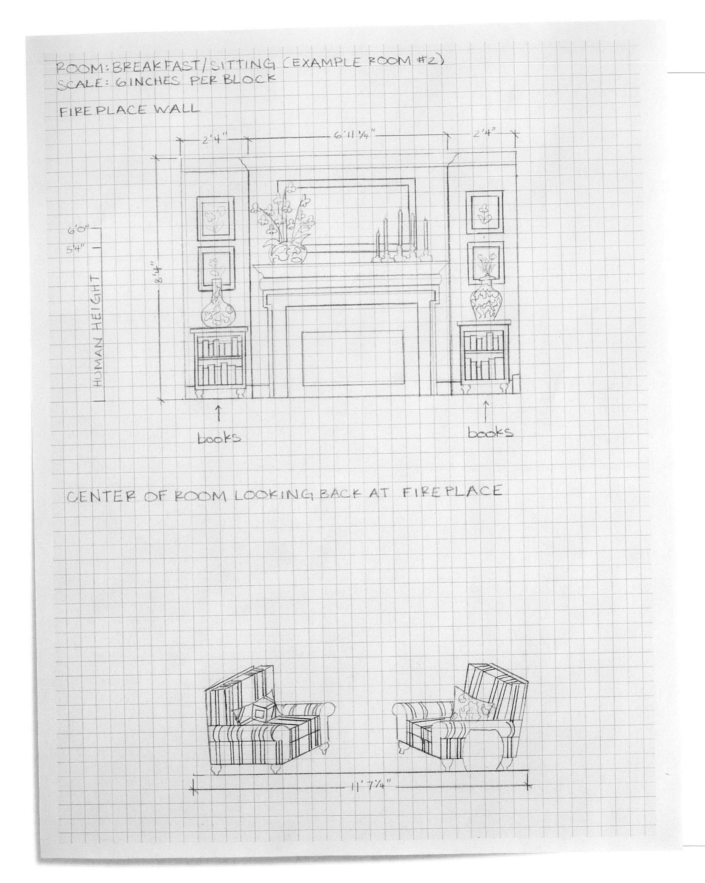

ROOM: BREAKFAST/SITTING (EXAMPLE ROOM #2)
SCALE: 6 INCHES PER BLOCK

FIREPLACE WALL

2'4"   6'11¼"   2'4"

6'0"
5'4"

8'4"

HUMAN HEIGHT

books   books

CENTER OF ROOM LOOKING BACK AT FIREPLACE

11'7¼"

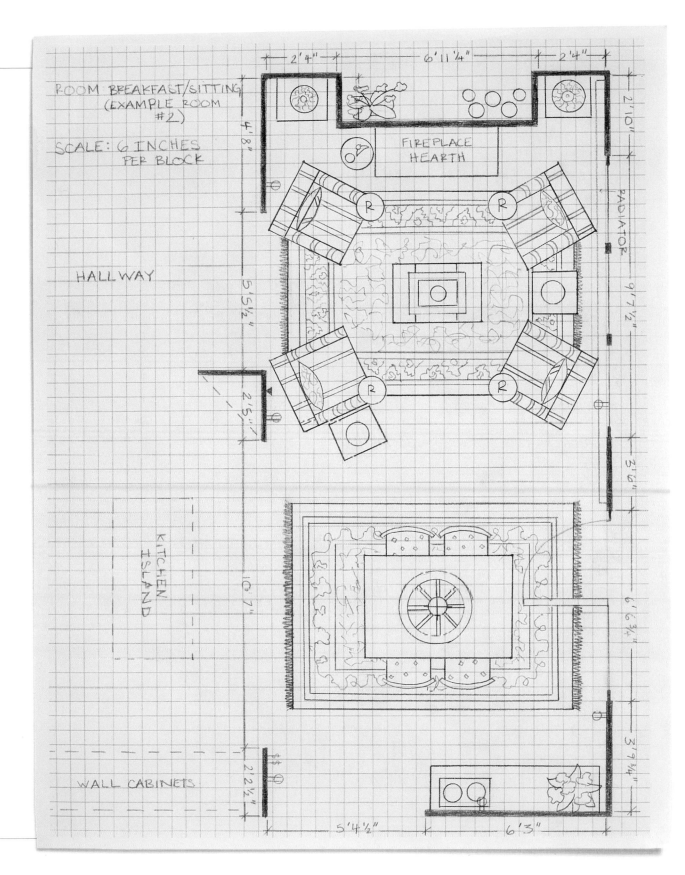

ROOM: BREAKFAST/SITTING
(EXAMPLE ROOM
#2)

SCALE: 6 INCHES
PER BLOCK

HALLWAY

FIREPLACE
HEARTH

RADIATOR

KITCHEN
ISLAND

WALL CABINETS

2'4"   6'11¼"   2'4"

2'10"

4'8"

5'5½"

9'7½"

2'5½"

3'6"

10'7"

6'6¾"

3'9¾"

2'2½"

5'4½"   6'3"

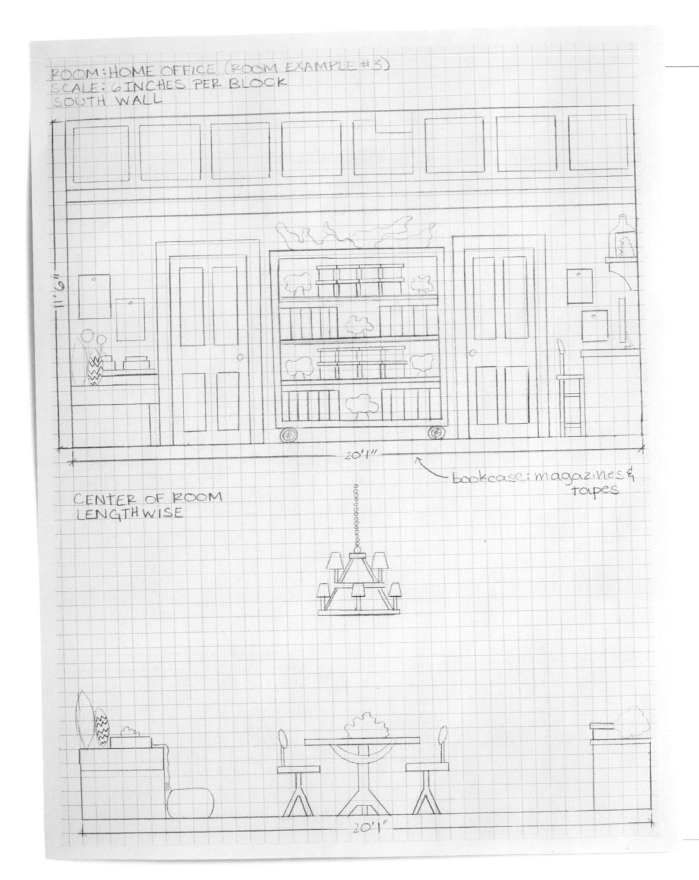

ROOM: HOME OFFICE (ROOM EXAMPLE #3)
SCALE: 6 INCHES PER BLOCK
SOUTH WALL

11'6"

20'1"

bookcase: magazines &
tapes

CENTER OF ROOM
LENGTHWISE

20'1"

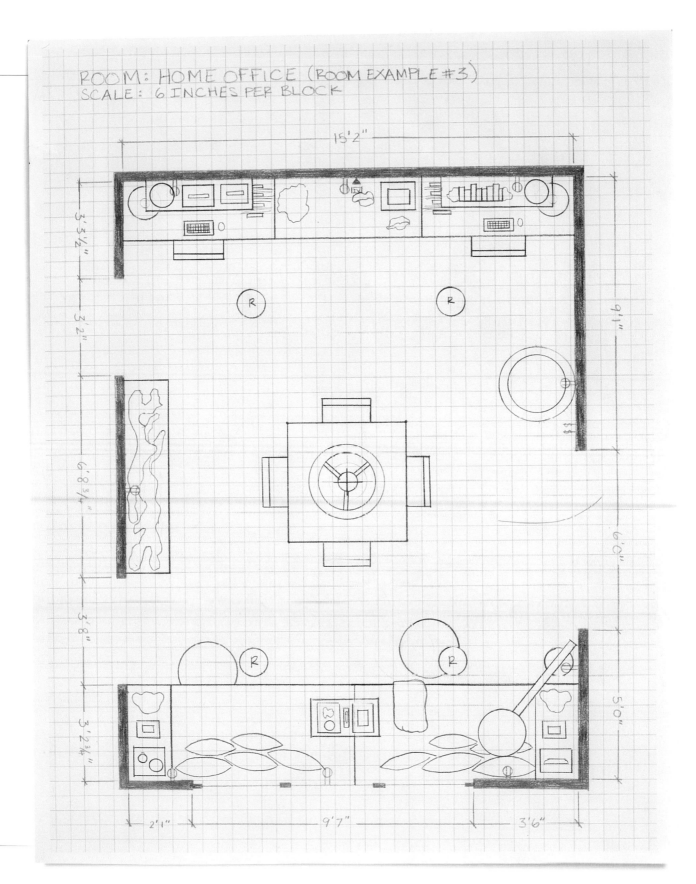

ROOM: HOME OFFICE (ROOM EXAMPLE #3)
SCALE: 6 INCHES PER BLOCK

15'2"

3'3½"

3'2"

6'8¾"

3'8"

3'2¾"

9'1"

6'0"

5'0"

2'1"

9'7"

3'6"

step: **11**

adding
texture

Theoretically you could layer textures or colors once you've finished with patterns because they're both characteristics. But if you haven't caught on yet, you're creating a coloring book of sorts with your room plan, and like with any coloring book, you don't start coloring until all the lines have been drawn. That's why you must layer on your textures before going color crazy.

WHY USE TEXTURES

Of the three — pattern, texture and color — texture is the last thing we notice. But don't take that to mean it's not important. While pattern and color add the spice, texture provides the base flavor of your room. It allows you to communicate softly — subtly — giving your room depth, because there's more to experience and soak up after the initial pomp of pattern and color is over.

So don't overlook texture. While it may be understated, it still gets noticed and affects how we feel in our rooms. Plus, some messages are best delivered in a whisper.

TYPES OF TEXTURES

Typically, when people talk about texture they're referring to the way it feels to touch. But when decorating, we're talking about the visual texture. How something *looks* like it should feel to the touch. Most of the time, things actually look how they feel. But from time to time, things will fool your eye.

Now all those textures — whether they feel as they look or not — can be grouped into categories. Six categories to be precise. And just like with patterns, if you can remember those categories, adding textures to your room will be a breeze.

Of course, I'll admit, that not every texture in existence can be represented by those six categories. But practically all can.

CHOOSING THE RIGHT TEXTURES

When it comes to selecting the textures for your room, there are seven things to consider: emotion, room size, materials, cleanability, stain concealment, durability and comfort.

Emotion. Thanks to your muse and style, you should already know what textures communicate the emotions you want to feel. So take out your muse and style sheets, and look under the texture section. Those are the textures you should use in your room.

Now there's always a chance that you forgot to list a texture or two, so if you find yourself drawn to a certain texture, don't be afraid to add it.

Room Size. If you want to make your ceiling feel lower (Trick 17, page 203) or room feel smaller (Trick 26, page 204), use texture. The more noticeable the texture, the smaller your room will feel. Just remember, there are many ways to make a room feel smaller. Texture is just one of them.

Materials. Most materials come in a wide variety of textures. But they rarely come in them all. That means the textures you can use in your room will be limited by the materials you plan to use.

Fortunately, you already have a good idea as to what materials you'll be using, thanks to your muse and style. Just look under the materials category on both your muse and style sheet to see which materials best evoke the emotions you want to feel. Use that list to help you determine what materials to use for each item in your room. Once you know the materials, choosing the texture of each item will be much easier.

Cleanability. Not all textures and materials are as cleanable as others. For example, smooth surfaces are far easier to clean than bumpy ones. So if you need some — or all — of your surfaces to be easy to clean, make sure you have at least

rough

smooth

shiny

matte

soft

bumpy

a texture or two on your list that fits the bill. If you don't, consider adding one.

Stain Concealment. If you're worried about stains, wear and pet hair, use a busy texture. The busier the texture, the harder it is to spot inconsistencies.

Comfort. Some textures are far more comfortable than others. For example, smooth is more comfortable than rough. Fluffy and soft are more comfortable than bumpy and prickly. If areas of your room need to be comfortable — like seating — make sure you have some comfortable textures and materials on your list.

HOW TO MIX TEXTURES

Mixing textures is like mixing patterns. It's all about the contrast. The more contrast you want, the more opposite the textures in your room should be. Whereas, the less contrast you want, the more alike the textures in your room should be.

PLACING TEXTURES

When it comes to placing textures, there are four things you should consider: your functional needs, desired emotional intensity, room size and visual grammar cocktail.

Functional Needs. The textures and materials you choose for each object in your room should correspond with what you functionally expect from each surface. For example, having a prickly floor or fluffy shower wall doesn't make much sense.

Emotional Intensity. Just as with pattern, there are two things that affect the intensity of the emotion communicated by texture. First, the more of a texture you use, the

stronger your emotional message will be. So when placing textures, the amount you use of each one should directly correspond with how much you want to feel the emotion it communicates.

And second, the more prominent the placement of the texture in your room, the more important the emotion it communicates will appear.

Room Size. If you decided to use texture to make your room appear smaller, be sure to place the texture in the spot necessary to create the optical illusion. Refer to page 200, trick 17 and 26, if your memory needs a kick start.

Visual Grammar Cocktail. The elements of your visual grammar cocktail tell you four important things when it comes to placing textures.

Balance tells you whether you should scatter the textures around your room symmetrically or asymmetrically.

Repetition tells you how often you should repeat the same textures in your room and whether or not each texture should be repeated identically or slightly different. For example, you could always use glass as smooth, or you could use glass, ceramic and silk for smooth.

Contrast tells you how much your textures should contrast with one another.

Movement tells you how you should place the same textures around your room in order to lead your eye from one place to another.

DRAWING IN YOUR TEXTURES

Now that you know how to select and place textures, it's time to draw — or rather, write — them in. Before doing so, make a copy of your most recent floor plan, elevations and ceiling layout. You know, the ones with patterns drawn in. That way, you can make multiple drafts.

1. DRAW TEXTURES ON YOUR ELEVATION

If your texture is very noticeable, draw it in. Otherwise, just write in the textures and materials you plan to use and where you want them to go. Remember every object in your room must have a texture and be made of a material.

If you're unsure of what materials you want all your decorative accessories to be, don't worry. You can figure that out later. For now, just write down what textures you want them to be.

As far as materials go, it's mostly important to know what you want for the functional areas of your room — the furniture, flooring, countertops, cabinetry, etc.

To see examples of textures drawn — and written — on elevations, turn the page.

2. DRAW TEXTURES ON YOUR FLOOR PLAN

Fill in the textures you've already chosen for each piece of furniture on your floor plan. Then write in what texture you want to use on the floor, carpeting or rugs. If your texture is very noticeable, draw it in.

To see examples of textures drawn — and written — on floor plans, turn the page.

3. DRAW TEXTURES ON YOUR CEILING LAYOUT

Write in what texture you want on the ceiling.

4. CREATE AT LEAST 3 MORE DRAFTS

You know the routine by now. Go back and make at least 3 more drafts.

5. CHOOSE THE BEST ONE

Look at all of the room plans you just created, and ask yourself which one feels best. Whatever it is, make a mental note. If you don't know, step away for awhile to let your emotions bubble to the surface. If you still can't decide, ask someone else what they think. But remember, only so you know how you feel.

If you still don't have a preference, you may not have created the best version yet. So go back to the drawing board.

Once you've found the one you love, ask yourself if it also functions best. If it does, you're ready to move on.

If it doesn't, then you have to decide if you're willing to make the sacrifice. If not, head back to the drawing board until you create a version that you love both functionally and emotionally.

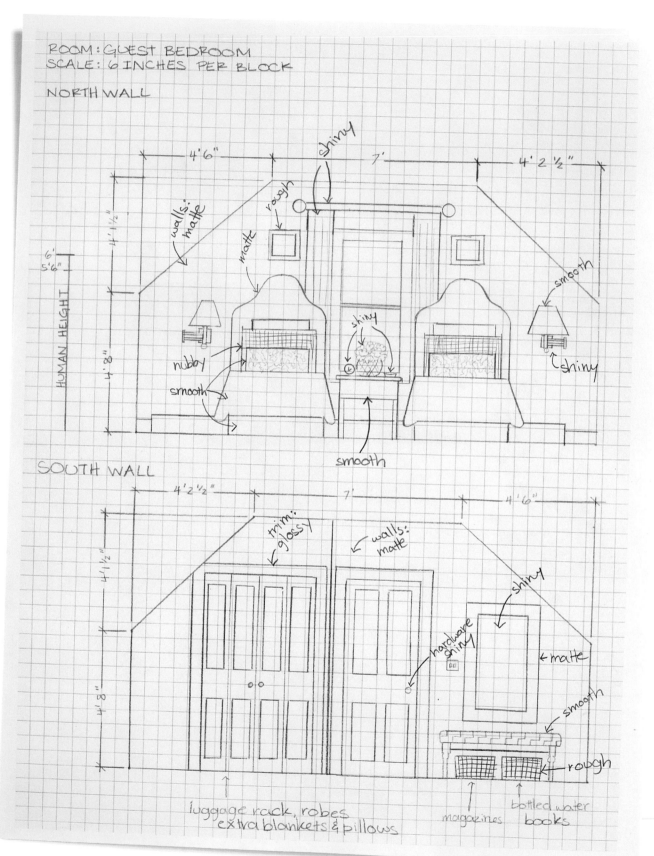

ROOM: GUEST BEDROOM
SCALE: 6 INCHES PER BLOCK

NORTH WALL

shiny

4'6"   7'   4'2½"

4'1½"

6'
5'6"

HUMAN HEIGHT

4'8"

walls: matte

rough

matte

smooth

shiny

nubby

smooth

shiny

smooth

SOUTH WALL

4'2½"   7'   4'6"

4'1½"

4'8"

trim: glossy

walls: matte

shiny

hardware shiny

matte

smooth

rough

luggage rack, robes
extra blankets & pillows

magazines

bottled water
books

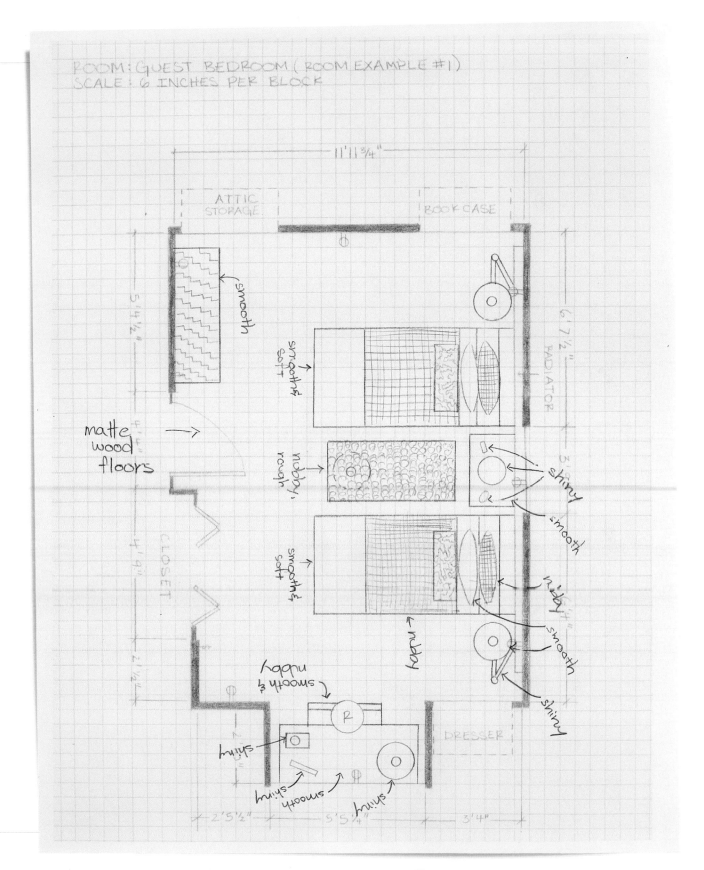

ROOM: GUEST BEDROOM (ROOM EXAMPLE #1)
SCALE: 6 INCHES PER BLOCK

11'11¾"

ATTIC STORAGE

BOOK CASE

smooth

matte wood floors

smooth & soft

nubby, rough

smooth & soft

CLOSET

shiny

smooth

nubby

smooth

shiny

nubby

nubby & smooth

shiny

shiny

smooth

shiny

DRESSER

RADIATOR

5'4½"

4'4"

4'9"

2'1½"

2'5½"

5'5¼"

3'4"

6'7½"

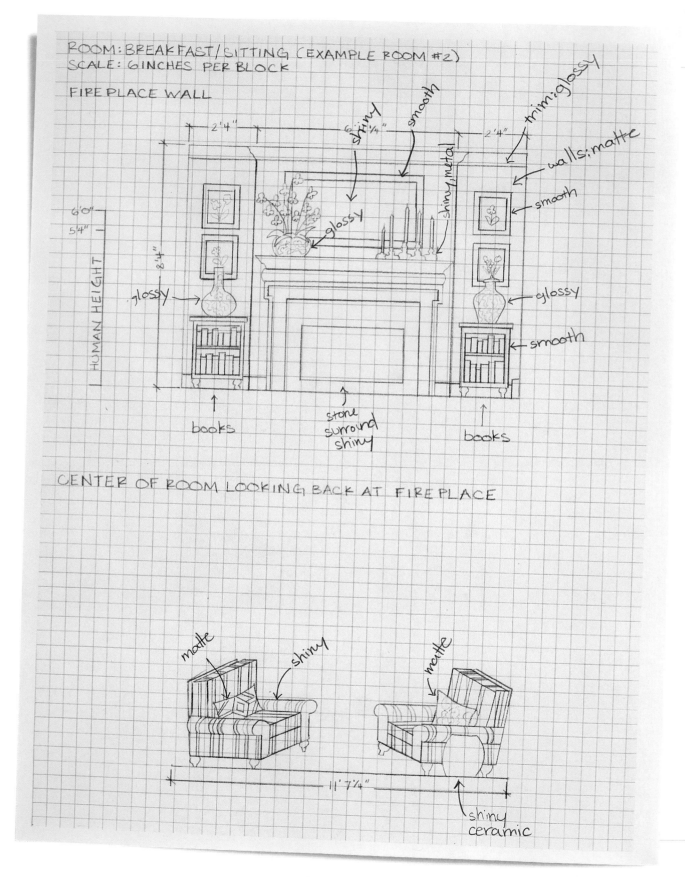

ROOM: BREAKFAST/SITTING (EXAMPLE ROOM #2)
SCALE: 6 INCHES PER BLOCK

FIREPLACE WALL

2'4"

6'¼"

shiny

smooth

trim: glossy

2'4"

walls: matte

shiny, metal

smooth

6'0"

5'4"

8'4"

glossy

glossy

HUMAN HEIGHT

glossy

glossy

smooth

books

stone
surround
shiny

books

CENTER OF ROOM LOOKING BACK AT FIREPLACE

matte

shiny

matte

11'7'¼"

shiny
ceramic

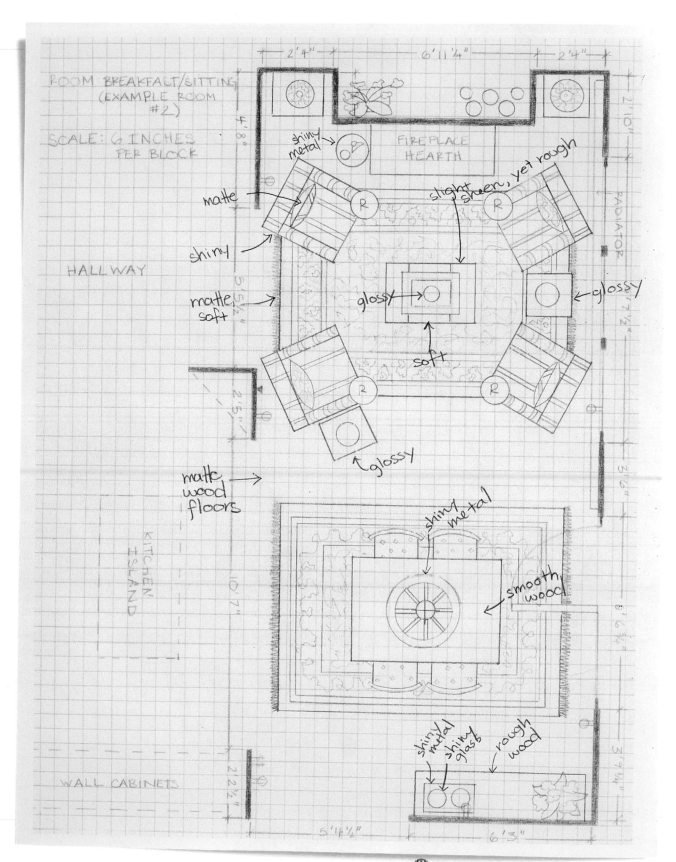

ROOM BREAKFAST/SITTING
(EXAMPLE ROOM #2)

SCALE: 6 INCHES PER BLOCK

2'4"   6'11¼"   2'4"

2'10"

4'8"

RADIATOR

HALLWAY

shiny metal

FIREPLACE HEARTH

matte

slight sheen, yet rough

shiny

5'5½"

matte soft

glossy

glossy

soft

2'5½"

R

R

R

R

glossy

1'7½"

3'6"

matte wood floors

KITCHEN ISLAND

shiny metal

10'7"

smooth wood

8'6¼"

WALL CABINETS

2'2½"

shiny metal   shiny glass   rough wood

3'4¼"

5'4½"   6'3"

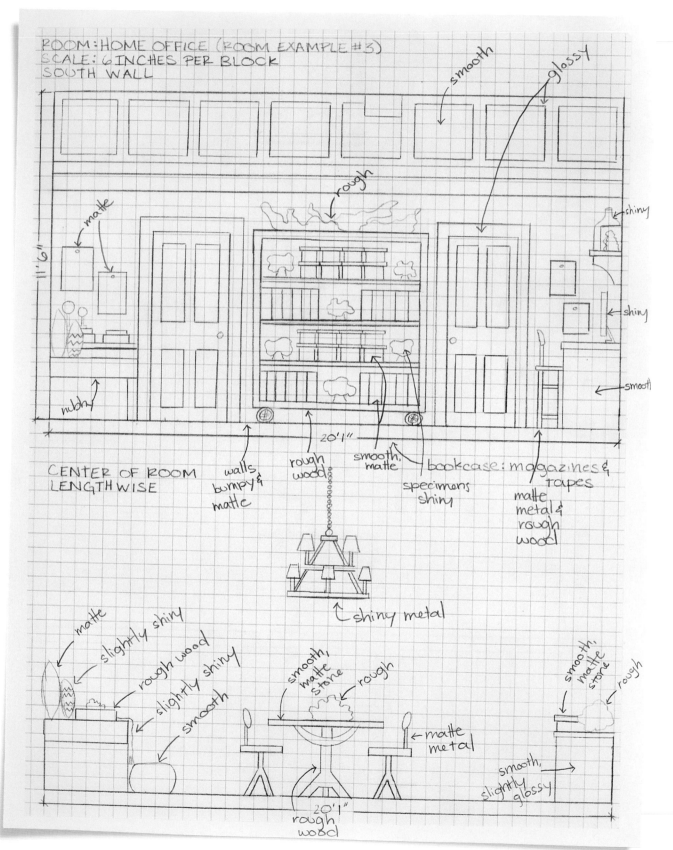

ROOM: HOME OFFICE (ROOM EXAMPLE #3)
SCALE: 6 INCHES PER BLOCK
SOUTH WALL

smooth

glossy

rough

matte

shiny

shiny

smooth

11'6"

nubby

20'1"

CENTER OF ROOM
LENGTHWISE

walls
bumpy &
matte

rough
wood

smooth,
matte

specimens
shiny

bookcase: magazines &
tapes

matte
metal &
rough
wood

shiny metal

matte
slightly shiny
rough wood
slightly shiny
smooth

smooth,
matte
stone

rough

matte
metal

smooth,
matte
stone

rough

smooth,
slightly
glossy

20'1"
rough
wood

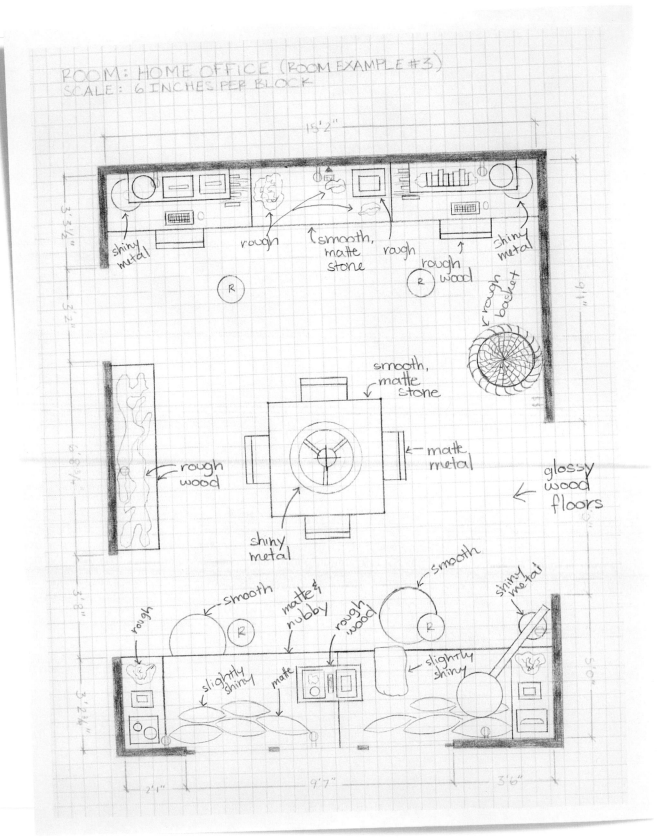

ROOM: HOME OFFICE (ROOM EXAMPLE #3)
SCALE: 6 INCHES PER BLOCK

15'2"

3'3½"
3'2"
6'8¾"
3'8"
3'2¾"

9'4"
5'0"

shiny metal

rough

smooth, matte stone

rough

rough wood

shiny metal

rough basket

smooth, matte stone

matte metal

glossy wood floors

rough wood

shiny metal

smooth

matte & nubby

rough wood

smooth

shiny metal

rough

slightly shiny

matte

slightly shiny

2'1"
9'7"
3'6"

12

adding
color

O f all the parts of decorating, color frustrates people the most. And anyone who's ever been in a paint aisle knows exactly what I'm talking about. There are so many choices.

And if you've ever tried to follow the expert's advice and use a color wheel, I feel your pain. Instead of feeling like there are too many choices, you suddenly feel like there are too few, because the color wheel only shows a handful of colors. For example, where's brown? Or taupe? Or greige? Or coral? Nowhere to be found.

That's why I say ditch the color wheel. And instead, well, let me show you.

WHY USE COLOR

Nothing — not pattern, not texture, not shape, not anything — communicates emotion as powerfully as color. And that's all because color is the easiest to notice.

With everything else, there's a lag. When we see pattern, our brains have to process all the different lines and colors in order to understand the meaning. With texture, it takes our brains a while to spot it. And that lag causes the emotion to get slightly diluted because we don't feel it immediately.

But with color, the emotion isn't diluted. We don't have to think about what we're seeing. We have absolutely no problem spotting it. We feel the emotion immediately, and it washes over us. That's why color has the power to evoke such an intense emotional reaction.

So if you want to drench people in a super strong emotion, use color. Bold, wonderful, evocative color. It will send the message home. Just remember, color is boisterous, not precise. If you want precision, that's what pattern's all about. With color, you get intensity.

TYPES OF COLORS

No matter what you do, your room will have color because everything has a color. And when it comes to what colors you can choose, the possibilities are endless. There are more colors in this world than we could ever imagine. Even if we close our eyes and try to picture a rainbow or paradise, we still can't picture them all. There's too wide of a spectrum. So to make understanding and remembering them easier, colors have been grouped into categories.

There are three ways in which they've been grouped. The first is by their intensity: dark or light, bright or dull. The second is based on what temperature they appear: warm or cool. The last is based on what general color they look most like: red, pink, orange, brown, yellow, green, blue, purple, black or white.

If you turn the page, you'll see examples of colors that fall in all of those categories except the ones based on general colors. Those everyone's familiar with.

When you turn the page, don't expect to see every color in the world. You'd need an entire book — or two or three — to showcase them all. What you're about to see is just a small sampling.

CHOOSING THE RIGHT COLORS

Seeing the abundance of color in our world gets most people excited and fills them with a sense of possibility. But when we have to choose a color, that's an entirely different story. The excitement quickly transforms into apprehension and frustration, because the number of possibilities is overwhelming. But that's only because you don't know what to base your decision upon. Everyone thinks you should choose whichever colors look best. But this far in, you should know that's not the case.

When you select colors for your room, the only things you should consider are your emotional needs, stain concealment needs and room size.

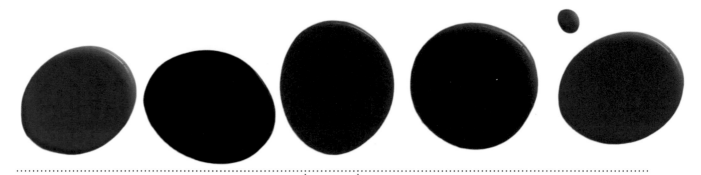

dark

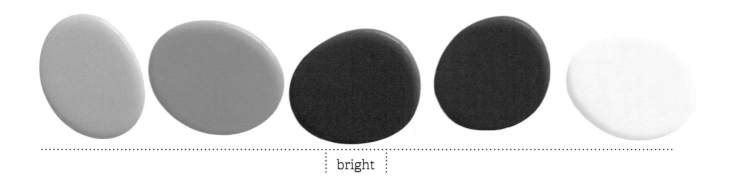

bright

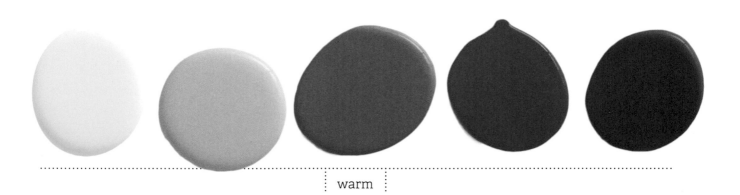

warm

light

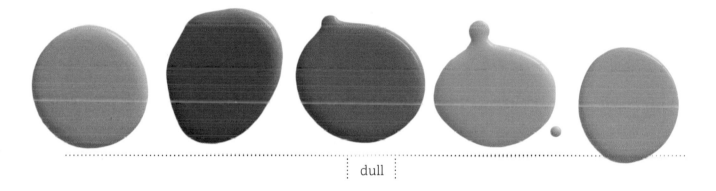
dull

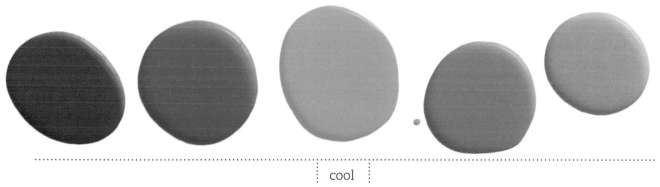
cool

Emotion. Ideally, you want the colors you choose for your room to perfectly communicate the emotions you want to feel. To determine what colors those are, you could go through each and every one to see which evokes the right emotion. But that would take forever. And pinpointing the perfect shade of blue or red or beige that best evokes what you want to feel is extremely difficult. Few people have the emotional understanding of color to be able to do that, which is why we have a muse.

Given that your muse evokes all the emotions you want to feel, the colors of it should as well. So to determine which colors you should use in your room, you simply have to look to your muse. Fortunately, you've already written down all the colors that compose it on your muse sheet.

Stain Concealment. If you're worried about stains, wear and pet hair, you may want to consider using at least one dark color in your room. The darker the color, the less stains and wear will show. That's why people avoid white sofas like the plague. They're incredibly hard to keep looking pristine. Of course, with modern day cleaners and materials being what they are, it's far easier to keep things stain-free than it used to be. But if you don't want to take the chance, consider adding a dark color if you don't already have one.

Room Size. Color is one way to trick your eye into seeing your room a different size. To refresh your memory on which colors do what, flip to 200 and pay close attention to Tricks 12, 13, 20, 20, 21, 22, 23 and 24.

CREATING COLOR SCHEMES

You already have a rough idea of what colors you'll be using in your room. The ones from your muse. Now it's time to refine them, because if you take them exactly how they are in the photograph, they may not translate well to your room. Sometimes you get lucky. And the colors you see are exactly what you should use.

But that's not always the case, because in comparison, your photo is very small and your room is very big. So the colors in your photo may be too intense for you to enjoy in your room.

Plus, sometimes the photo of our muse doesn't pinpoint exactly what we want to feel. It's close, but not quite there. In order to hone in on the emotions we really want, we must distill the colors.

Now, as we go through the refining process, don't think there's an ideal number of colors to hit. I know some people will try to tell you there is. Typically, they say it's around five or six, but that's completely untrue. Use as many colors as you want. They only say to use five or six because that number provides a nice amount of contrast. But that idea of "nice" is arbitrary. Some people like more. Some people like less. So use as many colors as you want, and most importantly, let your muse be your guide. It will tell you how many colors you need to evoke the emotions you want — whether that's one or twenty.

1. Cutting Colors. The first step in refining is to eliminate colors. You may not need to do this. Typically, you only need to cut colors when the photo of your muse includes things that don't particularly communicate the emotion you want to feel. For example, if your muse is an orange tree, you may not want to include the blue from the sky — even if it is in the picture — because it doesn't evoke what you want to feel.

Look closely at your muse and see if there are any colors that feel out of place. If there are, cut them from your color scheme.

2. Adding Neutrals. Sometimes our muses aren't composed of any neutral colors. For example, red roses or blueberries. But when we see those things in nature, we never see them in isolation. They're always surrounded by neutrals. So if you were to use only their colors in your room — like green and red, or blue — you'd end up with a very intense room that felt as if you were inside the rose or blueberry. That's perfectly fine if that's what you want.

But if that's not what you're going for — if you don't want the emotions to come off that strong and intense — add some neutral colors to your room. They'll act as a blank slate so the emotional colors from your muse stand out and get noticed — in a dose you prefer.

Most people consider whites, blacks, grays and browns to be neutral colors. If you were to add any neutral colors to your room, those would be the ones you'd probably choose. But sometimes people find very dark and light shades of green and blue to be neutrals as well — because they mimic the blank slates of our world — the sky and grass.

If you decide to add neutrals, choose whichever ones feel most natural with your muse and the colors you already have.

3. Selecting Shades. Now that you know what colors are in your color scheme, it's time to determine their shades. When we talk about the shade of a color, we're referring to how light or dark, and bright or dull it is.

If you're lucky, the shades of your colors are already perfect. But that's not always the case. Sometimes you need to tweak your colors a bit to make them more livable, add depth and create the desired amount of contrast in your room.

LIVABILITY. Like I said, the colors of your muse may look great on a tiny card, but when you put them in your room, they may be too intense. That's because the more of a color you use, the brighter and darker it will appear. If you plan to use a lot of a color in your room — like on your walls, cabinetry or big furniture pieces — you can evoke the same emotion of what you see in a little picture with a far lighter and duller color. So if you end up using an intense color from your muse in a large swath, you may want to tone it down a bit.

DEPTH. If your muse only had a couple colors and you're worried your room will appear flat, consider using two different shades of your colors. For example, a light blue and a bright blue. Doing that enables you to stay true to your original colors while having a bit more to work with.

When choosing what shades to use, look closely at your muse. Chances are the shades you should choose are in your picture. Very rarely does an object have a perfectly even color. Most of the time there is a subtle variation in a color, and it's that variation that provides the emotion.

CONTRAST. Pull out your visual grammar cocktail, and see if the amount of contrast in your color scheme matches the amount of contrast you want in your room. More than likely it does. But if it doesn't, it's time to tweak.

Which way you tweak your colors — darker, lighter, brighter or duller — depends on three things.

First, how you want your room to feel. The darker your room, the cozier, sexier and edgier it feels. The lighter your room, the airier, lighter and more cheerful it will feel. The brighter your room, the more energetic and fun it will feel. The duller your room, the more somber and melancholy it will feel.

Second, if you want to trick your eye into seeing your space a different size. That's discussed on page 200 if you need to brush up on how to do that.

Third, if you're worried about stains and wear, you may want to increase the darkness or brightness.

Just remember, when tweaking your color scheme, you still want to evoke the emotions of your muse. So don't go overboard. The further you stray from the original colors, the more you risk losing the overall emotion.

PLACING YOUR COLORS

When deciding where to place your colors, there are five things to take into consideration: desired emotional intensity, room size, stain concealment, perceived color intensity and visual grammar cocktail.

Emotional Intensity. Just as with pattern and texture, there are two things to consider when placing colors according to emotion. First, the more of a color you use, the stronger the emotion feel. So use the colors that communicate the emotions you most want to feel on the biggest areas of your room. Use the colors that communicate the emotions you least want to feel on the smallest areas of your room.

Second, the more important an emotion, the more prominent the placement of the color should be.

Room Size. If you decide to use color to fool your eye, then make sure you place the right colors in the right places in order to create your desired illusion. If you need a quick reminder as to which colors do what, flip to 200 and pay close attention to Tricks 12, 13, 20, 20, 21, 22, 23 and 24.

Cleaning Needs. If you decided to use color to camouflage stains, wear and pet hair, use your darkest colors on the areas bound to get dirtiest — like furniture, flooring and linens.

Perceived Color Intensity. We see color in terms of what it's next to. Just look below. Are the dots the same exact color and intensity?

Believe or not, they are. That's why the colors you pair together matter. Because what colors you place next to each other dramatically affects the way each are seen. The more alike colors are, the less intense and washed out they appear. Whereas the less alike they are, the more intense they will appear.

Fortunately, scientists have done quite a bit of research on this. The colors that stand out most next to one another are referred to as complimentary colors, and they're the ones that sit opposite each other on the color wheel. Unfortunately, despite naming them and having done all that research, scientists can't agree on which colors actually intensify each other the most. Why? They can't agree on which color wheel is right.

That's right. There are two different color wheels. So there are two different sets of complimentary colors:

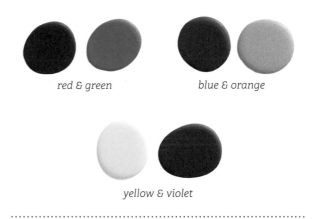

red & green   *blue & orange*

yellow & violet

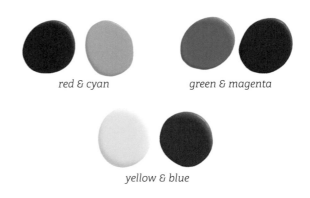

red & cyan   *green & magenta*

yellow & blue

Despite the two schools of thought, this gives you some guidance as to what color pairs appear most intense. And that's important to know when placing colors in your room, because it tells you what colors to place next to each other if you want to maximize their intensity. Or what colors not to place together if you don't want to increase their intensity.

Visual Grammar Cocktail. Just as with pattern and texture, the elements of your visual grammar cocktail tell you four important things when it comes to placing color.

Balance tells you whether you should scatter your colors symmetrically or asymmetrically around your room.

Repetition tells you how often you should repeat the same colors in your room.

Contrast tells you how much your colors should contrast with one another — as you already know.

Movement tells you how you should place the same colors around your room in order to lead your eye from one place to another. And that's very important, because aside from lines, color is the best way to create movement in a room. After coloring in your elevations and layouts, be sure to draw the visual path your colors create in your room. That way you'll know for sure you have the correct movement. If you need a refresher on how to do that, turn to page 144.

DRAWING IN YOUR COLORS

Now that you have your color scheme and know how to place the color in it, it's time to color in your plan. But don't do it on the version with your textures written in. Instead, use leftover copies of your pattern versions. If you drew in textures, add those to it before making copies.

To draw in color, you'll need colored pencils or markers. Ideally, you'd want to have the exact colors you imagine using in your room. But rarely does that happen, which means your elevation won't look exactly like how your room will end up. So don't freak out if it looks too bright or bold. It won't look like that in real life.

1. COLOR YOUR ELEVATION

Use the color scheme you created — and your new knowledge of how to place colors — to shade in each of your elevations. If you have patterns in your room, don't worry about figuring out exactly what colors will be in it. Instead, just choose one or two main colors.

2. COLOR YOUR FLOOR PLAN

Fill in the colors you chose for each piece of furniture. Color in what shade you want the floor to be.

3. COLOR YOUR CEILING LAYOUT

Color in your ceiling. Remember, the color of your ceiling affects how low or high your ceiling appears. If you need a refresher, flip to page 200 and look at Trick 19 and 20.

4. CREATE AT LEAST 3 MORE DRAFTS

Do I even need to say anything? I think you get this part by now.

5. CHOOSE THE BEST ONE

Selecting the best plan as far as color goes is all about listening to your gut. So which one does your gut say feels best to you?

If you're having a hard time deciding, you know the routine. Walk away. Give your emotions time to bubble to the surface. If you still can't decide, ask for a second opinion. Still don't love any? Ask yourself why. Then go back and make another version that fixes what was bothering you. Remember, don't go forward until you love what you have.

Once you've got a version you love, congratulations. You just finished creating your room plan. Talk about an accomplishment. You should be so proud of yourself. Proud *and* excited. Because now it's time to make it happen and see that room you've drawn come to life.

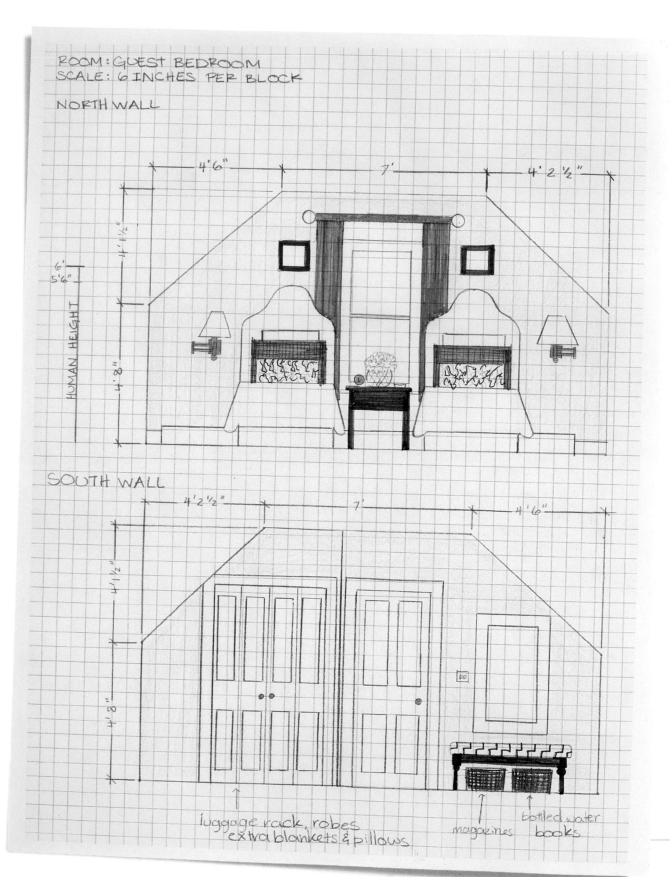

ROOM: GUEST BEDROOM
SCALE: 6 INCHES PER BLOCK

NORTH WALL

4'6"   7'   4'2½"

1'1½"

6'
5'6"

HUMAN HEIGHT

4'8"

SOUTH WALL

4'2½"   7'   4'6"

4'1½"

4'8"

luggage rack, robes
extra blankets & pillows

magazines   bottled water
books

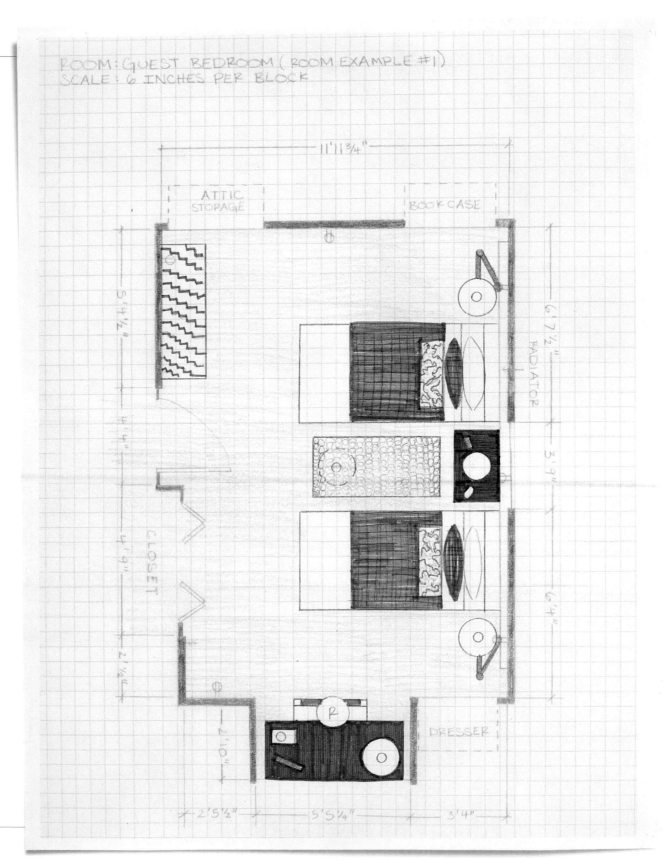

ROOM: GUEST BEDROOM (ROOM EXAMPLE #1)
SCALE: 6 INCHES PER BLOCK

11'11¾"

ATTIC STORAGE

BOOK CASE

RADIATOR

5'1½"

6'7½"

3'7"

4'1"

4'9"

CLOSET

6'4"

2'1½"

2'10"

DRESSER

2'5½"

5'5¼"

3'4"

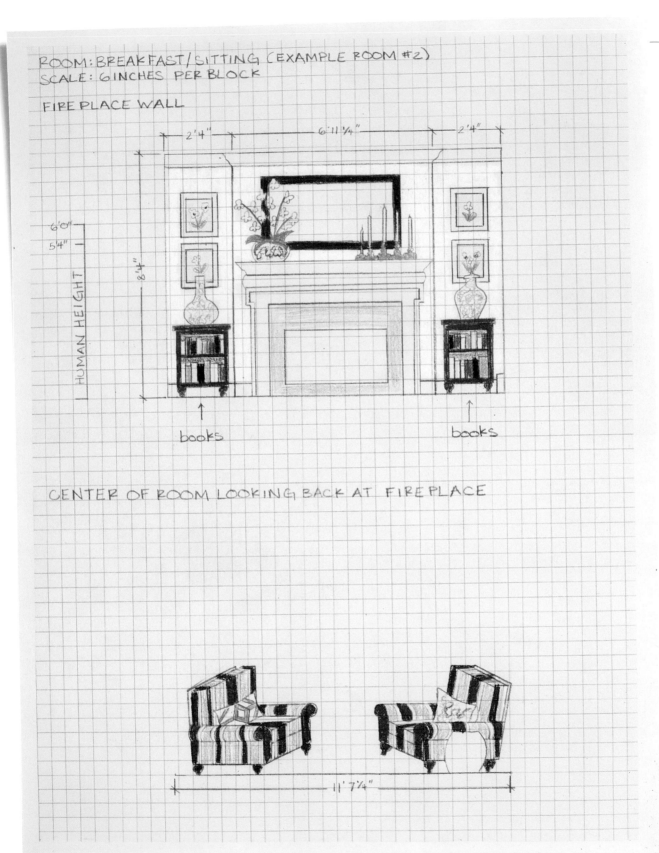

ROOM: BREAKFAST/SITTING (EXAMPLE ROOM #2)
SCALE: 6 INCHES PER BLOCK

FIREPLACE WALL

2'4"   6'11¼"   2'4"

6'0"
5'4"
8'4"

HUMAN HEIGHT

↑ books   ↑ books

CENTER OF ROOM LOOKING BACK AT FIREPLACE

11'7¼"

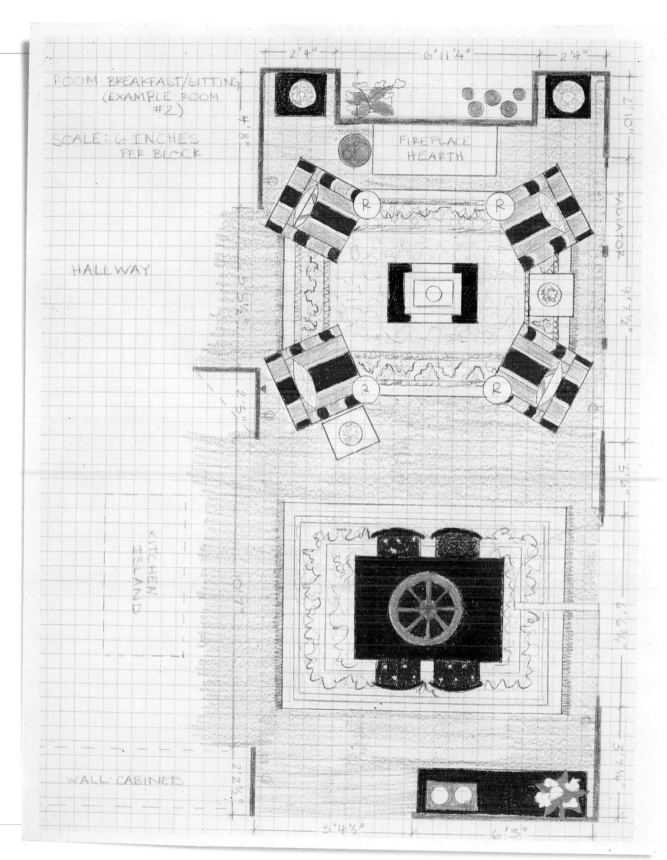

ROOM BREAKFAST/SITTING
(EXAMPLE ROOM
#2)

SCALE: 6 INCHES
PER BLOCK

HALLWAY

KITCHEN
ISLAND

WALL CABINETS

FIREPLACE
HEARTH

R

R

R

R

2'4"   6'11¼"   2'4"

2'10"

RADIATOR

9'7½"

5'6"

6'6¾"

3'9¼"

4'8"

5'5½"

2'5"

8'7"

2'2½"

5'4½"   6'3"

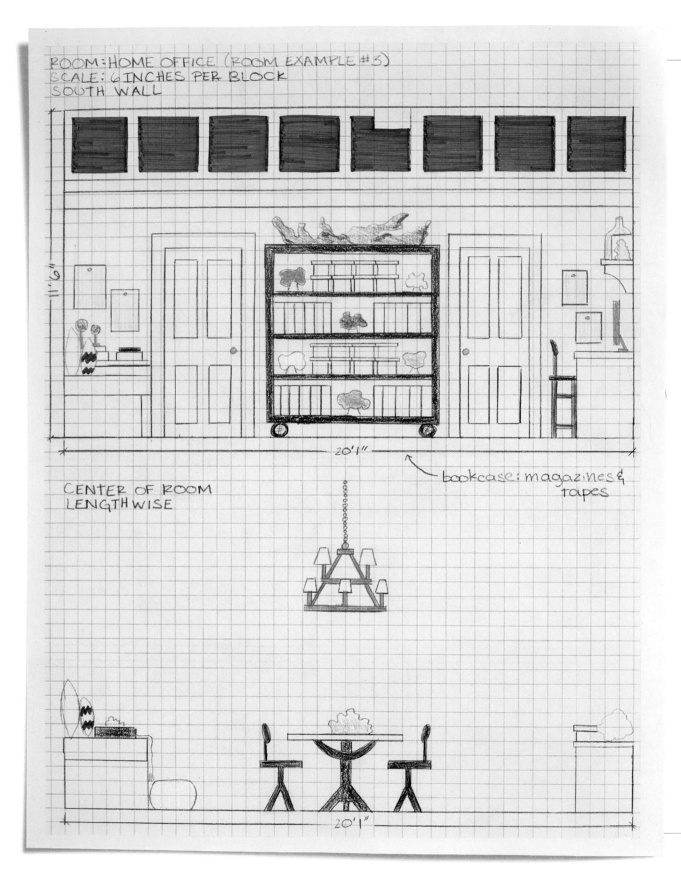

ROOM: HOME OFFICE (ROOM EXAMPLE #3)
SCALE: 6 INCHES PER BLOCK
SOUTH WALL

11'6"

20'1"

CENTER OF ROOM
LENGTHWISE

bookcase: magazines & tapes

20'1"

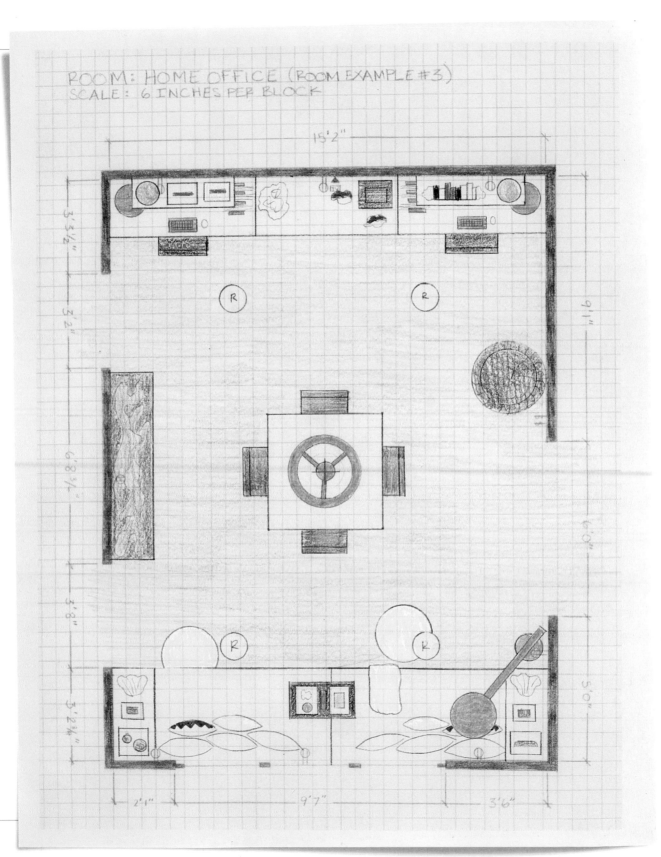

ROOM: HOME OFFICE (ROOM EXAMPLE #3)
SCALE: 6 INCHES PER BLOCK

PART THREE: MAKIN
HAPP

Scored
for
$10
on eBay.

Buy a
chandelier

As a child, I remember my mom and granny lamenting over how they couldn't find yellow kitchen towels anywhere. And that conversation didn't happen just once. I heard it on a three-month rotation year after year.

I guess yellow — or at least the shade they wanted — wasn't very popular when I was a kid.

And when it comes to decorating, popularity matters because the stores only stock what's trendy. And if you don't want what's trendy — like my mom and granny — you won't find it in the stores.

But that doesn't mean your plan is toast.

Like the Rolling Stones said,

> "You can't always get what you want. But if you try some times, you just might find you get what you need."

And that's the secret to making your plan come to life. Trying.

At the end of the day, talent isn't what separates a brilliantly executed room from a horrible one. It's effort. The harder you work — the longer you search — the more spectacular things you'll find. And the more spectacular things you find, the more amazing your room will be.

So don't give up on your plan, or decorating ability, if you don't immediately find what you want. Hit the pavement. Visit more than the standard stores. Put the effort in, and you'll get what you need.

"Oh, yes, you'll get what you need."

Even if it is just yellow kitchen towels.

step: **13**

setting your
budget

Most people will say setting your budget is the very first thing you should do when decorating. But I whole-heartedly disagree.

If you start out with a budget, you won't dream. You'll downgrade your wants based on what you think you can afford. But we don't decorate to compromise. We decorate to make our dream life a reality. And you have to know what your dream life is to make it come true. That's why you shouldn't even think — not even for a second — about your budget until you're finished creating your plan. That way you feel free to dream without any restraints.

Now you may think that logic is a recipe for disaster because you'll dream up a plan you can't afford. But I've learned that once you know what you truly want, nothing — not even a tight budget — will hold you back. And I can say that with confidence for two very good reasons.

One, when you decorate, the cost is almost always directly proportional to the size of your space. So the bigger the room, the bigger the budget. The smaller the room, the smaller the budget. And it just so happens that people who own large houses with large rooms tend to have larger budgets. Just as people who own small houses with small rooms tend to have smaller budgets. So more than likely, your budget is already proportional to the size of the room you need to decorate.

But even if it's not, I've seen time and time again, if there's a will, there's a way. As long as you're willing to work hard and think creatively, you can achieve practically any look on any budget.

Of course, I say that within reason. You can't redecorate an entire room for $10. You'd have to be the most resourceful person in the world. So when I say on any budget, I mean any *reasonable* budget.

And now that you're ready to make your plan come true, it's time we figured out what yours is.

SETTING THE MAGIC NUMBER

Your budget dictates what you can get for your room, which makes it a pretty important number. So you really want to think through what you're willing to spend. When doing that, there are two things to consider: your financial situation and your neighborhood's real estate value.

Your Financial Situation. When it comes to the home, everyone has a different amount they're willing to spend. Some feel their home is vitally important, so they're willing to scale back in other areas — like eating out, going to the movies, traveling or buying clothes — to increase their budget. Others, who don't value the home as much, aren't willing to sacrifice a thing to expand their decorating budget.

Whatever you decide, don't set your budget so high that you have to worry about paying the bills or putting food on the table. Living worry-free is far more important than living in a perfectly decorated home. Of course, I'm sure you already knew that, but I figured I should say it just in case.

Your Neighborhood's Real Estate Value. When decorating, there are two types of things you spend money on. The things you can take with you — like furniture, lamps, linens and accessories — and the things that stay fixed where they are — like flooring, tile, cabinetry, countertops, appliances and moldings.

If your plan requires spending lots of money on the latter, and you're thinking about selling your home in the not-so-distant future, you'll definitely want to take your neighborhood's real estate value into consideration.

You see, when you sell a home, you never want to be the most expensive home on the block. You rarely get what your home's worth, because the value of the other houses brings yours down. After all, half — if not more — of real estate is location, location, location. As a result, people are only willing to pay so much for a home in each neighborhood. And the highest price on the block is normally higher than they're willing to pay, because they don't feel like they're getting a good deal.

That's why it's important not to "overbuild" your home by adding expensive things you can't take with you, because you likely won't get your money back.

That's not to say it's all bad spending money on fixed items. Upgrading those areas of your home so that it fits with the value of other homes can help you sell it. Just don't spend too much.

If you don't plan on selling your home, or installing fixed items, there's no need to consider your neighborhood's market value.

Once you have a number you're comfortable spending, write it down.

ADJUSTING FOR UNEXPECTED COSTS

Unexpected costs are bound to pop up during a project, which is why many people suggest setting aside a portion of your budget specifically for those emergencies. That way, you don't have to hock any prized possessions to cover them.

But if you're like me, that way of thinking doesn't work. In the back of your mind, you know you have an extra chunk you can spend. And you'll spend it if you have a good enough reason, such as the perfect tile, fabric, sofa or chair.

That's why I don't plan for unexpected costs. Instead, I set a budget and stick with it. That way, I know for sure what I can't go over. To avoid unexpected costs springing up and ruining my day, I don't buy a thing — other than the bare minimum — until all projects are finished. That way, if they rip down the walls and find something awful, I can allocate more of my budget to that part without much worry.

Luckily, doing it that way doesn't push the timeline back much, because most unexpected costs are found early on. So you can often feel safe buying the other things you need

well before the projects are finished.

If you're redecorating a kitchen or bathroom, that method may not work for you, because you have to spend almost all of your budget on materials, cabinets and fixtures. In those cases, it's much smarter to set aside a portion of your budget for unexpected costs. How much you set aside depends on how much you like to gamble. Some set aside 10 percent. Others say 15 percent. And then there are those who say as much as 25 to 50 percent.

If you decide to set aside money for unexpected expenses, deduct it from your total budget now.

WHAT TO DO WHEN THE # IS TOO SMALL

If, after scouting for items, the total is more than you wrote down, you've got three options.

One, wait. Save up the money you need, and then implement your decorating plan. That way, you get exactly what you want without sacrifices.

Two, splurge on the things you feel are most important, skimp on the ones you don't and reuse any items you already have. Then over time, as you get the money, switch out the things you skimped on — or reused — for the versions you really want.

Three, buy each item for your room as you get the money.

Which you choose depends entirely on how long you're willing to wait to get exactly what you want. Unfortunately, I can't tell you how long that is. That depends completely on your budget and how good you are at saving. Both of which only you know.

The best advice I can give is to do whatever will make you happiest overall.

GUEST BEDROOM BUDGET:
(ROOM EXAMPLE #1)

$5,500

BREAKFAST/SITTING BUDGET:
(ROOM EXAMPLE #2)

$22,000

HOME OFFICE BUDGET:
(ROOM EXAMPLE #3)

$17,000

If you were to give yourself a 15% buffer for unexpected costs, the $17,000 budget would be reduced to: $14,450.

The do-not-exceed-no-matter-what numbers.

Buy oriental rugs.

Paint walls & moldings.

Insta. crown moldin...

Find an electrician.

Pot ...rchids in ...corative ...ntainers.

Buy ottoman.

step: 14

establishing your timeline

Hang artwork.

Buy a dining table & chairs.

Buy a chandelier.

The hardest part of bringing your plan to life isn't finding all the stuff you need or getting all the projects done. That part's easy. It's the coordinating — making sure everything arrives when you need it — that makes everyone's brain explode. There's just so much to keep track of, which is why it's so incredibly, unbelievably, vitally important to create a master list of the projects you must do, the things you must buy, and the order in which it must be done.

YOUR PROJECTS LIST

Look at your room plan, and list all of the projects. Start with the things that must be installed — like cabinetry, flooring, faucets, tile, countertops, molding and lighting.

Next, list all items that must be moved — like cable outlets, windows, doors or plumbing fixtures.

Then, list all of the things that must be painted. Walls. Ceilings. Trim.

Finally, list all of the things that must be hung, such as wallpaper and artwork.

14
timeline

PROJECTS TO-DO LIST

ROOM:

ORDER OF COMPLETION:

PROJECTS TO DO:

ORGANIZING YOUR PROJECTS LIST

When putting together a room, you don't complete the projects in random order. That would end in disaster because you'd tear up the work and have to do it all over again. And no one wants to do that, which is why you must complete the projects in the proper order — starting with the nitty-gritty jobs and working your way to the cosmetic tasks.

Go through your project list and order your tasks according to how they should be completed. That way, you know when each project must be done — and most importantly, in what sequence your materials must arrive.

STANDARD PROJECT ORDER

1. GET PERMIT IF NEEDED

2. DEMOLITION

3. ROUGH FRAMING
   *Add new walls, openings, windows or exterior doors.

4. PLUMBING, HEATING & NATURAL GAS

5. ELECTRIC

6. INSULATION

7. DRYWALL

8. HARDWOOD or TILE FLOORING
   *Install thick flooring. Thin flooring, such as linoleum or vinyl can be installed later. If you install hardwood flooring, don't have it finished yet — if possible. Hold off to avoid ruining it when doing other tasks — like those below — that have yet to be completed.

9. TRIM CARPENTRY
   *Interior doors, baseboards, casings and any other trim except those that are to be used on cabinetry.

10. PAINT
    *Paint ceiling first, walls second and trim last.

11. INSTALL CABINETS & APPLIANCES

12. INSTALL COUNTERTOPS.

13. TILE WALLS, CEILINGS or BACKSPLASHES

14. INSTALL HARDWARE
    *Door knobs, cabinet pulls, etc.

15. FINISH PLUMBING
    *Install faucets, toilets, etc.

16. FINISH HARDWOOD FLOORS

17. HANG WALLPAPER

18. FINISH ELECTRIC
    *Install light fixtures and put on switch plates.

19. HANG ARTWORK & OTHER ACCESSORIES

20. COLLAPSE FROM SHEER EXHAUSTION
    *And rejoice that it's finally finished.

PROJECTS TO-DO LIST

ROOM: HOME OFFICE

ORDER OF COMPLETION:	PROJECTS TO DO:
14	Switch out chandelier
10	Install cabinets.
12	Install countertops.
11	Put up shelves.
9	Build & install daybed.
4	Paint all walls with magnetic paint.
8	Paint back wall with dry erase paint.
6	Paint other 3 walls with regular paint.
3	Paint ceiling.
7	Paint trim.
1	Install French doors
2	Drywall.
5	Install decorative ceiling molding
13	Install cabinet & door hardware.

YOUR SHOPPING LIST

Take out your room plan, and make a list of every item you need to purchase. The lighting. The furniture. The fabrics. The accessories. The flooring. The molding. The cabinetry. The hardware. The appliances. Everything. And don't forget the paint.

Once you've created a thorough list, double check that you've listed everything you need.

14 timeline	SHOPPING LIST	ROOM:

NEEDED FOR PROJECTS:	LONG LEAD:	SHORT LEAD:	ITEMS NEEDED FOR ROOMS:
☐	☐	☐	
☐	☐	☐	
☐	☐	☐	
☐	☐	☐	
☐	☐	☐	
☐	☐	☐	
☐	☐	☐	
☐	☐	☐	
☐	☐	☐	
☐	☐	☐	
☐	☐	☐	
☐	☐	☐	

ORGANIZING YOUR SHOPPING LIST

Given that there are so many things you must buy for a room, it's important to figure out what must be bought when. That way, there is an order to your purchasing madness.

1. Find the Items Needed for Projects. Go through your list, and put a check next to all items needed for projects in the column aptly named "Needed for Projects."

2. Divide Items According to Lead Time. Buying decor isn't like buying groceries. Some things take a few weeks to arrive, and you need to know which those are so you can order them far enough in advance.

Go through your list using the chart of lead times below and put a check under the column "Long Lead" next to any item that will take longer than 2 weeks to get in. Then, put a check under the column "Short Lead" next to any item that will take less than 2 weeks to get in. If an item could take somewhere between, say 1-3 weeks, err on the side of caution and list it as a long lead item. It's always better to have it come early rather than late.

STANDARD LEAD TIMES

ANTIQUES:
same day

ACCESSORIES:
1-4 weeks
backordered: 2-6 weeks

CABINETRY:
stock & semi-custom: 3-6 weeks
custom: 4-12 weeks

COUNTERTOPS:
stock: 1-3 weeks
special order: 3-4 weeks

FABRICS:
in-stock: 1-2 weeks
backordered: 2-8 weeks

FURNITURE:
case goods: 2 - 6 weeks
custom case goods: 4-12 weeks
upholstered with stock fabric: 2-6 weeks
upholstered with specialty fabric: 6-8 weeks

FLOORING:
stock: 1-3 weeks
special order: 3-4 weeks

HARDWARE:
in-stock: 1-2 weeks
backordered or specialty: 2-4 weeks

LIGHTING:
stock: 1-3 weeks
backordered: 2-4 weeks
custom: 2-8 weeks

PAINT:
same day
special order: 1-2 weeks

TILE:
in-stock: 1-4 weeks
backordered or custom: 3-6 weeks

TRIM:
standard stock items: same day
special order: 1-2 weeks

timeline

SHOPPING LIST

ROOM: BREAKFAST SITTING

NEEDED FOR PROJECTS:	LONG LEAD:	SHORT LEAD:	ITEMS NEEDED FOR ROOMS:
☒	☐	☒	crown molding
☒	☐	☒	paint
☐	☒	☐	dining table
☐	☒	☐	dining chairs
☐	☐	☒	fabric for dining chairs
☐	☒		
☐	☐		
☐	☒		
☐	☐		
☐	☒		
☐	☐		
☒	☒		
☐	☐		
☐	☐		

ITEMS: NEEDED FOR PROJECTS, LONG LEAD
Chandelier

ITEMS: NEEDED FOR PROJECTS, SHORT LEAD
Crown Molding
Wall Paint
Trim Paint

ITEMS: LONG LEAD
Dining Table
Dining Chairs
Easy Chairs
Sideboard

ITEMS: SHORT LEAD
Dining Chair Fabric
Easy Chair Fabric
Ottoman Leather
Garden Seats

3. Make a Spread Sheet. Create a spreadsheet like the one on the bottom left and input the items you need in the appropriate categories. If you don't have spreadsheet software, visit Google Docs (docs.google.com). They offer free web-based spreadsheet software. To download a copy of the spreadsheet in Numbers, Excel or Google Docs, visit TheMeghanMethod.com.

ORGANIZING YOUR WORK FLOW

When it comes to when to do what, here are two things to consider. First, all the project items must arrive before the project starts. And two, if you want to put your room together as soon as your projects are finished, all the other things you need must arrive at that time.

There are two ways to make that happen. The easiest is to order all of the things you need at once, and store them until you're ready.

Unfortunately, most people don't have the space to do that. And if you fall in that category, you'll want to do things in this sequence:

1. Order Long-Lead Items Needed for Projects.

2. Order Short-Lead Items Needed for Projects.

3. Order Non-Project Long-Lead Items.

4. Order Non-Project Short Lead Items.

* To determine when to do each, look at the estimated lead time for the items you want and back calculate from the date you need them. Be sure to give yourself at least an extra week for items to arrive. That way you have time to switch any wrong items accidentally sent or change any items you don't like.

Now, how long your projects will take completely depends on whether you plan to do the work yourself or hire it out. If you plan to do the work yourself, get detailed instructions for each project and based on the instructions, estimate how long you think each will take. Then double — or triple — that time, because it will definitely take longer. And remember, if you work, you'll only have weekends and nights to do the projects, which makes completion take much longer.

If you plan to hire someone, know that the timeline they give you could change if something goes wrong.

For more information on hiring and DIYing, turn to page 359.

IF YOU'RE ON A DEADLINE

Most of the time, putting together a room is a get-it-done-as-soon-as-you-can-whenever-that-may-be type of thing. But every once in awhile, someone needs the room finished by a certain date — like for a graduation, anniversary, birthday, holiday or baby's birth.

If that's you, ask yourself: Do I have enough time to get my long-lead materials?

If not, you have two choices. Either trash the idea of getting your room done in time, or buy things off the showroom floor. Keep in mind, when you buy off the showroom floor, you can't always get what you want. You're limited to the colors and finishes they have in stock. And while that sacrifice may seem okay in the short run, in the long run, it may not be so good because you have to live with it. All the time. So before you rush the process, ask yourself: Is it worth it?

If you can get all the materials you need in time, ask yourself: Can the projects be *completed* in time?

If not, you have only two options. Trash the idea of getting your room done on time, or cut down on the number of projects. If you're leaning toward the latter, ask yourself if making that sacrifice is really worth it.

Just a few of the things you should take when scouting.

step:

15

scouting for items

Now that you have a plan, you could go out shopping and buy each item you need. But after all your hard work, buying things piecemeal doesn't ensure you get the best combination.

For that, you must scout.

You must go into the stores, scope out your options and take photos of each item. Then, once you've returned home, mix and match those photos until you find the perfect combination. The combination that makes your gut sing.

And doing that — scouting to find the best options — ensures your plan turns out the best it possibly can, which often is better than you could have ever imagined. So what do you say? Let's do your plan justice. Let's go scouting.

Download the entire spreadsheet from TheMeghanMethod.com.

GETTING YOUR LIST IN ORDER

To scout efficiently and effectively, you must have the proper list. One that details exactly what you need and offers you a place to keep track of all of your options. Fortunately, you've already started the list on page 331. Now, we just need to add to it.

Ideal Dimensions. When scouting, it's essential to know what size each item must be, because it keeps you from wasting time on items that are too big or too small. And more importantly, it prevents you from returning home with them.

So next to the first column on your list, "Items to Buy," add a second column titled "Ideal Dimensions." In that column, fill in the dimensions from your plan for each item you need. Remember to include the height, width and depth.

ITEMS: NEEDED FOR PROJECTS, LONG LEAD	IDEAL DIMENSIONS	REQUIREMENTS
Chandelier	28"W, 17"T	Brass

ITEMS: NEEDED FOR PROJECTS, SHORT LEAD	IDEAL DIMENSIONS	REQUIREMENTS
Crown Molding	5" - 6"	
Wall Paint	n/a	Yellow, no VOC
Trim Paint	n/a	White, no VOC

ITEMS: LONG LEAD	IDEAL DIMENSIONS	REQUIREMENTS
Dining Table	60"W, 42"D, 30"T	Wood
Dining Chairs	18"W, 24"D, 34"T	Wood, Upholstered Seat
Easy Chairs	30"W, 30"D, 34"T	Comfortable
Sideboard	69"W, 18"D, 36"T	Shelf and Drawer Storage
Ottoman	36"W, 24"D, 20"T	Leather
Book Table	18"W, 18"D, 30"T	Storage for Books

ITEMS: SHORT LEAD	IDEAL DIMENSIONS	REQUIREMENTS
Oriental Rug under Table	7" x 10"	Durable, Neutral
Oriental Rug under Seating	7" x 10"	Durable, Neutral
Garden Seats	18"W, 18"D, 25"T	White

Requirements. In addition to dimensions, you must also remember each item's requirements. This includes what type of storage it should have, what level of durability or cleanability it must meet, and what pattern, texture and color it should be.

Next to the column, "Ideal Dimensions," add a third column, "Requirements." Under that column, list all the requirements you have for each item.

Options. For each item, you'll find a number of options, and remembering all of them taxes your brain like you would not believe. That's why it's vitally important to have a place to list those options.

So next to the column, "Requirements," make a fourth column, "Options." Under that column, you'll list each option for each item. If you find the option in a brick-and-mortar store, you must list where you found it along with a brief description. If you find the option from an online source,

simply copy and paste the URL of the item in that column.

Price. In order to stay on budget, you must keep track of the prices. That way, you can easily tell if a combination breaks the bank.

So next to the column, "Options," create a fifth column, "Price." Under that column, fill in the price of each option.

Lead Time. Buying things for your home is not like buying groceries. You don't walk out with your purchases. Often, you must wait a few weeks before it arrives. Knowing how long it will take to get the item — which is referred to as lead time — is crucial. As you already know, it tells you when to purchase each item in order to stay on schedule.

So next to the column, "Price," add a sixth column, "Lead Time." Under that column you should fill in the lead time for each item.

WHERE TO SCOUT

Many people believe the most important part of decorating is creating a fantastic plan. But here's the truth. You could have the best decorating plan in the world, but if you can't find the stuff you need to make it happen, it's absolutely worthless. Just a scribbled sketch on cheap paper.

That's why the ability to scout and source great products is heralded by many in the industry as being one of the most important decorating talents. The better you are at sourcing interesting items, the better your room will turn out.

Now doing that is far more difficult for the average person, because unlike interior designers, we don't have access to the special trade stores filled with row after row of unique, jaw-dropping items.

But don't let that get you down. There are tons of wonderful stores open to the general public.

Brick-and-Mortar Stores:

ANTIQUE STORES. Hands down, one of the most popular

Got from an antique mall for only $25.

places for interior designers to shop are antique stores, because they're always full of wonderfully unique and interesting items. Of course, the general public doesn't seem to share the same enthusiasm. When most people hear the word antique, they assume it means expensive. But that's not always the case. A number of things sold by antique stores are relatively inexpensive, partly because not all items are in high demand, and partly because not everything is a true antique. They're not old enough. A true antique must be over 100 years old. So don't be afraid to visit antique stores. They offer some of the most unique pieces you'll find — and some of the greatest deals.

Just be sure to do your research before you go. If you don't know the current value of an item, it's easy to get swindled into paying more than it's worth. So before heading out, do a quick internet search of your required items to see what they sell for online. Or — at very least — take a smart phone with you when shopping. That way, if you see an item you like, you can do an internet search right in the store. If you find the prices online lower, don't be afraid to ask the owner if he or she is willing to barter. Sometimes you get lucky, and they are.

Now keep in mind, the items you find in antique stores vary greatly depending on where you live. For example, in New England you'll find lots of early American and traditional decor. In Florida — especially Miami — you'll find lots of Art Deco. In Los Angeles, you'll find lots of Hollywood Regency. Where you live greatly influences the types of items you'll find in your local antique stores.

If you're not a fan of the styles found in your antique stores, don't be discouraged. Try the online antique stores listed on page 337.

ARCHITECTURAL SALVAGE. If you want to find unique doors, windows, mantles, columns, tiles, bathtubs or any other architectural item, look into architectural salvage

Found for $150 at antique store sale.

stores in your area. They sell spectacular items removed from old homes.

AUCTIONS & ESTATE SALES. Auctions and estate sales sell items like you'd find in an antique store. But since they're sold auction style, sometimes you can get them at a much lower price — well, if there isn't a big turnout for the sale. Just make sure you set a spending limit, because it's easy to get caught up in the excitement of the auction. Also, show up early. Each piece is often available for inspection before the show, and you want to take advantage of that. You don't want to buy an item that looks good far away, only to find its drawers won't open when you bring it home.

FLEA MARKETS. If you want to see a huge variety of vintage, antique and handmade items all at once, flea markets are the place to go. Sometimes they're held indoors, but often they're outside. So bring a raincoat, wellies and an umbrella if it looks like it's going to rain, and make sure you wear comfortable shoes. If you want to see all the vendor booths, you're going to do a lot of walking. But the most important thing to remember is to get there early. The best things go fast. And if you see something you like, don't be afraid to haggle.

$50
Craigslist
find

CONSIGNMENT STORES. Consignment shops work as a middle man selling people's used furniture and accessories. Typically, the items they sell are in good condition, so if you're on a tight budget, you can score some great discount finds.

THRIFT STORES. If you need to find things on the cheap, thrift stores are the place. Just know, finding something worthwhile is like searching for a jewel in the rough. But it can be done. My editor, Veronica Hill, let me in on her mom's secret. To find the best stuff, go to the thrift stores in expensive areas.

GARAGE & YARD SALES. If you live somewhere warm, you can find garage sales year-round. But in places with a cold, hard winter, garage sales typically only happen in the summer. If you're lucky enough to be decorating when they're going on, stop by. Sometimes you get lucky. Garage sales can be treasure troves of unique items at very low prices. And if you're willing to haggle, they can go even lower. After all, people having garage sales want to get rid of their stuff. So if you give them a decent offer, more often than not they take it.

BOUTIQUE STORES. Practically every town and city has a number of boutiques unique to their area. Typically, boutiques carry new items made by small manufacturers and local artists, which means you're bound to find interesting pieces. But, be warned. Those interesting items often come with a high price tag.

INTERIOR DESIGNERS. If you want to order a fabric, wallpaper or other item offered to the trade only, visit an interior designer's showroom. In addition to trade-only items, some sell pieces that didn't work on previous jobs, which can be a great way to scoop up fashionable finds.

SPECIALTY STORES. Most people always go to the home improvement centers and chain stores first. But in most places, there are a number of local stores that specialize in just one particular item, such as furniture, lighting, appliances, cabinetry, hardware, wallpaper and so on. And those specialty stores carry a wider variety of products compared to what you'd find at the chains. Plus, they tend to be far more knowledgeable about the products because they work with them day in and day out. That's why it's smart to check out those stores first, because you'll get to see the biggest selection. Plus, it's nice to help the small guy and support the local economy.

CHAIN STORES. This is where you go if you want new, reasonably priced or trendy products. Chain stores carry what is currently popular and hip. And while some designers turn their noses up at them, there are a number of wonderful products carried by chain stores. So don't cross them off your list. You'd be surprised. Sometimes the best option for your room is from a chain store.

HOME IMPROVEMENT CENTERS. If price is an issue and you want something new, big box stores are the place to go.

They often offer the lowest prices on new items, but not always. I've been shocked to find that some specialty stores are able to beat the chain store prices. So don't make any assumptions. Always shop around and get prices from each type of store.

Internet Stores:

ONLINE ANTIQUE MALLS. These may be one of my favorite places to shop, because they allow you to see antiques from a number of vendors across the country. You can't find a better antique selection. Some of the most popular antique conglomerate sites are 1stdibs.com, Rubylane.com, GoAntiques.com and BondandBowery.com.

ONLINE ANTIQUE STORES. There are a number of brick-and-mortar antique stores who have an internet presence as well. To find them, do an online search for the product you want. You may have to search through a few pages of results, but you'll find them.

EBAY, CRAIGSLIST & ETSY. I can't tell you how often I use these sites. They're absolutely wonderful places to find amazing stuff. eBay.com is the place to discover all of those hard-to-find items because practically anything can be found there. Craigslist.org is a great place to score cheap finds. In fact, the desk in the guest room, pictured to the left, was a Craigslist find that only cost $50. And no, that's not a typo. Etsy.com is the place to go if you want anything handmade, vintage or unique.

ONLINE SAMPLE SALES. A number of websites, such as OneKingsLane.com, Eziba.com, JossandMain.com, Gilt.com and BeyondtheRack.com, have popped up offering daily home good sales. Typically, each sale is associated with one specific retailer, and more than one sale is featured each day. To find out about the sales, you must join the websites. Once you're a member, you receive daily e-mail alerts telling you about that day's sales.

On certain days, One Kings Lane features sales from interior designers' personal inventories of things never used on jobs. Amazing items can be found at those sales. Another site offering a similar service is DecoratorTagSale.com. They're often sold at a discount, which makes it a great place to scoop up stylish finds.

ARTIST WEB STORES. Many artists have popped up online — selling everything from pottery, furniture, paintings or metalware. Finding them can be difficult, but when you do, it's well worth it. When searching, type words like "handmade," "artist," and "custom" along with the item you're looking for.

BOUTIQUE WEB STORES. There are a number of online stores replicating the selection you'd find at a brick-and-mortar boutique store — unique, new items that are hard to find anywhere else.

WAREHOUSE WEB STORES. These stores sell a ginormous selection of one product — like lamps or knobs. Finding them couldn't be simpler. Typically, when you do an internet search for an item, they're the first websites that come up.

CHAIN STORES ONLINE PRESENCE. Most chain stores have an online presence, but be warned. They don't always carry all of the items online. Some things are only in stores. Similarly, you can't always find all the items in the stores. Sometimes they're only offered online. If you want to see a chain store's full selection, visit them both online and in person.

For a list of tons of decor stores, visit
TheMeghanMethod.com.

WHAT STORES TO VISIT FIRST

It's highly unlikely that one store will have the best option for every single thing you need. That's why when you scout, you don't go to just one store. You go to several. And the more stores you visit, the better, because you're more likely to find all those items you've been dreaming about.

Of course, visiting tons of stores — whether in person or online — can take up quite a bit of time. That's why it's important to visit them in the most efficient order.

First: Online Stores Selling New Items. When you scout for items, you don't buy anything. You just look — except when it comes to one-of-a-kind items, like antiques. If it's your best option, you buy it because there's no telling if another one will come on the market, and if you don't get it, someone else will.

But, as I said, it must be your best option. And the only way to know that is if you scout everywhere else first before visiting a single antique store, flea market, consignment shop or any other place selling one-of-a-kind items.

That's why the first places you should scout are those selling new items. But don't go to the bricks-and-mortar stores first. Start your search online. For one, it's easier. Two, it has the widest selection. Three, it allows you to scope out a store's selection before wasting a trip there. And three, knowing what's available online — and at what price — gives you a scouting baseline, which makes it easier to know which items in the bricks-and-mortar stores are worth your time.

Second: Boutique, Specialty & Chain Stores. After visiting all the online stores selling new things, it's time to visit the brick-and-mortar stores doing the same.

Third: Online Stores Selling One-of-a-Kind Items. After scouting the new items that are available, it's time to visit those selling one-of-a-kind items. Always do it online first. That way you get a sense of what types of antiques and handmade goods are available at what price, which is very helpful when you go to antique stores, flea markets, estate sales or auctions. It keeps you from getting swindled and helps you when haggling.

If during your online search you find something perfect, and there are no others like it, get it. But before you do, make sure it really is perfect. If you have any doubt, hold out. It's far better to see how all your options fit together before buying anything. All too often, the thing you think looks best on its own ends up being the worst option when put next to everything else in your room.

Now, if you want to lump your brick-and-mortar shopping into one day, visit all the online stores selling one-of-a-kind items beforehand. Just remember what I said about holding back unless it's absolutely perfect.

Fourth: Antique, Consignment, Thrift, Flea Market, Auction & Estate Sales. Finally, it's time to visit all the brick-and-mortar stores selling one-of-a-kind items. You know the deal. If you spot something that's absolutely perfect — far better than all the other options you've found — scoop it up. But if you feel even the slightest hesitation, wait. As I said, it's far better to see all your items together before making a decision.

WHEN TO SHOP

The biggest sales always occur right before new inventory comes in, because stores need to clear the floor to make room for new models. So they have a sale. Take furniture, for example. You'll typically find the lowest prices in January and July because the new inventory usually arrives in February and August.

If you want to know when the stuff you want will go on sale, and are too shy to inquire outright, ask, "When do new floor models come in?"

Start looking for sales one month ahead of the date they

give.

Of course, if you're not shy — which you shouldn't be, because there's no shame in trying to get the best deal — just ask outright if any sales are coming up. I highly recommend doing that, because there's nothing worse than buying a full-priced, high-ticket item only to find out one week later it's selling for half-off.

If you're shopping online, do a quick internet search using the name of the company selling the item you want and the words "coupon code," "promotional code" or "discount code." You'd be surprised how often you find one that isn't promoted on the company's website. And if you're lucky enough to find one, you can save quite a bit. So make it a habit when shopping online to always search for coupon codes before pressing that order submit button.

WHAT TO BRING WHEN SCOUTING

Decor scouting is no different than Boy Scouting. You should always be prepared. And when it comes to decor scouting, being prepared entails having a bag filled with:

Your Shopping List. Do I even need to explain why? You don't know what you need if you don't have your list — not to mention, you won't remember all your other options. And if you don't remember all your options, how do you know if that awesome one-of-a-kind thing you just found is worth getting?

Your Emotional Wants, Muse & Style Sheets. After looking at tons of items, it's difficult to tell the maybes from the nos. That's why it's important to bring your emotional wants, muse and style sheets along with you. They remind you of exactly what you need.

Now, in addition to those sheets, it's also smart to bring along the photos of your muse and a few of your favorite style example photos. And not just to help you determine which items do and don't feel right. Having them with you can save time. Instead of wasting countless hours looking through every item in a store, you can just point to the picture and ask a salesperson, "Do you have anything like this?"

More often than not, they can take you to exactly what you need. And if they don't have it, they'll tell you, and you can move on.

Your Plan. Every once in awhile when scouting, you run across something truly spectacular. Something that perfectly fits all your emotional wants for your room. Only there's one problem. You don't have anything like it in your plan. In those instances, don't walk away and sigh, "If only."

Take out your plan and see if there's a way to switch things around so that your wonder item works. There's no reason to miss out on something you love if you can find a way to make it fit — especially when finding something you truly love is so rare.

A Tape Measure. Not all places are nice enough to write the dimensions of each item on their tiny sale tag. In fact, many don't, which means you'll need a tape measure. If you're going furniture shopping, don't bring one of those puny little 3-foot yo-yos. Bring one big enough to do the job. a 10-15 footer.

A Camera. If you're shopping in brick-and-mortar stores, take a camera. As good as you think your memory is, trust me, it's not good enough. After seeing hundreds of different items, they all blend together and you forget all the intricate — and not so intricate — details of each piece. And you need to know exactly how each of your options look in order to determine which is best.

So take your camera, and take a picture of every single item that might work. Better yet, take photos of each item from every angle. The more photos you have, the easier it will be to make a decision.

Now, if you're shopping online, obviously there's no need to take a camera. Instead, for each item you think may work, save the photo in a file folder. That way you can easily browse through your options without opening up a bunch of browser windows. Just be sure to rename the file so that you remember where it came from. If you don't remember, you'll end up opening all the browser windows again.

A Notebook & Pen. There's quite a bit of information you have to remember for each option you find: where it came from, its dimensions, delivery details and price. And after a long day of finding many options, you're bound to mix the information up. That's why it's extremely important to bring a notebook and pen along, and write down the information for each item.

Samples. If you've already visited a few stores and have samples, take them with you. That way, you have a better idea of how everything will work together.

WHAT TO ASK FOR

If you're shopping in a brick-and-mortar store, it's not enough to just walk in, click your camera, take some notes and walk out. Because unlike online, in person you don't get the little descriptive paragraph and list of features and options handed to you. For those, you have to ask, and here's what you'll need.

Samples. If you want to see the actual color of an item, you must have a sample because pictures don't always get colors right. And when making sure your color combinations work, you need to see the actual color. That's why you should always ask for samples. If they don't have any on hand, ask how you can get one. Can they ship one to you? Can you order one online? Do whatever you have to do to get a sample of things too big to take home.

Obviously, places selling one-of-a-kind items won't be able to give you a sample. For those, just take a good picture.

Options. Stores are limited by floor space, which means they can't display all of the options. Instead, they pick the options they think will sell best. So to know if you can get different furniture feet on a sofa, or different stain colors for a table, you have to ask.

And it's not just little decorative details that they don't show. Often a number of furniture pieces never make it onto the showroom floor. For those, you have to look in a book. So ask to view all of their furniture books, then ask to see all of the decorative detail options for each item you're interested in.

Installation Details. If you're purchasing something that must be installed, make sure to inquire about the installation requirements. After all, there's absolutely no use considering something that can't be installed in your home.

Price. Some places are sneaky about the prices and don't put them out in the open, and they do that for one of three reasons. The first is to create the illusion of luxury. People immediately assume things without a price are extremely expensive. The second is to make you think their product is exclusive — that only those who don't have to ask for the price can afford it. And the third is to give them the chance to sell you on it, so that by the time you see the price you want the item so bad it doesn't matter. You'll spend whatever it takes because they've whipped you into a frenzy.

And in all those instances, they're doing it for selfish reasons, so don't be ashamed to ask for the price. It's your right as the customer to know how much something costs.

Delivery Details. You already know it's important to ask about lead time. That's why you have a special column for it on your shopping list.

But there are two other important delivery questions to ask. First, is the item backordered? You'd be surprised how often that happens.

And second, do they deliver? Sometimes, you have to pick up the items yourself, and if they're big, that could be an issue.

Deals. You already know about this one. Always ask about any deals or sales that are coming up. There's no reason to pay full price if you can pay less.

WORKING WITH SALES PEOPLE

There are many helpful sales people who are an absolute pleasure to work with. And then there are those who believe they're a design expert. And as a design expert, it's their duty to guide you — a mere peon with no taste — in the right direction. Often, that direction entails a number of disparaging comments about your choices, followed by strong declarations of what you must buy because it will look oh-so-much better.

And whatever you do, don't listen to them. They don't know what they're talking about. You are the only person who knows what's right for you. And you're allowed to like whatever you like. So don't let them make you feel bad — especially when you'd probably hate the stuff they'd pick for their home.

If they try to push you in a different direction, tell them politely you don't need any design advice. Your mind is already made up. You simply need their assistance in getting it.

If they continue pushing, ask to work with someone else. You're not required to work with the first person who assists you.

And if there is no one else, hold your ground and stay polite — especially the polite part. I know how hard it is in those situations to keep your temper from boiling over, but do what you gotta do to keep it under control. Because if they treat you that badly when you're nice, just think of how they treat people they don't like. And like it or not, they're your ticket to getting what you want. So do what your momma told you — kill them with kindness.

Afterward, you can write a completely honest review recounting how unsatisfied you were with your shopping experience.

WHAT ITEMS TO FIND FIRST

When you scout, it's always smarter to start with the items available in the least amount of colors. That way, you never have to double back and pick things out again. Instead, you build your entire scheme off the hardest-to-find item, knowing you'll be able to find each additional item you need in a shade that works, because it's available in far more colors. When it comes to hard-to-find items, these take the cake:

1. Patterned Rugs. Many designers start every project by choosing the rug, because rugs are available in so few patterns — which limits your color choices greatly. If you want a patterned rug or carpet, you should look for it first.

2. Artwork. Finding artwork you love is extremely difficult — especially in the colors you want. That's why some designers start every design where artwork is a main feature by scouting for artwork first.

3. Patterned Tile. There's an extremely limited selection of patterned tile out there — probably far smaller than that of rugs and artwork. But since few people make patterned tile the focal point of their room, rarely does anyone start by selecting it. If patterned tile is the main feature of your room, by all means scout for it first.

4. Patterned Wallpaper. After patterned tile, rugs and artwork, patterned wallpaper is the next hardest item to find.

5. Patterned Fabric. While there are numerous types of fabric available, you can still have a difficult time finding the pattern you want in the color you need. After you've found the patterned rugs, tile, wallpaper and artwork that you need — if any — for your room, search for fabric next.

6. Natural Stone Tile or Slabs. Stone only comes in so many colors. Be sure to look for it fairly early in your scouting, preferably right after you find the items above.

After you've found options for all necessary items listed above, you're safe to move forward. Now, there are always exceptions — like if you want a colored refrigerator. But for the most part, you won't run into any problems.

Just be sure to select paint last. Dead last. It's available in the most color options. In fact, you can have paint made in any color you can imagine.

HOW TO FIND WHAT YOU WANT

When most people shop for decor, they walk into a showroom, see the hundreds of different options and become completely overwhelmed not knowing what to pick.

But that's not going to happen to you, because you have a plan. And your plan gives you a set of criteria to judge every one of those items. When you walk into a showroom, all you've got to do is look at each item and see if it meets your criteria. If it does, you have an option worth considering. If it doesn't, move on.

You'll be surprised at how fast it goes. Within a matter of minutes you can spot all the items worth considering and be out the door. So kiss feeling overwhelmed goodbye. You'll be walking through the showrooms with confidence, because you know exactly what you want. All you need to do is ask yourself the following six questions:

1. Does it Feel Right? When you walk through a store, you could analyze every single item, but that would take forever. Instead, let your gut weed out all the items that won't work. You know, the ones that aren't your style. And trust me, you won't have a problem spotting them, because when you see them you'll think, "Ew," or something along those lines. If you have that reaction, just keep on walking.

Only stop and analyze the items you're drawn to — the ones that feel right. When you find one, pull out your emotional needs, muse and style sheets to make sure the item will feel right in your room. After all, all items you're drawn to will. The emotions you want to feel in your room are only one small part of your life. During other times, you want to feel other things. So your gut will be drawn to a wide variety of items. And it's your job to weed out the ones that don't fit with what you want for your room.

So look at the item. Does it feel like the emotions you want to feel? Not sure? Look at its amount of ornamentation, overall shape and texture. Does it fit with your muse and style? If you need some extra guidance, compare it to the photos of your muse and style.

If it doesn't feel right, move on. But if it does, you're ready to ask yourself the next question.

2. Is it in Your Price Range? When you find an item that feels right, look at its price tag. There's no point in falling for something that's out of your league. You'll only get hurt in the end. If the number you see makes your eyeballs explode, quickly move on and don't get attached.

3. Is it the Right Size? If the item is within your price range, check to see if it's the right size. If it's not, there's no point in wasting time on it.

Look at its tag and see if the size is listed. If not, pull out your measuring tape and go to town. Remember, if the item isn't a built-in, it's okay for it to be a bit smaller or bigger than your ideal dimensions. If you really love it and it just misses your ideal dimensions, don't cross it off just yet.

4. Does it Meet Your Requirements? If the item is within the size range you need, make sure it meets all of your requirements. Does it have the right type of storage? Is it as durable and cleanable as you need? Is it the right size, shape, texture and color?

If it doesn't meet your criteria, move on. Well, except when durability, cleanability or color are your hang-ups, because there may be ways around those.

As far as durability and cleanability go, ask for two samples of the item. Take them home and test them yourself. Scratch it with a knife. Rub it with lemon. Spill grape juice on it. Try cleaning it — if possible. Then see how it compares with the untouched sample. The results will tell you how durable and cleanable the item truly is. Just remember, before testing, always check to see if there are any protective coatings you can put on the item. If there are, apply them to your sample before testing. It's the only way to get accurate results.

When it comes to color, see if you can have the item refinished. Having it repainted, stained or reupholstered can completely change its personality — and most importantly, its look.

5. Does it Functionally Work? If the item meets your requirements, test it. Use the item like you would at home.

If it's a storage piece, open all the doors and drawers. Make sure they work smoothly. If they don't, move on if it's a new piece. But if it's old, see if it can be saved.

If it's seating, sit on it, and stay for awhile. Make sure it's really comfortable. Don't get up until you're 100-percent convinced.

Now what happens if you fall completely head-over-heels in love with something that's either not the right size or doesn't meet your requirements? Well, you have two options. Pine for it from afar, or see if you can rework your plan to incorporate the item. Your second option is always

the best, because it's very rare to find something you love beyond reason. And if you're lucky enough to have that happen, do whatever it takes to make it work — even if that means creating an entirely new plan. Sometimes the best things are those we can't imagine, and it takes seeing it to know what is right.

INSIDER TIPS FOR FINDING SPECIFIC ITEMS

Sometimes, in order to get what you want, you need a little insider information.

Rugs & Carpets. If you can't find an area rug you love or in the size you need, you can always have a carpet you like made into one. And don't think it has to be a solid color. There are a number of patterned carpets available.

Another option is to get a natural fiber rug — like seagrass — cut and bound to size. Again, don't think it has to be a solid color. Many people paint patterns on natural fiber rugs.

If neither of those options sound good, have a custom area rug made. Just know, they're typically pretty expensive. But it never hurts to check around.

Cabinetry. Practically all cabinet manufacturers supply cabinet retailers with a special book that details all of the options. The types of base cabinets. The types of wall cabinets. The specialty cabinets. The decorative trim. The feet. The filler strips. Everything you can imagine.

The only problem is many cabinet retailers never let you see that book. Instead, they ask you to give them the dimensions for your room, and then they figure out what's best for you. If you already have a plan, they'll take it and decide which cabinets and trim best fit your design. But that doesn't cut it.

What a salesperson picks out isn't necessarily best. They'll choose what they think looks good — not what you think looks good. And you won't know any better, because you'll think it's the best they can do. After all, how do you know what you can get if you don't see the book?

So ask them for it. Tell them you want to see every option available so you can make a good decision. Then ask them to explain any terminology or size information you don't understand.

When you look at the books, you'll find cabinetry widths are typically sold in 3-inch increments. So you can have a 9-inch, 12-inch, 15-inch, 18-inch, 21-inch, 24-inch, 27-inch, 30-inch, 33-inch and 36-inch cabinets. If you need a size somewhere in between, what you do depends on the type of cabinets you choose.

If you go with a custom line — which tends to be the most expensive — the cabinets will be made to the sizes you need. Custom lines tend to have the most trim options.

If you go with a semi-custom line — which tends to be mid-range in terms of pricing — you'll likely have to use the standard cabinet sizes. But they do offer a number of decorative fillers to cover any gaps, in addition to a number of other decorative trim pieces.

If you go with stock cabinets — which tends to be the cheapest — you have the least options. What you see is what you get. They only come in standard sizes, and they don't offer many decorative trim options.

Which type of cabinetry you choose depends completely on your budget. And if you can't afford expensive cabinetry, don't worry. You can still dress your cabinets up.

Most cabinets are just plain boxes with doors. To make them appear special, the decorative details are layered on top or inserted between. For example, extra doors are often attached to the end of cabinetry, crown molding is added to the tops, and legs are sandwiched in between cabinets to make them look more like furniture. If you want to get really fancy, you can have small trim pieces attached to the bottom of wall cabinets or double-layer your crown molding to make it appear larger. Do whatever it takes to make your cabinets look the way you want.

Keep in mind, you don't have to get the decorative details from the same place you get your cabinets. It's easier, because you don't have to worry about matching the finish. But just because it's easier doesn't mean it's the best option. Sometimes you can find better trim pieces online or at your local lumber yard. If you decide to go that route — especially if you go with stock cabinets and want any type of decoration — know that the trim will come completely unfinished, which is a benefit. That way, you can have it stained or spray painted to match. And I promise, you won't be able to tell that your cabinets and trim didn't come from the same place.

Just look on page 391. Do you think those legs came with the cabinetry? Guess again. I bought the legs unfinished for a fraction of what I would have paid through a cabinet company and sprayed them to match the cabinets.

So when it comes to trim, don't worry if the cabinetry company doesn't have what you want. You can always find it elsewhere and have it refinished. The main thing you should focus on is selecting the right door styles. And when it comes to door styles, there are two things to remember.

One, always ask the cost. You'll be shocked to find some are far more expensive than others — even if they're in the same cabinetry line. So before you get your heart set on a style, ask how much it'll set you back.

Two, don't worry if your door looks too plain. You're looking at it in isolation. When that door is repeated over and over again with nice hardware, it will suddenly appear far less plain. But don't take my word for it. Find pictures of kitchens with similar door styles to make sure you'll like it.

Stone Slabs. If you're planning to use a stone slab for anything in your home — a backsplash, countertop, fireplace surround, shower or tub — don't go off the sample. Stone varies dramatically. One piece of the same exact stone can look drastically different than another. And we're talking I-can't-believe-it's-the-same-stone different, because the color, the veining, and the flecks can all be off. So whatever you do, don't base your decision on a sample.

The only way to ensure you get exactly what you want is to pick out the slab yourself. When you visit a stone retailer, tell them you want to see the slabs. When you go to where the slabs are stored, you'll often find the same types of stones are often stacked, leaning up against one another with only the slab on top visible. And don't make the mistake of assuming the ones behind it look identical. They may not.

So if you're interested in a particular type of stone, have them move each slab so you can see each one. Be sure to take a picture of each one you see, because it's rare to see all of them at once, standing side by side. Typically, they move each one individually. So the only way to compare them is through pictures.

Now, when you look at the slabs, keep in mind they're not always polished. Unpolished stones look very different than polished ones. If you want to see what the slab will look like polished, throw a bit of water on the slab and use your hand to rub it around. What you see is close to how the stone will look when it's polished.

Of course, you don't have to have your stone polished. If you want a duller look, you can always have it honed. Also, the stone doesn't have to be an inch- to two-inches thick. You can have two slabs sandwiched together for a thicker profile. Or, if you're willing to spend a pretty penny, have the stone cut extra thick. Be sure to ask the salespeople about all the special options available before making your decision.

Upholstery. While the furniture salespeople may imply that you must purchase the fabric for your pieces there, often that's not the case. Most upholstery manufacturers allow you to have your pieces covered in any fabric you want. All you have to do is have your piece covered in muslin — which is the term used to say, "this piece is being covered with an outside fabric."

If you decide to do that, you will need to supply the furniture company with the fabric. Ask how many yards will be needed to cover your piece. If your fabric has a pattern on it, be sure to tell the furniture manufacturer what the size of the pattern's repeat is. It will affect how many yards will be needed to cover your piece. Once you get the correct amount of fabric, get it to the furniture manufacturer as soon as possible. Within a matter of weeks, your new piece will magically arrive in the fabric you really wanted — not some fabric you chose because you didn't think you had any other options.

You also have the option to use more than one fabric on your piece. You can use one on the front, one on the back and another on the cushion. You can even use a different fabric on the welting.

Be sure to tell them how you want the pattern — if there is one — oriented on your piece. If you don't tell them, it may not show up the way you want.

When selecting the fabric, don't make the mistake of using a drapery-grade fabric. It's nowhere near strong enough. For upholstery, you need fabric that can undergo a certain amount of abuse, and those fabrics are known as upholstery-grade fabrics. Within upholstery-grade fabrics, each fabric is graded in terms of how much abuse it can take. Be sure to choose an upholstery grade fabric strong enough to withstand the amount of abuse you plan to give it.

Next, ask about furniture leg options. Often, you can get a number of different feet styles and colored stains.

Tables & Chairs. We all assume that if we purchase a chair, it will be the right height for the dining table or desk we buy. But guess what? That's not always the case.

The first time I picked out a desk chair, the seat was only 5 inches below the underside of the desk, which made for a snug fit when sitting. A bit too snug.

Ideally, the height difference between a chair seat and underside of a desk or table should be around 8 inches. When shopping for a table and chairs to pair together, measure their heights. You don't want to scrape your knees every time you sit at the dinner table.

Pillows, Bedding & Drapes. Despite there being a number of lovely pillow, bedding and drapes available, sometimes you can't find one you want. That's why designers often have them custom made. And shockingly, it's not all that expensive. In fact, having custom pillows, bedding and drapes made can sometimes be cheaper than buying ones off the rack. And considering you can have them made exactly how you want, it's practically an offer you can't refuse.

And when I say exactly how you want, I'm not kidding. You can have fabric sewn in different patterns. Piping or welting or fringe added on. Buttons or sequins or beads sewn on. Whatever you can imagine, it can be done. Just be sure to draw it up. Clearly show exactly what you want, where you want it and the exact size you want it to be. That way, there are no communication errors.

If you decide to have pillows made, specify the size insert you want to use.

If you want your pillow to be an odd shape, you can even have that made. Just realize you can't take the cover off to clean it, because they'll have to stuff the pillow like a stuffed animal.

As for who to hire, finding a local seamstress or tailor is always your best bet because they're almost always the cheapest. If you go through an interior designer or furniture showroom, they typically bid it out, which causes the price to go up. To be safe, get multiple bids.

Paint. Whatever you do, don't pick your paint color in the store. You're bound to choose the wrong one, because the lighting there is likely different than the lighting in your home. And lighting greatly affects the way we see colors. So the colors you see in the store are not how they will look in your home.

The only way to know what color will look right is to take samples home. And I'm not talking about those little tiny paper cards. They're too small to get an idea of how the color will look on your walls, and the color on the chip often looks a bit different than the actual paint. If you want to see how the color will really look, you need to get actual samples of the paint. Liquid samples.

When it comes to choosing samples, remember colors always appear brighter and darker on your walls than they do on the chip. That's because on your walls, they cover a much bigger area — which makes the color look more intense. So choose samples that are lighter than what you think you want. More often than not, that ends up being the color you really want. Ideally, you should bring home at least three samples. Maybe more. The more colors you bring home, the more options you have, and the less trips you need to make back and forth to the paint store.

When you get home with the samples, don't make the mistake everyone makes. Don't paint the color directly on your wall. If you do, you have to live with it. And unless you're repainting the very next day, that will get old fast.

Instead, paint each sample on thick, white poster board. Then, once it's dry, hang it on your wall using painter's tape. Move it around the room to see how the color will look on each wall and against the floor. Also, pay attention to how the color changes in different lighting — morning, afternoon and evening. The color you like at night may not look so good during the day.

If you don't like the samples you brought home, don't sweat it. You can make your own color using the leftover paint in each sample. Just pour some of each color you want to combine in a jar. Shake and stir vigorously until the color is completely blended. Then, paint it on a piece of poster board. If you like what you see, take the poster board into the paint store. They'll use it to create a custom color just for you. If you have a shirt, hat, piece of fabric or mug that is the exact color you want, you can take that in and they'll match it for you.

WHEN YOU CAN'T FIND WHAT YOU WANT

Sometimes, no matter how hard you try, you can't find what you want. In those cases, you have five choices.

One, be patient. The thing you want may surface in the next few months. Then again, maybe it won't. Before deciding to hold out, go to all the places that most likely sell the item and ask the store owners or managers what the chances are of it coming in. If the consensus seems good, wait. If not, reconsider because you may end up waiting for a very long time.

Two, get a stand in. If the item you want isn't built in like cabinetry, tile or countertops, consider a less expensive substitute. That way, you have something to use until the perfect item pops up down the road.

Three, scope out other options that achieve the same effect. For example, say you want a patterned wallpaper, only you can't find the pattern in the color you want. You can always achieve a similar look by hiring a faux finisher to paint the pattern on your walls or having a fabric you like paper-backed — which allows the fabric to be hung on your walls like wallpaper.

Four, go custom. And I promise, it's not always as expensive as you think. There are a number of talented craftsmen in your area looking for work. Cabinet makers. Furniture makers. Weavers. Glass blowers. Stone carvers. Blacksmiths. They can make whatever you want. Tables. Tapestries. Glass pendants. Fireplace mantels. Decorative stands.

For the Home Office Example Room, I had a stand custom made by a local blacksmith, and it cost just about the same as one would have from a store. So don't be afraid to get quotes for custom work. You may be surprised by how reasonable the pricing is, and you can't beat getting exactly what you want.

If you do go custom, make sure to draw precise plans. If you don't, the artisan will create what they think looks best, and that may not be what you like best.

Five, alter your plan. Unfortunately, sometimes your only

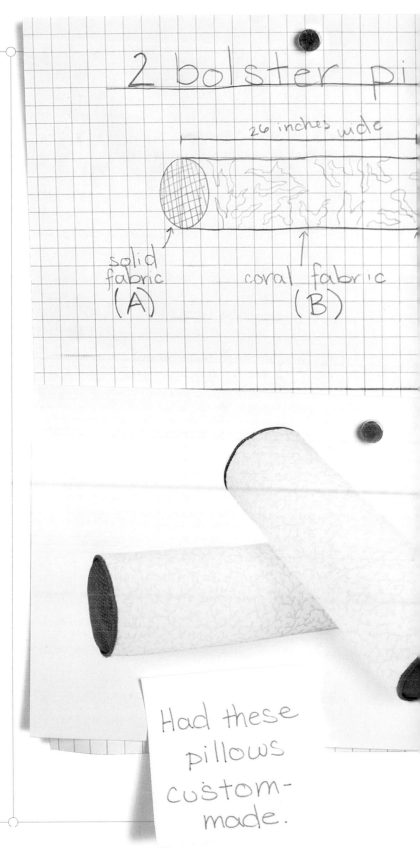

alternative is to rearrange things so you can take advantage of what is available. That could mean making small surface changes like switching the pattern from your rug to your sofa, or completely overhauling your plan and starting from scratch. Either way, hit the drawing table until you create a new version you absolutely love.

WHEN YOU'VE FOUND ENOUGH OPTIONS

Ideally, you want to find a few options for every item on your list. That way, you have flexibility when trying to create the perfect combination.

But, that's not always possible. Sometimes, no matter how hard you look, you can only find one thing that works for what you need. And that's okay. You can only find what's there.

So just do your best. And once you're completely satisfied with all your options, you can stop searching and start deciding which will make the cut.

IF YOU DECIDE TO HAVE ITEMS REFINISHED

Before you move on, decide if any pieces need to be refinished. If they do, the overall price of the item will change. It'll cost you its original price — plus the cost to refinish it. Calculate that number in order to determine what combination of items you can afford.

For each item you plan to refinish, add its refinishing cost to its original price. That refinishing cost will completely depend on what you need done.

Painted. If you plan to have something painted, you have two options: use a brush or a sprayer. Using a brush is the budget option, because all you need is paint and a paintbrush. But know that it will leave brushstrokes no matter how good of a painter you are.

A sprayer provides a perfectly-even, brushstroke-free finish, much like that on a car or brand-new painted cabinetry. To get that flawless finish, it'll cost you just a bit more because you have to hire someone to do it, or rent the equipment yourself.

If you decide to hire someone, get multiple quotes to ensure you get both the best price and end result possible.

If you decide to do it yourself, know that you must have a large work space and lots of tarps because when you spray, it goes everywhere.

Stained. If you plan to have something stained, you can either do it yourself or have a furniture refinisher do it for you. Staining it yourself isn't all that hard. It's the stripping of its current finish that's difficult, and perfectly matching one stain to another is no walk in the park either.

If you need to do either of those two things and don't consider yourself particularly handy, consider hiring a furniture refinisher. Just remember to call around and get multiple quotes before choosing someone.

Reupholstered. If you plan to reupholster a small piece of furniture such as an ottoman, stool or dining room chair cushion, you can do it on your own fairly easily. I recovered the bench on page 377 — with the help of an extra set of hands.

If you have pieces with numerous upholstery seams — like a sofa or sitting chair — don't even try it. Upholstering is a very complicated job. And if you've never done it before, it's best to leave it to professionals.

If you decide to upholster a difficult piece, call up several places for quotes before making a decision. Just be warned, reupholstering an item can be expensive, because sometimes pieces need to have their padding and springs replaced, as well as the fabric. So don't let your eyeballs pop out of your head if the number comes back high.

CREATING YOUR PICTURE BOARD

When deciding what options to use in your room, don't worry about how they look individually. You'll never see them that way. All that matters is how they look together. That's why interior designers create mood and picture boards. To get a taste of how the room will look and make it easy to see which options work the best.

And that's exactly what we're going to do.

But first things first. Decide whether you want a real or virtual picture board. Making a real one can be more of a hassle because you have to print actual photographs of your options. But if you're not computer savvy — or lack a large monitor — that may be your best option.

Once you've decided which type you're going to do, it's time to create.

1. Select Your Items. Take out — or open up the files — of your option photos. For each item you need, select your favorite option. Don't think about it. Use your gut, and choose the ones you're drawn to first.

2. Arrange the Photos. Arrange all the photos you chose together in a collage. Try to position them as you'd see them in your room. The items going in the center of your room should be in the center of your collage. The items going on the floor should be at the bottom of your collage. And so on.

If you don't like the way the combination looks, switch out items one at a time until you do. You'll be surprised by how much the overall look can change by switching out just one item.

3. Determine its Total. Once you have a combination you like, total up the cost. Remember, you can't blow your whole budget on the items in your room. You must have enough money left for your projects.

If the combination is within your budget, move on. If not, switch out items until you find a combination you like that is within your budget.

4. Take a Photo or Screenshot. Once you find a combination you like and can afford, take a photo or screen shot. That way, you can compare all the combinations to see which you like best.

5. Create at Least Three More. You should know the drill by now. The only way to know which combination is best is to create multiple versions. Switch out items one-by-one, and when you find a combination you like, determine its total and if it's within budget. Then take its picture. Continue doing this until you've created as many combinations as possible.

6. Choose the Best One. Often, the best combination will jump right out at you. It'll be the one you keep being drawn to. The one you can't help but love.

But every once in awhile, you'll find yourself torn between two, and more often than not, your indecision is due to a war over the two essential parts of decorating: function and emotion.

One combination functionally works better. The other feels better. Ideally, you want both. So how do you choose?

Listen to your gut. Some people value function more. Others value emotion more. And your gut will tell you which one you are by irrationally pulling for one version or the other. Whichever one you slightly favor is the one that will probably make you happiest.

If you can't tell which one your gut favors, do what I suggested on page 221. Ask for a second opinion. Your reaction to their answer — joy or disappointment — will tell you which one you prefer.

If you still can't decide, you haven't created the right combination. So go back to the drawing board. If you've found one you love, congratulations. Now you just have to make sure it will actually work the way you want it to.

TOTAL FOR ALL ITEMS INCLUDING
THOSE NEEDED FOR PROJECTS:

$5,235

FOR PLANTS
CONTEMPORARY BOTANICAL MASTERWORKS

138

SW 6908
Fun Yellow

SW 6909
Lemon Twist

ARCHITECTURAL
Plants

christine shaw

PORARY BOTANICAL MASTERWORKS

TOTAL FOR ALL ITEMS INCLUDING
THOSE NEEDED FOR PROJECTS:

$21,225

TOTAL FOR ALL ITEMS INCLUDING
THOSE NEEDED FOR PROJECTS:

$16,927

DRAWING YOUR FINAL PLAN

Once you've found the combination you love, redraw your floor plan, elevations and ceiling layout. That way, you know everything will actually work together in both size and looks. When drawing them up, use the actual size, shape, color, texture and pattern of each item. Don't worry about getting it perfect. Stick drawings are still fine. You just need to know for sure that the combination you created will indeed work. And more importantly, that you'll definitely like it all together.

TAPING OUT YOUR ROOM

Now, you don't have to do this part, because redrawing your plans with the dimensions of each item will tell you if the sizing will work. But if this is your first time decorating and you're nervous about making a mistake, try it. Taping out your room allows you to see exactly what it will look and feel like with the items you chose.

And I'll be honest, even if it's not your first time, doing this is a good idea. After seeing your room taped out, you'll know without a doubt if you love your plan. And that's very important to know before spending all that money.

To tape out your room, you'll need your newly drawn floor plan, painter's tape, scissors and a measuring tape.

1. Tape out all Furniture on the Walls. To determine where a piece of furniture should be located on your wall, first measure the distance it should be away from one wall. Put a marker piece of tape there. Measure the height it should be from the floor. Put a marker piece of tape there. Where the two pieces of tape intersect is where the corner of the item should be. Use that spot to locate all corners of the piece. Then connect the dots with tape.

If your piece has curves, locate the tallest point of the curve, and where the curve begins and ends. Then, rip off small pieces of tape and slightly angle each piece as you stick it on the wall. Use those small pieces to connect the dots of the curve. If your piece is circular, locate four points of the circle. Then, fill in the dots using small pieces of tape.

2. Tape out Furniture on the Floor. Tape out the location of each furniture piece on the floor the same way as you did on the walls. First locate the corners, then connect the dots with tape.

3. Tape out Lighting and Accessories. Do it the same way as you did with the furniture. First locate the corners, then connect the dots with tape. When you're finished, your room should look something like those to the right.

Don't feel like your taped versions should be perfect. A rough idea is all you need.

Once you have everything taped out, soak it up. Walk around. Experience the room.

Do you have enough space? Is it easy to get around? Does it feel right? Do the focal points draw your attention? Does the room feel balanced? Does it look proportional?

If you're not happy with the way something is, sit on it for a day or two. Sometimes it's just a shock seeing your room in a different way. If you still don't like it, go back to your plan and fix it.

But if you're happy — if you love everything about it — congratulations. You've finished scouting. You've conquered the part of decorating that terrifies people, and are well on your way to having your room completed.

Before you move on, you might want to hold out for a few days — maybe a week — to make sure that feeling stays. That is, unless you're on a tight deadline or are worried a special piece will be scooped up. Then, move right ahead. But if you have the time, sit on it to make sure your affection for the combination grows, not wanes.

Just don't keep the painter's tape up longer than a few days. You don't want it to meld to your wall and rip down a piece of drywall or paint with it.

That's how you create a curve. But you don't have to be that detailed. A rough idea will do. •·······························>

Taping out your room will give you a really good idea of how your room will look. Just be sure to set aside enough time to do it. You'll need at least an hour.

Not using the right tools is one of the biggest mistakes made by DIYers.

step:

16

hiring & DIYing

After figuring out what items to put in their rooms, people get trigger happy and want to buy everything right away. But hold up. Before you buy a single thing, you must first make sure all those things that need to be installed can actually be installed in your situation and most importantly, that the cost to install them won't break the bank. The only way to determine that is to decide whether you're going to hire it out or do it yourself.

TO HIRE OR TO DIY

There are four main things to consider when deciding between hiring and DIYing: cost, time, tools and skill level.

Cost. Before you assume it's too expensive to hire someone, ask for a bid. Many small jobs aren't as expensive as you'd think, such as installing a new light. If you can't afford to hire someone, you've got two options. Either do it yourself or select cheaper items so that more of your budget can be used to hire someone.

Time. To do a project yourself, you need time — lots of it because practically all DIY jobs take far longer than you'd think. If you don't have much free time and want the job done fast, consider hiring someone.

Tools. You can have all the time in the world, but if you don't have the right tools, you can't do the job. Sometimes the cost of buying the right tools is more than it costs to hire someone. So before you decide to do it yourself, find out how much the tools cost to rent or buy. If it's practically as much as it would cost to hire someone, delegate the job. More pinball time for you.

Skill Level. When it comes to DIY work, everyone always makes the same mistake. They assume they have what it takes to do the job and jump in headfirst only to find half-

way through they don't. And it's not because they lack talent. It's because they lack experience.

Most remodeling jobs aren't exceptionally difficult. They just require practice to do well. If you think you can hack it without practice, test yourself.

Get a small amount of the materials you need for the job, and practice doing it on a scrap piece of plywood or drywall. If you like the outcome, you're good to go. If not, try again or considering hiring someone.

Just know, the majority of errors that do-it-yourselfers make are from either using the wrong tools or skipping an important step. If you do decide to try it again, do some extra research to determine where you went wrong.

Now there are some things you should never test, such as anything electrical. As my dad, Tim Carter, award-winning remodeler and author of the syndicated newspaper column "Ask the Builder," always says, "Electricity is the silent killer."

One faulty wire is enough for a house to burn down. So if you've never worked with electricity, don't start now.

WHAT TO KNOW WHEN HIRING

There are four easy steps you should always follow when hiring someone to work on your home. First, locate the best. Second, get bids. Third, see their work. Finally, create a contract.

1. Find the Best. Finding contractors, electricians, plumbers and painters is like finding a buffalo. Your best bet is to go to their watering hole, which is where they get their supplies. And no, I'm not referring to a big box home improvement center. I'm talking about where the professionals go. The lumber yards. The electrical supply companies. The plumbing supply companies. And the stores devoted just to paint. That's where you'll find the best.

So go there, and ask the owner or manager for a list of the top three contractors, plumbers, electricians — whatever you need — they would hire to work on their home. Tell them you want the people who always pay their bills on time, who always seem to have a lot of business and who, from what they hear, always do a good job. The people they list are the people you should consider hiring. More than likely, they're the best in your area.

2. Get Bids. Now that you know who to consider, it's time to give out bids. Before you do, draw up a plan and a complete list of specs. Fortunately, you already have the plan. You just need to make a copy with the details they need. For example, if you want cabinets installed, only draw the cabinets. There's no need to draw your kitchen table or chairs.

When it comes to creating the specs, list each item you need installed and where it should go. Write down what level of quality you expect. Do you want the molding joints to be perfect? The paint lines to be razor-straight? The grout lines between the tile completely identical? Write down exactly what you want them to do.

You should also research the correct way for the job to be done. That way, you know what steps should be taken and what products should be used during the installation. That entire process, along with the supplies that should be used, must be included in your specification. If you're unsure of the correct process, there are a number of places that sell detailed instructions or checklists that specify exactly how a job should be done. My dad's website, AsktheBuilder.com, is one of them. And no, I don't get any kickbacks from him. Not even a penny. Although, maybe I should bring that up next time I see him for dinner.

It's also a good idea to include how you want them to work. Do you expect them to work in silence? Put down plastic sheeting or drop clothes to protect your floors? Only use certain bathrooms? Write that down as well.

Finally, include if you're working on a tight deadline. If you are, state that all materials must be on site and inspected before any work begins. That way you don't end up with a giant hole in your ceiling the night before a big dinner party — because the parts aren't arriving until a week later.

As you write each of those specifications, be very clear. Many people skip this part because they don't think it's important. However, specifications are the most important part of hiring. Nothing frustrates contractors or electricians more than a customer who isn't specific. They can't read your mind. They don't know what you expect, which means they end up assuming, and you know what happens when people assume. You don't get what you want. Then you get angry, and whoever you hired gets frustrated because you didn't communicate clearly.

So take the specifications very seriously. You've worked this hard. You deserve to get it done right. Fortunately, you already have the most difficult part of creating specifications figured out: exactly what products you want installed. Most people don't know that before hiring people, which infuriates contractors because they have to hold up jobs waiting for the homeowners to make decisions. If you hand a reputable contractor or tradesman a clear, concise and extremely detailed specification, they will thank you. They will appreciate you. They will feel like it's a pleasure working with you.

So do it. Create a clear specification. Make copies of it and your plan. Call up the three or more people that were suggested to you. Tell them you want a bid. They should ask to come over and see your place so they can inspect the site-specific challenges. When they do, hand them the plan and specifications. Tell them when you want their bid, and then wait.

Be wary of bids that come in right away. Sometimes they're extremely high, because the person's hoping you'll jump on it before you hear any other bids. Other times it's too low, because the person didn't take the time to consider everything.

The amount of time you should wait for a bid is directly proportional to the size of the job. The more work that needs to be done, the more time the person needs to price things out. For a small paint job, 48 hours is normally sufficient. For a big remodel, they may need three weeks. So be patient.

3. Visit Their Work. When you get the bids back, you'll probably receive a range of numbers. Typically, you'd think the highest is best, but that's not always the case. If some of the numbers are too big for your budget, don't worry. Only focus on the ones you can afford. For those, ask the person if you can see some of his or her work.

When looking, pay close attention to the details. How clean and precise are they? If they are up to your standards, you've got a good candidate. If none of them are up to your standards, start the whole process over again. This time, try a different watering hole.

If you're left with more than one good candidate, ask for referrals. Based on what you receive and how you feel about each one, decide who is best. If they were able to get this far in the vetting process, you probably can't make a bad decision. More than likely, both will do a good job.

4. Create a Contract. Many people skip the contract, assuming the contractor, painter or plumber will do what they promise. But when promises are broken, you lose. Whereas, when a contract is broken, you win. So create a contract and include all of the specifications and payment details.

And don't ever — e-v-e-r — give a contractor or worker money upfront. The only time it's acceptable is if they are buying supplies. And even then, it's far better for you to purchase the supplies. Sadly, there are contractors who will take your money, use it on something else and never show up again. So to be on the safe side, say you'll provide all the materials.

If it's a small job that only takes a day or two, pay when the job is completed according to the specifications. If it's a long job, create a payment schedule. And don't make the mistake of paying according to how much time has gone by. There are workers who will dilly-dally around halfheart-

edly on the job, waiting for each week's payment to come in. Then, they'll split right before the job is supposed to be done, leaving you with a half-finished room.

If you need to make a payment schedule, only pay according to how much work has been done. Specifically state in your contract when this task is completed according to the specifications, you get this much money. And so on. Do that for each part of the job. When you're finished, you'll be ready to sign and hire your new contractor, painter, plumber, electrician or whoever it is you need.

WHAT TO KNOW WHEN DIYING

Everyone thinks they can slap on a tool belt and become a weekend warrior. But more goes into it than that. A lot more. To get your projects done well and right, there are a number of things you must do: research, practice, make a list, schedule twice the time, get help, use the right tools and push through.

Research. At the very beginning of my dad's building career, a woman hired him to install crown molding. Being young and cocky, he took the job — despite never having installed crown molding before in his life. My dad was quickly humbled. After three hours of making wrong cut after wrong cut, the woman came outside and said, "You've never done this before, have you?"

Then, she fired him.

Despite his bruised ego, my dad headed straight for the library. He checked out every single book he could find on how to cut crown molding, and quickly became a pro at installing it. And I'm not just saying that because I'm his daughter. As I stated above, he's won numerous remodeling awards and writes a syndicated building column. Ironically, he has written quite a bit on how to install crown molding.

And it's all because he did the research. At the beginning of his career, he was as useless with a hammer as Barney

Fife with bullets. But through research, he learned how to do every home project the right way.

So take a page from my dad's book, and most importantly, learn from his mistake. Always research how to do a project and what you'll need before you attempt it. Always.

Practice First. Through interviews with professionals I've discovered the secret of professionals. They practice. A lot.

Make a List. Many first-time do-it-yourselfers spend more time driving back and forth to the hardware store than they do on the job. And unless you have a fancy little hot rod, no one likes driving that much. So don't follow in their footsteps. Before you start a job, make a list of all materials and tools you need. That way, you only have to go to the store once.

Schedule Twice the Time. As a general rule, we tend to *overestimate* our abilities and *underestimate* the complexity of projects. So unless you've done the project before, it's going to take you at least twice as long to finish as you think it will — if not longer.

And I don't care what the time estimates are online or how long your research told you it will take. It's always better to be safe than sorry. Not to mention, those estimates normally assume everything goes smoothly. But rarely does the first project go smoothly. There are almost always bumps in the road.

So before starting a project, ask yourself realistically how long you think it will take. Then double it. That way you're not surprised when you have to miss the big football game or spend the second weekend in a row working on that blasted, time-sucking project. Instead, you'll know what you're getting into and can plan ahead.

Don't Start Until You Have Everything You Need. Many rookies start a project only to get halfway in and realize they don't have everything they need. Then, they go to the store and learn what they need is on backorder for the next six weeks. That doesn't cut it. If you're going to rip apart your bathroom, cut a hole in your wall, or do anything that you don't want to live with for six weeks, don't start the project until you have every little thing you need. And it's not enough to have boxes. You must open every one to make sure they didn't pack the wrong part, or leave it out. Only when you know you have everything, should you begin.

Get Help. Four hands are better than two. Six hands are better than four. And eight hands are better than six. Get some help. The more help you have, the faster your job will go. If you need help getting help, lure them with food. Bake brownies. Order pizza. Throw in some beers. They'll come.

Although, you might want to tell people they can't have the beers until the job is done. If you don't, you may end up with crooked crown molding and people hanging from your old chandelier — instead of your new chandelier hanging from your ceiling.

Now, in the rare cases when food doesn't work, offer to return the favor. Mow their lawns. Babysit their hellions. Host the Super Bowl party into eternity. Only a fool who enjoys driving back and forth to the hardware store, visiting the emergency room or both inflicts large DIY jobs upon themselves.

Use the Right Tools. If what you're doing is ridiculously hard and you find yourself wondering, "How in the heck do people flipping do this?" you're probably using the wrong tools. It's a common error — one I've made many, many times — that stems from being both ignorant and cheap.

Fortunately, the ignorant part can easily be fixed. Once you feel something is too difficult, go buy the right tool. Better yet, before you start a project ask people with experience what tool they'd recommend for the job. And just so you know, people at the big box home centers rarely have experience. To find someone who really knows, go to a lumber yard or local hardware store. If the people working there don't know, they might be nice enough to ask a local builder, who happens to be in the store, on your behalf. If you want that to happen, the best time to visit the store is early in morning before all crews need to report to work. Now, if you're the shy type, you can research online. It just might take awhile to find what you need to know. But it's always worth a try before walking out the door. I personally like to do both, because I've found the more info you get, the better off you are.

As for the cheap part, just know that cheap tools make your life miserable and often make your final product come out looking half as good. If you want the job to be as easy, fast and professional as possible, get the right tools. You'll thank yourself for it. And if the right tools will break the bank, borrow them from a friend or rent them.

Push Through. There's a moment of panic and darkness that sets in during any large project. When the room has been cleared out and torn apart. When you're living in boxes scattered all over your house. When everywhere you look is a never-ending mess.

And you're tired. Bone tired. Every muscle in your body aches. And no matter how hard you work, everything you do seems to make the room look worse.

Whatever you do, don't give up.

One of the saddest sights in the world is a decorating job half done. Where a homeowner, once bright-eyed and bushy-tailed, loses all hope. It always happens at the same point: right before thing are about to turn around and look good.

But if you keep at it, I promise, it will get better. And you need to remember that, because no matter how bad your room looks when you start out, it can — and will — get worse if you plan to do big projects. Sometimes people crack when they see that "worse" and start thinking it was a stupid idea. But you have to push through.

I know this sounds crazy and overdramatic right now,

but once you're in the belly of the beast surrounded by dust and debris, you'll thank me. Every amateur DIYer needs to hear "you can do it." If you keep pushing through, you will see improvement. Your room will look better. The pain will be worth it. And you will be so unbelievably proud of yourself when it's finished.

So whatever you do, don't stop halfway through. Halfway is the hardest part. If you push through, you will reach glory. Keep pushing. It will get better, one blasted nail at a time.

HANDLING FREAK OUTS

Regardless of whether you've hired or DIYed your job, whenever something new comes in there's always a chance a freak out will happen.

You know, where you walk in your room and think, "Oh my gosh. What was I thinking? That looks horrible."

If that happens, your initial reaction will be to get rid of it as soon as possible. But don't you dare. What you're looking at isn't the finished product. So step back. Take a deep breath, and try to visualize what it will look like with everything else in the room.

Many people lose faith in their plan when they see their room halfway done, because after all the work, they're afraid to move forward. But trust your gut. If you're just nervous, stick with your plan.

But if it feels like somethings wrong — really wrong — listen. Ask yourself what you don't like. Then, based on your answer, fix whatever you feel is wrong.

Just whatever you do, don't beat yourself up. Everyone — and I do mean everyone — makes mistakes when they're getting started. And even when you have tons of experience, you can't expect to get it right every time.

So give yourself a break. You're not decorating deficient. You're just learning. And the more you learn — the more mistakes you make — the better you'll get. Think of it as earning your decorating stripes.

step:

17

shopping

You're going to have a lot of these. Make sure you hold onto them.

Partial receipt text visible:

HOME COMFORT LLC
RT 25B
CENTER HARBOR, NH. 0322

I.D.: 111773400091171102009
#: 2311718023

CARD
******6292 *
E
#: 8   INV: 000008   TIME: 12:36
JUL 22, 09
#: 633   AUTH: 015432

RESPONSE: Y
RESS AND 5 DIGIT ZIP MATCH

$0.00
+ $0.00
$2,850.00

OTAL $2900.00

I AGREE TO PAY ABOVE TOTAL AMOUNT
ACCORDING TO CARD ISSUER AGREEMENT
(MERCHANT AGREEMENT IF CREDIT VOUCHER)

CUSTOMER COPY

From Sales
Thanks for shopping with us!

7945

7/22/2009 2:16 PM   Deposit Receipt #8624
Store

Home Comfort Design Center
PO Box 1552, Senters Market
Center Harbor, NH 03226
603-253-6660

Bill To:
Meghan Carter
6136 Market Drive
Cincinatti, Ohio 23215

Cashier: Sheryl

Subtotal $0.00
Local Sales Tax   0 % Tax   + $0.00
RECEIPT TOTAL: $2,900.00

Credit Card: $2,900.00
MasterCard

Total Deposit Taken: $5,750.00
Balance Outstanding: $0.00

Now that you know exactly which items you want for your room and that they'll all work, it's time to whip out your wallet and start buying. Of course, if you need to pause or take a deep breath before doing so, I completely understand. You're about to make some very big purchases that require lots of dough. You should be nervous.

But remember, you love everything on that list. You tested it all out and know it works, so there really shouldn't be anything to worry about. But just in case, let's check the return policies.

RETURN POLICIES

Take out — or open up — the spreadsheet for your favorite room version. Once it's out, make a new column next to "Price" titled "Return Policy." Fill in the return policy for each item on the list. Doing this is not just to ease your conscious. When you have dozens of things arriving, it's easy to forget which ones have to go back, and when, if you don't like them. That's why it's so handy having a nice, neat, little list detailing exactly when each item must be returned.

If an item can't be returned — because not all can — don't write "none" in the category. Instead, brainstorm a backup plan for the very slim chance that you don't like it when it arrives. That way, you can skip the whole blame-yourself-while-freaking-out-about-what-a-mistake-you-made stage and move straight to doing something productive. Because let's face it — when things start arriving, you'll have too much going on to stress out. That's why you need a backup plan now. And it could be anything. Sell it on eBay. Give it as a Christmas present. Use it in another room. Whatever will ease your guilt most — or provide you with enough cash to replace the thing you hate — is the one to choose. Once you've made up your mind about what you'll do, write it under the "Return Policy" column.

BUYING EACH ITEM

Once you finish writing in all the return policies and backup plans, your stress about buying each item should be somewhat — if not completely — eliminated. So what are you waiting for? Start buying.

After purchasing each item, record when it is supposed to be delivered in a new column next to "Return Policy" labeled "Delivery Dates." That way, you can easily keep track of when everything is supposed to arrive, which may not seem all that important now. But in a few weeks, when a certain item hasn't arrived, you won't have to scour through e-mails and receipts to figure out when it should have.

In addition to writing the expected delivery date, make note if you need to be there to inspect the item upon delivery. Doing that is very important because some items, like furniture, must be inspected for damage as soon as they arrive. If you're not there to inspect it, you may forfeit your right to return an item that was damaged during delivery. So be sure to make note of each delivery you must be present for, because you don't want to forget.

CREATING A RECEIPT FILE

Once all of your items have been purchased, hold onto those receipts and treat them like gold. They're your proof of purchase. If an item doesn't show up, you'll need them. If you want to return something, you'll need them. And most importantly, if you ever need to make an insurance claim because something happens to your home, having them will make it much easier because you can prove the exact value of each piece. If you're going to invest all that money in your home, make sure it's actually protected.

Put all of those receipts in a file. If you really want to be safe, take a photo of each piece when it arrives. That way, you have both the receipts and the photos of each item to prove you actually bought them and that they were indeed in your home.

The bare minimum you should include in your room file are all your samples and plans. But it doesn't hurt to hang onto your worksheets, muse photos and anything else you use to create your room.

E-mail copies of the receipts and photos to yourself and a close friend or person currently living in your home. After all, if something were to happen to your home, more than likely your receipt folder and computer might get damaged too. So there's a good possibility you'd have to access them from a remote location, hence the e-mail.

Also, check your insurance policy to see if there is anything else you'll need to prove ownership.

KEEPING TRACK OF ARRIVALS

When you purchase many things at once, they arrive at your home like a deluge. And if you don't keep track of what's arrived, you'll forget, which can be a really bad thing for two reasons. One, if you don't like something, you may not realize it until after it's too late to return it. And two, if something doesn't show up, you won't notice until it's time to put your room together.

That's why next to the "Delivery Date" column of your spreadsheet, make a new column titled "Arrived." Then, when each package shows up, fill in the date it came in. That way, you know it did indeed come, and you can easily check if you can still return it.

If any items that don't need to be inspected on arrival show up damaged, take a photo of it in its packaging. Contact the company right away with a nice note and let them know you have photos. The company should offer to send a new item right away free of charge.

INSPECTING UPON ARRIVAL

When inspecting items on arrival, don't let the delivery men or women rush you. Take your time to thoroughly inspect each piece. Just in case you miss something in the heat of the moment, take a picture of each item either on or next to the delivery truck. That way if it does have damage from delivery, and you don't notice it before the delivery people leave, you can prove it.

CREATING YOUR ROOM FILE

Once everything has been ordered, most people throw out their room samples. But don't you dare. Those room samples are invaluable. If you ever decide to change anything in your room — paint, flooring, or a chair — you'll need those samples.

So hold onto them. Put them in a special room file. I like using expandable file folders. That way, I can easily take all the samples with me if I ever need to go shopping. You can use whatever works best for you. A box. A bin. Whatever. As long as you keep those samples. While you're at it, throw your room plan in with it. That way, you can look back at what you created with pride years down the road. Plus, if you hold onto them, you'll never have to remeasure your room again — which is incentive enough alone.

Download the entire spreadsheet from: •·····
TheMeghanMethod.com.

RETURN POLICY	DELIVERY DATE	NEEDS INSPECTION UPON ARRIVAL	ARRIVED
3 weeks	May 20 - 24		
Sell on E-bay or Craigslist	May 18	Yes	May 18
2 months	May 16		May 17
3 weeks	May 19		May 19
Sell on E-bay or Craigslist	May 26	Yes	

We're
almost
finished!

Just
one, last
step.

• Hooray!

step:

18

putting it all together

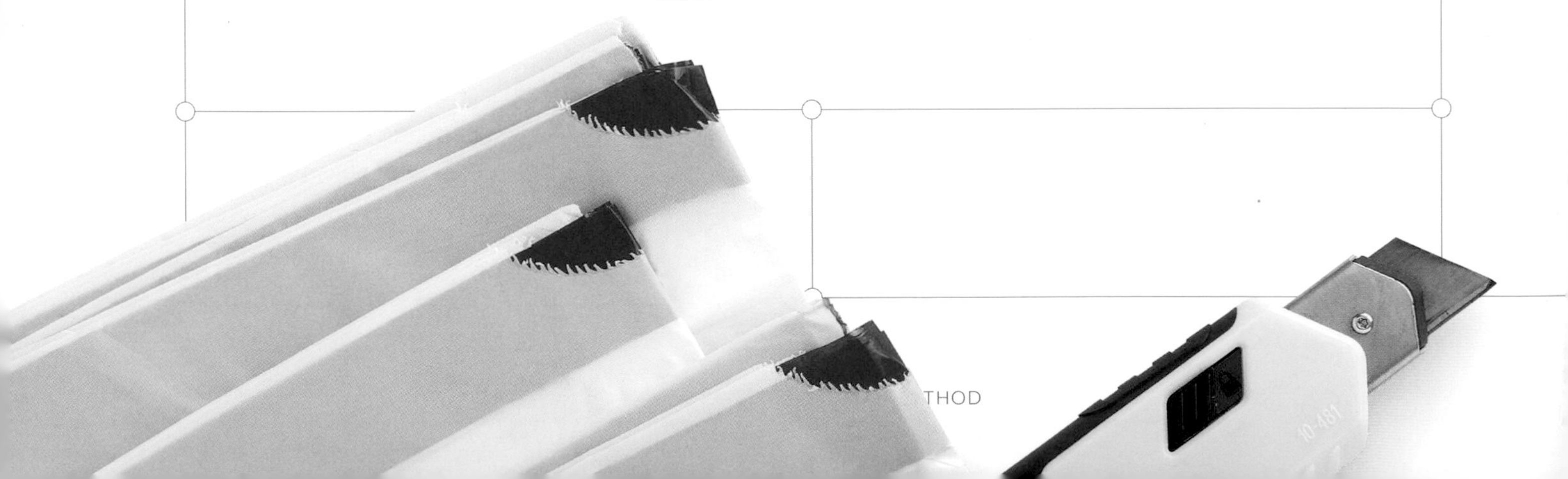

THOD

Only in our dreams — and the edited reality of makeover TV — do rooms come together in a matter of seconds. In real life, putting together a room takes work. Lots of work.

Linens don't come magically pressed. Boxes don't open themselves. Artwork doesn't arrive hung on your walls. Accessories don't show up with their gunky sale sticker residue removed. And furniture doesn't always come pre-assembled.

So if you only set aside 5 minutes to put together your room, you'll be in for a rude awakening. It's going to take longer than 5 minutes. A lot longer. To avoid disappointment and frustration, set aside an entire morning or afternoon to put your room together. Better yet, make a whole day of it. That way, you have enough time to thoroughly clean your room, move everything in, do all those little things that need to be done and still have time to sit back in amazement and enjoy what you created.

But first, you've got to put your room together.

WHAT YOU'LL NEED

To avoid making trips to the store, these are the things you should have on hand when putting your room together:

Light Bulbs. Not having the right light bulbs on hand when putting together a room is like getting an electronic gift without batteries. A real bummer. Make sure you have all the light bulbs you need ready and waiting.

Gunk Remover. There are few things more frustrating than leftover sticker gunk. It seems companies haven't caught onto that yet, because a number of them still put impossible-to-remove stickers on their items. So be prepared to battle the gunk.

Steamer, Iron or Cheater Spray. There is nothing quite as disheartening as opening a case of linens that look so beautiful in their packages only to find them deeply creased and crumpled when removed. So if you have linens in your room, you'll need something that effectively removes wrinkles.

I personally prefer a steamer because I get frustrated ironing big things on small ironing boards. But I'll be honest, if those cheater sprays didn't irritate my skin, I'd probably choose those. After all, what's easier than spritz, spritz, pull.

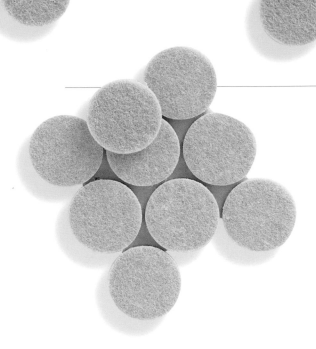

Floor Protectors. You know what they are. They're those little felt pieces with an adhesive back. Get a lot of them, because you can use them anywhere. The feet of your furniture. The bottoms of lamps and knick-knacks. The backs of paintings and mirrors. Put them on anything you think might scratch your floors, tables or walls. And be sure to stock up. You want to have enough.

Rug Pad. Rug pads keep your rug from slippin' and a slidin', movin' and a groovin'. So if you have an area rug in your room, it's a good idea to have a rug pad.

Photo Hangers. And a hammer. And a pencil. And a tape measure. And painter's tape. That's what you need to make hanging art, mirrors and anything else easy.

Put the painter's tape generally where the wall hanger should go. That way, you don't have to write on your freshly finished walls. Use the tape measure to determine exactly where the photo hanger should be hung. Then, mark the placement of the hanger on the painter's tape. Once you have the placement marked, all you have to do is hammer in the photo hanger and gently pull off the tape.

When purchasing your photo hangers, be sure to select the correct ones. Photo hangers are sold according to size,

and the ones you purchase must be big enough to hold the weight of whatever you're hanging. If it's not, your brand-new item may come crashing to the floor — taking anything in its path with it.

Scissors or Razor Knife. You already know boxes don't open themselves, so keep a scissors or razor knife close by.

Large Garbage Bag. Putting together your room is like Christmas morning, with paper and boxes and packaging everywhere. And if you don't tame the trash, you'll end up buried in it, so keep a garbage bag close at hand. Better yet, make it two. If you really want to score bonus points, have one for cardboard, another for plastic and a third for trash. That way, you already have everything sorted to recycle.

Dust Cloths. All those boxes, papers and packing peanuts throw up a lot of dust. And even though your things are new, they won't look like it after you've finished unpacking everything. So keep a dust cloth on hand to use after everything has been unpacked and all the trash has been removed. With one swipe, your room will sparkle like it should.

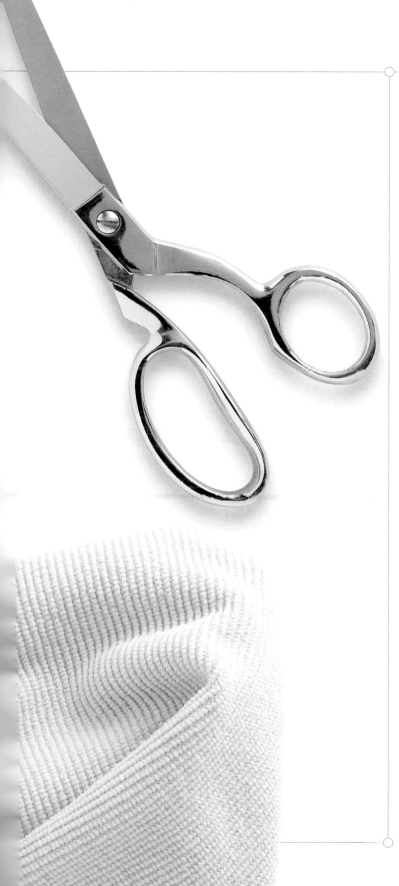

DAMAGE CONTROL

Ideally, after putting everything together, you'll sit back amazed thinking, "I can't believe I created something this beautiful."

But it doesn't always work out that way. Sometimes the reaction is more like, "What have I done?"

If that's what happens, it's okay. Don't panic. Step back. Breathe. Ask yourself calmly why you don't like it. Are you just shocked? Or does it not feel good to you?

Give yourself a few days to decide. If you still hate it — if your gut tells you it's wrong — well, that's what returns, Goodwill and Craigslist are for.

As I said in the DIY section, page 363, it's impossible to get it right all the time. No one bats one thousand. Even interior designers make mistakes — more often than they like to admit.

So don't blame yourself.

Making a mistake doesn't mean you're a bad decorator. If anything, it should teach you to trust your gut. Nine out of the 10 decorating mistakes I've made were simply because I let my logical brain talk me out of my gut instinct. The other one out of 10 were simply oversights from rushing things along too fast.

And neither of those reasons — not one of them   has anything to do with a lack of talent. So don't blame yourself. Mistakes are natural, human and necessary. You need them to learn and improve. The more mistakes you make, the better decorator you will become.

Use what you've learned from your mishap to find replacements you'll love. Once they arrive, you can finally sit back and look at your room in amazement. Because you did it. You created a spectacular room. Bravo.

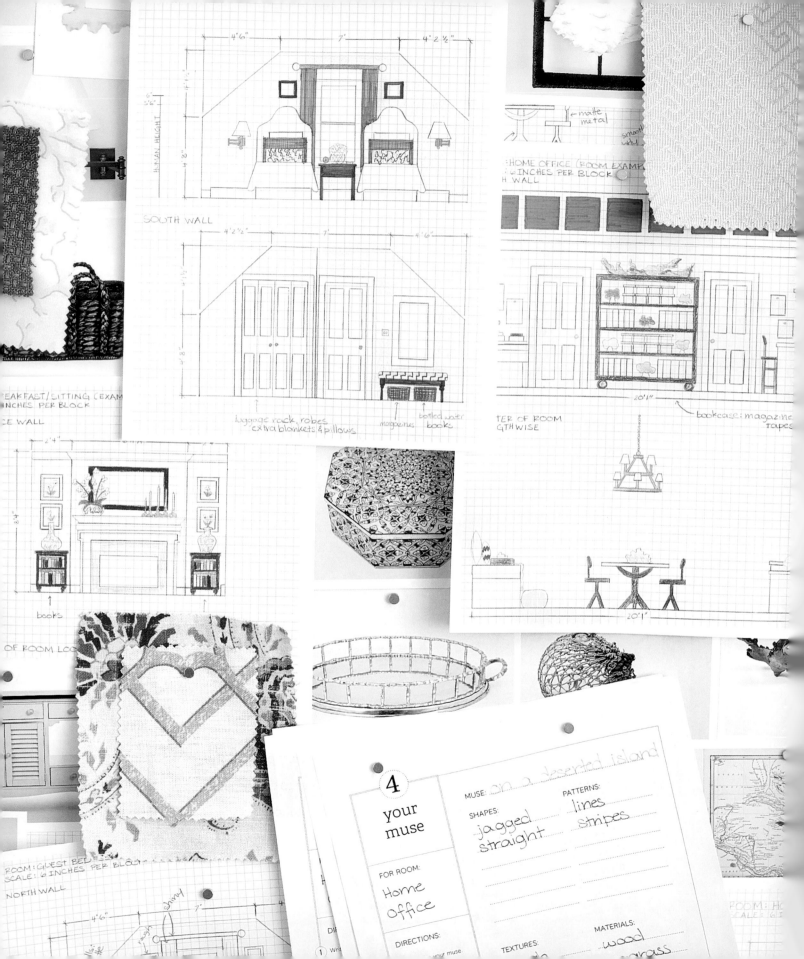

4'6"   7'   4' 2 ½"

HUMAN HEIGHT
5'6"

SOUTH WALL

4' 2 ½"   7'   4'6"

4'8"

luggage rack, robes
extra blankets & pillows

magazines   bottled water
books

...EAKFAST/SITTING (EXAM...
...INCHES PER BLOCK

...E WALL

...HOME OFFICE (ROOM EXAMP...
...6 INCHES PER BLOCK
...H WALL

matte metal

smooth...

...TER OF ROOM
...GTH WISE

bookcase: magazine...
tapes...

20'1"

2'4"

8'4"

books

...OF ROOM LOO...

20'1"

...ROOM: GUEST BED...
SCALE: 6 INCHES PER BLOCK

NORTH WALL

4'6"   7'   3'...

④
your
muse

FOR ROOM:
Home
office

DIRECTIONS:
① Wri...
...your muse...

MUSE: ...on a deserted island

SHAPES:
jagged
straight

PATTERNS:
lines
stripes

TEXTURES:

MATERIALS:
wood
...rass

ROOM: HO...
SCALE: 6 I...

the end result

NO WORDS could adequately describe what it's like seeing your finished room for the first time. The joy. The relief. The excitement. The wonder. It's like living in a dream. You can barely believe what's in front of you is real, because it *looks* too spectacular. It *feels* too spectacular.

But it is. It's 100-percent real. And it's all yours.

So soak it up. Revel in it. Let yourself get lost. And most importantly, start making all those aspirations come true. After all, that's what all that hard work was for. So get to it. Live your dream life. Do all those things you wanted to do, because there's nothing holding you back now.

....

After all those examples, I wasn't going to leave you hanging. When you turn the page, you'll see how they turned out. But before you do, I want to be clear. These rooms are not meant to be exemplars of what "good" rooms looks like.

As you should know by now, there is no such thing. Good — like beauty — is in the eye of the beholder. So while the people living in those rooms love them, you may hate them. And that's okay.

I didn't include those rooms to push an aesthetic on you. I simply wanted you to see the visual process of starting with aspirations and using them to create a room. So view the following photos for what they are. Simply examples. Not ideals.

room example 1:

GUEST BEDROOM

{ Used by two kid or adult guests
who may or may not be related. }

(left) The desk gives guests the perfect place to apply makeup, catch up on e-mails or write post cards. The pegs, to the right of the desk, provide guests with a place to hang outfits for the next day.

....

(above) Upon walking in the door, guests can set their belongings on the bench. When they get ready to leave, the bench serves as a place to sit and put on shoes, while the mirror enables them to check themselves.

....

(top right) Sitting on the nightstand is a tiny alarm clock for those early mornings and a small dish for corraling any jewelry taken off before bed.

....

(right) On rainy days and restless nights guests can entertain themselves with books and a leather-bound, board game that adorn the small in-wall bookcase.

room example 2:

BREAKFAST/SITTING

{ Used by a couple and
any guests they may have. }

(*previous two pages*) With places to display pottery on the sideboard, terrariums filled with mini orchids and selaginella were used on the book tables instead of the vases depicted in the original plan.

....

(*left*) Perfect for board games, breakfast and brunch, the table can seat up to six — which is nice for when guests drop by. With a decorative bowl filled with lemons in the center, the table is always festive for impromptu gatherings.

(*above*) With five drawers and two hidden shelves, the sideboard neatly stores napkins, tablecloths, candles, small serving dishes, cards and board games. On top, decanters sit ready for afternoon cocktails with guests.

....

(*next two pages*) Bright and cheerful, the four easy chairs draw people — even on sunny days — to curl up with a book, enjoy the view or gather for conversations. And in the dead of winter, they provide the perfect pick-me-up.

room example 3:

HOME OFFICE

{ Used by two people who primarily work from home. }

(*previous two pages*) If you noticed, the room isn't exactly like the plan. A spectacular, green specimen couldn't be found for a centerpiece. So a large coral from a vintage collection was used instead. A two-tier chandelier in the right size couldn't be found either. So a single tier version was chosen. But the bookcase is exactly as imagined: spacious, open and rough.

(*top left*) A large, floor lamp provides bright light for late-night and dreary-day reading.

(*left*) The tray houses everything needed when reading: a box filled with stickies and highlighters for marking spots to remember when reading, a pen atop a decorative pen holder for taking notes, and the latest magazines.

(*right*) The large daybed doubles as a sofa for lounging and a bed for afternoon naps and overflow guests.

(*left*) After four coats of magnetic paint, artwork, notes, inspiration and any other pieces of paper can be hung by magnets on all four walls, making them the perfect canvases for displaying and working on projects. The back wall, above the desks was painted with dry erase paint. So whenever an idea strikes — or something must be remembered — it can be scribbled on the board. And when it's no longer needed, it can easily be erased, leaving a pristine, white wall of opportunity and potential behind. Best of all, the dry erase markers and erasers are neatly tucked away in the hinged brown box — allowing for one-handed, two-action access.

(*above*) Each desk has everything needed close at hand: a lamp for when it's late or cloudy; a pen — on a decorative pen holder — and notepad for jotting quick thoughts; a toast rack for sorting mail and papers; a phone for when an e-mail just won't do; a covered mug for staying hydrated without risk of spilling; reference books overhead for the rare times an internet search doesn't suffice; envelopes, stamps, checks, rubber bands, tape and other necessities — hidden behind the doors — for paying bills and other tasks; files stored in the center cabinet for organizing the paper trail of life; and a computer for doing everything else.

before you go

THANKS FOR STICKING WITH ME. Decorating is a messy, chaotic, sometimes frustrating and completely time-consuming process. But if you've made it this far, you know how satisfying it is. That all the hard work pays off — *and not just in terms of beauty.*

Through this process, I hope you've found your true style. I hope you've discovered you're more talented and creative than you ever thought you were. I hope you realized you can turn anything — absolutely anything — you can imgaine into reality. And most importantly, I hope you've learned to trust yourself — to tune out everyone else and focus on the one voice that truly matters. Your own.

In this busy, complicated world, we can't rely on others to believe in us. We must do it ourselves. We must believe our opinions matter. We must believe we're worthy of our dreams. And above all else, we must pursue those dreams with a passion, because they're what make life worth living. And I hope this book helped you get them. That it helped you create a home you love — a home where all your dreams and aspirations can come true.

That's what I wish for you.

Until next time,

index

Library of Congress Cataloging-in-Publication Data

Carter, Meghan Alexis.
The Meghan Method : the step-by-step guide to decorating your home in your style / by Meghan Carter.
p. cm.
ISBN: 978-0-9829387-0-6
1. Interior decoration.   I. Title.
NK2115 .C325 2011
747   dc22
          2011920038

PRINTED IN AMERICA.

FIRST EDITION

TEXT, DESIGN, ILLUSTRATIONS & PHOTO STYLING BY: Meghan Carter

PHOTOGRAPHY BY: Brent Walter, except for those disclosed below*

EDITED BY: Veronica Hill

*ADDITIONAL PHOTO CREDITS:
Christena Walter: Ocean, 7; Mountain, 58; Tiger, 62; Graffiti, 62; Horse, 62; New York, 63; Produce, 63; Orange Tree, 65;
Ocean Water, 71; Pumpkins, 70; Two Tulips, 73; Mountain, 138
Tim Carter: Mountain, 6 & 19; Winter Wonderland, 60; Fall Tree, 62; Sunrise, 63; Mountain, 63; Steering Wheel, 70

FABRICS:
Animal Print, 274, Highland House; Blues (3), 270, Anichini; Botanical, 273, GP&J Baker; Checks, 273, Pinecone Hill; Floral, 273, Lee Jofa; Geometric, 276, Serena & Lily; Houndstooth, 276, Thibaut; Ikat, 274, Fabricadabra; Jacobean, 270, Lee Jofa; Novelty, 275, Lauren Hunt; Plaid, 273, Duralee; Shiny, 290, Ralph Lauren; Southwestern, 275, Kravet; Stripe, 276, GP&J Baker; White Bumpy, 293, Stroheim; Yellow and White, 270, Calico Corners;

SPECIAL ACKNOWLEDGMENTS:
Jeane Carter, Kathy Carter, Kelly Carter, Tim Carter, Christena Walter, Christopher Walter & Lawrence Walter

7 drawing your layout — YOUR VISUAL GRAMMAR
DIRECTIONS: Check the

BALANCE: ☐ symmetrical ☐ asymmetric

7 drawing your layout — YOUR W
DIRECTIONS: List

TASK:

8 drawing your elevations — EMO
DIREC

RANK: ITEMS ASSOCIATED WITH MUSE

7 drawing your layout — YOUR GRAM
DIRECTION

RANK: POTENTIAL FOCAL POINTS BASED

7 drawing your layout — LIN
DIREC

EXTENDED STAY VANTAGE POINTS:

8 wing your vations — PERISHA
DIRECTIONS: L

CESSORIES I CAN MAINTAIN:

Get all the worksheets used in this book

plus extensive lists of decor stores, blogs & magazines

from:
TheMeghan Method.com

7 rawing your layout — POTE
DIRECTION

NEEDED:

7 drawing your layout — LAYOUT
DIRECTIONS: R

NUMBER OF ASPIRATIONS UNABLE TO DO: ☐ 0

our — ELEVATIO
DIRECTIONS: Ra

☐ ideal

7 rawing your layout — PR
DIRE

TOP PLAYER PICKS

8 drawing your elevations — FUNCTIONA
DIRECTIONS: List the

FUNCTIONAL ACCESSORIES :

14 timeline — PROJECTS T

ORDER OF COMPLETION: PROJECTS TO DO:

7 rawing your layout — M
DIR

AYS:
the doorways your item must

8 drawing your elevations — MEANIN
DIRECTIONS: List and

RANK: MEANINGFUL ACCESSORIES :

14 timeline — SHOPPING L

Want more?
Visit me at:

Meghan Carter.com

You'll find
instructional videos
and articles that
expand on the
topics in this book,
as well as
details on the latest
happenings
and where to see
me speak.

*To buy
this book
visit:
The Meghan
Method.com

I can't wait for you
to stop by!